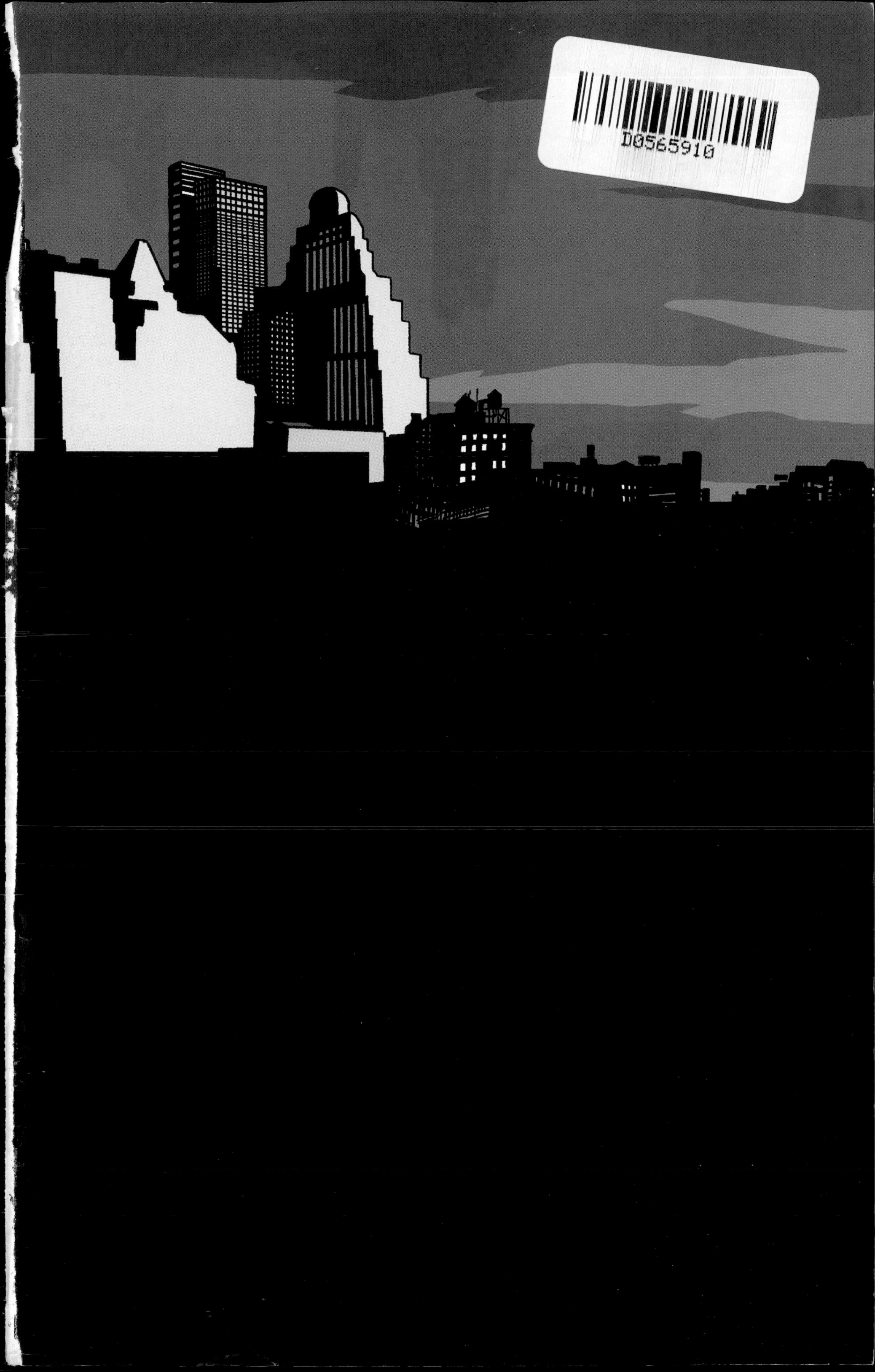

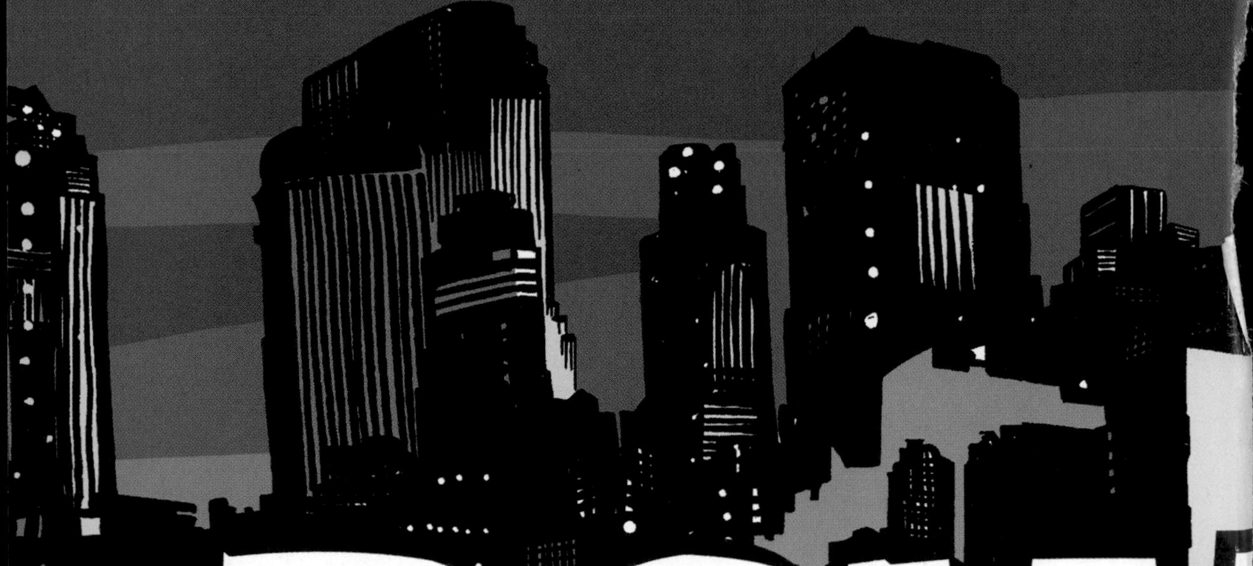

POW

CREATED AND

BRIAN MICHAEL BENDIS

COLOR ART BY
PAT GARRAHY
SEPARATION ASSISTS BY OJO CALIENTE STUDIOS

LETTERING BY
GARRAHY AND BEND

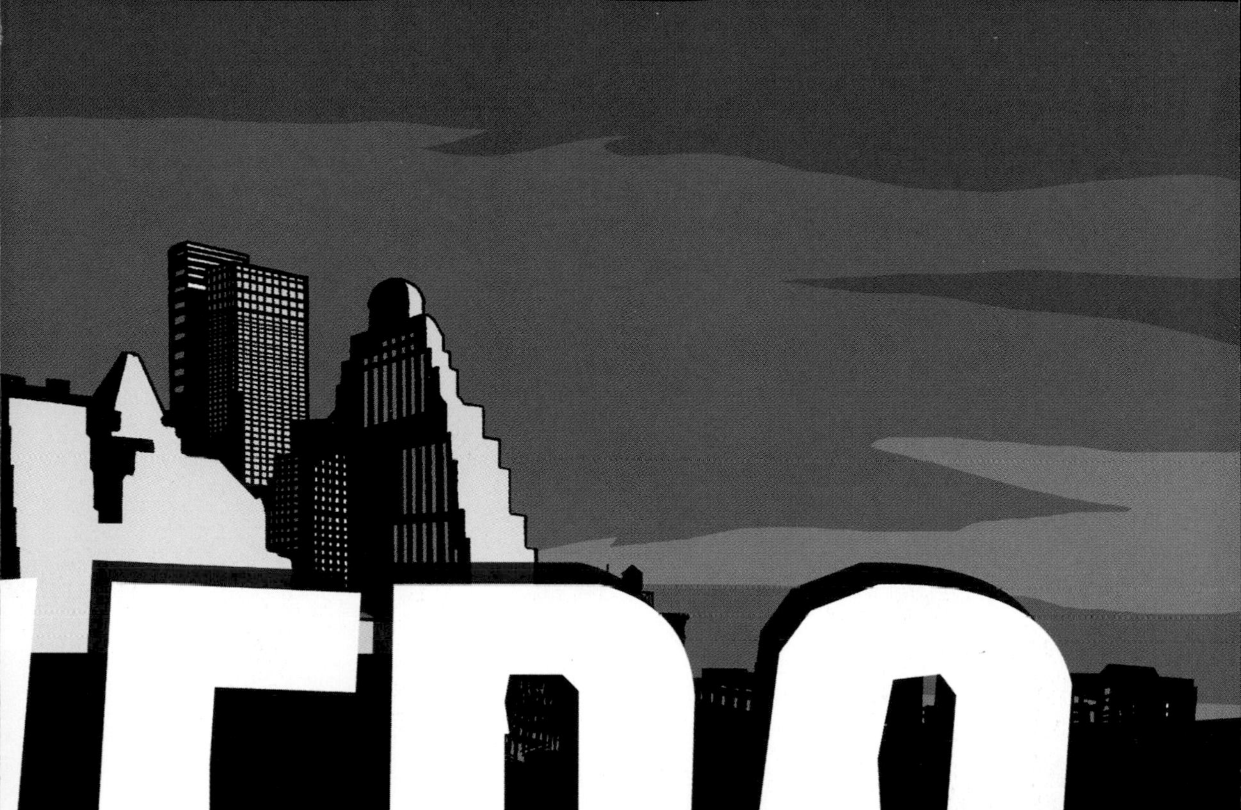

ERS

PRODUCED BY

AND **MIKE AVON OEMING**

EDITOR
KC MCCRORY

BUSINESS AFFAIRS
ALISA BENDIS

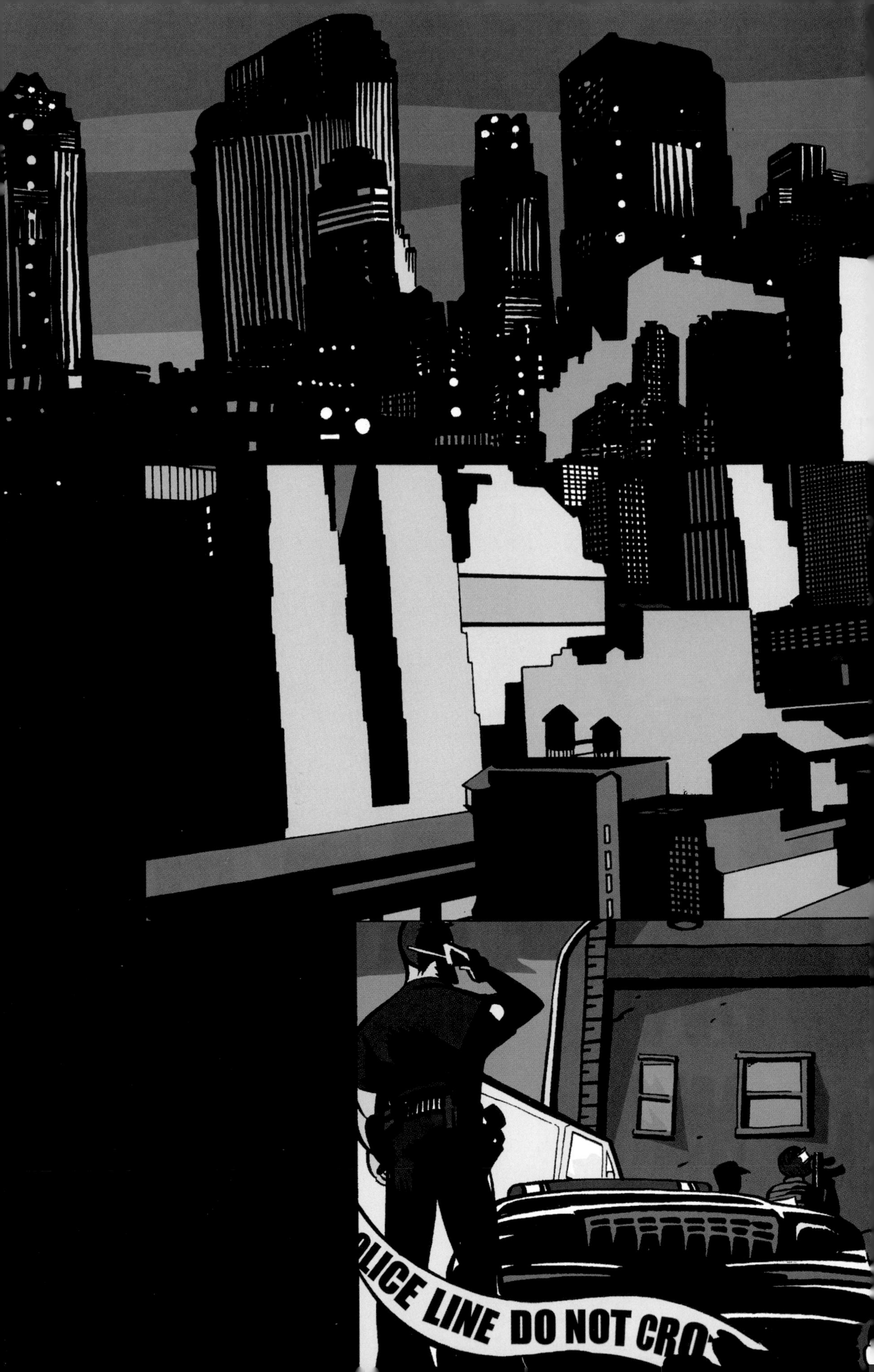
OLICE LINE DO NOT CRO

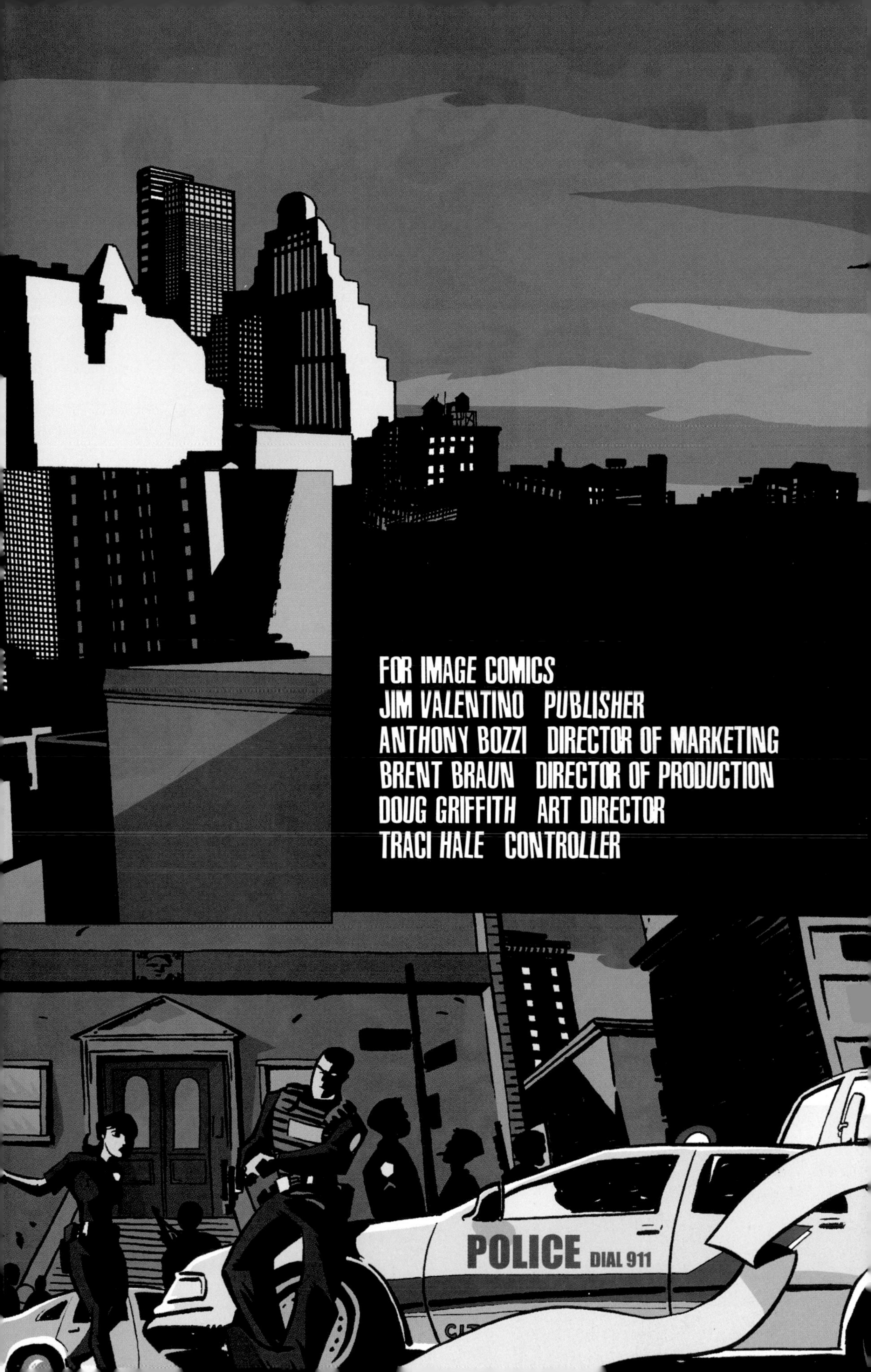
POLICE DIAL 911

FOR IMAGE COMICS
JIM VALENTINO PUBLISHER
ANTHONY BOZZI DIRECTOR OF MARKETING
BRENT BRAUN DIRECTOR OF PRODUCTION
DOUG GRIFFITH ART DIRECTOR
TRACI HALE CONTROLLER

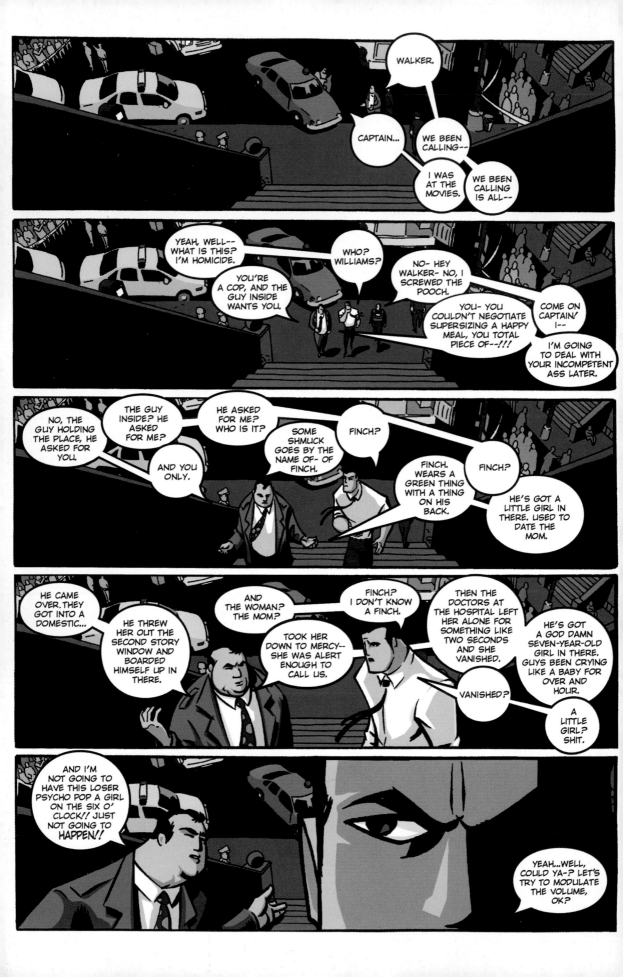

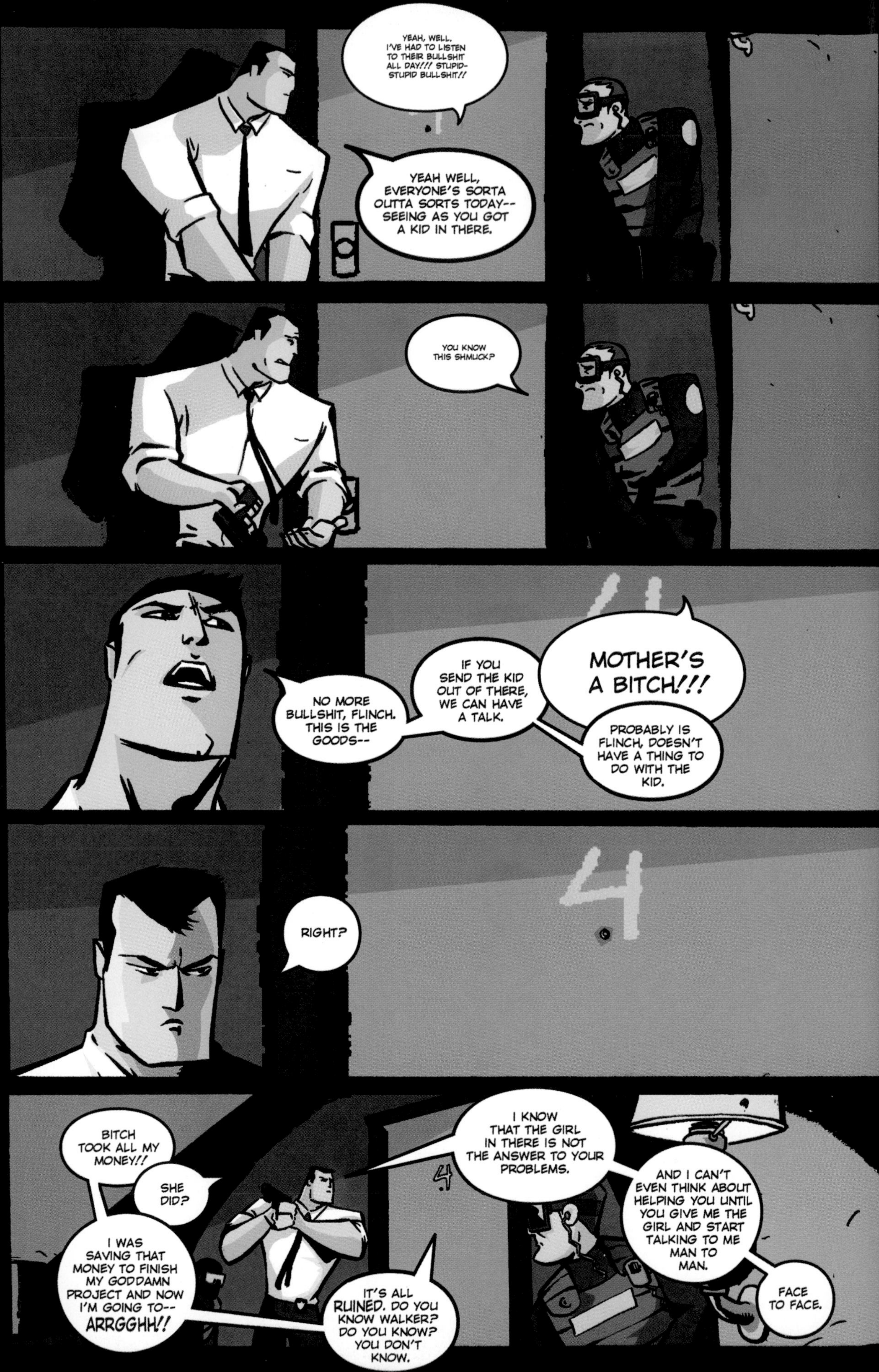

YEAH, WELL, I'VE HAD TO LISTEN TO THEIR BULLSHIT ALL DAY!!! STUPID-STUPID BULLSHIT!!
YEAH WELL, EVERYONE'S SORTA OUTTA SORTS TODAY-- SEEING AS YOU GOT A KID IN THERE.
YOU KNOW THIS SHMUCK?
NO MORE BULLSHIT, FLINCH. THIS IS THE GOODS--
IF YOU SEND THE KID OUT OF THERE, WE CAN HAVE A TALK.
MOTHER'S A BITCH!!!
PROBABLY IS FLINCH, DOESN'T HAVE A THING TO DO WITH THE KID.
RIGHT?
BITCH TOOK ALL MY MONEY!!
SHE DID?
I WAS SAVING THAT MONEY TO FINISH MY GODDAMN PROJECT AND NOW I'M GOING TO-- ARRGGHH!!
IT'S ALL RUINED. DO YOU KNOW WALKER? DO YOU KNOW? YOU DON'T KNOW.
I KNOW THAT THE GIRL IN THERE IS NOT THE ANSWER TO YOUR PROBLEMS.
AND I CAN'T EVEN THINK ABOUT HELPING YOU UNTIL YOU GIVE ME THE GIRL AND START TALKING TO ME MAN TO MAN.
FACE TO FACE.

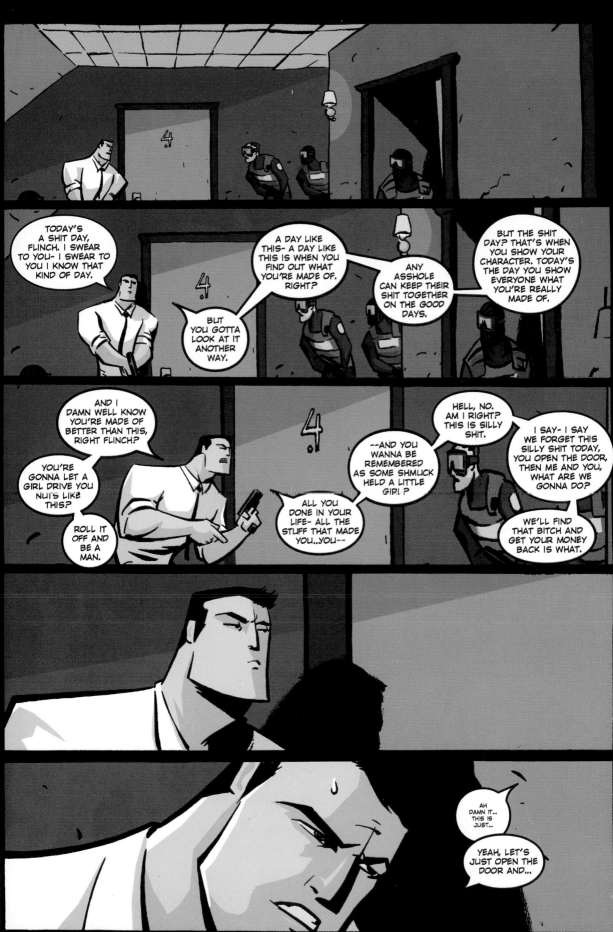

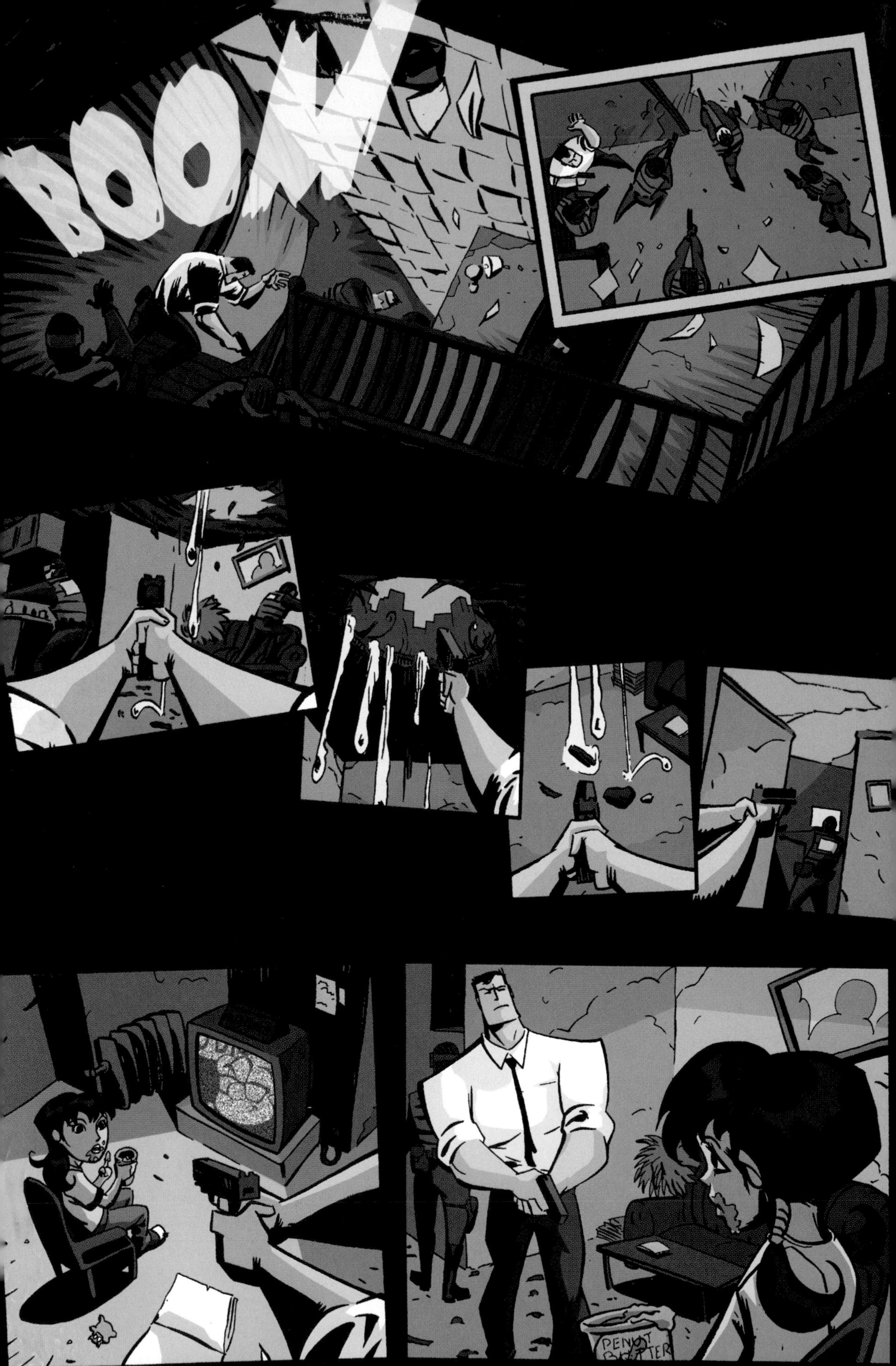
BOOM

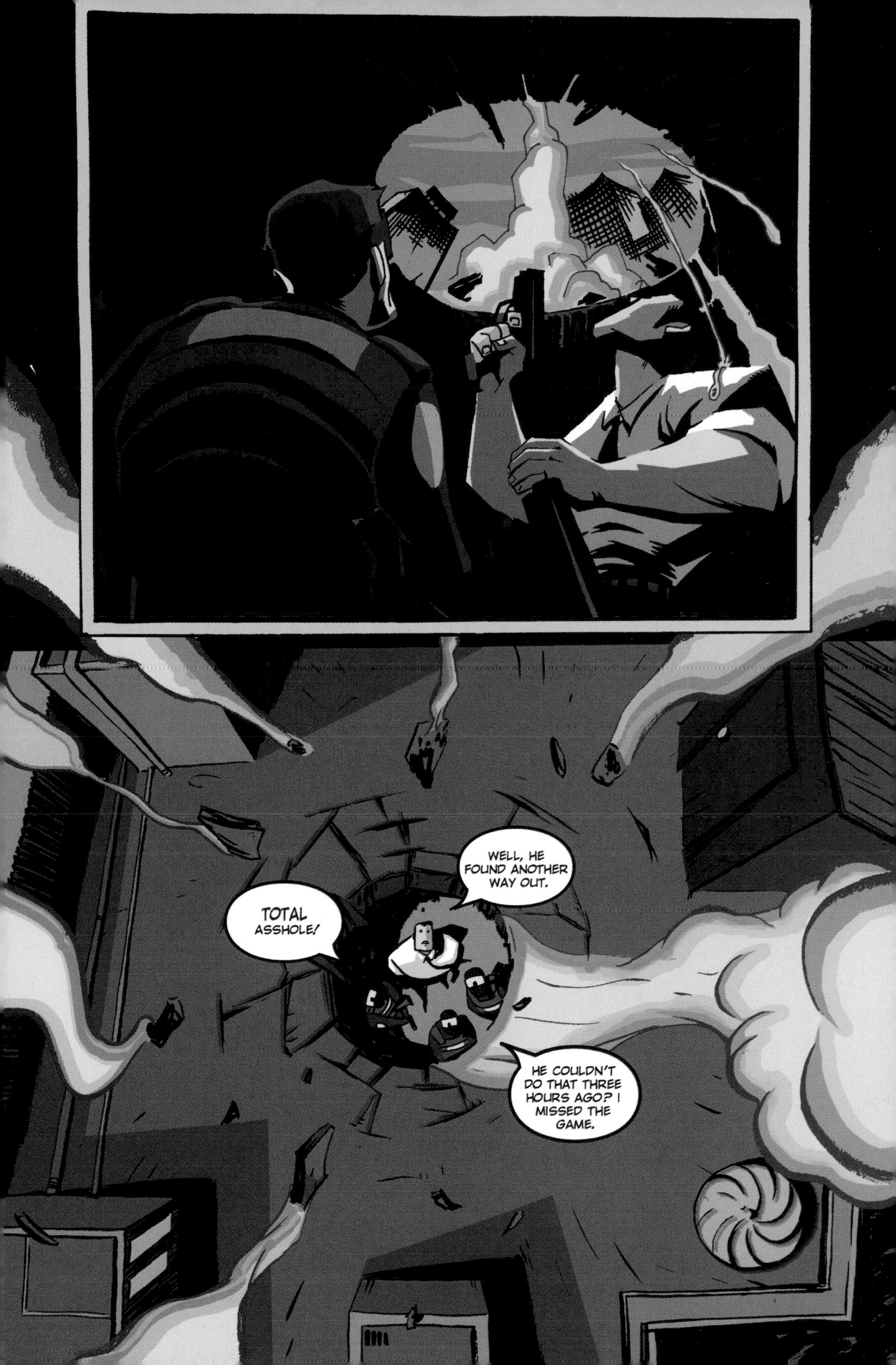
WELL, HE FOUND ANOTHER WAY OUT.
TOTAL ASSHOLE!
HE COULDN'T DO THAT THREE HOURS AGO? I MISSED THE GAME.

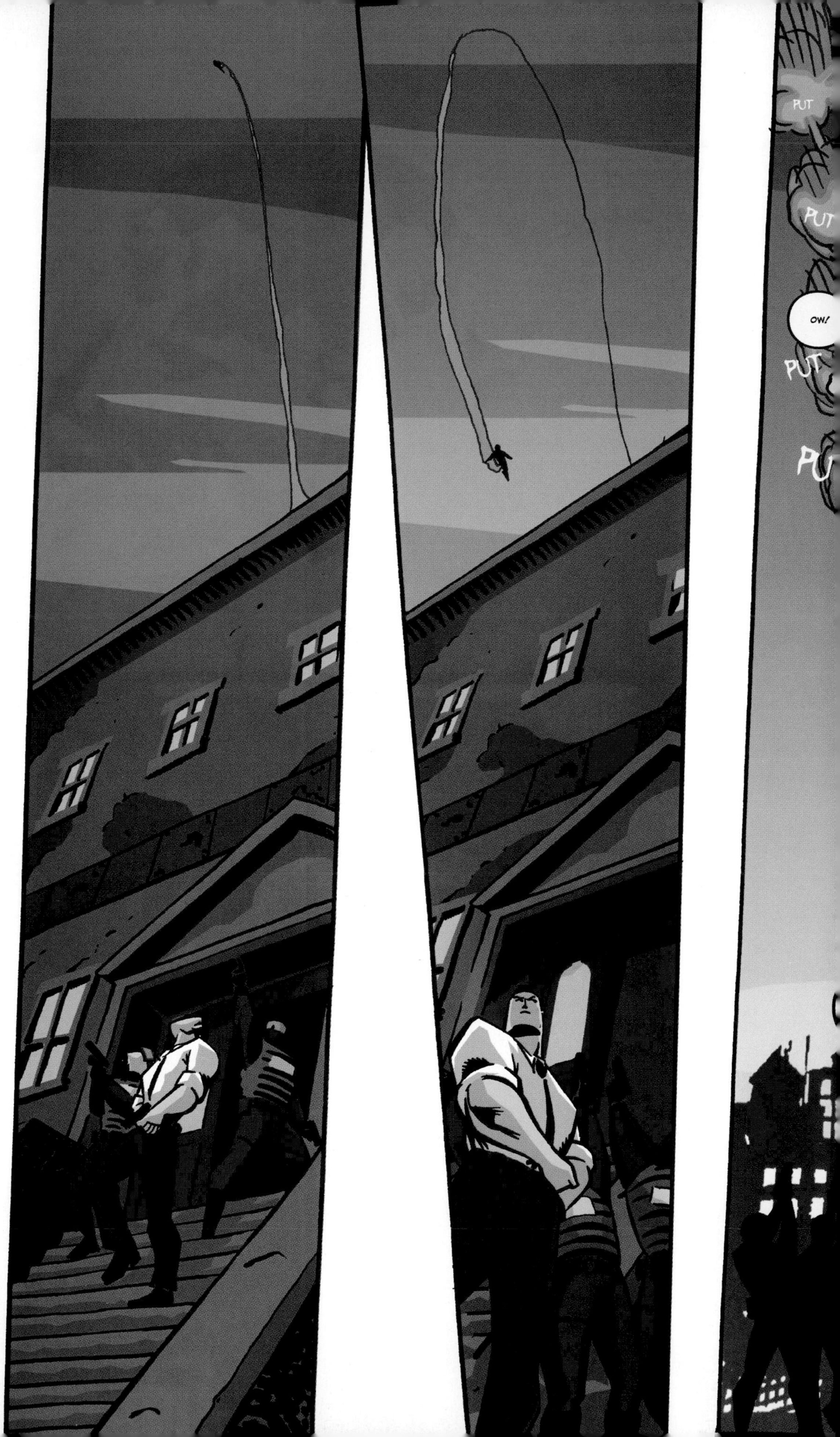
PUT
PUT
OW!
PUT
PU

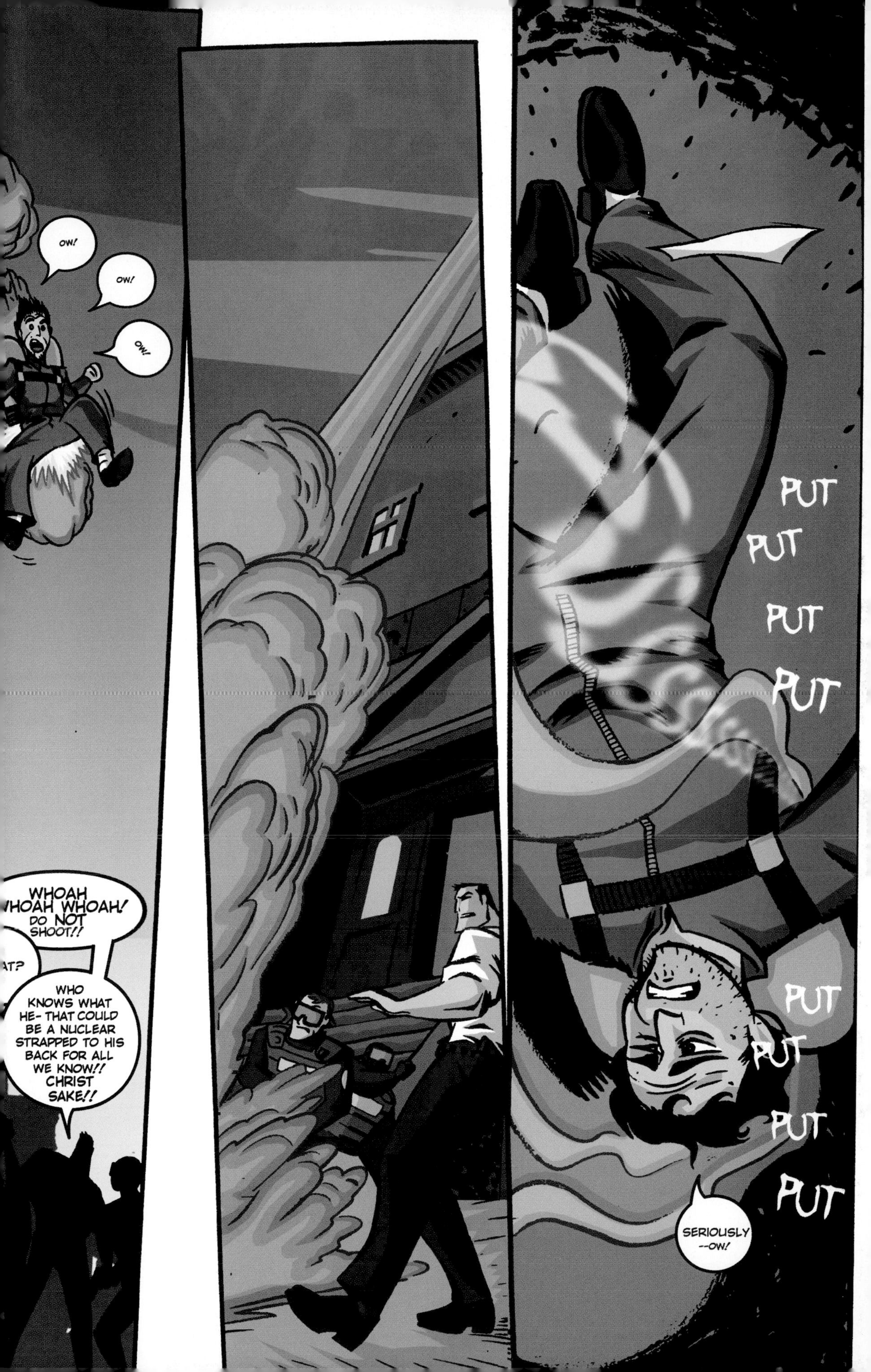

OW!
OW!
OW!
WHOAH WHOAH WHOAH! DO NOT SHOOT!!
AT?
WHO KNOWS WHAT HE- THAT COULD BE A NUCLEAR STRAPPED TO HIS BACK FOR ALL WE KNOW!! CHRIST SAKE!!
PUT PUT PUT PUT
PUT PUT PUT PUT
SERIOUSLY --OW!

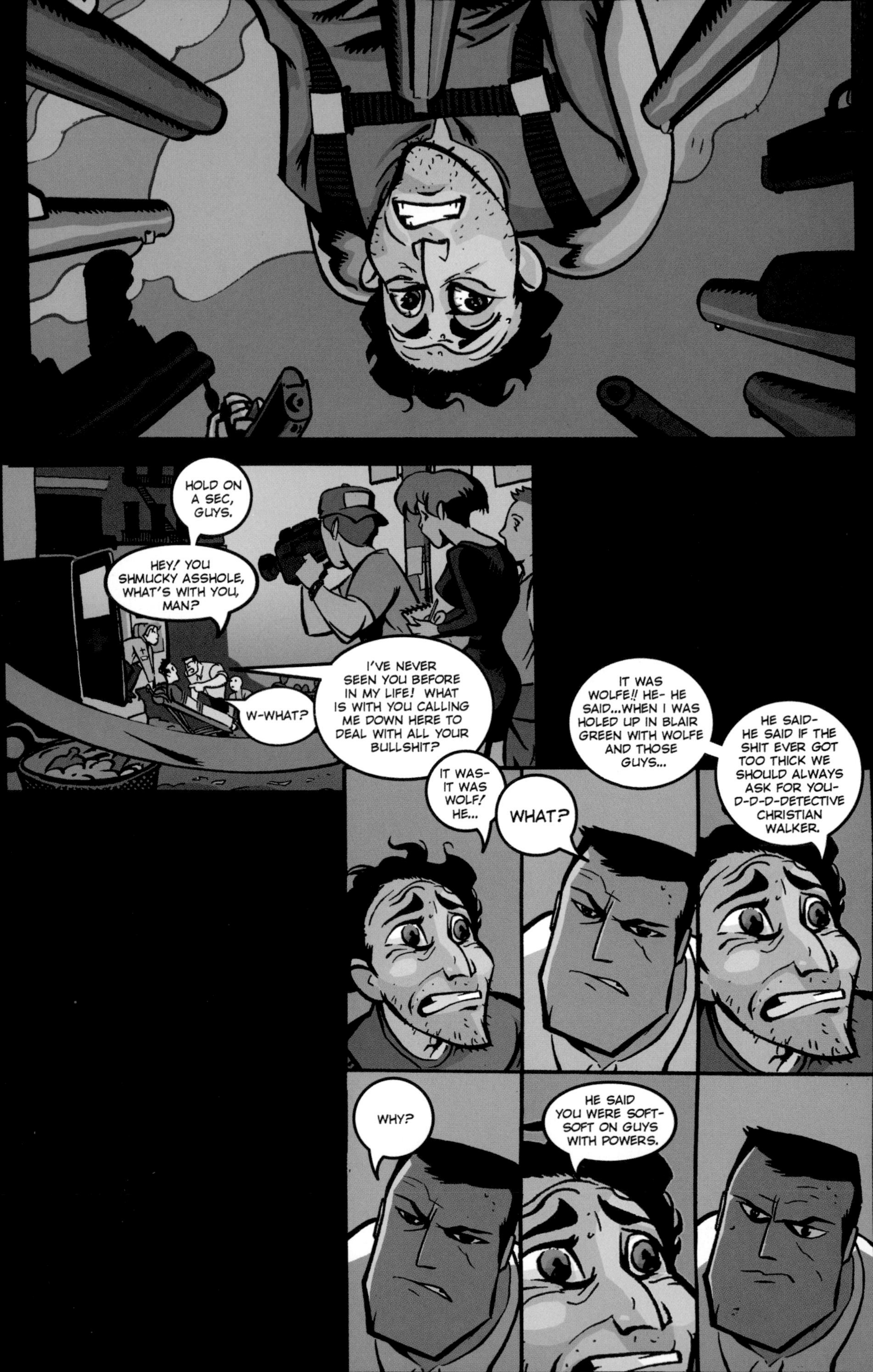
HOLD ON A SEC, GUYS.
HEY! YOU SHMUCKY ASSHOLE, WHAT'S WITH YOU, MAN?
W-WHAT?
I'VE NEVER SEEN YOU BEFORE IN MY LIFE! WHAT IS WITH YOU CALLING ME DOWN HERE TO DEAL WITH ALL YOUR BULLSHIT?
IT WAS- IT WAS WOLF! HE...
WHAT?
IT WAS WOLFE!! HE- HE SAID...WHEN I WAS HOLED UP IN BLAIR GREEN WITH WOLFE AND THOSE GUYS...
HE SAID- HE SAID IF THE SHIT EVER GOT TOO THICK WE SHOULD ALWAYS ASK FOR YOU- D-D-D-DETECTIVE CHRISTIAN WALKER.
WHY?
HE SAID YOU WERE SOFT- SOFT ON GUYS WITH POWERS.

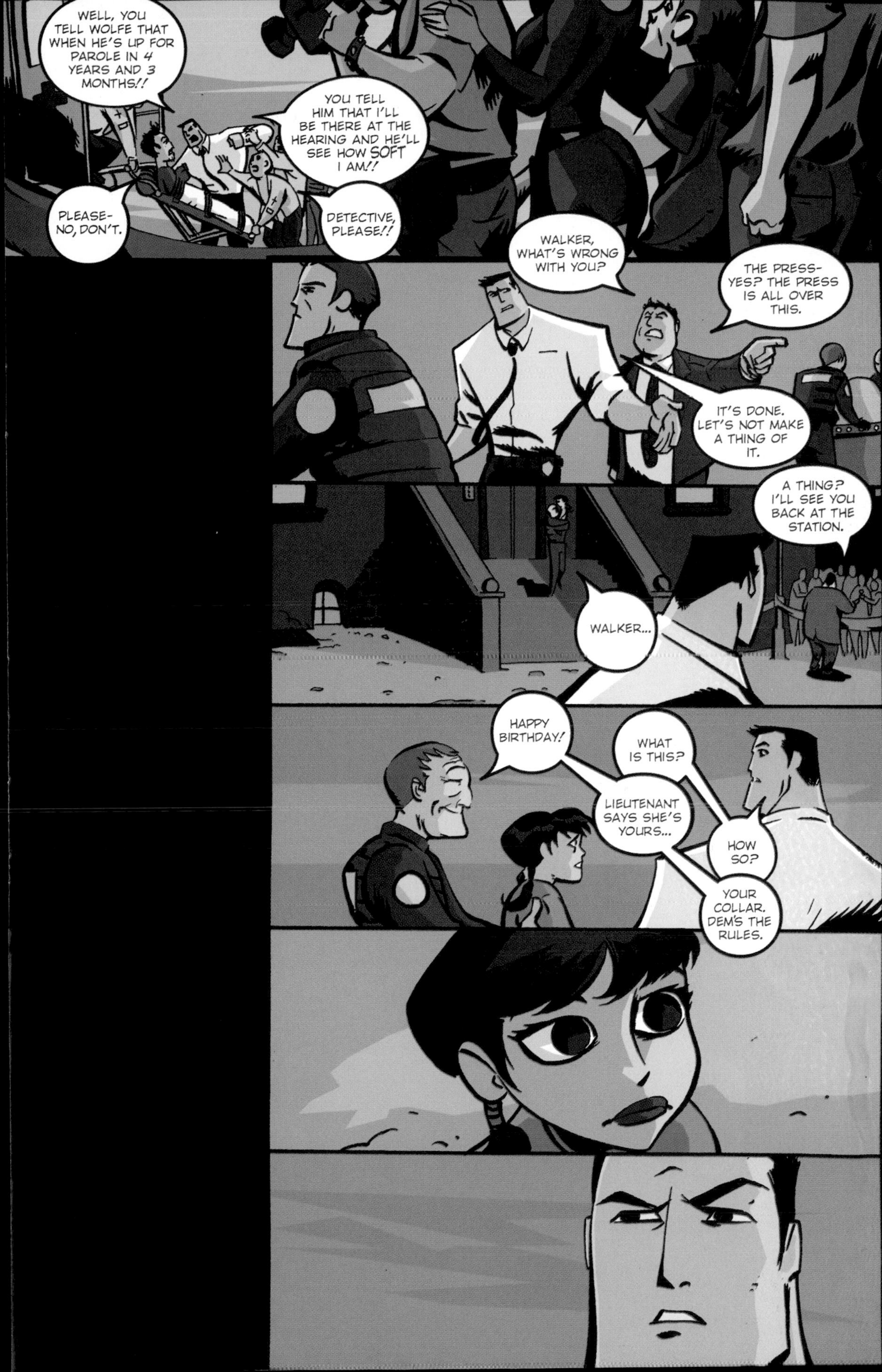
WELL, YOU TELL WOLFE THAT WHEN HE'S UP FOR PAROLE IN 4 YEARS AND 3 MONTHS!!
YOU TELL HIM THAT I'LL BE THERE AT THE HEARING AND HE'LL SEE HOW SOFT I AM!!
PLEASE-NO, DON'T.
DETECTIVE, PLEASE!!
WALKER, WHAT'S WRONG WITH YOU?
THE PRESS-YES? THE PRESS IS ALL OVER THIS.
IT'S DONE. LET'S NOT MAKE A THING OF IT.
A THING? I'LL SEE YOU BACK AT THE STATION.
WALKER...
HAPPY BIRTHDAY!
WHAT IS THIS?
LIEUTENANT SAYS SHE'S YOURS...
HOW SO?
YOUR COLLAR. DEM'S THE RULES.

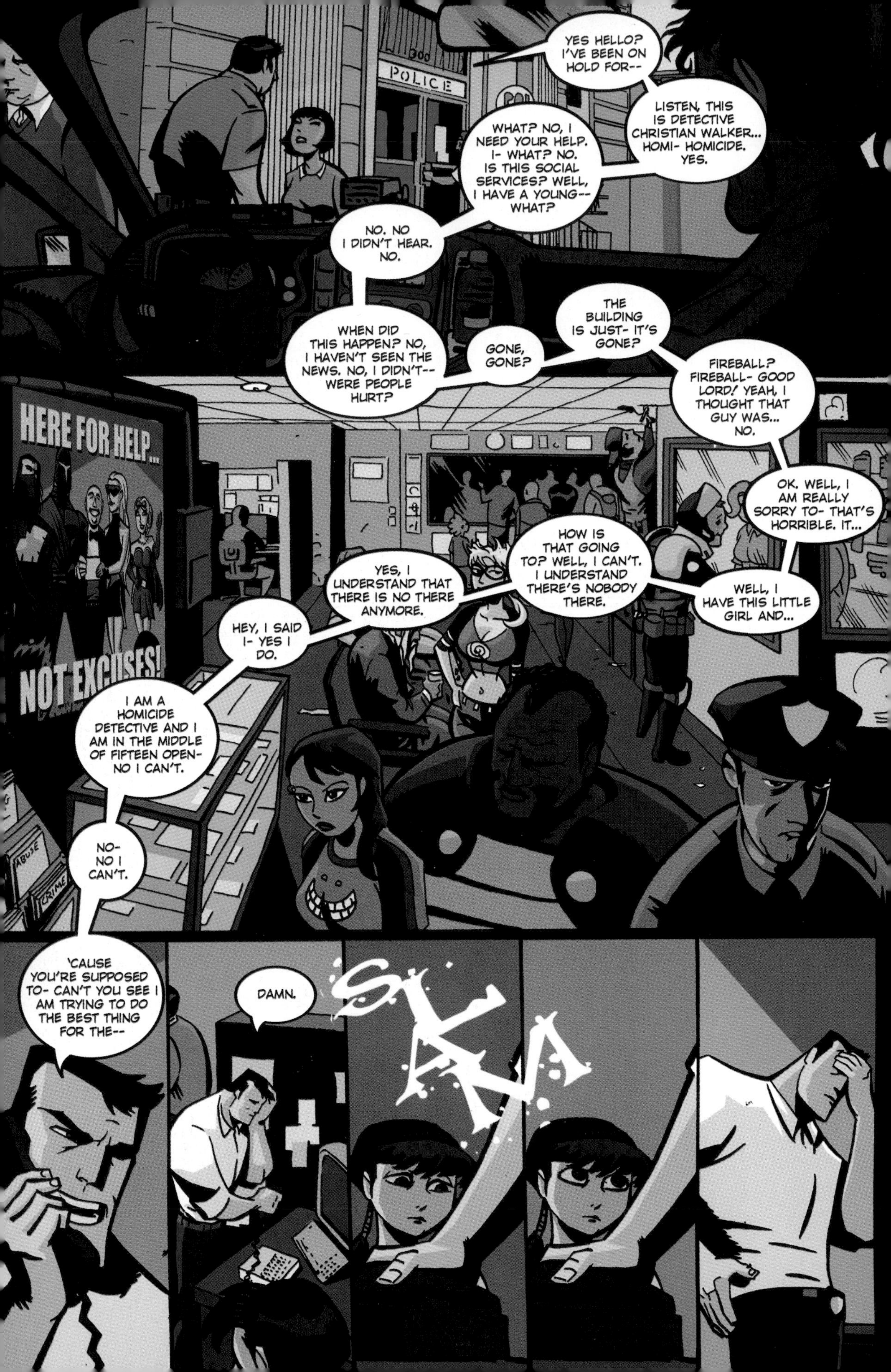
POLICE
YES HELLO? I'VE BEEN ON HOLD FOR--
LISTEN, THIS IS DETECTIVE CHRISTIAN WALKER... HOMI- HOMICIDE. YES.
WHAT? NO, I NEED YOUR HELP. I- WHAT? NO. IS THIS SOCIAL SERVICES? WELL, I HAVE A YOUNG-- WHAT?
NO. NO I DIDN'T HEAR. NO.
WHEN DID THIS HAPPEN? NO, I HAVEN'T SEEN THE NEWS. NO, I DIDN'T-- WERE PEOPLE HURT?
GONE, GONE?
THE BUILDING IS JUST- IT'S GONE?
FIREBALL? FIREBALL- GOOD LORD! YEAH, I THOUGHT THAT GUY WAS... NO.
OK. WELL, I AM REALLY SORRY TO- THAT'S HORRIBLE. IT...
WELL, I HAVE THIS LITTLE GIRL AND...
HOW IS THAT GOING TO? WELL, I CAN'T. I UNDERSTAND THERE'S NOBODY THERE.
YES, I UNDERSTAND THAT THERE IS NO THERE ANYMORE.
HEY, I SAID I- YES I DO.
I AM A HOMICIDE DETECTIVE AND I AM IN THE MIDDLE OF FIFTEEN OPEN- NO I CAN'T.
NO- NO I CAN'T.
HERE FOR HELP...
NOT EXCUSES!
ABUSE
CRIME
'CAUSE YOU'RE SUPPOSED TO- CAN'T YOU SEE I AM TRYING TO DO THE BEST THING FOR THE--
DAMN.
SLAM

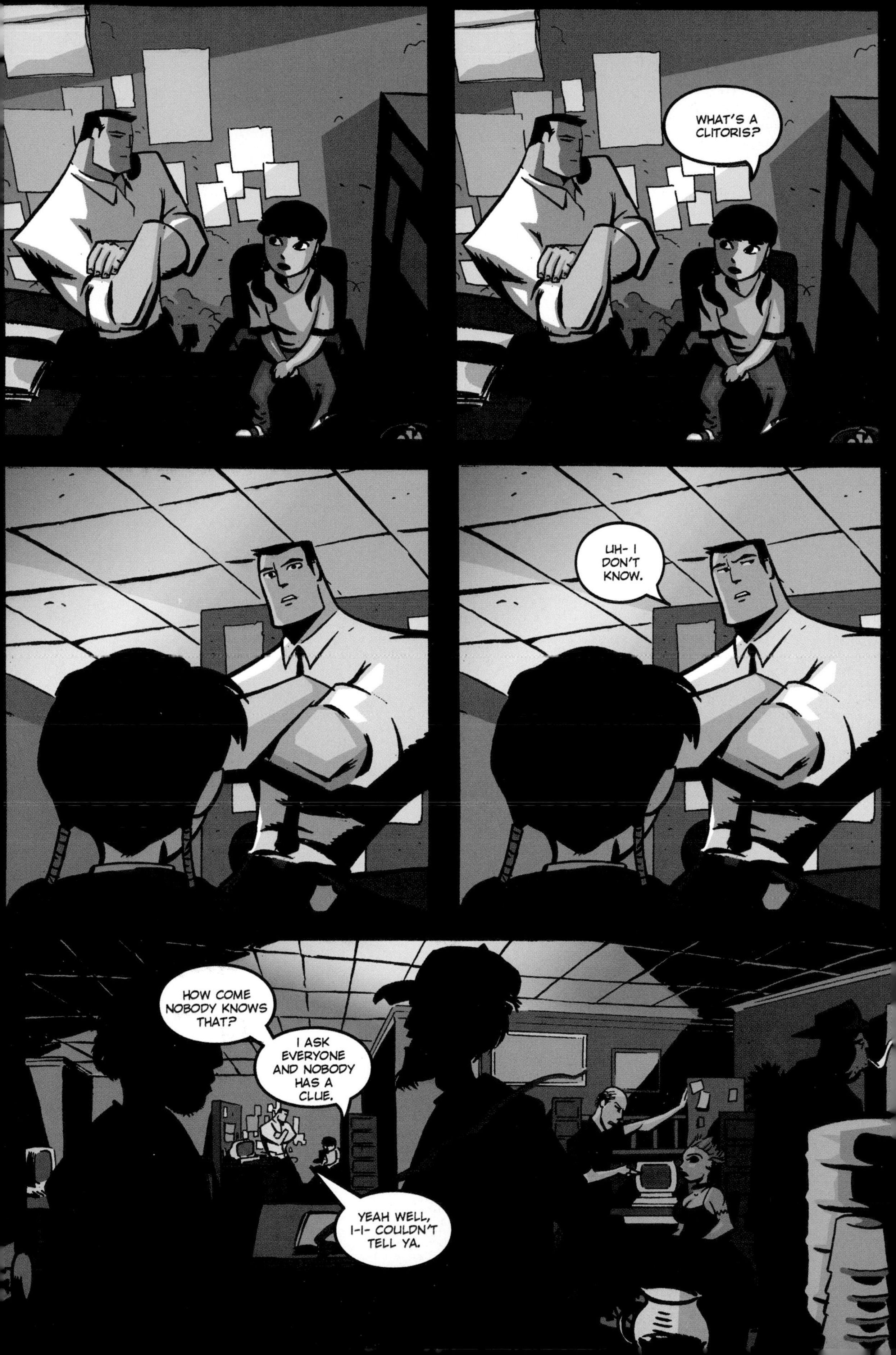
WHAT'S A CLITORIS?
UH- I DON'T KNOW.
HOW COME NOBODY KNOWS THAT?
I ASK EVERYONE AND NOBODY HAS A CLUE.
YEAH WELL, I-I- COULDN'T TELL YA.

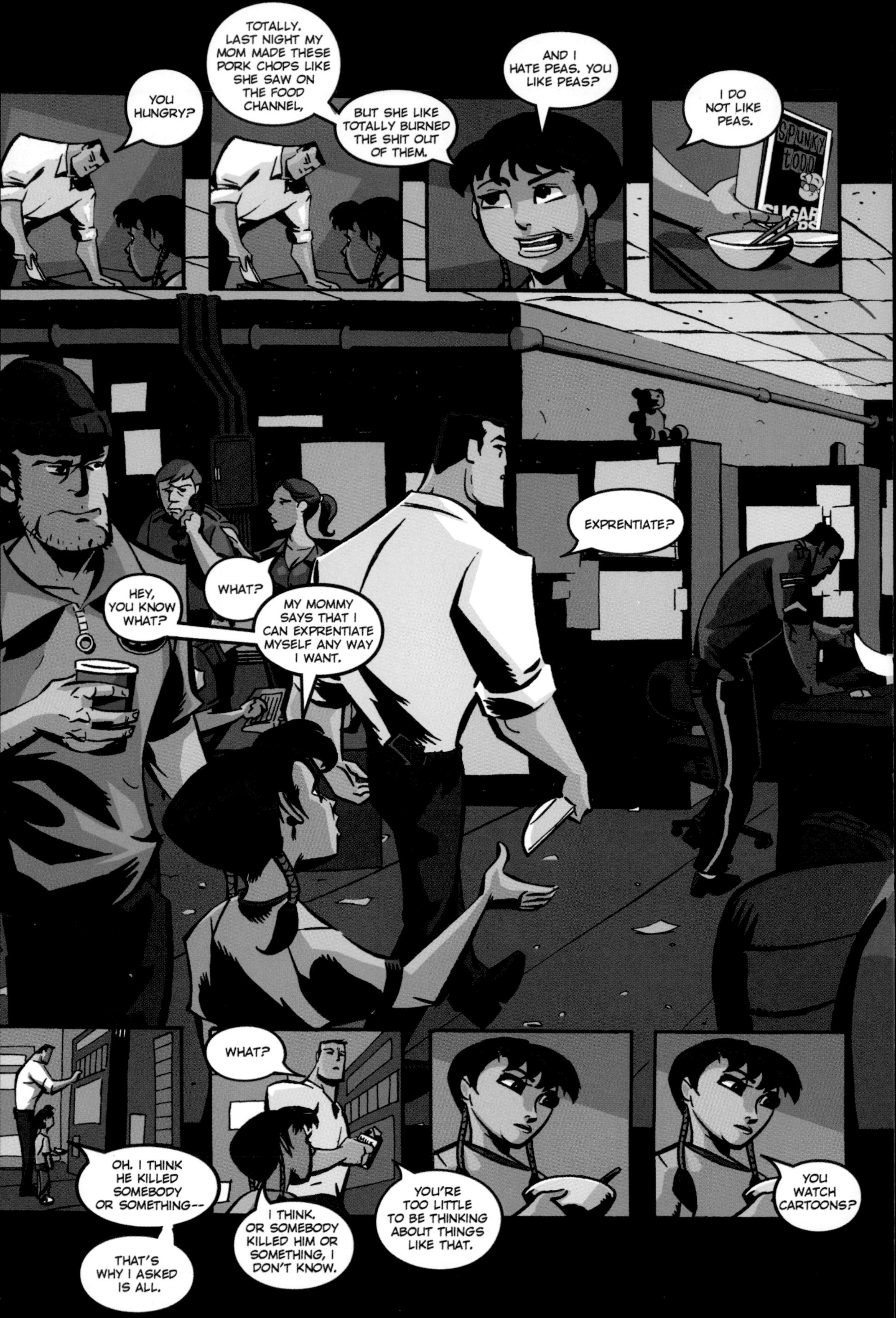
YOU HUNGRY?
TOTALLY. LAST NIGHT MY MOM MADE THESE PORK CHOPS LIKE SHE SAW ON THE FOOD CHANNEL,
BUT SHE LIKE TOTALLY BURNED THE SHIT OUT OF THEM.
AND I HATE PEAS. YOU LIKE PEAS?
I DO NOT LIKE PEAS.
SPUNKY TODD
SUGAR
HEY, YOU KNOW WHAT?
WHAT?
MY MOMMY SAYS THAT I CAN EXPRENTIATE MYSELF ANY WAY I WANT.
EXPRENTIATE?
WHAT?
OH. I THINK HE KILLED SOMEBODY OR SOMETHING--
THAT'S WHY I ASKED IS ALL.
I THINK. OR SOMEBODY KILLED HIM OR SOMETHING, I DON'T KNOW.
YOU'RE TOO LITTLE TO BE THINKING ABOUT THINGS LIKE THAT.
YOU WATCH CARTOONS?

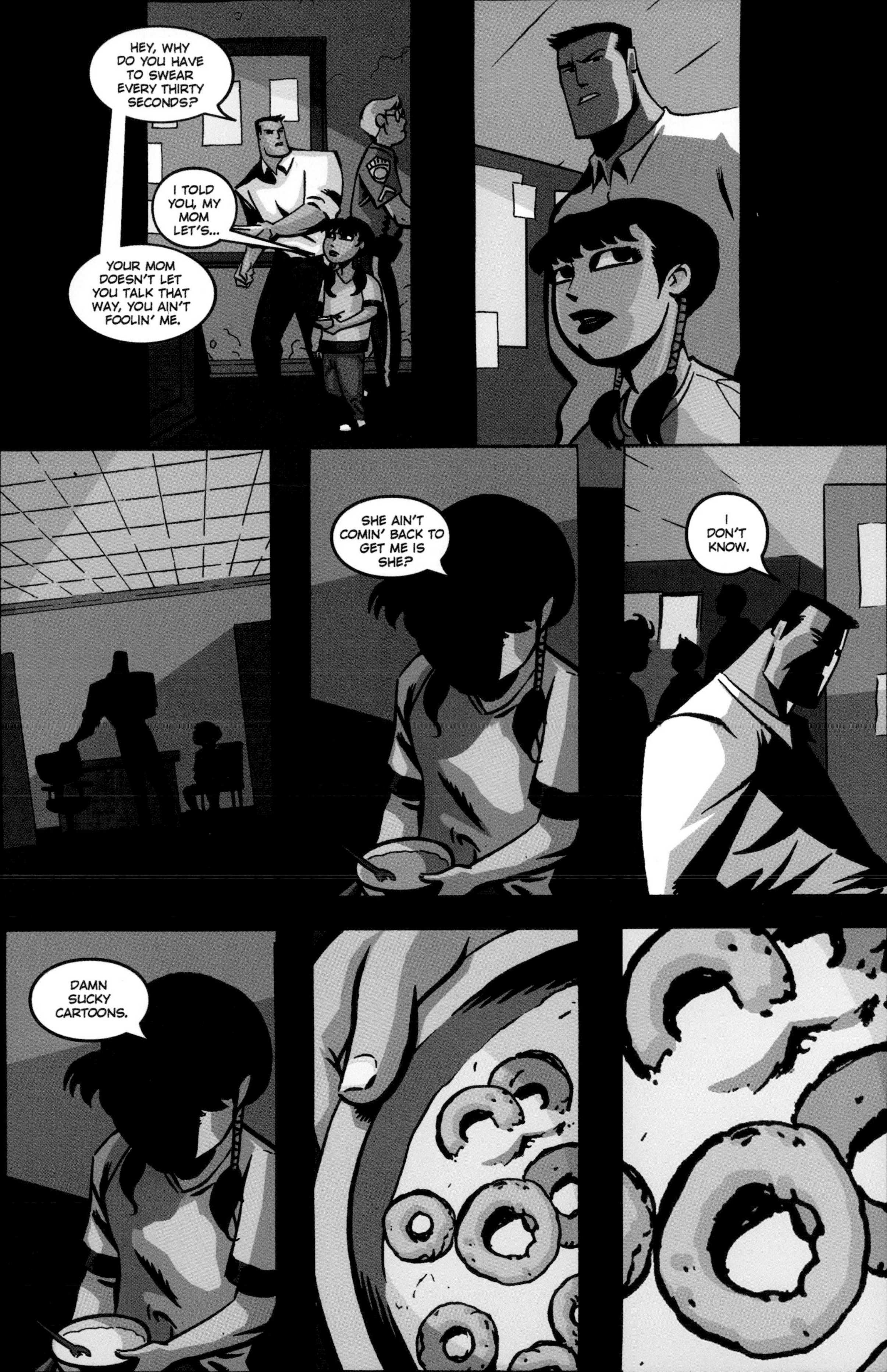
HEY, WHY DO YOU HAVE TO SWEAR EVERY THIRTY SECONDS?
I TOLD YOU, MY MOM LET'S...
YOUR MOM DOESN'T LET YOU TALK THAT WAY, YOU AIN'T FOOLIN' ME.
SHE AIN'T COMIN' BACK TO GET ME IS SHE?
I DON'T KNOW.
DAMN SUCKY CARTOONS.

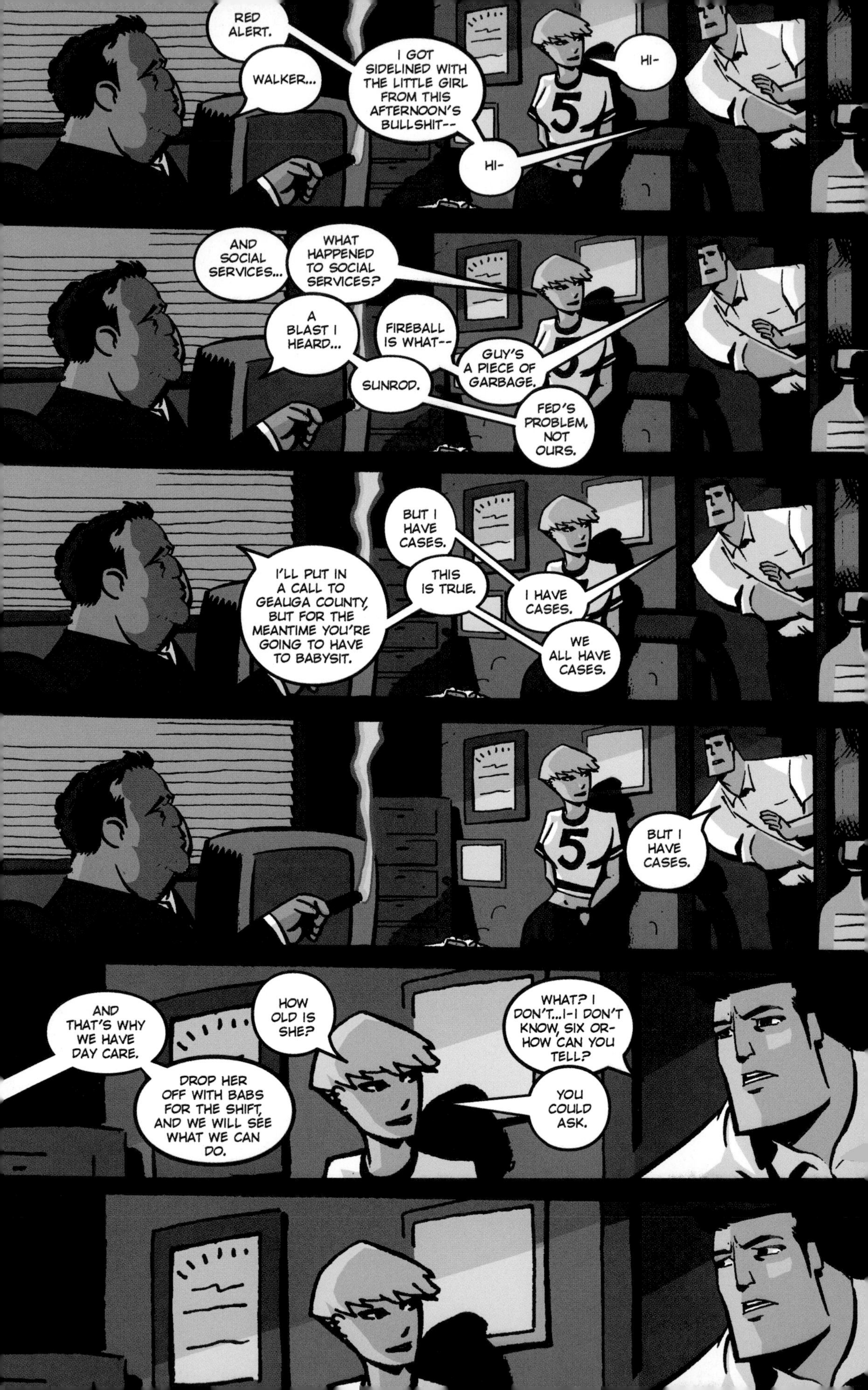
RED ALERT.
WALKER...
I GOT SIDELINED WITH THE LITTLE GIRL FROM THIS AFTERNOON'S BULLSHIT--
HI-
HI-
AND SOCIAL SERVICES...
WHAT HAPPENED TO SOCIAL SERVICES?
A BLAST I HEARD...
FIREBALL IS WHAT--
SUNROD.
GUY'S A PIECE OF GARBAGE.
FED'S PROBLEM, NOT OURS.
I'LL PUT IN A CALL TO GEAUGA COUNTY, BUT FOR THE MEANTIME YOU'RE GOING TO HAVE TO BABYSIT.
BUT I HAVE CASES.
THIS IS TRUE.
I HAVE CASES.
WE ALL HAVE CASES.
BUT I HAVE CASES.
AND THAT'S WHY WE HAVE DAY CARE.
DROP HER OFF WITH BABS FOR THE SHIFT, AND WE WILL SEE WHAT WE CAN DO.
HOW OLD IS SHE?
WHAT? I DON'T...I-I DON'T KNOW, SIX OR- HOW CAN YOU TELL?
YOU COULD ASK.

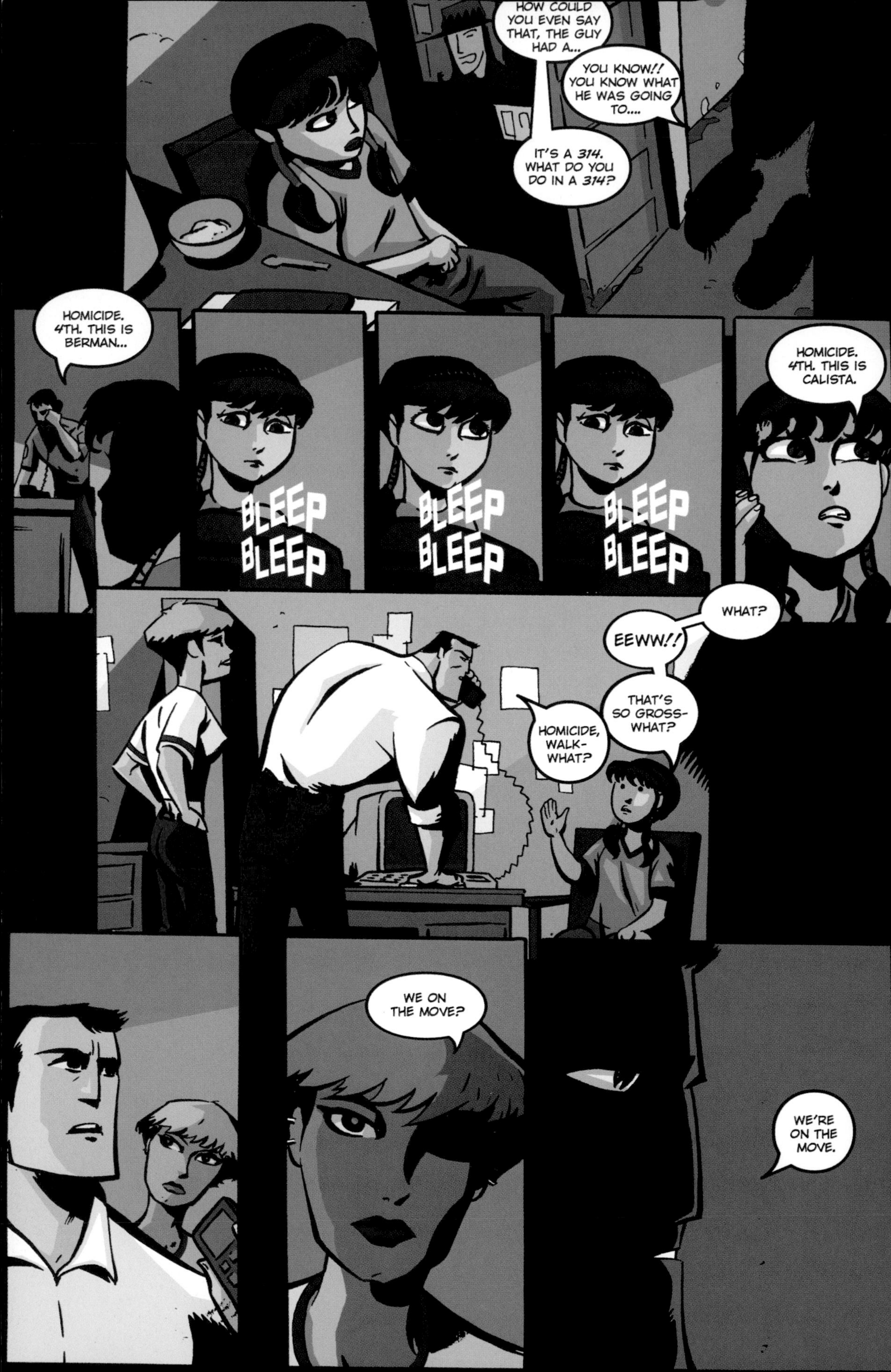
HOW COULD YOU EVEN SAY THAT, THE GUY HAD A...
YOU KNOW!! YOU KNOW WHAT HE WAS GOING TO....
IT'S A 314. WHAT DO YOU DO IN A 314?
HOMICIDE. 4TH. THIS IS BERMAN...
BLEEP BLEEP
BLEEP BLEEP
BLEEP BLEEP
HOMICIDE. 4TH. THIS IS CALISTA.
WHAT?
EEWW!!
THAT'S SO GROSS-WHAT?
HOMICIDE, WALK-WHAT?
WE ON THE MOVE?
WE'RE ON THE MOVE.

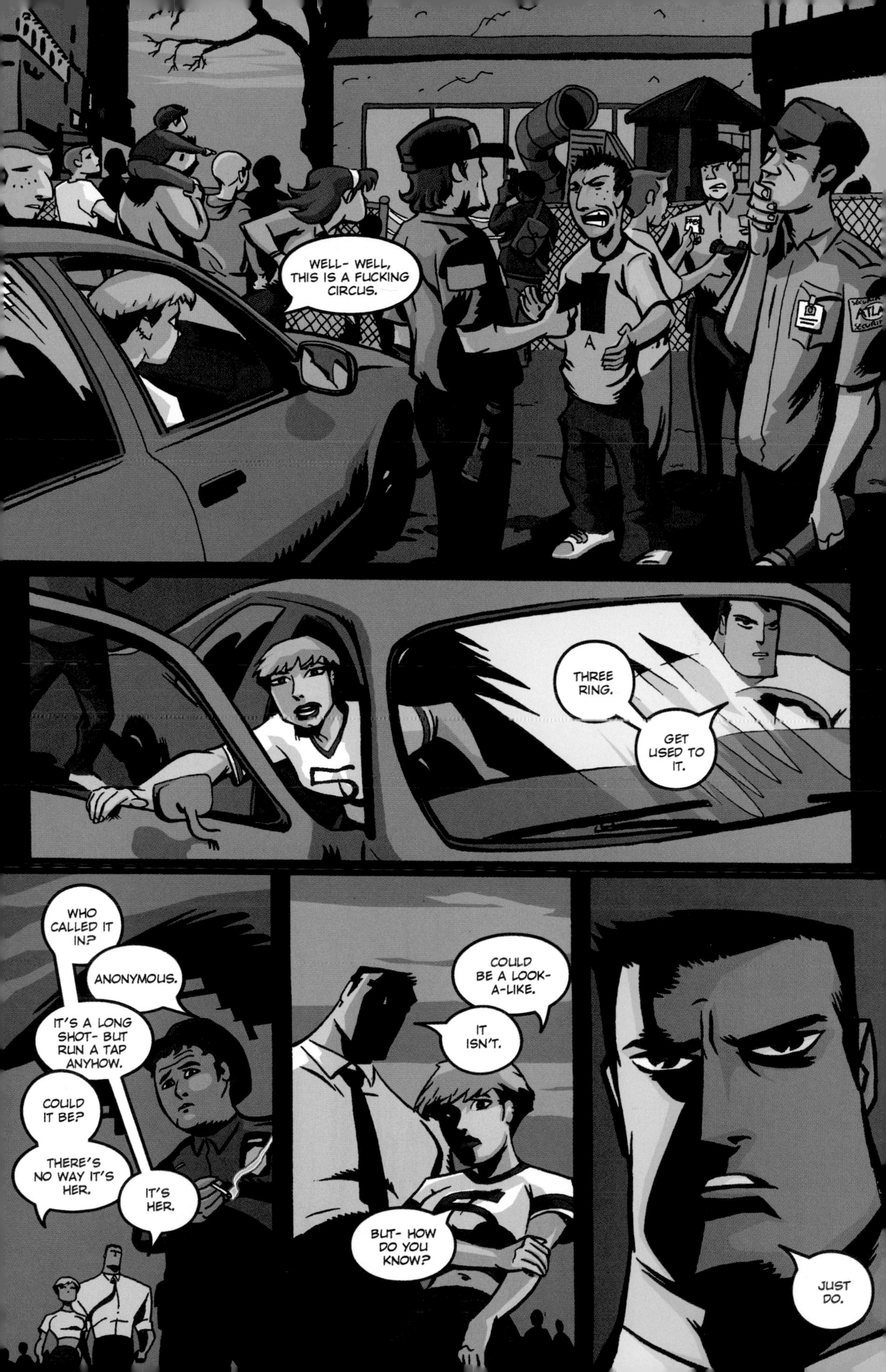
WELL- WELL, THIS IS A FUCKING CIRCUS.
THREE RING.
GET USED TO IT.
WHO CALLED IT IN?
ANONYMOUS.
IT'S A LONG SHOT- BUT RUN A TAP ANYHOW.
COULD IT BE?
THERE'S NO WAY IT'S HER.
IT'S HER.
COULD BE A LOOK-A-LIKE.
IT ISN'T.
BUT- HOW DO YOU KNOW?
JUST DO.

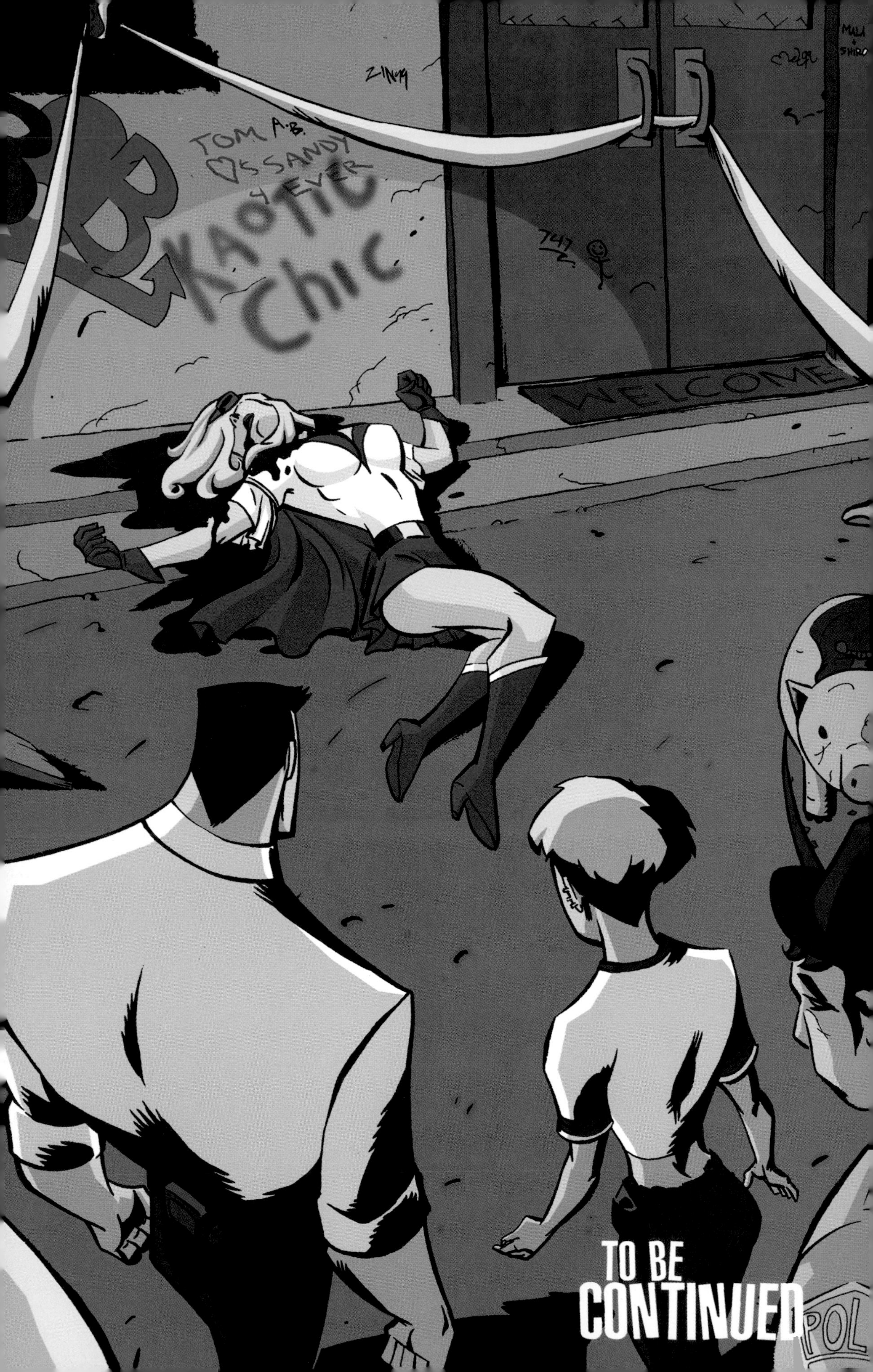
TOM A.B. ♡s SANDY 4 EVER
KAOTIC Chic
747
WELCOME
TO BE CONTINUED

A PAIR OF RED LEATHER BOOTS. SIZE FOUR.

ITEM 476-99.

WHAT IS THIS? I GUESS IT'S HER CAPE.

ITEM 476-003.

IT'S HER CAPE.

HAD TO REMOVE THESE WITH A HACK SAW AND A BLOW TORCH.

HAD TO GET THEM OFF.

TWO STEEL ARM BANDS.

ITEM 476-000

A BLOW TORCH?

HER TUNIC...

OR COSTUME OR WHATEVER--

SIGH...

ITEM NUMBER 476-006

THAT'S SO- SO SAD.

YEAH--

CAN YOU TELL US HOW YOU'RE FEELING?

SNIFF... I FEEL BAD.

SHE- SHE WAS SO BEAUTIFUL.

AS YOU CAN IMAGINE, DAVID, THE MOOD AT MORRISON ELEMENTARY IS GRIM INDEED.

IT IS HERE AND AT SCHOOLS ALL OVER THE WORLD THAT THIS TERRIBLE LOSS IS BEING FELT THE MOST.

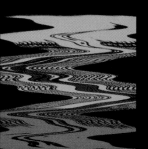

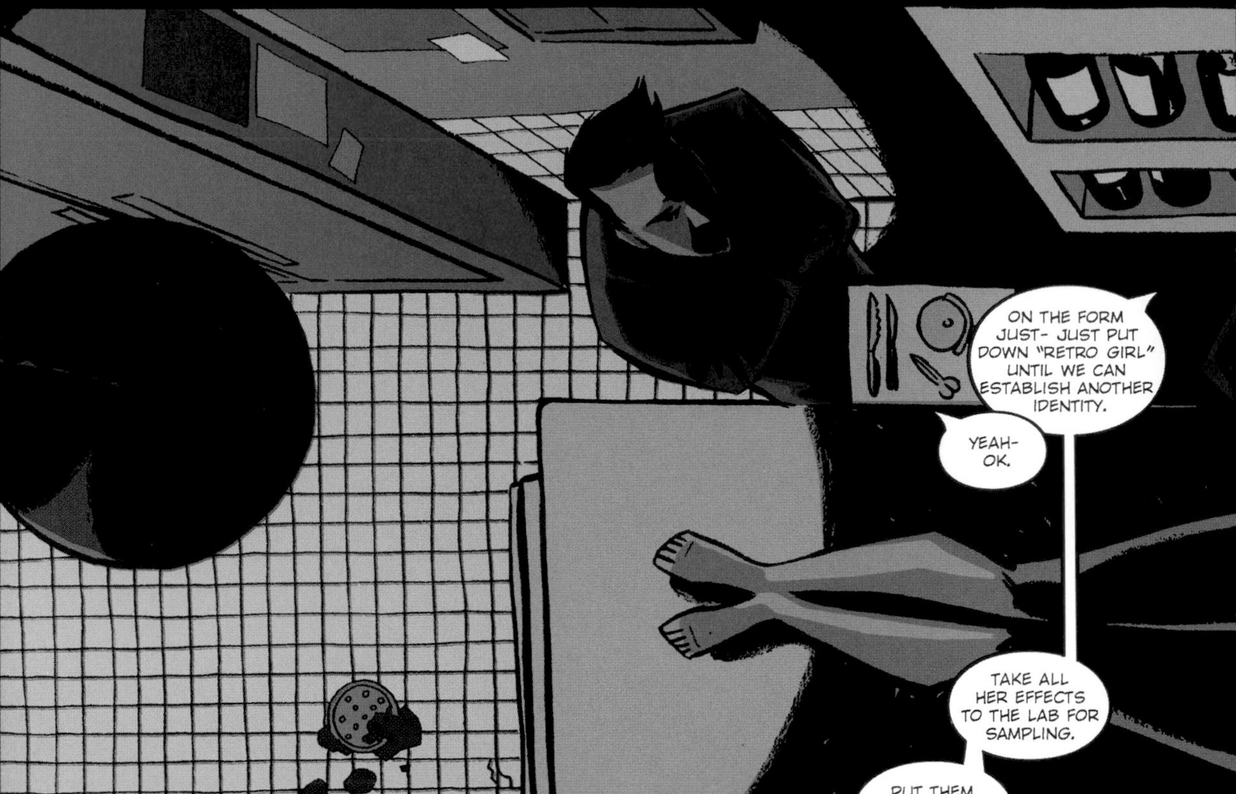
ON THE FORM JUST- JUST PUT DOWN "RETRO GIRL" UNTIL WE CAN ESTABLISH ANOTHER IDENTITY.
YEAH- OK.
TAKE ALL HER EFFECTS TO THE LAB FOR SAMPLING.
PUT THEM THROUGH FIBERS AND WHAT NOT--
YEAH...OF COURSE.

IF YOU ARE JUST JOINING US, WE ARE CONTINUING OUR EXTENSIVE ROUND-THE-CLOCK COVERAGE. THE LEAD STORY OF COURSE...

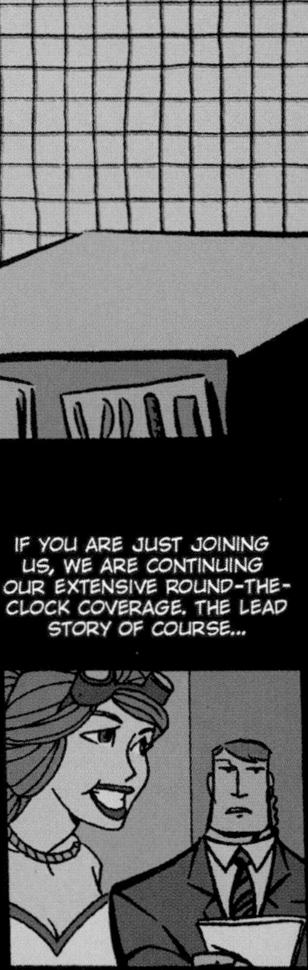

RETRO GIRL IS DEAD.

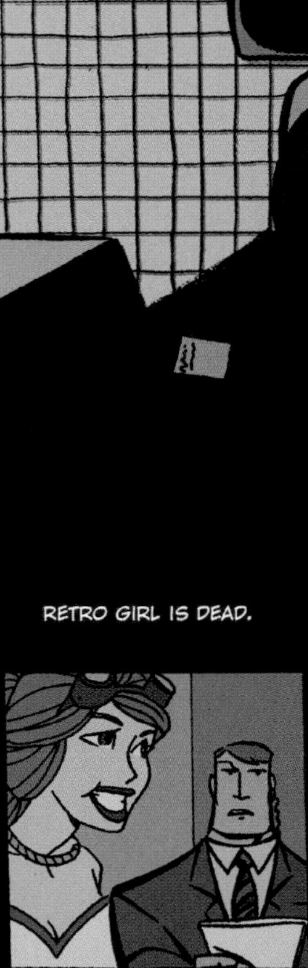

WE ARE STILL AWAITING OFFICIAL WORD FROM THE CORONER'S OFFICE FOR DETAILS CONCERNING THIS HARROWING TRAGEDY.

WE PLAN TO CONTINUE WITH OUR EXCLUSIVE COVERAGE UNTIL THAT TIME.

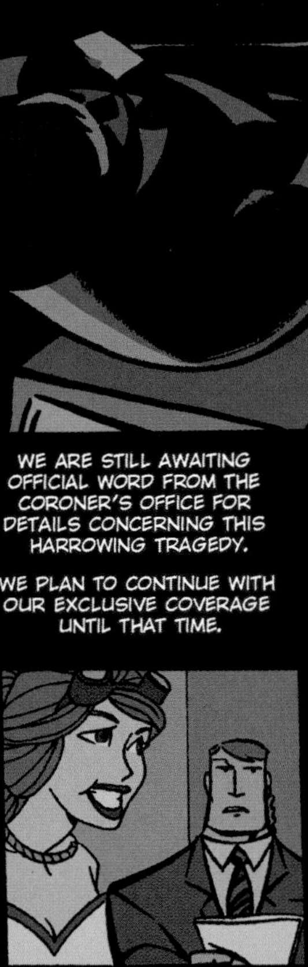

SOME OF THE IMAGES YOU ARE ABOUT TO SEE MIGHT DISTURB AND SHOCK YOU. IF YOU ARE OF WEAK CONSTITUTION OR HAVE CHILDREN PRESENT, WE URGE YOU TO TURN AWAY.

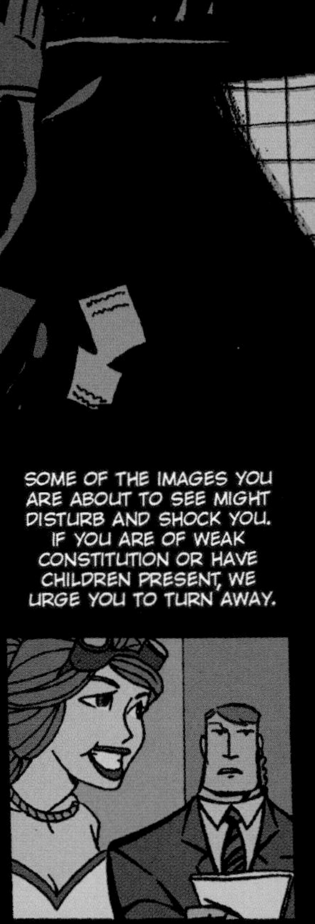

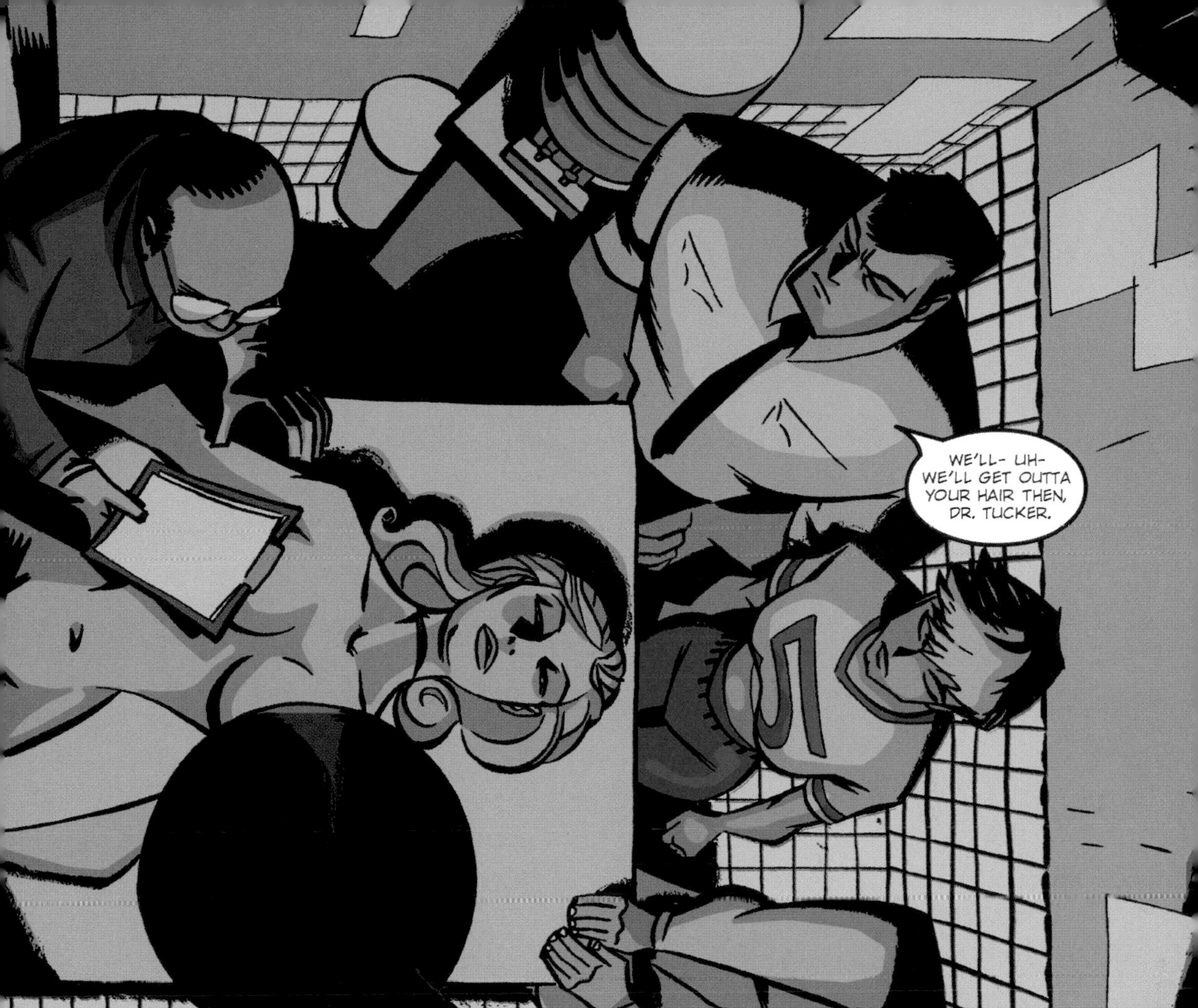
WE'LL- UH- WE'LL GET OUTTA YOUR HAIR THEN, DR. TUCKER.

IT WAS JUST UNDER THREE HOURS AGO, EASTERN STANDARD TIME, THAT WE RECEIVED WORD THAT THE FALLEN BODY OF RETRO GIRL WAS FOUND LYING DEAD ON THE PLAYGROUND OF MORRISON ELEMENTARY.

THESE EXCLUSIVE IMAGES WHERE TAKEN JUST MOMENTS BEFORE POLICE ARRIVED, CLOSING BOTH THE PLAYGROUND AND THE SCHOOL TO THE PUBLIC.

THE CAUSE AND INCIDENT OF HER DEATH REMAINS A MYSTERY. WAS IT AN ACCIDENT THAT BEFELL ONE OF OUR NATION'S MOST BELOVED AND REVERED HEROES?

OR DID SHE BECOME YET ANOTHER VICTIM OF THE VIOLENT WORLD THAT SHE HAD SO BOLDLY SWORN TO PROTECT?

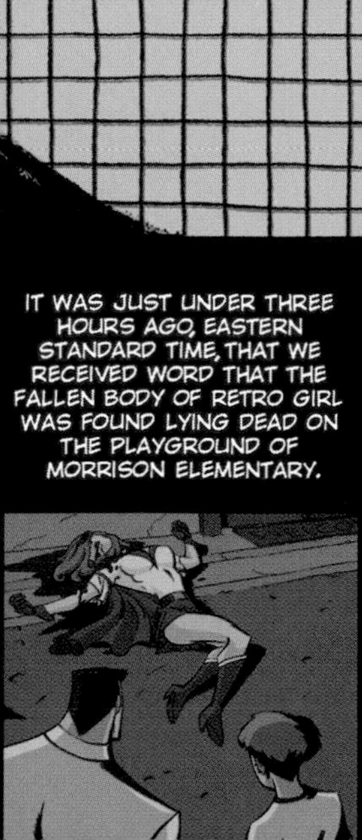

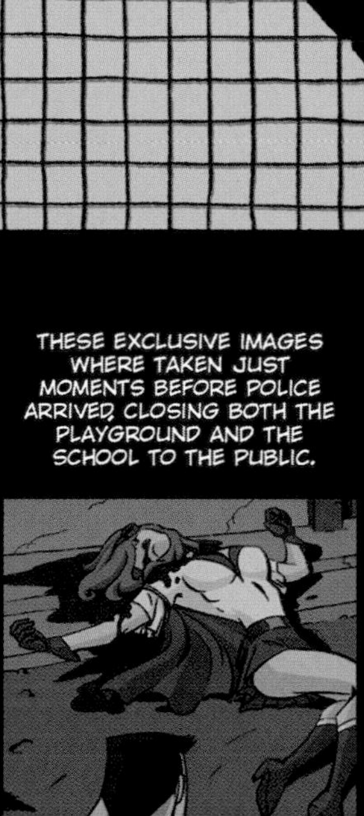

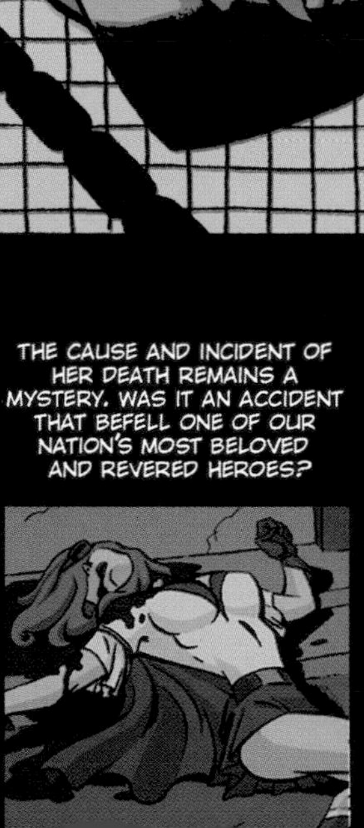

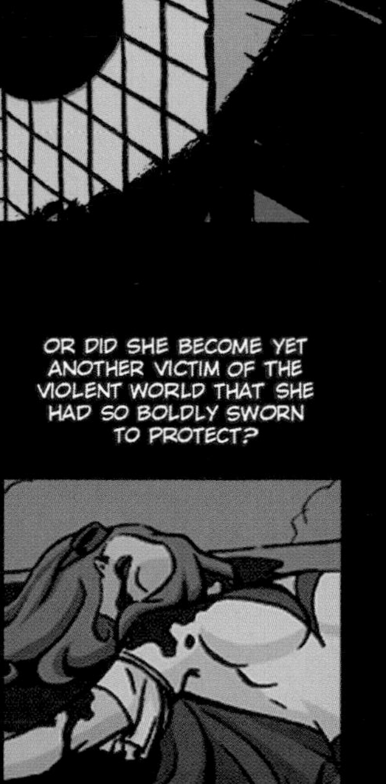

YEAH, OK. I GET IT.

WELL, THEN.

WE SHOULDN'T BE SO QUICK TO SLAP LABELS ON EVERYTHING IN THIS WORLD, SHOULD WE?

THING OF IT IS--

I MEAN-- I WANT TO DO MY JOB.

I WANT TO LOOK MY FRIEND WALKER HERE IN THE FACE AND BE ABLE TO ANSWER EVERY QUESTION THAT COULD POSSIBLY POP INTO HIS THICK COP-LIKE HEAD...

THE THING IS I-I-I CAN'T WHEN IT COMES TO STUFF LIKE THIS. THERE'S NO TEXTBOOK. THERE'S NO MANUAL.

I HAVE TO RETRAIN MYSELF EVERY DAY.

I MIGHT AS WELL THROW MY M.D. IN THE GARBAGE!

DO YOU HAVE ANY IDEA WHAT IT'S LIKE EVERY GODDAMN DAY?

WHAT THE FUCK?

IT'S WORTHLESS.

YEAH, WELL...

THROW IT OUT!! BYE BYE!!

FUCKING SPACE LIZARDS AND ORANGUTANS WITH LASER GUNS.

I MEAN- I MEAN- I MEAN-

HERE'S YOUR BREAKFAST, SIR.

OH, THANK GOD.

PEOPLE STARTED RUNNIN' ALL AROUND, AND THEN ONE OF THE TOUR GUIDES, SHE STARTS CRYIN'- CRYIN' RIGHT INTO THE P.A. SYSTEM...

TELLING EVERYONE THAT THERE WAS A BOMB. RIGHT HERE ON THE ROOF, DONTCHA KNOW?

IT WAS ON THAT FATEFUL DAY- RIGHT HERE AT THIS POWER CONTROL SWITCH ON THE ROOF OF THE UNITY BUILDING...

WE EVENTUALLY FOUND OUT THAT THE TERRORIST ORGANIZATION RUN BY THE INFAMOUS KAMEEL MASINKONI HAD MADE GOOD--

--HIS LONG-STANDING PROMISE OF RETALIATION TO OUR COUNTRY'S ALLEGIANCE WITH THE REBEL FORCES THAT REMOVED HIM FROM POWER--

SO, EVERYBODY STARTS RUNNING AROUND LIKE CHICKENS WITH THEIR HEADS CUT OFF, MY GRANDSON IS A-HUGGIN' MY LEG. THE DOORS ARE LOCKED. THE ELEVATORS AREN'T WORKIN'. ALL HELL HAD BROKEN LOOSE.

MASINKONI HAD MADE GOOD--

BRINGING THE TERRORIST WAR OF HIS COUNTRY RIGHT ONTO AMERICAN SOIL.

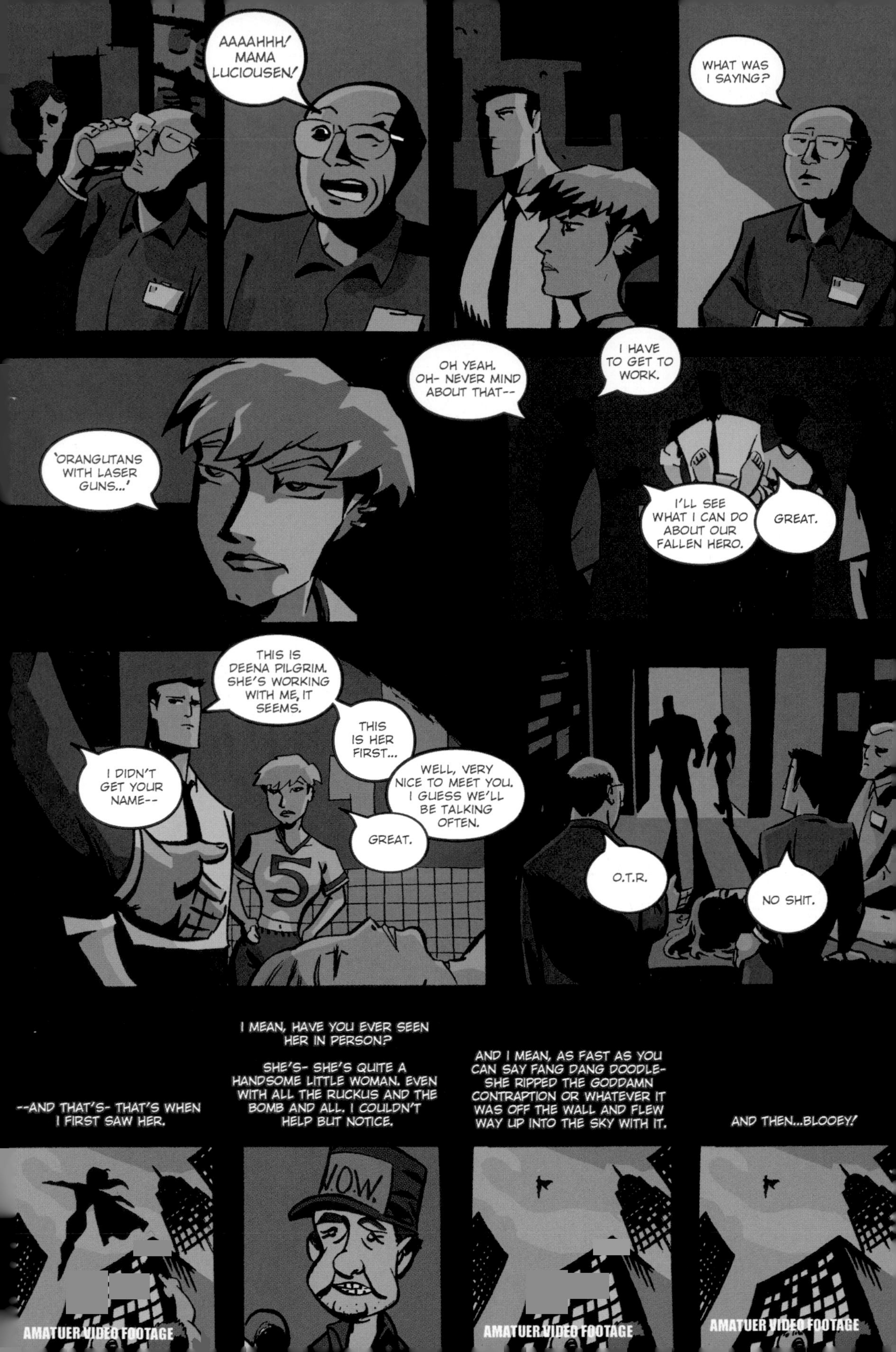
AAAAHHH! MAMA LUCIOUSEN!
WHAT WAS I SAYING?
'ORANGUTANS WITH LASER GUNS...'
OH YEAH. OH- NEVER MIND ABOUT THAT--
I HAVE TO GET TO WORK.
I'LL SEE WHAT I CAN DO ABOUT OUR FALLEN HERO.
GREAT.
THIS IS DEENA PILGRIM. SHE'S WORKING WITH ME, IT SEEMS.
I DIDN'T GET YOUR NAME--
THIS IS HER FIRST...
WELL, VERY NICE TO MEET YOU. I GUESS WE'LL BE TALKING OFTEN.
GREAT.
O.T.R.
NO SHIT.
--AND THAT'S- THAT'S WHEN I FIRST SAW HER.
AMATUER VIDEO FOOTAGE
I MEAN, HAVE YOU EVER SEEN HER IN PERSON?
SHE'S- SHE'S QUITE A HANDSOME LITTLE WOMAN. EVEN WITH ALL THE RUCKUS AND THE BOMB AND ALL. I COULDN'T HELP BUT NOTICE.
W.O.W.
AND I MEAN, AS FAST AS YOU CAN SAY FANG DANG DOODLE- SHE RIPPED THE GODDAMN CONTRAPTION OR WHATEVER IT WAS OFF THE WALL AND FLEW WAY UP INTO THE SKY WITH IT.
AMATUER VIDEO FOOTAGE
AND THEN...BLOOEY!
AMATUER VIDEO FOOTAGE

IT- LISTEN- I DON'T KNOW IF YOU'VE EVER HAD THE EXPERIENCE, BUT...BEING SAVED- UP IN THE AIR LIKE THAT IT- IT'LL CHANGE YOU.

YOU- YOU REALIZE HOW BIG IT ALL IS...

BUT WHO WAS RETRO GIRL, THE PERSON?

WHAT BROUGHT UPON HER UNTIMELY AND TRAGIC DEATH THAT HAS THE NATION MOURNING TODAY?

AS WE STAND OUTSIDE THIS DOWNTOWN DISTRICT POLICE STATION WAITING FOR OFFICIAL COMMENT ON THIS TRAGIC EVENT...

ALL WE CAN DO IS WAIT AND WONDER...AND MOURN.

WE'LL BE RIGHT BACK.

BACK TO YOU IN THE STUDIO...

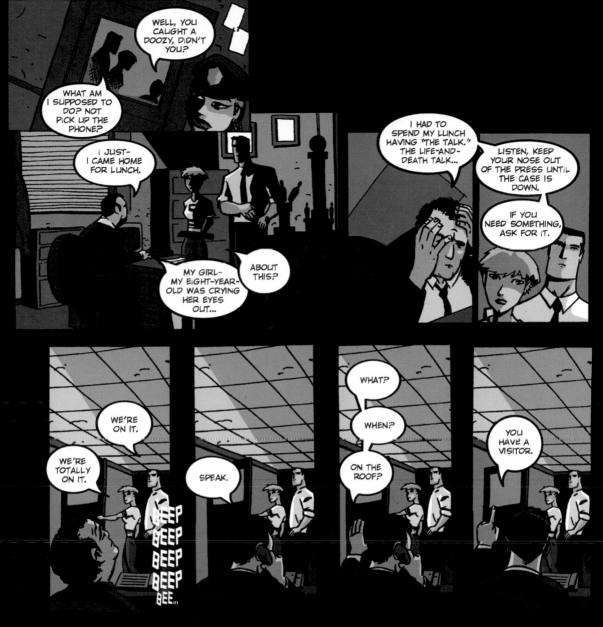

IF YOU'RE JUST JOINING US, WE ARE CONTINUING OUR ROUND-THE-CLOCK COVERAGE OF THIS TRUE AMERICAN TRAGEDY.

THE YOUNG PIXIE KNOWN ONLY TO HER PUBLIC AS RETRO GIRL HAS BEEN FOUND DEAD ON THE PLAYGROUND OF MORRISON ELEMENTARY.

THE CAUSE OF HER DEATH IS STILL UNKNOWN, BUT NUMEROUS REPORTS BELIEVE THAT SHE WAS FOUND WITH A FATAL WOUND TO THE NECK AND THROAT AREA...

WE HAVE COLLEEN MCBRIDE OUTSIDE THE JUSTICE CENTER WAITING FOR OFFICIAL WORD FROM POLICE AND AUTHORITIES.

BUT IN THE MEANWHILE, HERE IS ROGER SANDERS WITH A LOOK BACK AT THE POWERFUL LEGACY OF RETRO GIRL.

LIKE MANY OF THE COLORFUL CHARACTERS THAT SURROUND OUR CITY, REALLY VERY LITTLE IS KNOWN ABOUT RETRO GIRL.

MOST OF WHAT WE KNOW IS WHAT SHE HAS LET US KNOW.

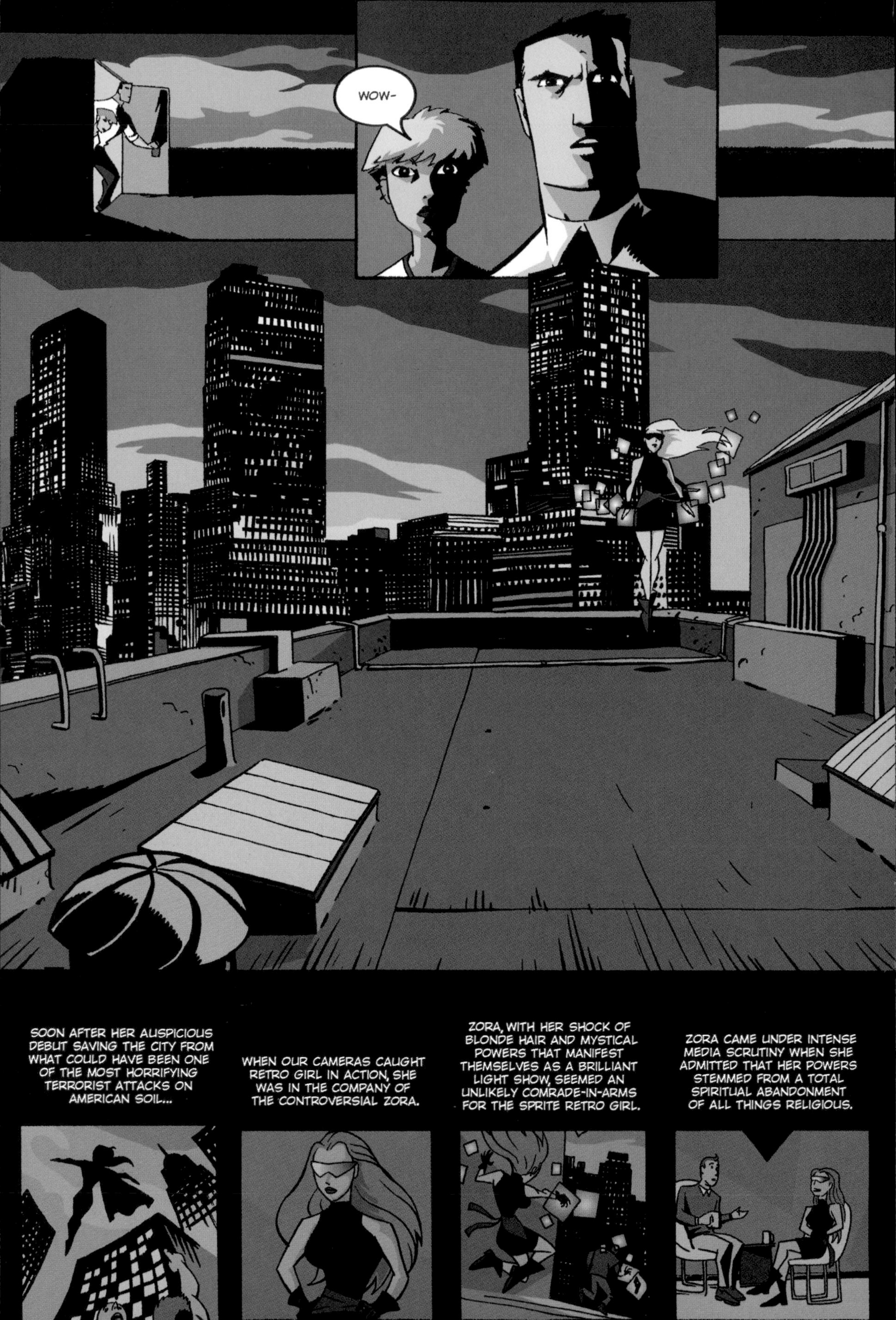
WOW-
SOON AFTER HER AUSPICIOUS DEBUT SAVING THE CITY FROM WHAT COULD HAVE BEEN ONE OF THE MOST HORRIFYING TERRORIST ATTACKS ON AMERICAN SOIL...
WHEN OUR CAMERAS CAUGHT RETRO GIRL IN ACTION, SHE WAS IN THE COMPANY OF THE CONTROVERSIAL ZORA.
ZORA, WITH HER SHOCK OF BLONDE HAIR AND MYSTICAL POWERS THAT MANIFEST THEMSELVES AS A BRILLIANT LIGHT SHOW, SEEMED AN UNLIKELY COMRADE-IN-ARMS FOR THE SPRITE RETRO GIRL.
ZORA CAME UNDER INTENSE MEDIA SCRUTINY WHEN SHE ADMITTED THAT HER POWERS STEMMED FROM A TOTAL SPIRITUAL ABANDONMENT OF ALL THINGS RELIGIOUS.

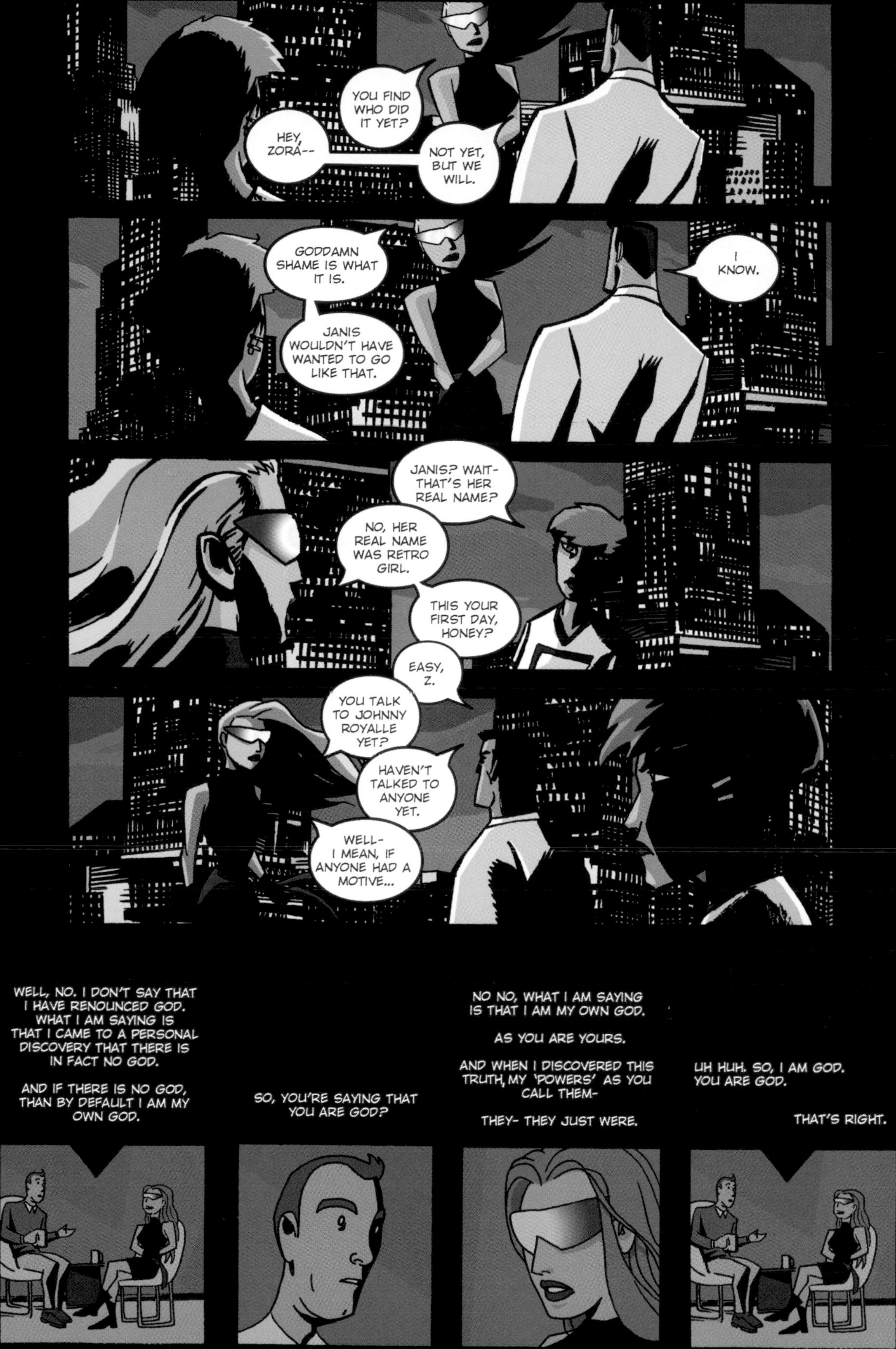
YOU FIND WHO DID IT YET?
HEY, ZORA--
NOT YET, BUT WE WILL.
GODDAMN SHAME IS WHAT IT IS.
JANIS WOULDN'T HAVE WANTED TO GO LIKE THAT.
I KNOW.
JANIS? WAIT- THAT'S HER REAL NAME?
NO, HER REAL NAME WAS RETRO GIRL.
THIS YOUR FIRST DAY, HONEY?
EASY, Z.
YOU TALK TO JOHNNY ROYALLE YET?
HAVEN'T TALKED TO ANYONE YET.
WELL- I MEAN, IF ANYONE HAD A MOTIVE...
WELL, NO. I DON'T SAY THAT I HAVE RENOUNCED GOD. WHAT I AM SAYING IS THAT I CAME TO A PERSONAL DISCOVERY THAT THERE IS IN FACT NO GOD.
AND IF THERE IS NO GOD, THAN BY DEFAULT I AM MY OWN GOD.
SO, YOU'RE SAYING THAT YOU ARE GOD?
NO NO, WHAT I AM SAYING IS THAT I AM MY OWN GOD.
AS YOU ARE YOURS.
AND WHEN I DISCOVERED THIS TRUTH, MY 'POWERS' AS YOU CALL THEM-
THEY- THEY JUST WERE.
UH HUH. SO, I AM GOD. YOU ARE GOD.
THAT'S RIGHT.

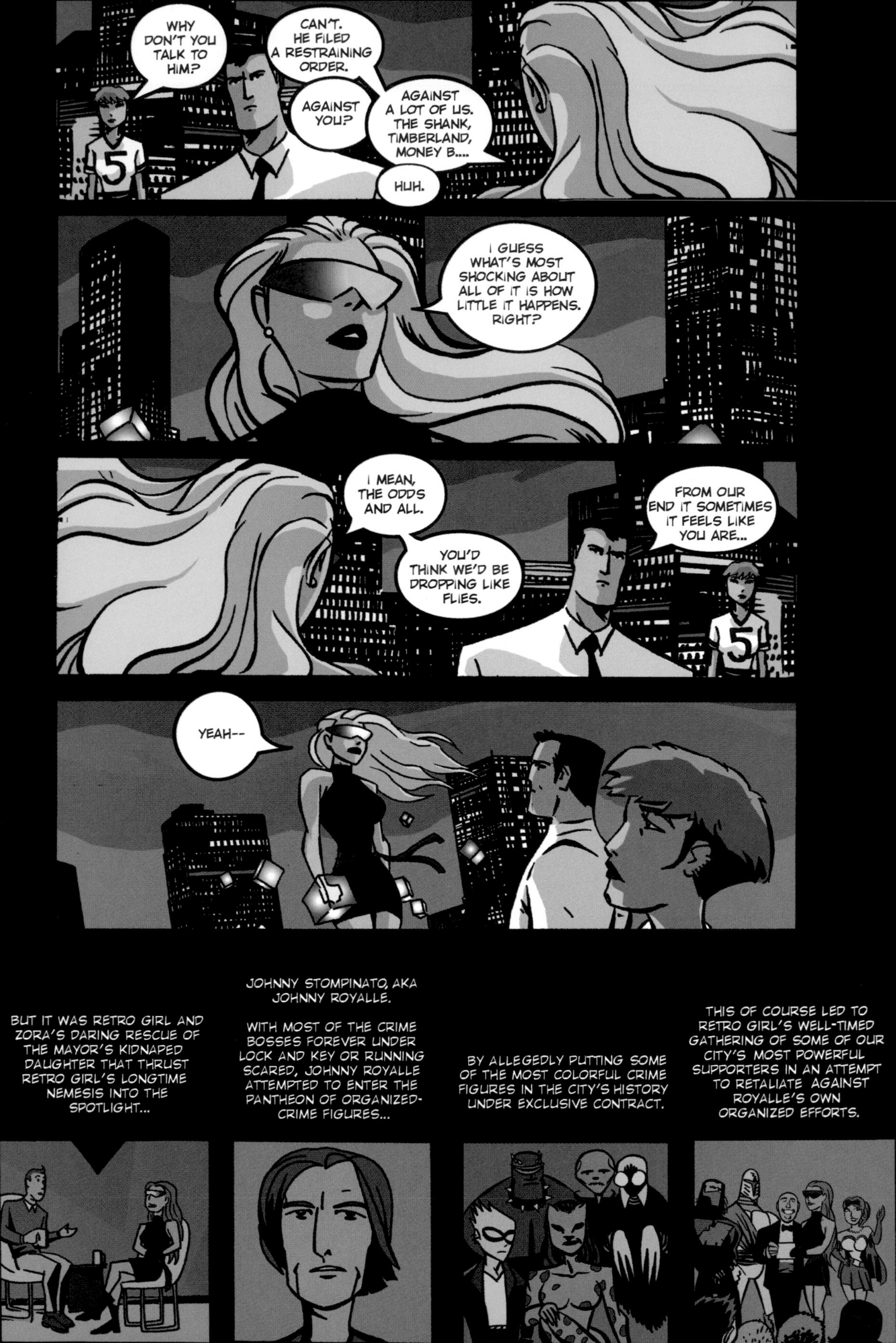

WHY DON'T YOU TALK TO HIM?
CAN'T. HE FILED A RESTRAINING ORDER.
AGAINST YOU?
AGAINST A LOT OF US. THE SHANK, TIMBERLAND, MONEY B....
HUH.
I GUESS WHAT'S MOST SHOCKING ABOUT ALL OF IT IS HOW LITTLE IT HAPPENS. RIGHT?
I MEAN, THE ODDS AND ALL.
YOU'D THINK WE'D BE DROPPING LIKE FLIES.
FROM OUR END IT SOMETIMES IT FEELS LIKE YOU ARE...
YEAH--
BUT IT WAS RETRO GIRL AND ZORA'S DARING RESCUE OF THE MAYOR'S KIDNAPED DAUGHTER THAT THRUST RETRO GIRL'S LONGTIME NEMESIS INTO THE SPOTLIGHT...
JOHNNY STOMPINATO, AKA JOHNNY ROYALLE.
WITH MOST OF THE CRIME BOSSES FOREVER UNDER LOCK AND KEY OR RUNNING SCARED, JOHNNY ROYALLE ATTEMPTED TO ENTER THE PANTHEON OF ORGANIZED-CRIME FIGURES...
BY ALLEGEDLY PUTTING SOME OF THE MOST COLORFUL CRIME FIGURES IN THE CITY'S HISTORY UNDER EXCLUSIVE CONTRACT.
THIS OF COURSE LED TO RETRO GIRL'S WELL-TIMED GATHERING OF SOME OF OUR CITY'S MOST POWERFUL SUPPORTERS IN AN ATTEMPT TO RETALIATE AGAINST ROYALLE'S OWN ORGANIZED EFFORTS.

IT WAS HERE AT THE CORNER OF E STREET AND COMBS THAT THE FEUD FOR CONTROL OF THE CITY CAME TO ITS VIOLENT CONCLUSION.

THE DETAILS OF WHAT HAPPENED THAT DAY WERE NEVER DIVULGED TO THE PUBLIC. ALL WE KNOW FOR SURE IS THAT MANY OF THE FIGURES INVOLVED DISAPPEARED FROM PUBLIC EYE, MAYBE FOREVER.

WHETHER VOLUNTARY RETIREMENT OR LIVES LOST IN BATTLE FOR OUR CITY'S FUTURE...

WE HAVE NEVER AGAIN HEARD FROM TWILIGHT, DIAMOND, SSAZZ, OR THE B.9. FOMFOM.

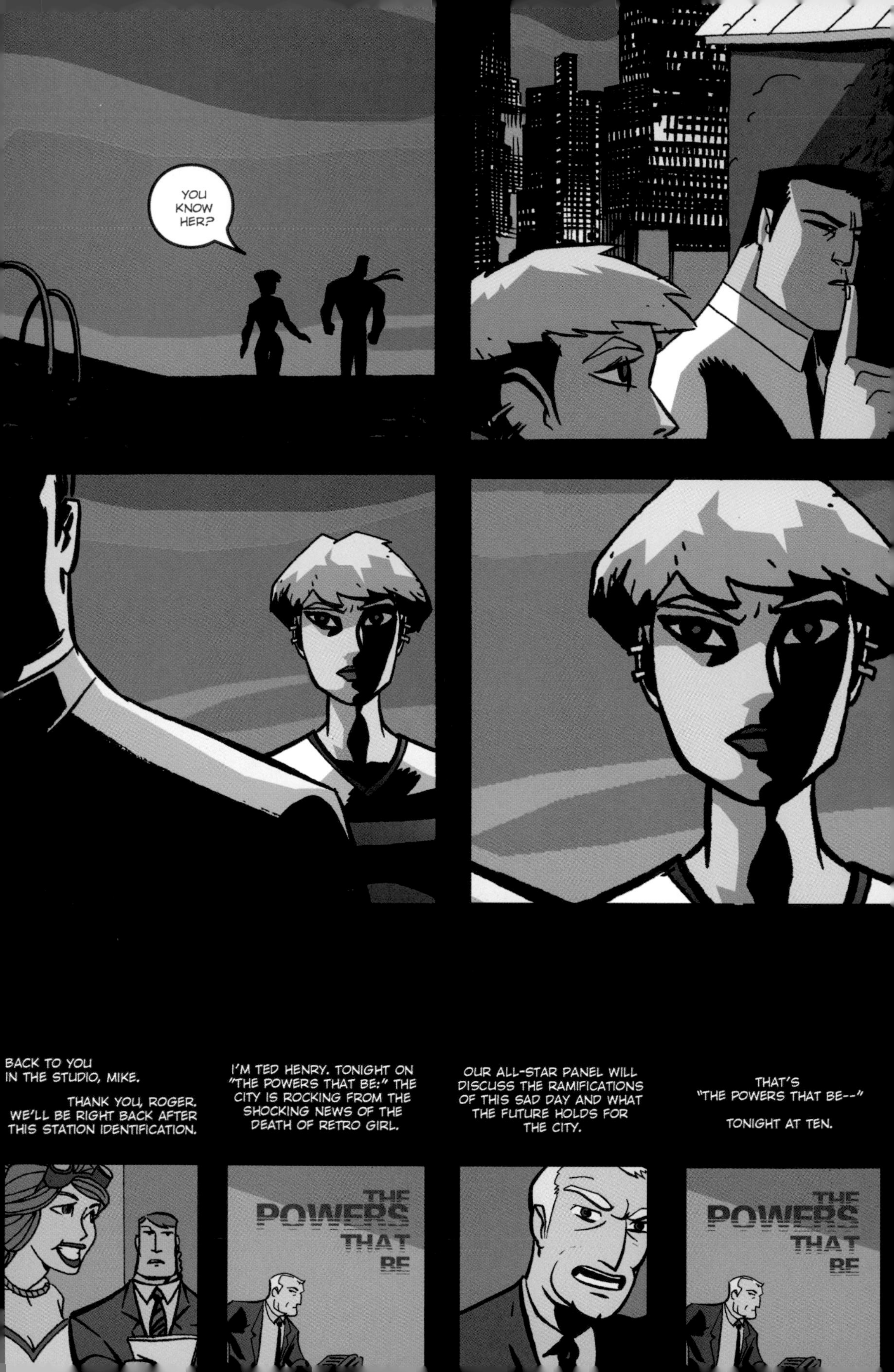
YOU KNOW HER?
BACK TO YOU IN THE STUDIO, MIKE.
THANK YOU, ROGER. WE'LL BE RIGHT BACK AFTER THIS STATION IDENTIFICATION.
I'M TED HENRY. TONIGHT ON "THE POWERS THAT BE:" THE CITY IS ROCKING FROM THE SHOCKING NEWS OF THE DEATH OF RETRO GIRL.
THE POWERS THAT BE
OUR ALL-STAR PANEL WILL DISCUSS THE RAMIFICATIONS OF THIS SAD DAY AND WHAT THE FUTURE HOLDS FOR THE CITY.
THAT'S "THE POWERS THAT BE--"
TONIGHT AT TEN.
THE POWERS THAT BE

STANDING WITH ME IS
THE SUPERINTENDENT
OF CITY SCHOOLS,
CLAYTON MANZERICK.

YES, WE DECIDED TO GIVE
THE KIDS THE REST OF
THE DAY OFF TO REFLECT
AND GRIEVE THIS
TERRIBLE LOSS.

WHAT WE HOPE WILL
HAPPEN IS THAT PARENTS
WILL ENGAGE THEIR CHILDREN
IN A DISCUSSION ABOUT THE
TRAGEDY AND HELP THEIR
LITTLE MINDS GAIN SOME
PERSPECTIVE.

CAN YOU TELL US MR.
SUPERINTENDENT, WHETHER
ANYBODY HERE AT THE
SCHOOL SAW ANYTHING
THAT WOULD HELP POLICE
WITH THEIR INVESTIGATION?

NO. NOTHING THAT
I AM AWARE OF.

WHY'S THAT, SIR?

BECAUSE THEY ARE
THE FUTURE.

ALRIGHT.

WHAT'S MOST IMPORTANT
NOW IS THAT WE FOCUS
ON THE CHILDREN.

THE CAUSE OF HER DEATH IS STILL UNKNOWN, WE CONTINUING OUR COVERAGE OF THE DEATH OF RETRO GIRL JUST A FEW HOURS AGO.

WE HAVE COLLEEN MCBRIDE OUTSIDE THE JUSTICE CENTER WAITING FOR OFFICIAL WORD FROM POLICE AND AUTHORITIES.

STILL NO WORD FROM AUTHORITIES HERE AT THE JUSTICE CENTER.

WE HAVE RECEIVED UNCONFIRMED REPORTS THAT AN AUTOPSY IS ALREADY UNDER WAY AND THAT ZORA HAS BEEN SPOTTED ON THE ROOF OF THE JUSTICE CENTER.

NOW WHETHER ZORA WAS HERE TO HELP WITH THE INVESTIGATION OR TO PAY HER RESPECTS IS STILL UNCLEAR.

IS THERE ANY WORD ON WHO IS CONDUCTING THE INVESTIGATION?

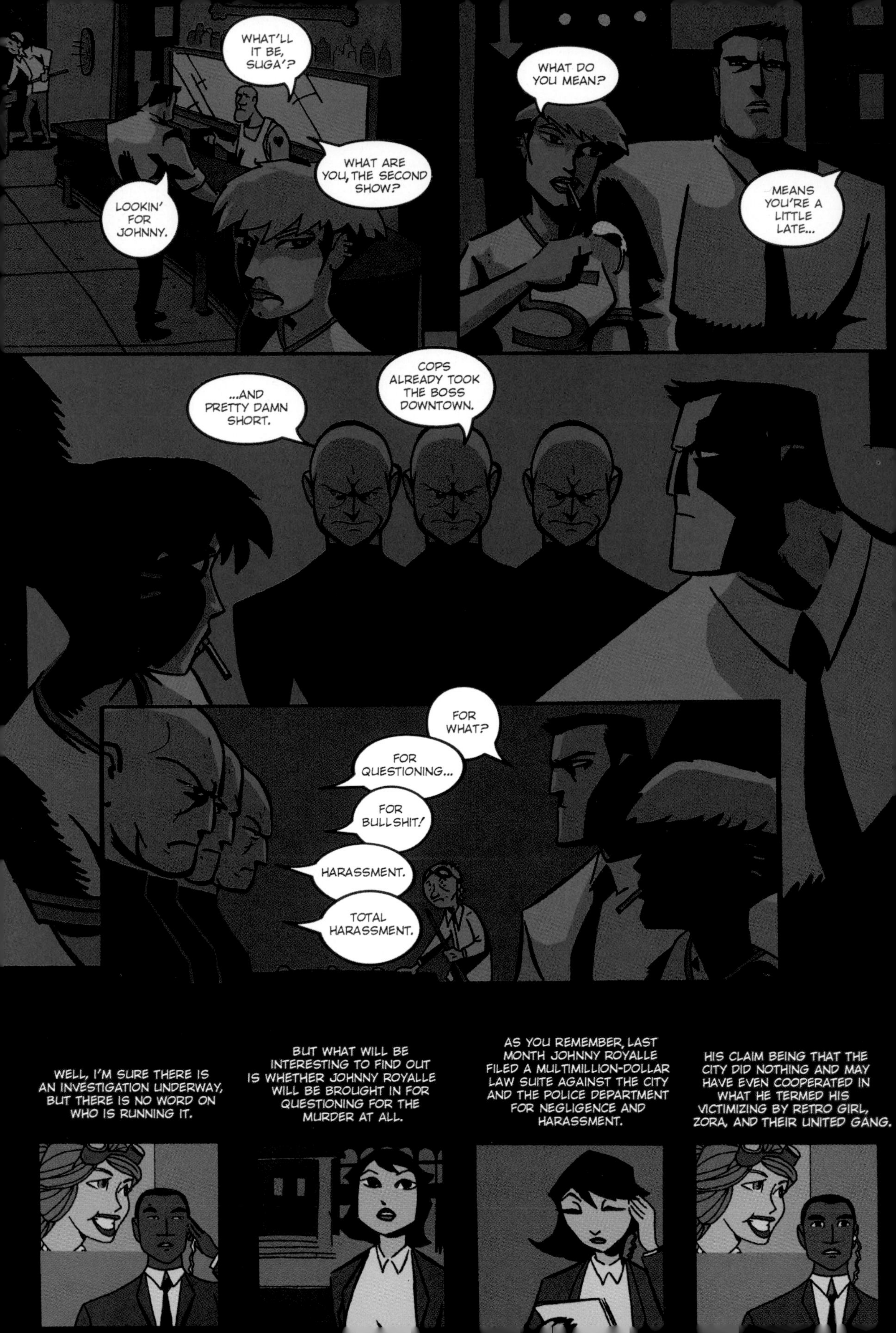
WHAT'LL IT BE, SUGA'?
WHAT ARE YOU, THE SECOND SHOW?
LOOKIN' FOR JOHNNY.
WHAT DO YOU MEAN?
MEANS YOU'RE A LITTLE LATE...
...AND PRETTY DAMN SHORT.
COPS ALREADY TOOK THE BOSS DOWNTOWN.
FOR WHAT?
FOR QUESTIONING...
FOR BULLSHIT!
HARASSMENT.
TOTAL HARASSMENT.
WELL, I'M SURE THERE IS AN INVESTIGATION UNDERWAY, BUT THERE IS NO WORD ON WHO IS RUNNING IT.
BUT WHAT WILL BE INTERESTING TO FIND OUT IS WHETHER JOHNNY ROYALLE WILL BE BROUGHT IN FOR QUESTIONING FOR THE MURDER AT ALL.
AS YOU REMEMBER, LAST MONTH JOHNNY ROYALLE FILED A MULTIMILLION-DOLLAR LAW SUITE AGAINST THE CITY AND THE POLICE DEPARTMENT FOR NEGLIGENCE AND HARASSMENT.
HIS CLAIM BEING THAT THE CITY DID NOTHING AND MAY HAVE EVEN COOPERATED IN WHAT HE TERMED HIS VICTIMIZING BY RETRO GIRL, ZORA, AND THEIR UNITED GANG.

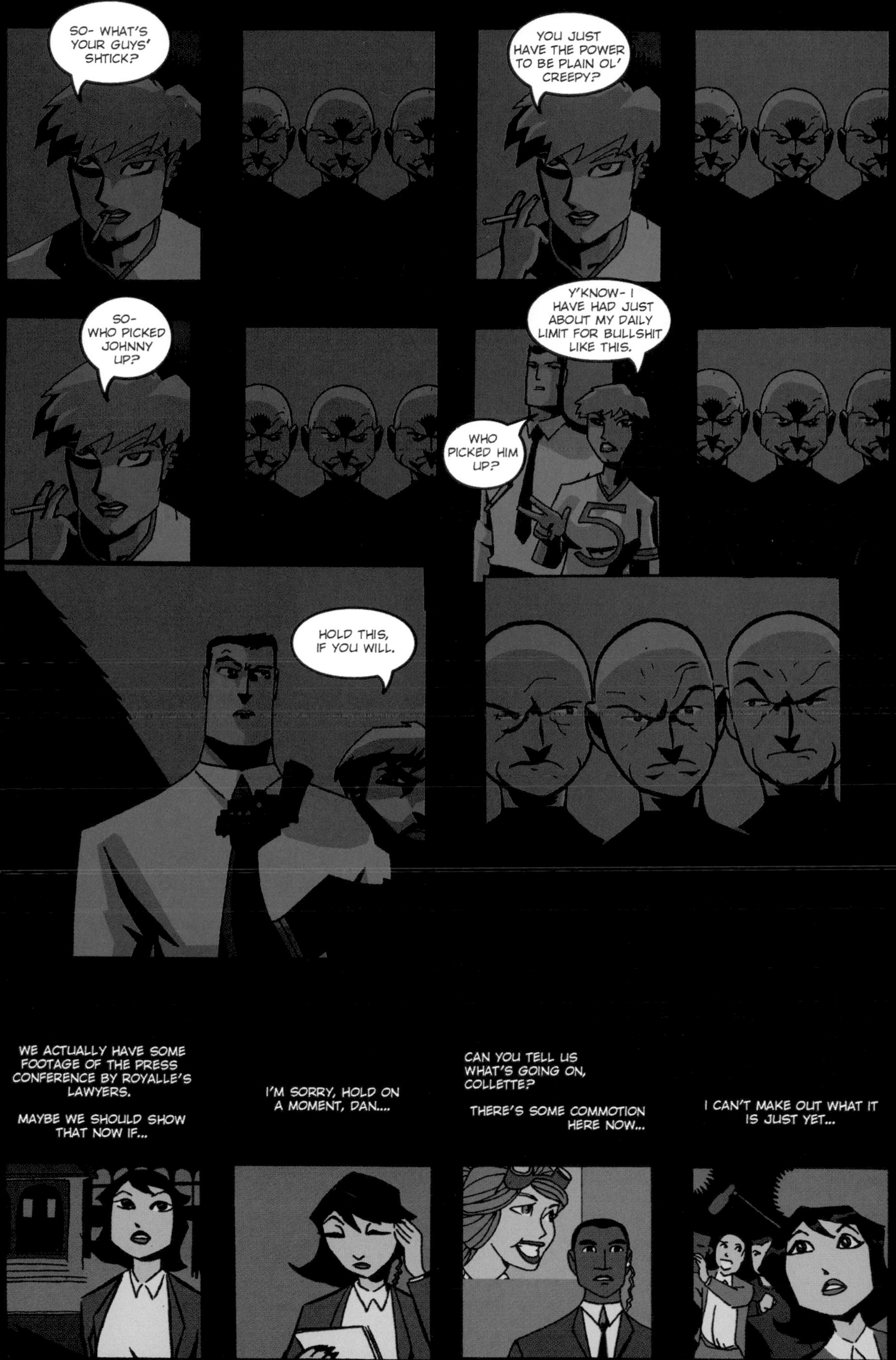
SO- WHAT'S YOUR GUYS' SHTICK?
YOU JUST HAVE THE POWER TO BE PLAIN OL' CREEPY?
SO- WHO PICKED JOHNNY UP?
Y'KNOW- I HAVE HAD JUST ABOUT MY DAILY LIMIT FOR BULLSHIT LIKE THIS.
WHO PICKED HIM UP?
HOLD THIS, IF YOU WILL.
WE ACTUALLY HAVE SOME FOOTAGE OF THE PRESS CONFERENCE BY ROYALLE'S LAWYERS.
MAYBE WE SHOULD SHOW THAT NOW IF...
I'M SORRY, HOLD ON A MOMENT, DAN....
CAN YOU TELL US WHAT'S GOING ON, COLLETTE?
THERE'S SOME COMMOTION HERE NOW...
I CAN'T MAKE OUT WHAT IT IS JUST YET...

WHAP

SMACK

SMACK

CRREK

BOBBY, TURN THE
CAMERA AROUND.

HOLD ON.

NOT ON ME, AROUND.

WE'RE- WE'RE TRYING TO-
TO GET IN HERE--

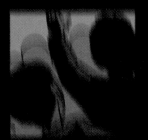

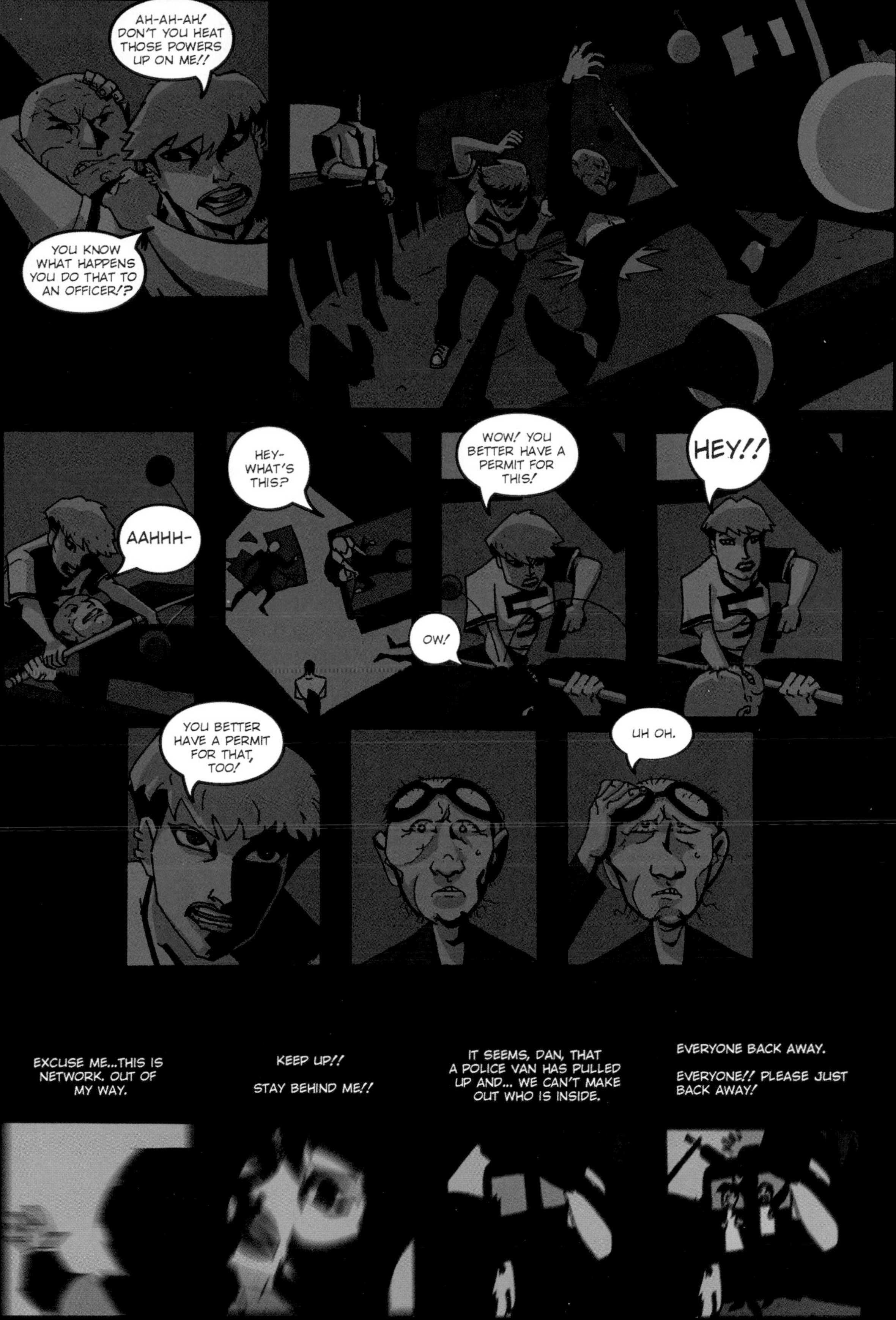
AH-AH-AH! DON'T YOU HEAT THOSE POWERS UP ON ME!!
YOU KNOW WHAT HAPPENS YOU DO THAT TO AN OFFICER!?
AAHHH-
HEY-WHAT'S THIS?
WOW! YOU BETTER HAVE A PERMIT FOR THIS!
OW!
HEY!!
YOU BETTER HAVE A PERMIT FOR THAT, TOO!
UH OH.
EXCUSE ME...THIS IS NETWORK. OUT OF MY WAY.
KEEP UP!!
STAY BEHIND ME!!
IT SEEMS, DAN, THAT A POLICE VAN HAS PULLED UP AND... WE CAN'T MAKE OUT WHO IS INSIDE.
EVERYONE BACK AWAY.
EVERYONE!! PLEASE JUST BACK AWAY!

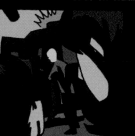

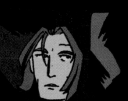

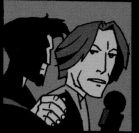

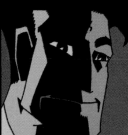

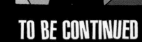

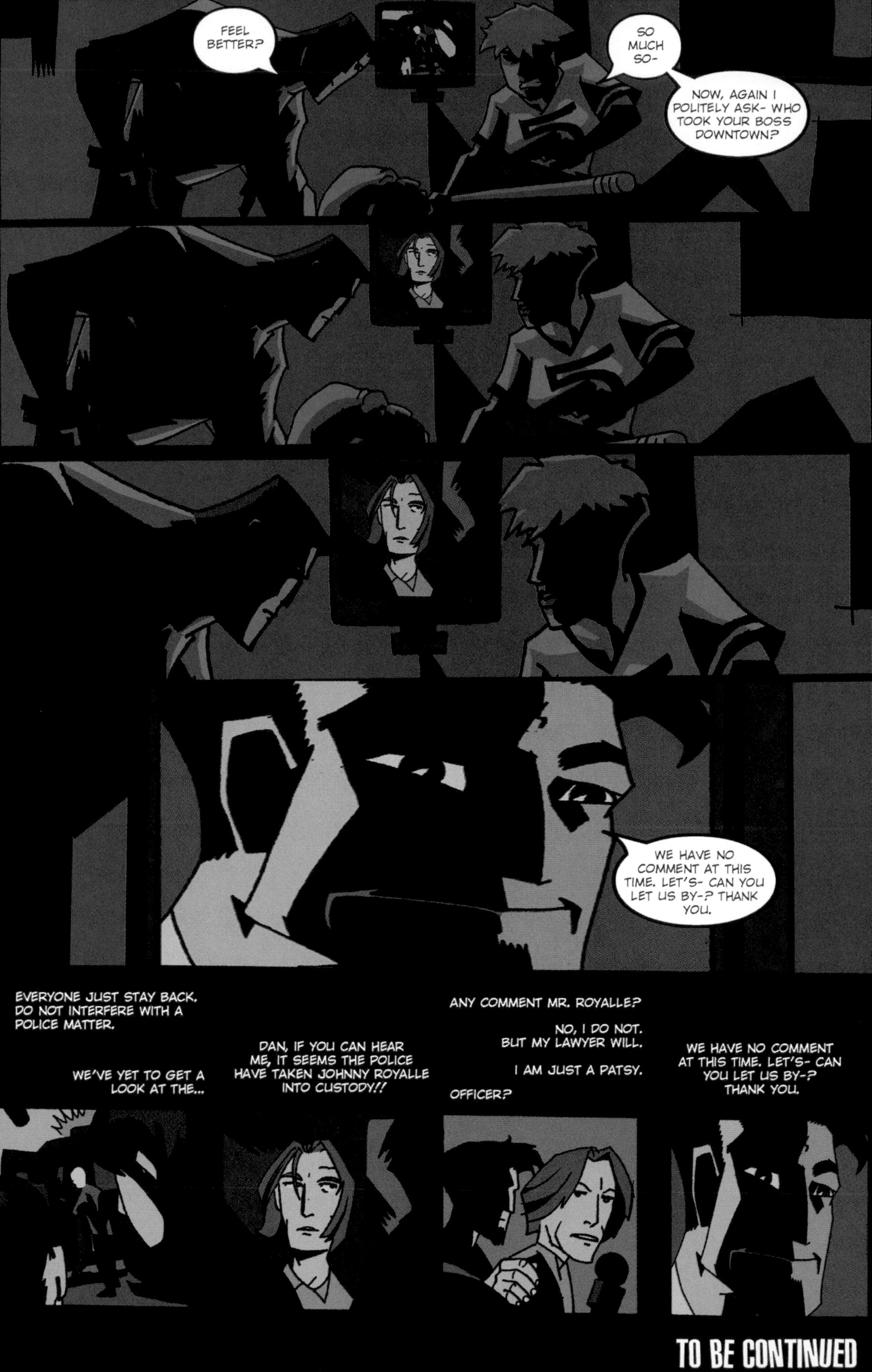
FEEL BETTER?
SO MUCH SO-
NOW, AGAIN I POLITELY ASK- WHO TOOK YOUR BOSS DOWNTOWN?
WE HAVE NO COMMENT AT THIS TIME. LET'S- CAN YOU LET US BY-? THANK YOU.
EVERYONE JUST STAY BACK. DO NOT INTERFERE WITH A POLICE MATTER.
WE'VE YET TO GET A LOOK AT THE...
DAN, IF YOU CAN HEAR ME, IT SEEMS THE POLICE HAVE TAKEN JOHNNY ROYALLE INTO CUSTODY!!
ANY COMMENT MR. ROYALLE?
NO, I DO NOT. BUT MY LAWYER WILL.
I AM JUST A PATSY.
OFFICER?
WE HAVE NO COMMENT AT THIS TIME. LET'S- CAN YOU LET US BY-? THANK YOU.
TO BE CONTINUED

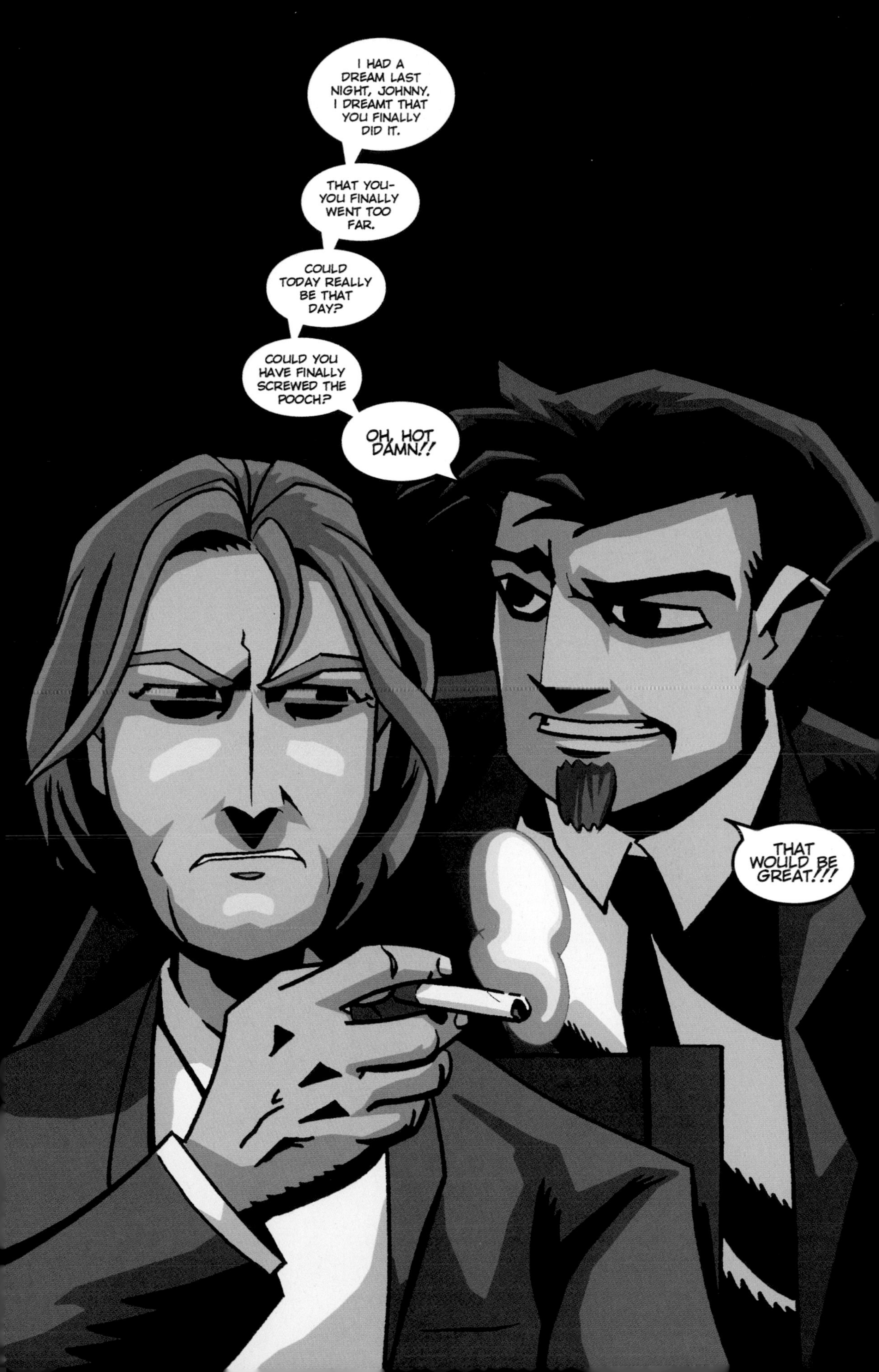
I HAD A DREAM LAST NIGHT, JOHNNY. I DREAMT THAT YOU FINALLY DID IT.
THAT YOU- YOU FINALLY WENT TOO FAR.
COULD TODAY REALLY BE THAT DAY?
COULD YOU HAVE FINALLY SCREWED THE POOCH?
OH, HOT DAMN!!
THAT WOULD BE GREAT!!!

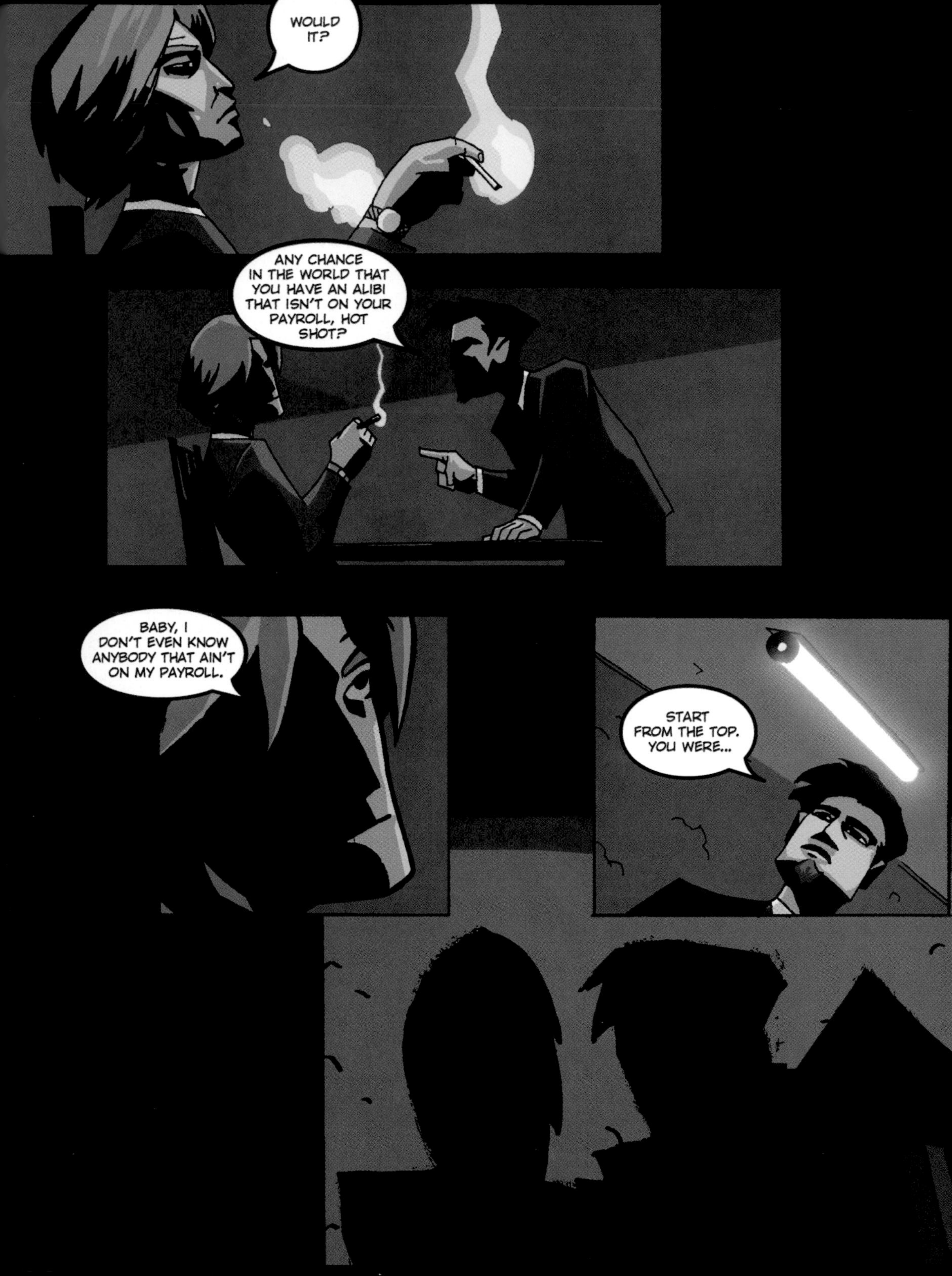
WOULD IT?
ANY CHANCE IN THE WORLD THAT YOU HAVE AN ALIBI THAT ISN'T ON YOUR PAYROLL, HOT SHOT?
BABY, I DON'T EVEN KNOW ANYBODY THAT AIN'T ON MY PAYROLL.
START FROM THE TOP. YOU WERE...

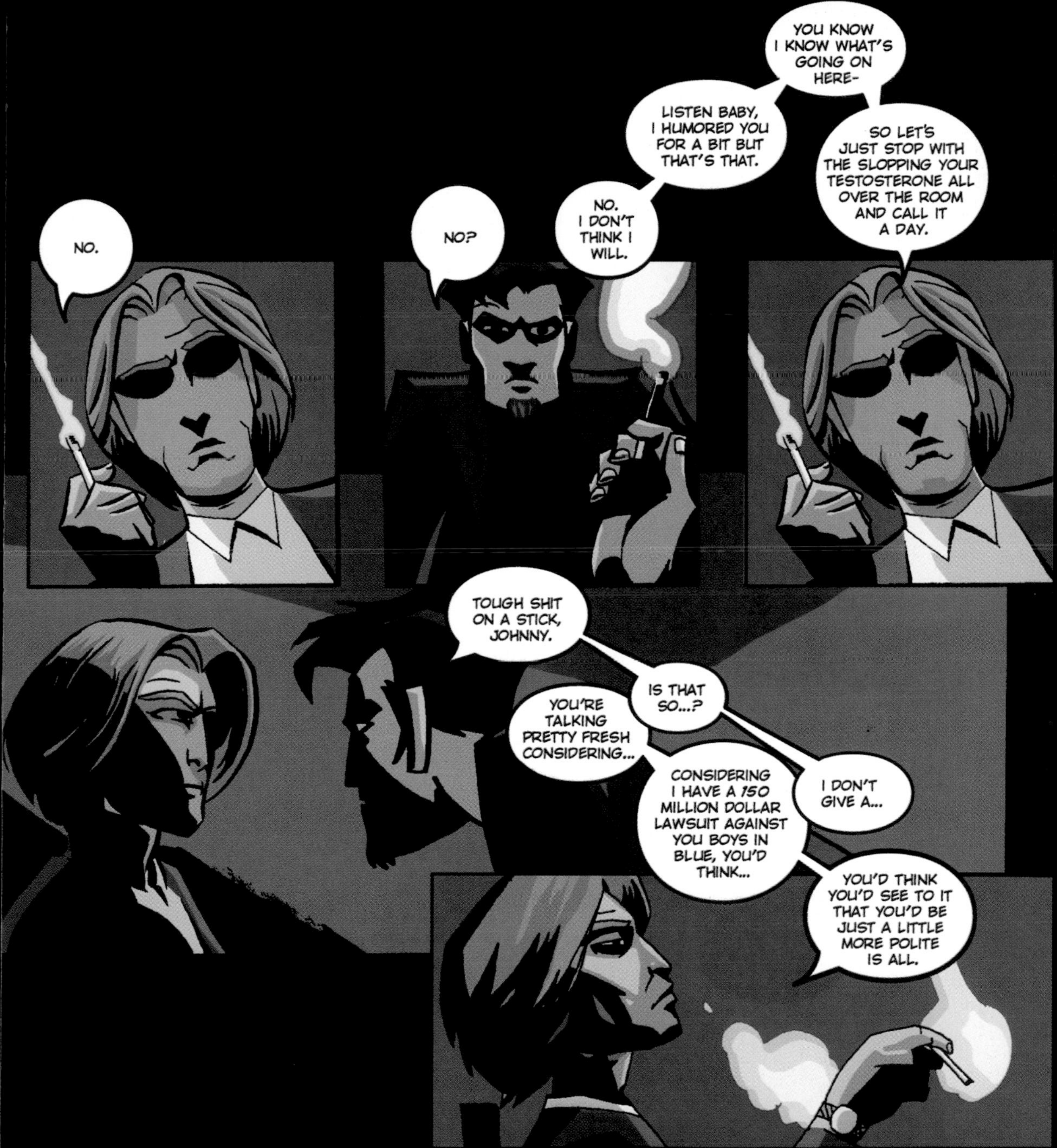
NO.
NO?
NO. I DON'T THINK I WILL.
LISTEN BABY, I HUMORED YOU FOR A BIT BUT THAT'S THAT.
YOU KNOW I KNOW WHAT'S GOING ON HERE-
SO LET'S JUST STOP WITH THE SLOPPING YOUR TESTOSTERONE ALL OVER THE ROOM AND CALL IT A DAY.
TOUGH SHIT ON A STICK, JOHNNY.
IS THAT SO...?
I DON'T GIVE A...
YOU'RE TALKING PRETTY FRESH CONSIDERING...
CONSIDERING I HAVE A *150* MILLION DOLLAR LAWSUIT AGAINST YOU BOYS IN BLUE, YOU'D THINK...
YOU'D THINK YOU'D SEE TO IT THAT YOU'D BE JUST A LITTLE MORE POLITE IS ALL.

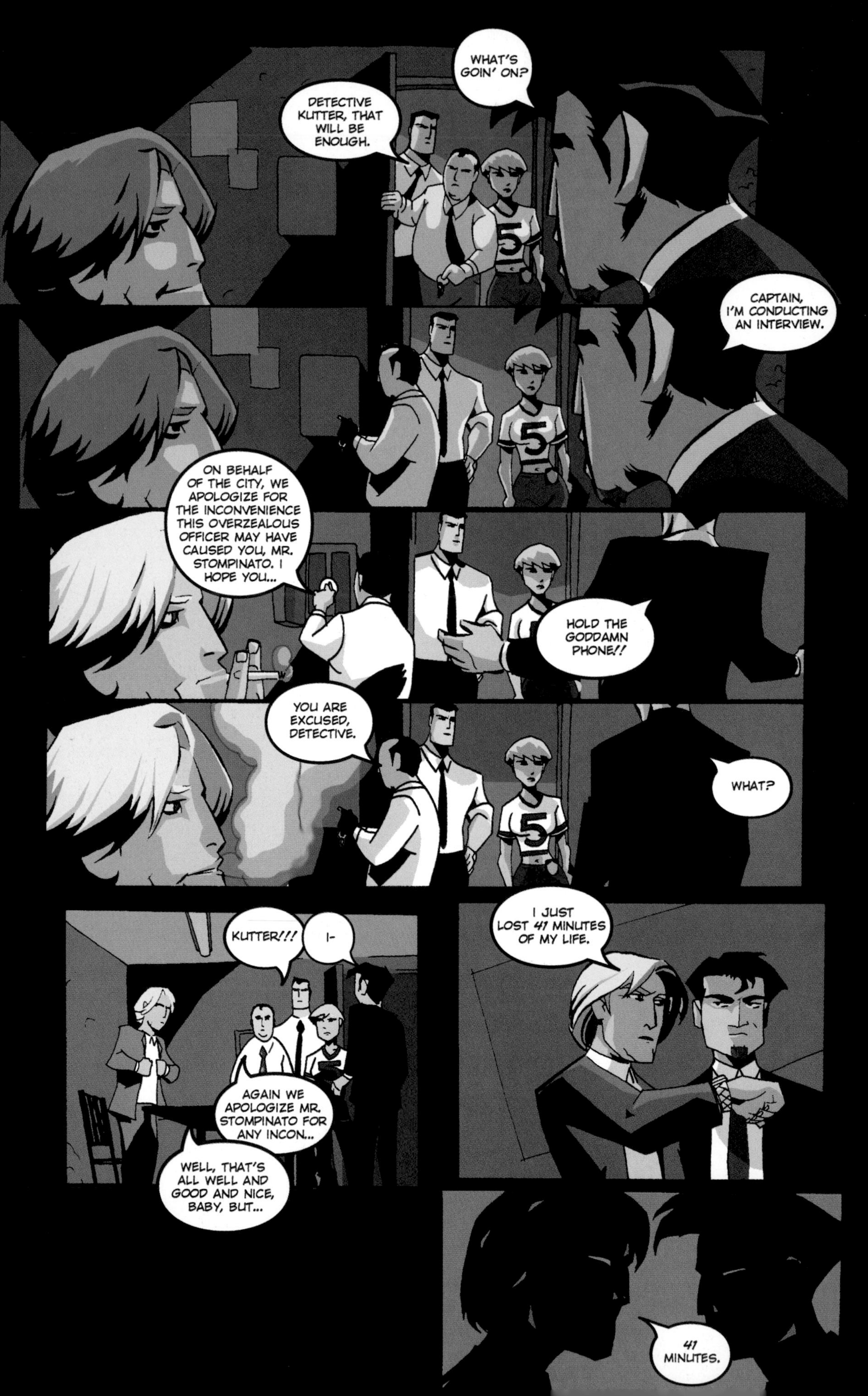
WHAT'S GOIN' ON?
DETECTIVE KUTTER, THAT WILL BE ENOUGH.
CAPTAIN, I'M CONDUCTING AN INTERVIEW.
ON BEHALF OF THE CITY, WE APOLOGIZE FOR THE INCONVENIENCE THIS OVERZEALOUS OFFICER MAY HAVE CAUSED YOU, MR. STOMPINATO. I HOPE YOU...
HOLD THE GODDAMN PHONE!!
YOU ARE EXCUSED, DETECTIVE.
WHAT?
KUTTER!!!
I-
AGAIN WE APOLOGIZE MR. STOMPINATO FOR ANY INCON...
WELL, THAT'S ALL WELL AND GOOD AND NICE, BABY, BUT...
I JUST LOST 41 MINUTES OF MY LIFE.
41 MINUTES.

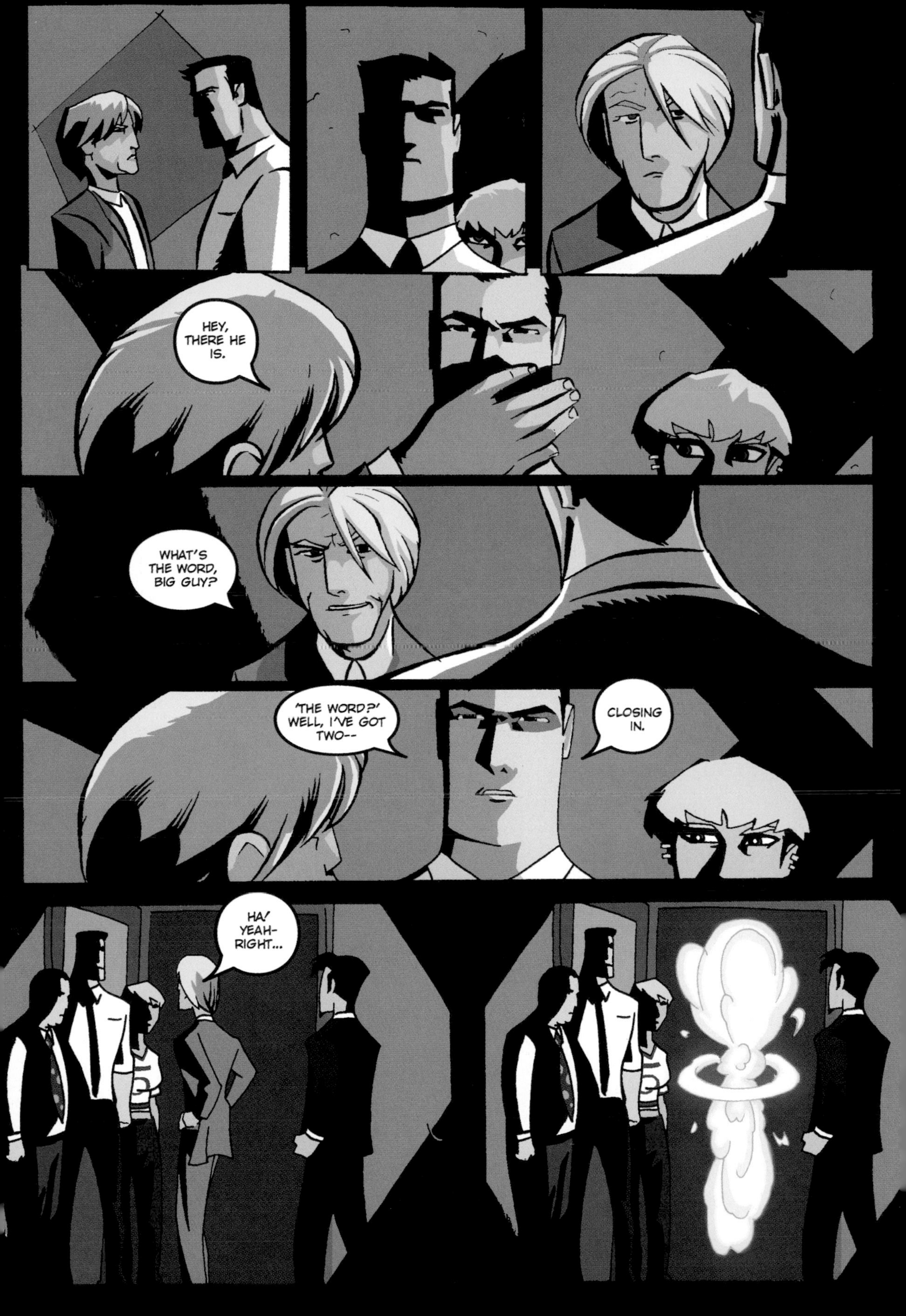
HEY, THERE HE IS.
WHAT'S THE WORD, BIG GUY?
'THE WORD?' WELL, I'VE GOT TWO--
CLOSING IN.
HA! YEAH-RIGHT...

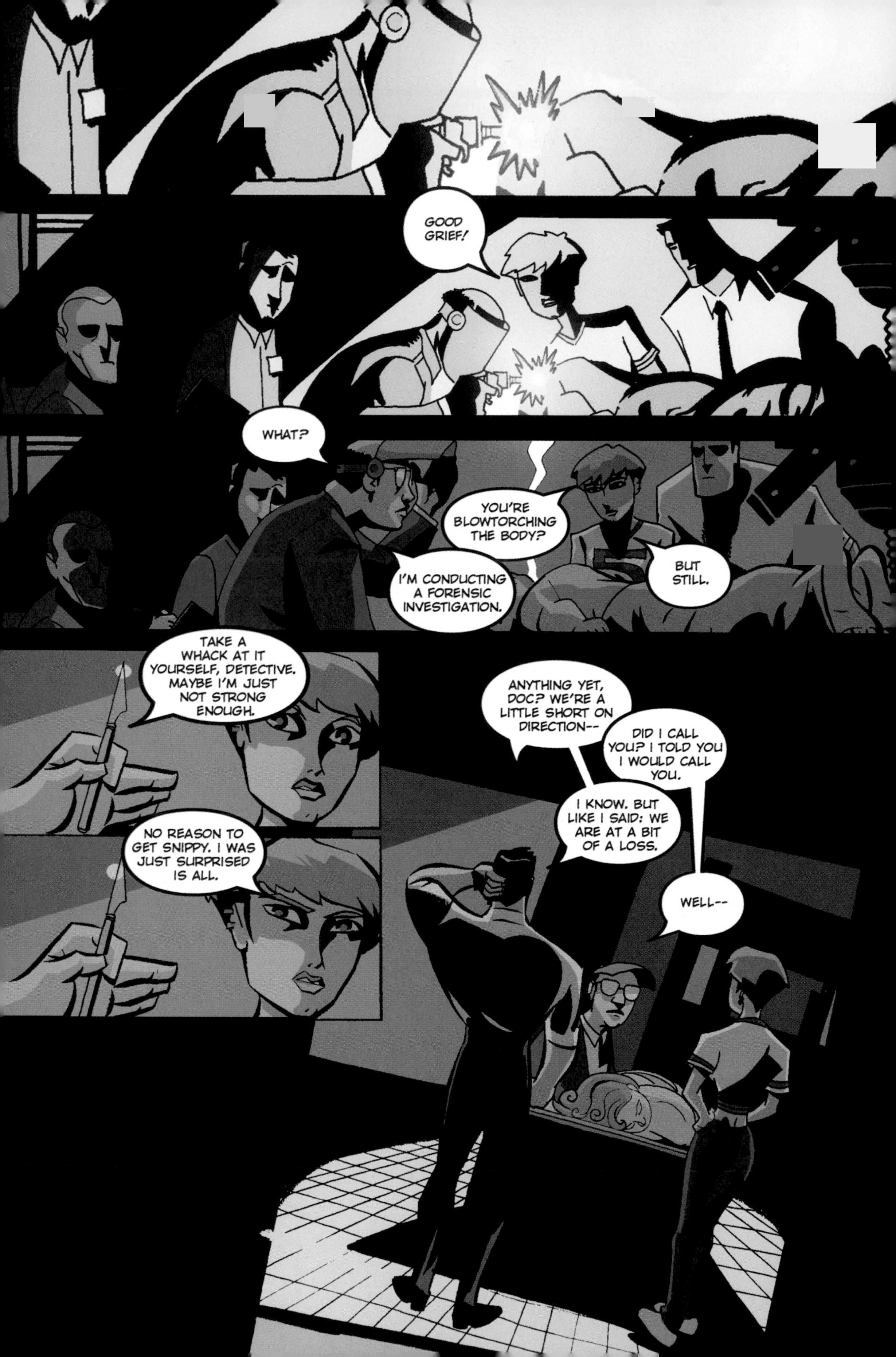
GOOD GRIEF!
WHAT?
YOU'RE BLOWTORCHING THE BODY?
I'M CONDUCTING A FORENSIC INVESTIGATION.
BUT STILL.
TAKE A WHACK AT IT YOURSELF, DETECTIVE. MAYBE I'M JUST NOT STRONG ENOUGH.
NO REASON TO GET SNIPPY. I WAS JUST SURPRISED IS ALL.
ANYTHING YET, DOC? WE'RE A LITTLE SHORT ON DIRECTION--
DID I CALL YOU? I TOLD YOU I WOULD CALL YOU.
I KNOW. BUT LIKE I SAID: WE ARE AT A BIT OF A LOSS.
WELL--

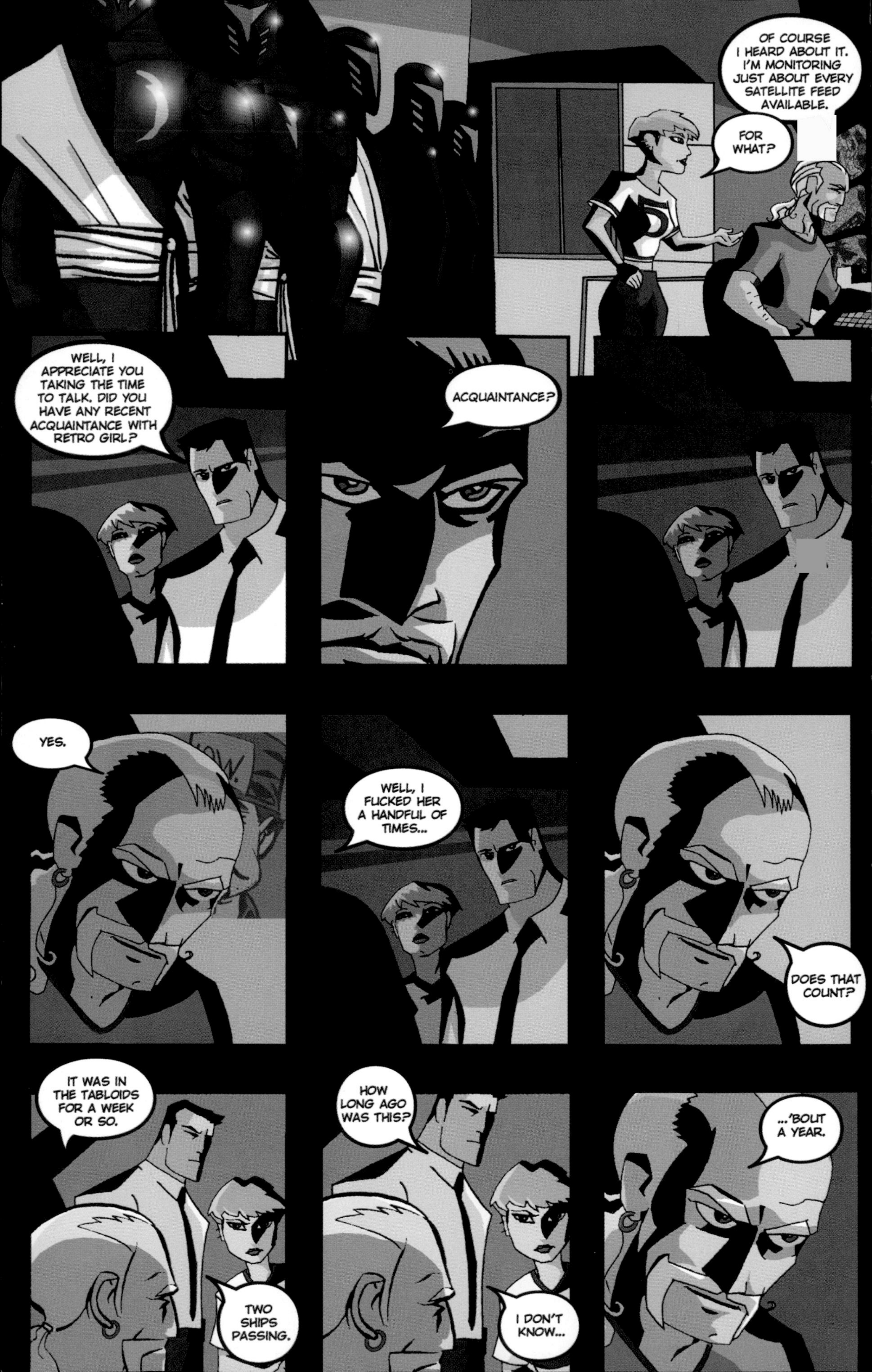
OF COURSE I HEARD ABOUT IT. I'M MONITORING JUST ABOUT EVERY SATELLITE FEED AVAILABLE.
FOR WHAT?
WELL, I APPRECIATE YOU TAKING THE TIME TO TALK. DID YOU HAVE ANY RECENT ACQUAINTANCE WITH RETRO GIRL?
ACQUAINTANCE?
YES.
WELL, I FUCKED HER A HANDFUL OF TIMES...
DOES THAT COUNT?
IT WAS IN THE TABLOIDS FOR A WEEK OR SO.
TWO SHIPS PASSING.
HOW LONG AGO WAS THIS?
I DON'T KNOW...
...'BOUT A YEAR.

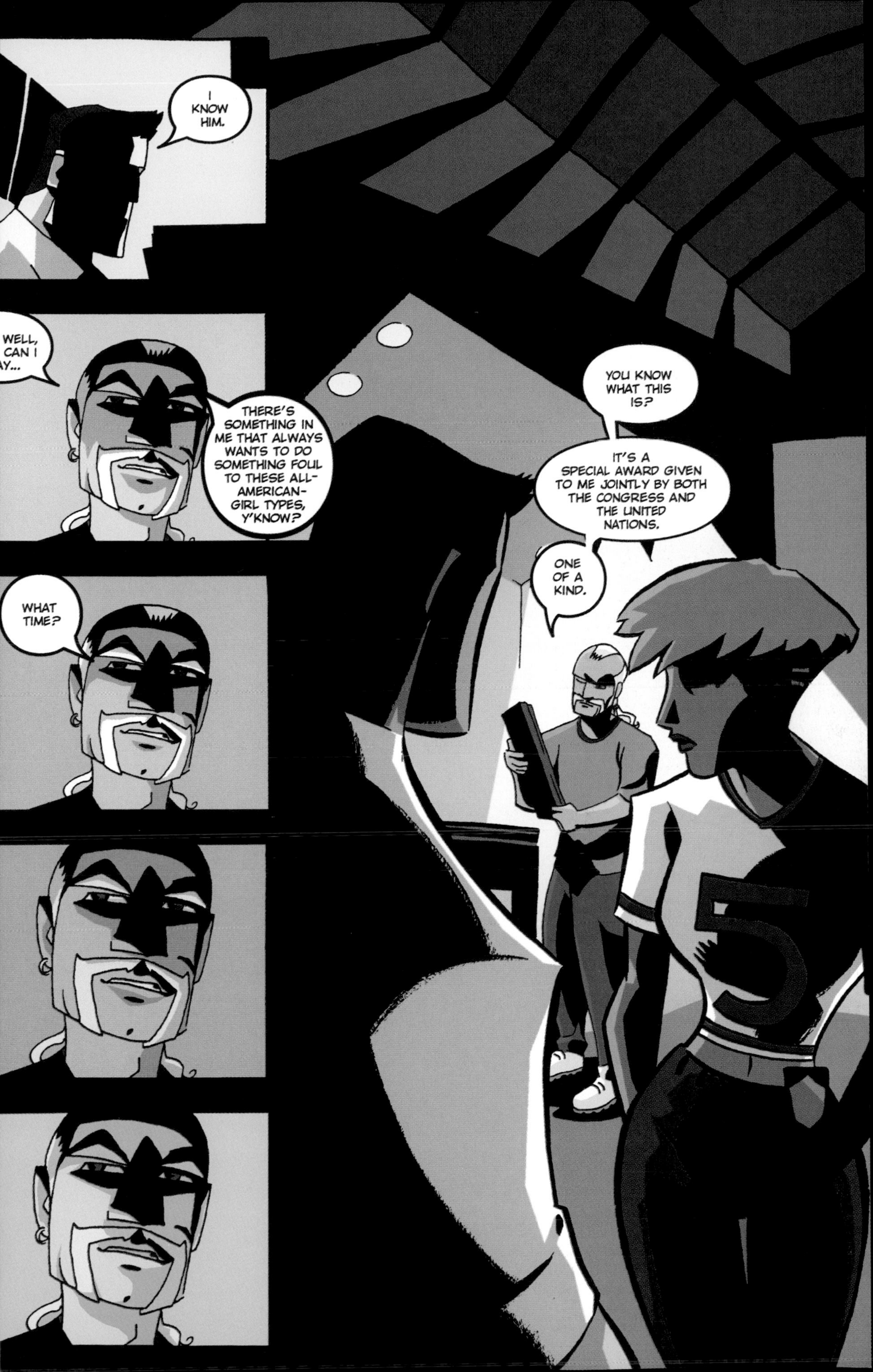
I KNOW HIM.
WELL, CAN I SAY...
THERE'S SOMETHING IN ME THAT ALWAYS WANTS TO DO SOMETHING FOUL TO THESE ALL-AMERICAN-GIRL TYPES, Y'KNOW?
WHAT TIME?
YOU KNOW WHAT THIS IS?
IT'S A SPECIAL AWARD GIVEN TO ME JOINTLY BY BOTH THE CONGRESS AND THE UNITED NATIONS.
ONE OF A KIND.
5

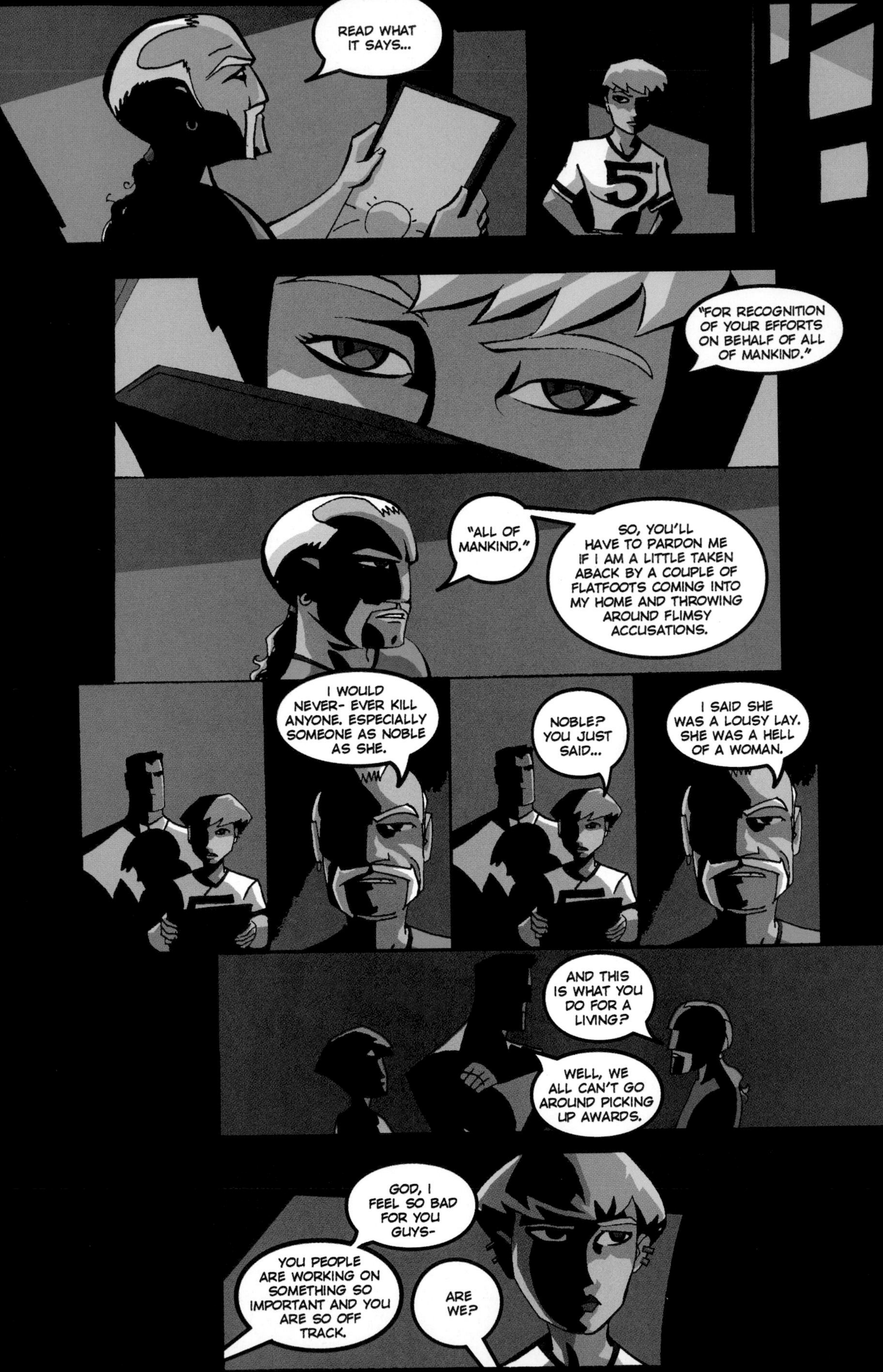
READ WHAT IT SAYS...
"FOR RECOGNITION OF YOUR EFFORTS ON BEHALF OF ALL OF MANKIND."
"ALL OF MANKIND."
SO, YOU'LL HAVE TO PARDON ME IF I AM A LITTLE TAKEN ABACK BY A COUPLE OF FLATFOOTS COMING INTO MY HOME AND THROWING AROUND FLIMSY ACCUSATIONS.
I WOULD NEVER- EVER KILL ANYONE. ESPECIALLY SOMEONE AS NOBLE AS SHE.
NOBLE? YOU JUST SAID...
I SAID SHE WAS A LOUSY LAY. SHE WAS A HELL OF A WOMAN.
AND THIS IS WHAT YOU DO FOR A LIVING?
WELL, WE ALL CAN'T GO AROUND PICKING UP AWARDS.
GOD, I FEEL SO BAD FOR YOU GUYS-
YOU PEOPLE ARE WORKING ON SOMETHING SO IMPORTANT AND YOU ARE SO OFF TRACK.
ARE WE?

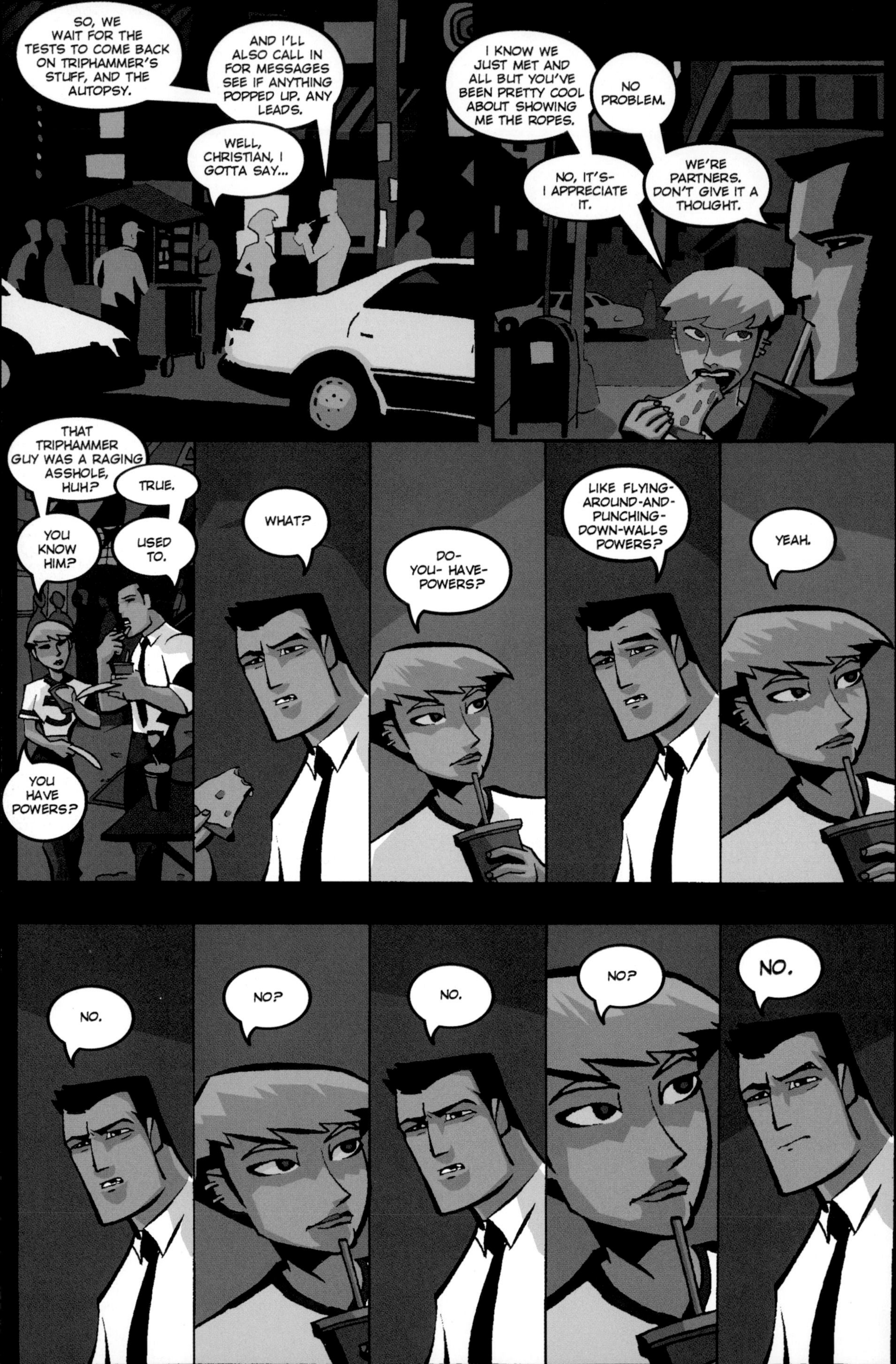

SO, WE WAIT FOR THE TESTS TO COME BACK ON TRIPHAMMER'S STUFF, AND THE AUTOPSY.
AND I'LL ALSO CALL IN FOR MESSAGES SEE IF ANYTHING POPPED UP. ANY LEADS.
WELL, CHRISTIAN, I GOTTA SAY...
I KNOW WE JUST MET AND ALL BUT YOU'VE BEEN PRETTY COOL ABOUT SHOWING ME THE ROPES.
NO PROBLEM.
NO, IT'S- I APPRECIATE IT.
WE'RE PARTNERS. DON'T GIVE IT A THOUGHT.
THAT TRIPHAMMER GUY WAS A RAGING ASSHOLE, HUH?
TRUE.
YOU KNOW HIM?
USED TO.
YOU HAVE POWERS?
WHAT?
DO- YOU- HAVE- POWERS?
LIKE FLYING-AROUND-AND-PUNCHING-DOWN-WALLS POWERS?
YEAH.
NO.
NO?
NO.
NO?
NO.

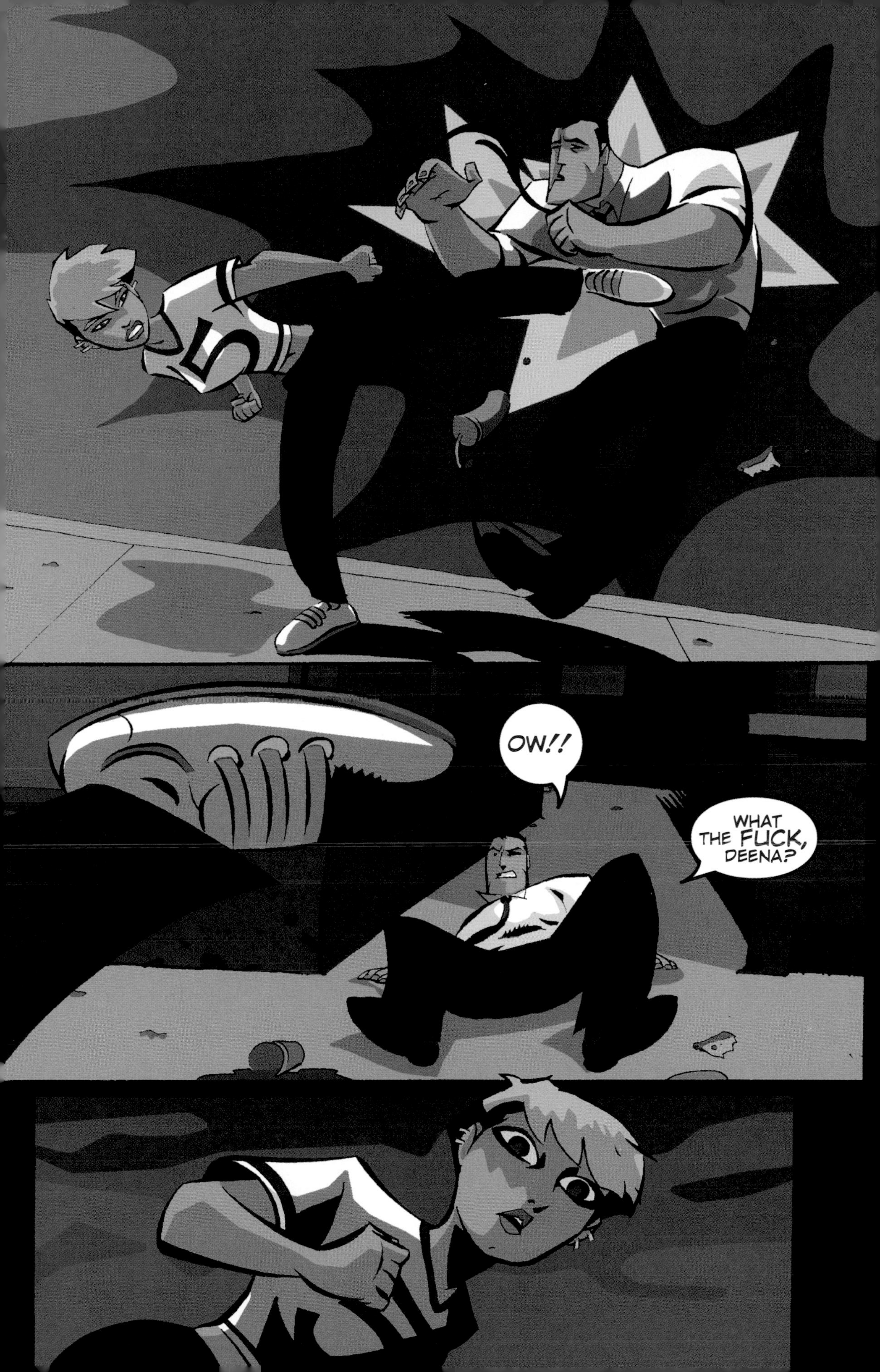
OW!!
WHAT THE FUCK, DEENA?

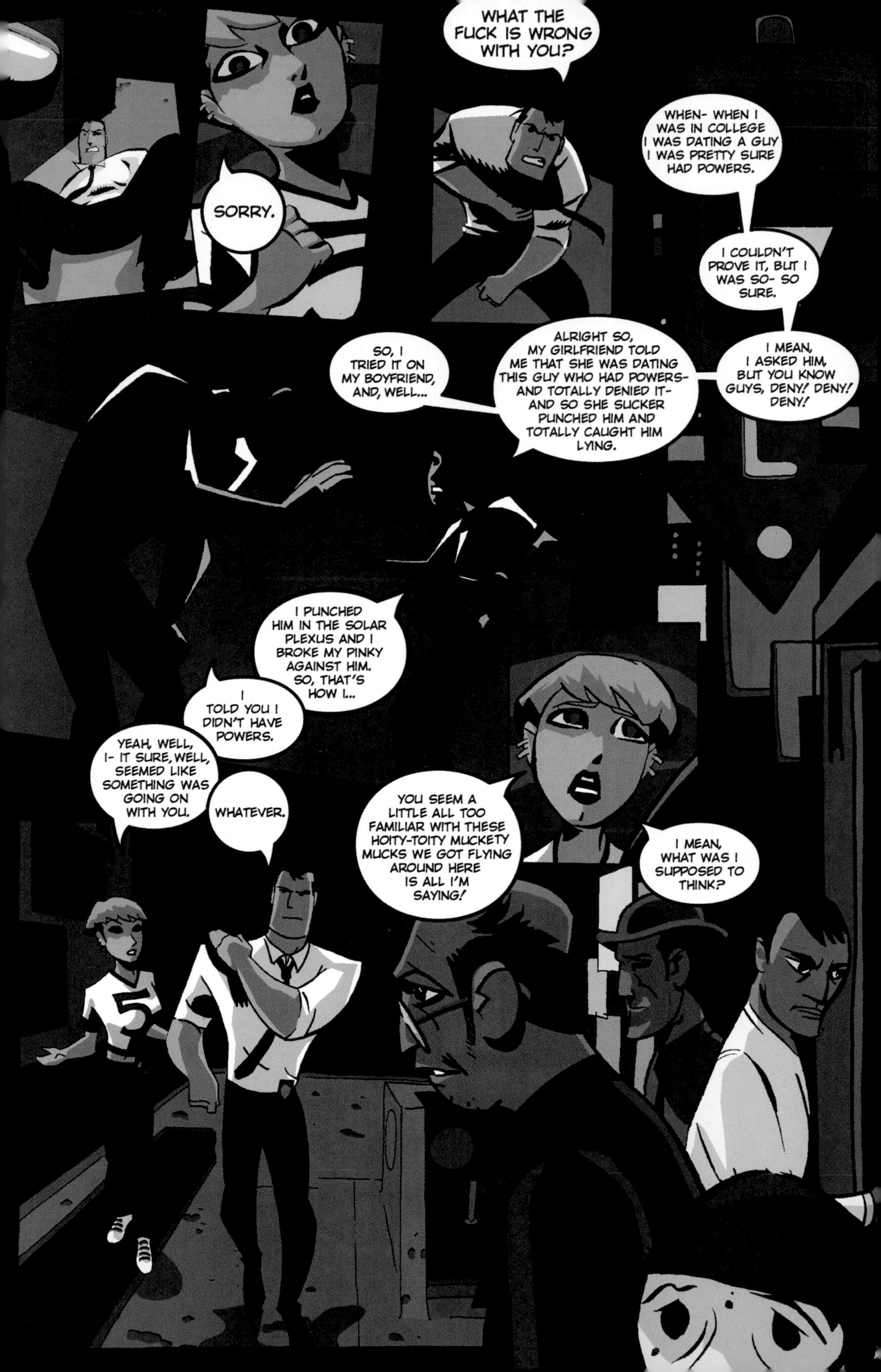
SORRY.
WHAT THE FUCK IS WRONG WITH YOU?
WHEN- WHEN I WAS IN COLLEGE I WAS DATING A GUY I WAS PRETTY SURE HAD POWERS.
I COULDN'T PROVE IT, BUT I WAS SO- SO SURE.
I MEAN, I ASKED HIM, BUT YOU KNOW GUYS, DENY! DENY! DENY!
ALRIGHT SO, MY GIRLFRIEND TOLD ME THAT SHE WAS DATING THIS GUY WHO HAD POWERS- AND TOTALLY DENIED IT- AND SO SHE SUCKER PUNCHED HIM AND TOTALLY CAUGHT HIM LYING.
SO, I TRIED IT ON MY BOYFRIEND, AND, WELL...
I PUNCHED HIM IN THE SOLAR PLEXUS AND I BROKE MY PINKY AGAINST HIM. SO, THAT'S HOW I...
I TOLD YOU I DIDN'T HAVE POWERS.
YEAH, WELL, I- IT SURE, WELL, SEEMED LIKE SOMETHING WAS GOING ON WITH YOU.
WHATEVER.
YOU SEEM A LITTLE ALL TOO FAMILIAR WITH THESE HOITY-TOITY MUCKETY MUCKS WE GOT FLYING AROUND HERE IS ALL I'M SAYING!
I MEAN, WHAT WAS I SUPPOSED TO THINK?

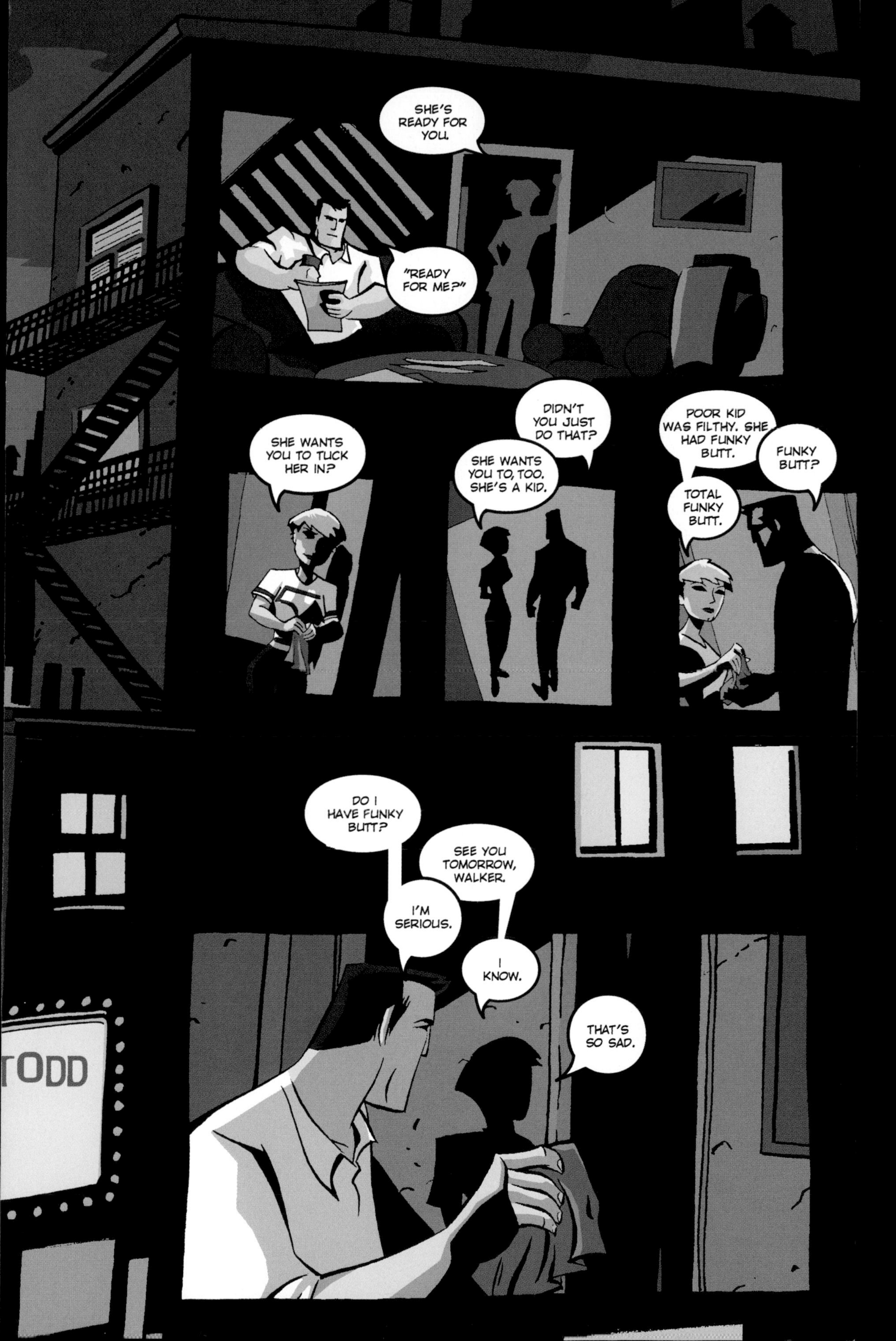
SHE'S READY FOR YOU.
"READY FOR ME?"
SHE WANTS YOU TO TUCK HER IN?
DIDN'T YOU JUST DO THAT?
SHE WANTS YOU TO, TOO. SHE'S A KID.
POOR KID WAS FILTHY. SHE HAD FUNKY BUTT.
FUNKY BUTT?
TOTAL FUNKY BUTT.
DO I HAVE FUNKY BUTT?
SEE YOU TOMORROW, WALKER.
I'M SERIOUS.
I KNOW.
THAT'S SO SAD.
TODD

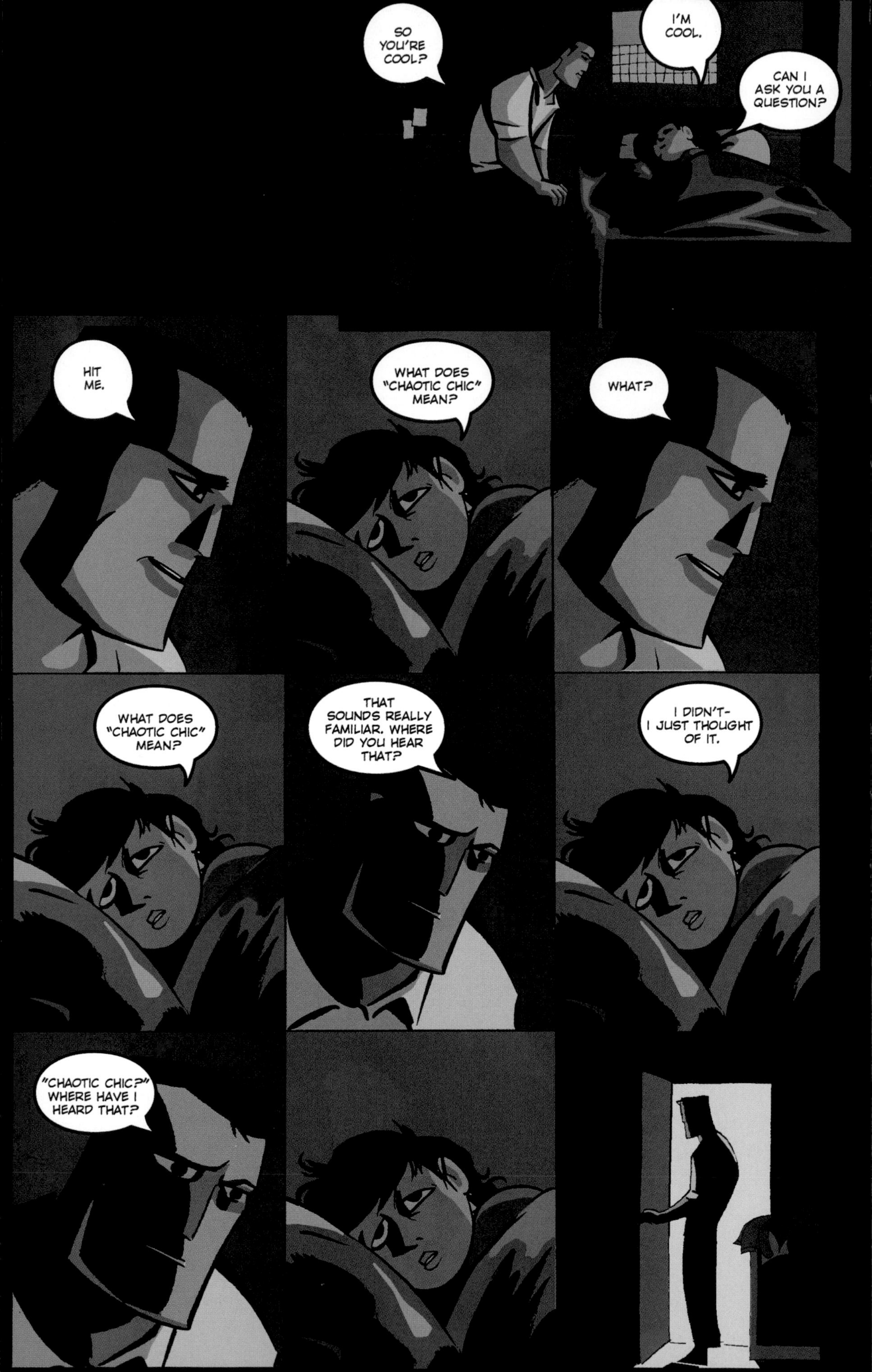
SO YOU'RE COOL?
I'M COOL.
CAN I ASK YOU A QUESTION?
HIT ME.
WHAT DOES "CHAOTIC CHIC" MEAN?
WHAT?
WHAT DOES "CHAOTIC CHIC" MEAN?
THAT SOUNDS REALLY FAMILIAR. WHERE DID YOU HEAR THAT?
I DIDN'T- I JUST THOUGHT OF IT.
"CHAOTIC CHIC?" WHERE HAVE I HEARD THAT?

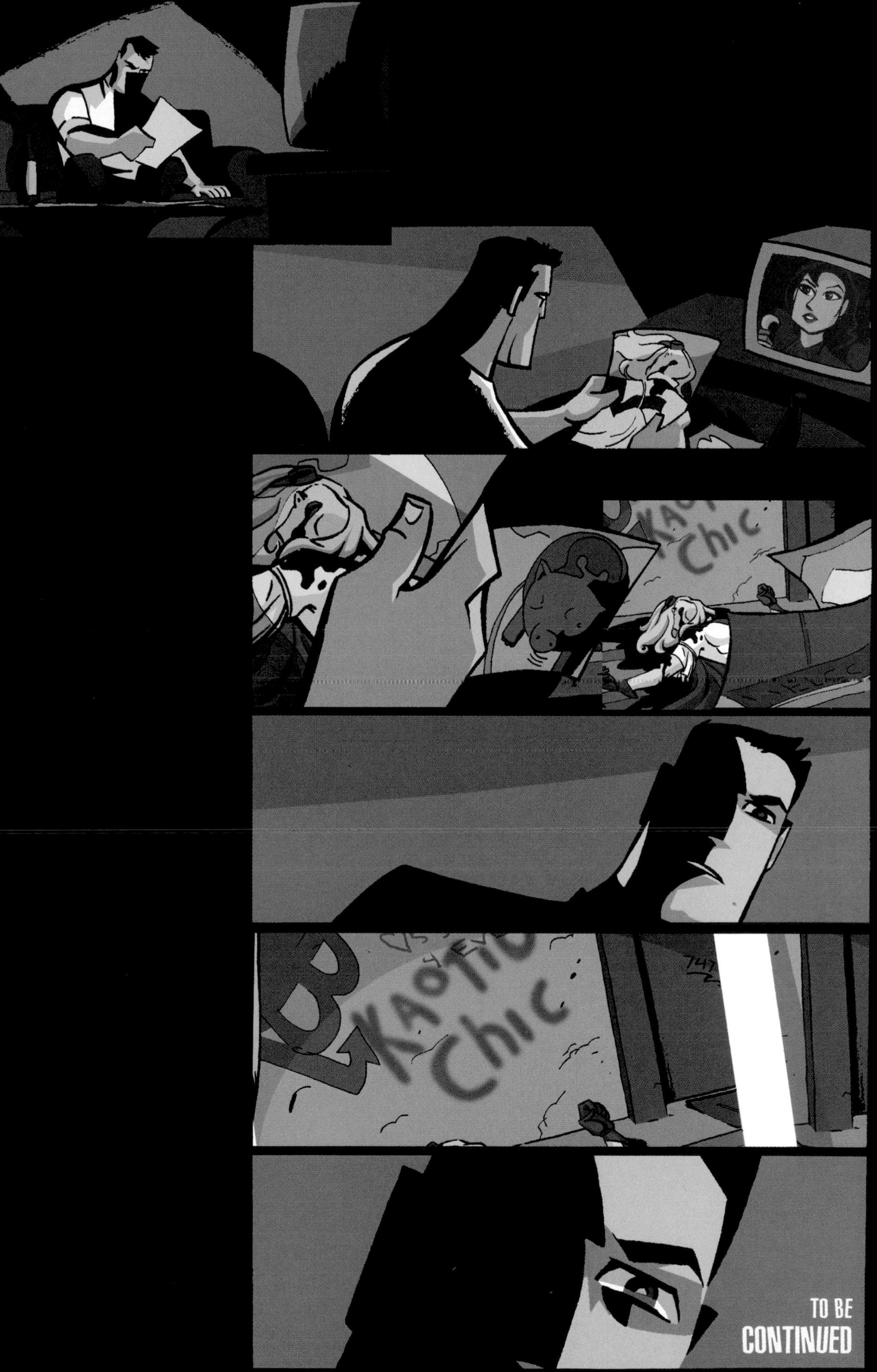
TO BE
CONTINUED

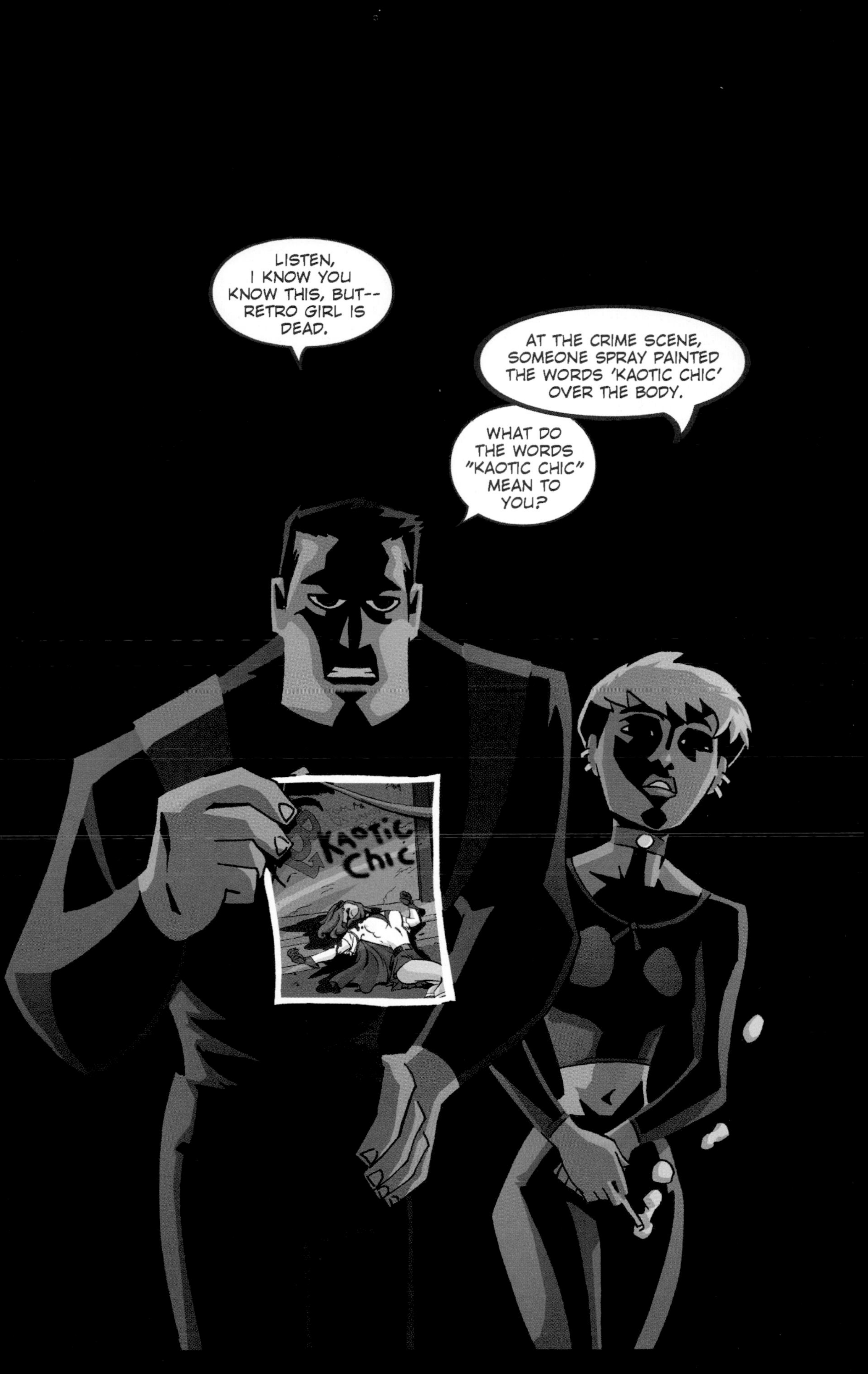
LISTEN, I KNOW YOU KNOW THIS, BUT-- RETRO GIRL IS DEAD.
AT THE CRIME SCENE, SOMEONE SPRAY PAINTED THE WORDS 'KAOTIC CHIC' OVER THE BODY.
WHAT DO THE WORDS "KAOTIC CHIC" MEAN TO YOU?
KAOTIC CHIC

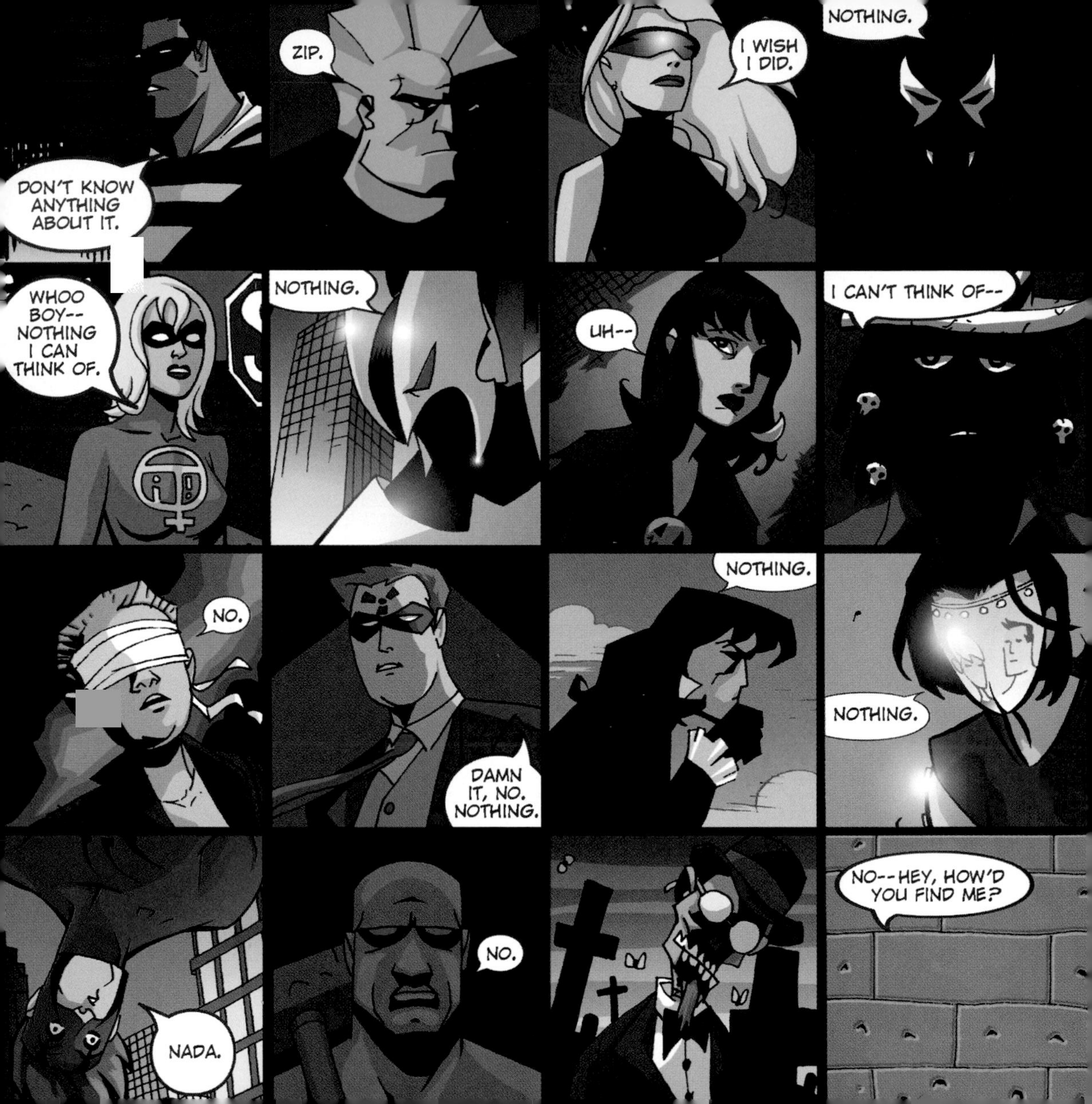
DON'T KNOW ANYTHING ABOUT IT.
ZIP.
I WISH I DID.
NOTHING.
WHOO BOY-- NOTHING I CAN THINK OF.
NOTHING.
UH--
I CAN'T THINK OF--
NO.
DAMN IT, NO. NOTHING.
NOTHING.
NOTHING.
NADA.
NO.
NO--HEY, HOW'D YOU FIND ME?

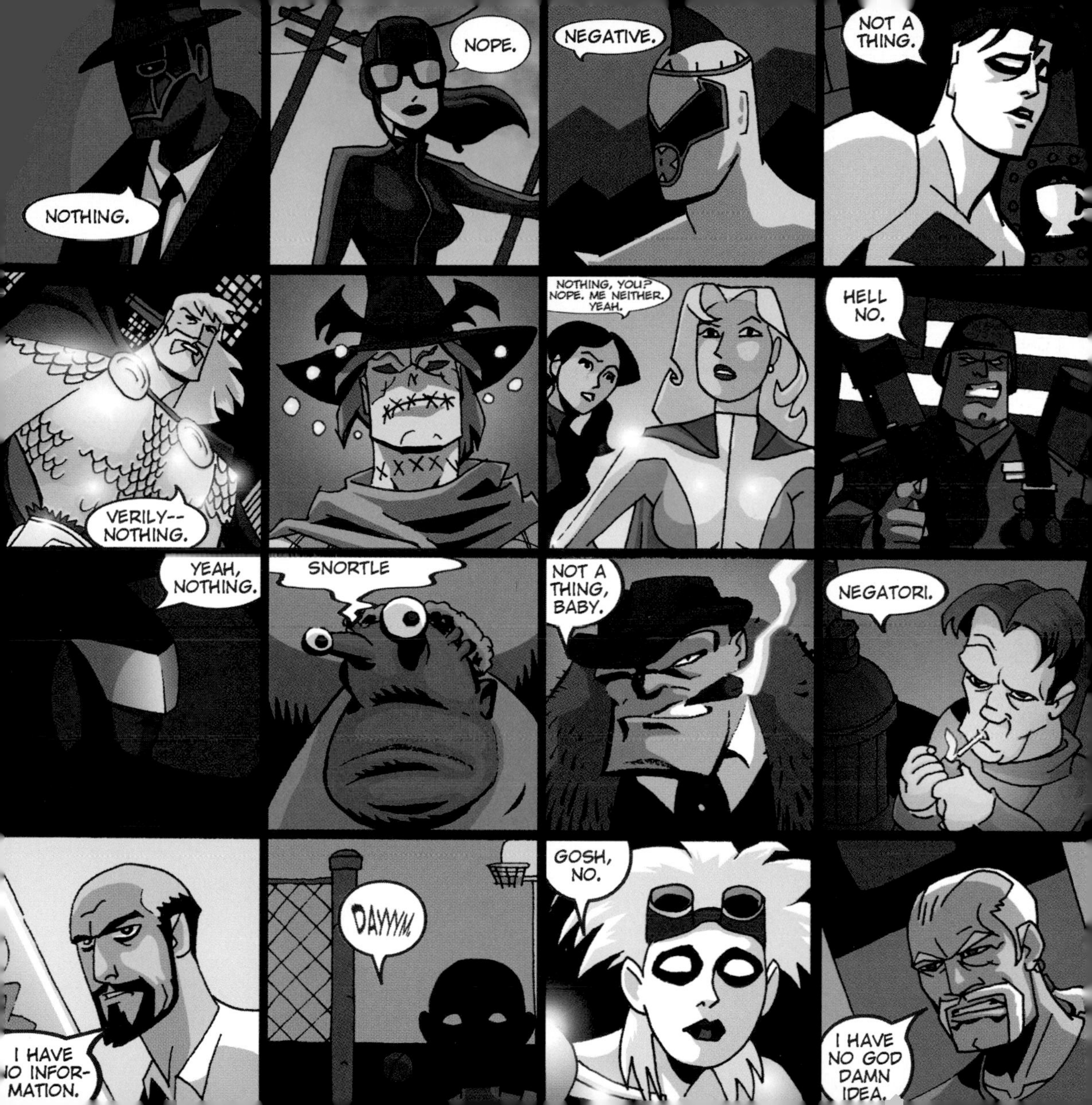
NOTHING.
NOPE.
NEGATIVE.
NOT A THING.
VERILY-- NOTHING.
NOTHING, YOU? NOPE. ME NEITHER. YEAH.
HELL NO.
YEAH, NOTHING.
SNORTLE
NOT A THING, BABY.
NEGATORI.
I HAVE IO INFOR- MATION.
DAYYYM.
GOSH, NO.
I HAVE NO GOD DAMN IDEA.

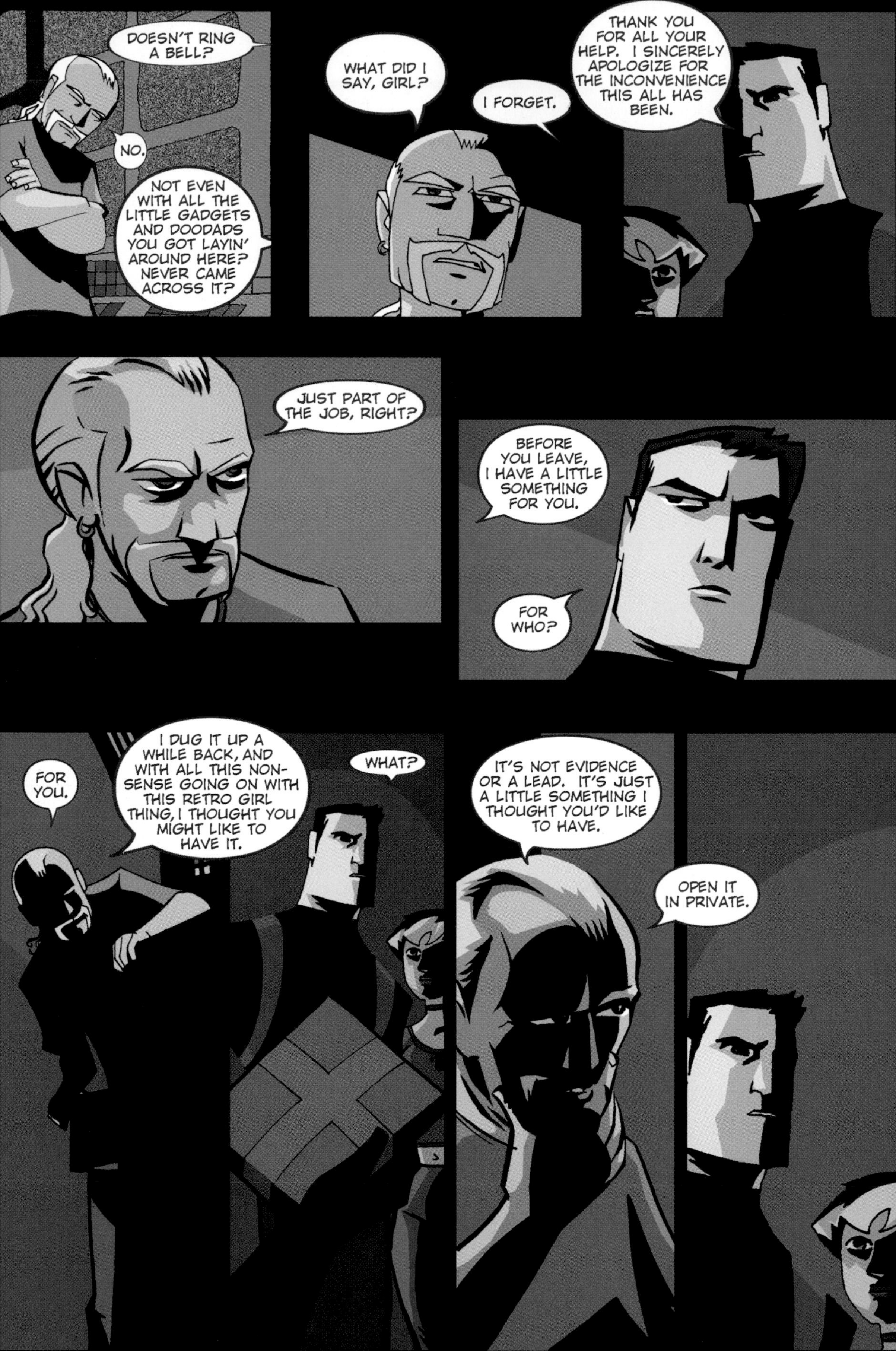
DOESN'T RING A BELL?
NO.
NOT EVEN WITH ALL THE LITTLE GADGETS AND DOODADS YOU GOT LAYIN' AROUND HERE? NEVER CAME ACROSS IT?
WHAT DID I SAY, GIRL?
I FORGET.
THANK YOU FOR ALL YOUR HELP. I SINCERELY APOLOGIZE FOR THE INCONVENIENCE THIS ALL HAS BEEN.
JUST PART OF THE JOB, RIGHT?
BEFORE YOU LEAVE, I HAVE A LITTLE SOMETHING FOR YOU.
FOR WHO?
FOR YOU.
I DUG IT UP A WHILE BACK, AND WITH ALL THIS NON-SENSE GOING ON WITH THIS RETRO GIRL THING, I THOUGHT YOU MIGHT LIKE TO HAVE IT.
WHAT?
IT'S NOT EVIDENCE OR A LEAD. IT'S JUST A LITTLE SOMETHING I THOUGHT YOU'D LIKE TO HAVE.
OPEN IT IN PRIVATE.

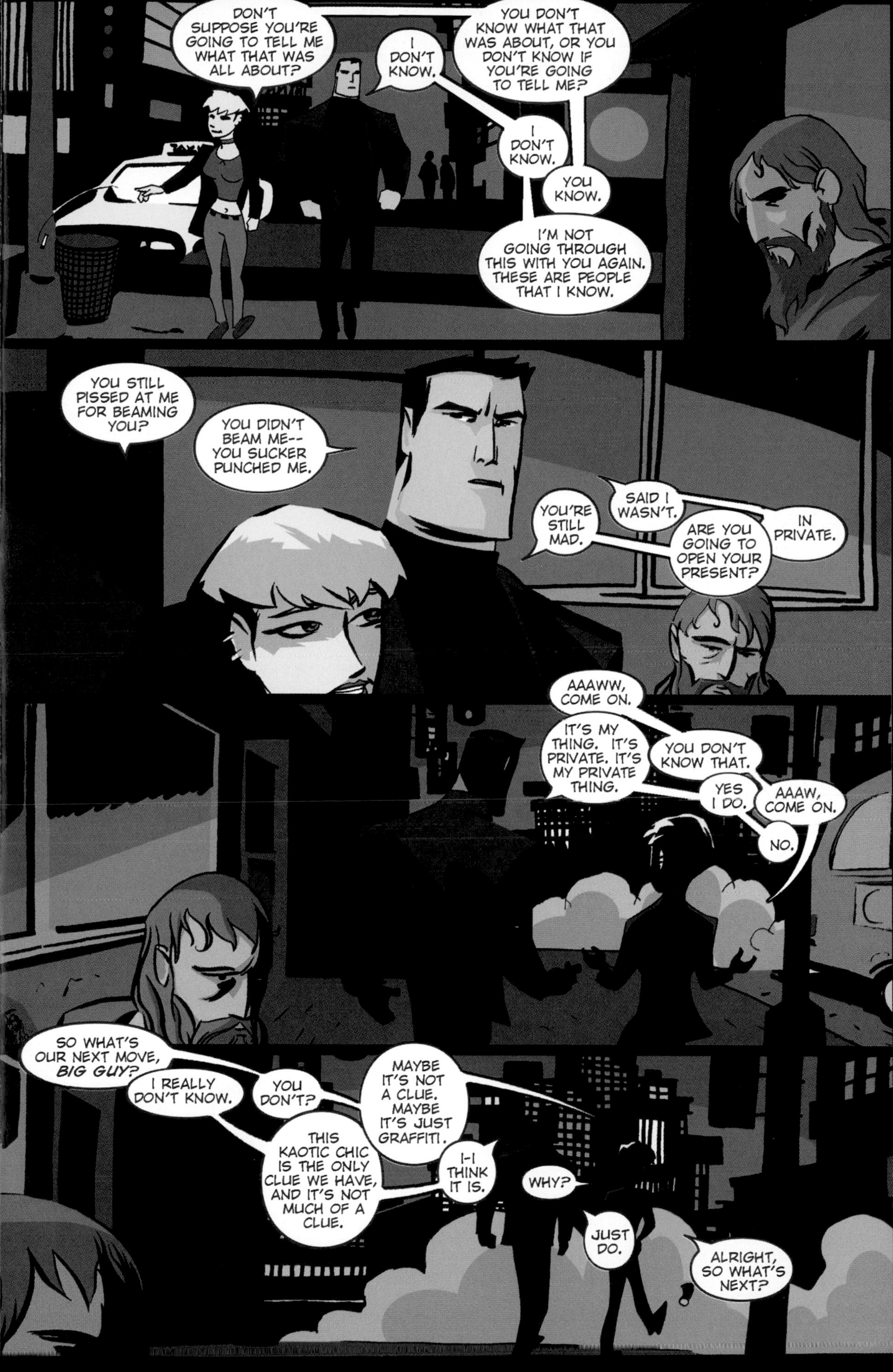
DON'T SUPPOSE YOU'RE GOING TO TELL ME WHAT THAT WAS ALL ABOUT?
I DON'T KNOW.
YOU DON'T KNOW WHAT THAT WAS ABOUT, OR YOU DON'T KNOW IF YOU'RE GOING TO TELL ME?
I DON'T KNOW.
YOU KNOW.
I'M NOT GOING THROUGH THIS WITH YOU AGAIN. THESE ARE PEOPLE THAT I KNOW.
YOU STILL PISSED AT ME FOR BEAMING YOU?
YOU DIDN'T BEAM ME-- YOU SUCKER PUNCHED ME.
YOU'RE STILL MAD.
SAID I WASN'T.
ARE YOU GOING TO OPEN YOUR PRESENT?
IN PRIVATE.
AAAWW, COME ON.
IT'S MY THING. IT'S PRIVATE. IT'S MY PRIVATE THING.
YOU DON'T KNOW THAT.
YES I DO.
AAAW, COME ON.
NO.
SO WHAT'S OUR NEXT MOVE, *BIG GUY?*
I REALLY DON'T KNOW.
YOU DON'T?
THIS KAOTIC CHIC IS THE ONLY CLUE WE HAVE, AND IT'S NOT MUCH OF A CLUE.
MAYBE IT'S NOT A CLUE. MAYBE IT'S JUST GRAFFITI.
I-I THINK IT IS.
WHY?
JUST DO.
ALRIGHT, SO WHAT'S NEXT?

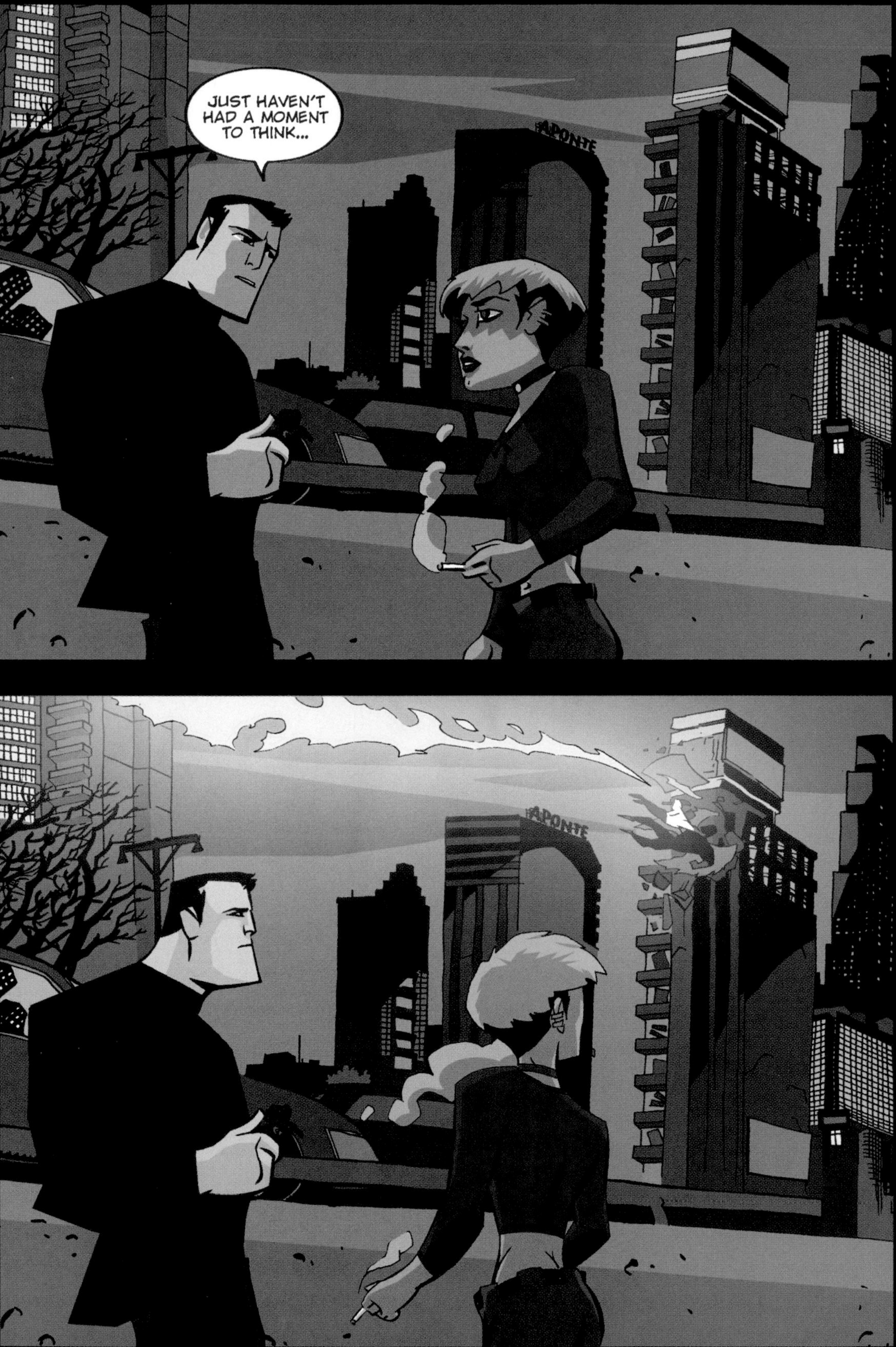
JUST HAVEN'T HAD A MOMENT TO THINK...
APONTE

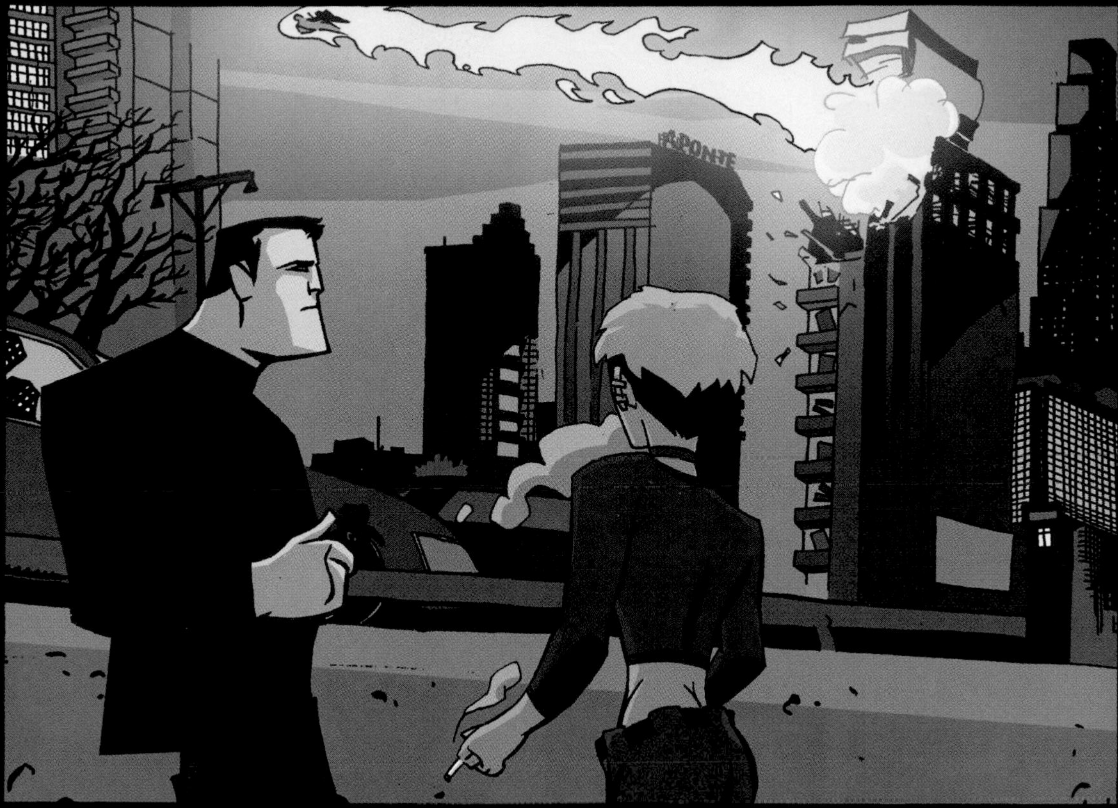

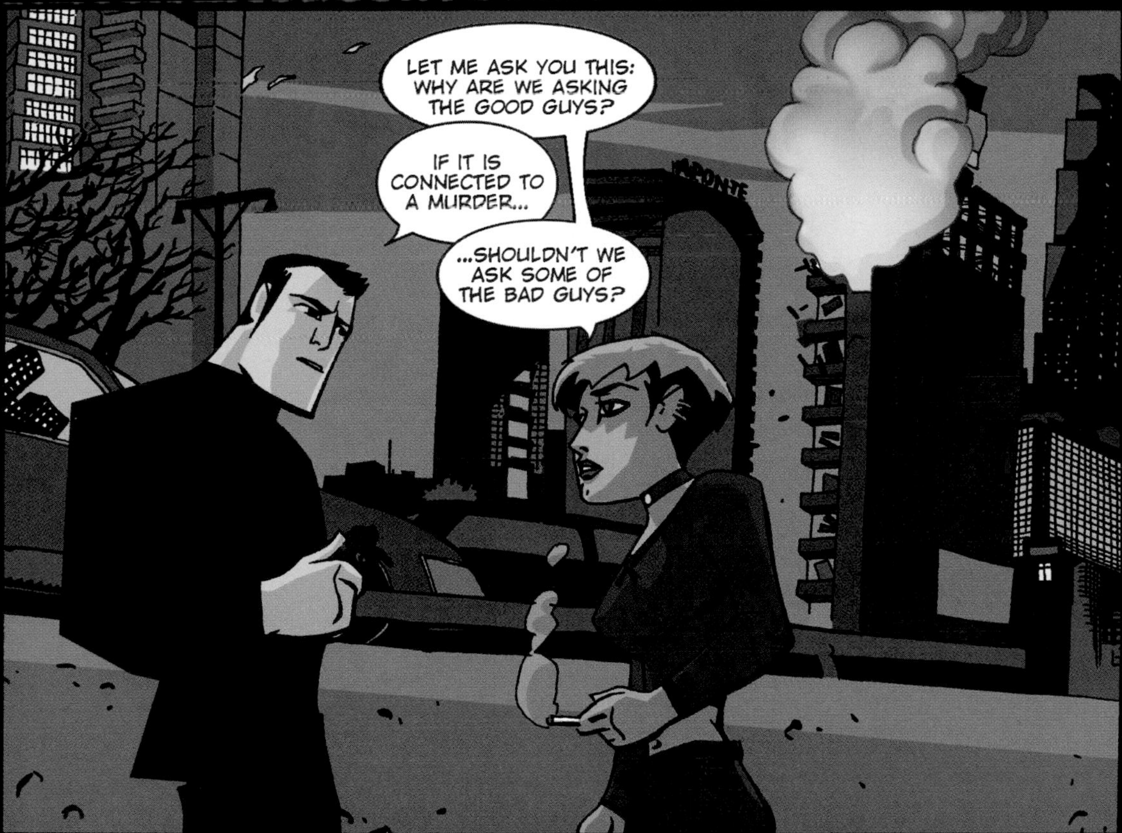
LET ME ASK YOU THIS: WHY ARE WE ASKING THE GOOD GUYS?
IF IT IS CONNECTED TO A MURDER...
...SHOULDN'T WE ASK SOME OF THE BAD GUYS?

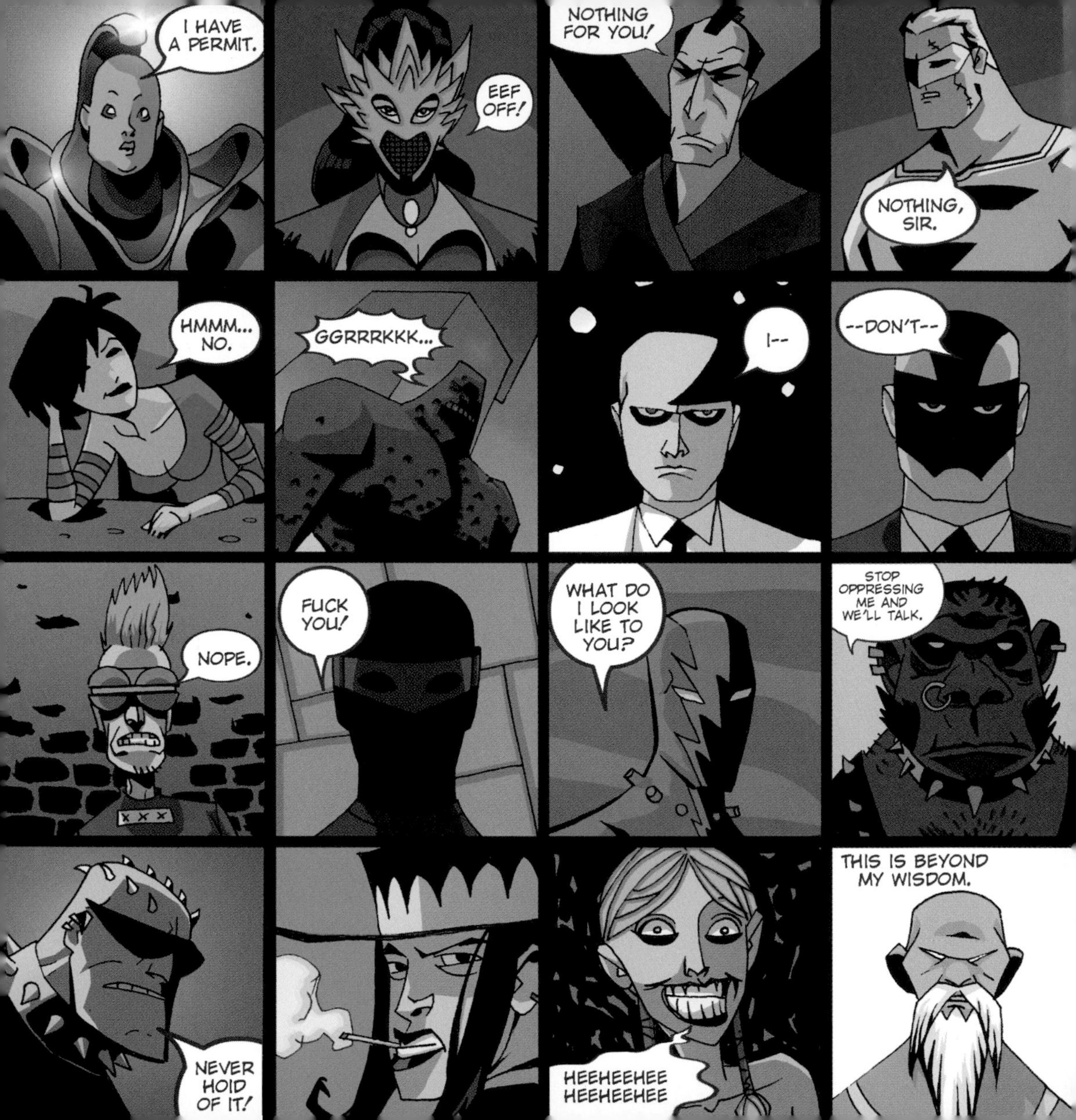
I HAVE A PERMIT.
EEF OFF!
NOTHING FOR YOU!
NOTHING, SIR.
HMMM... NO.
GGRRRKKK...
I--
--DON'T--
NOPE.
FUCK YOU!
WHAT DO I LOOK LIKE TO YOU?
STOP OPPRESSING ME AND WE'LL TALK.
NEVER HOID OF IT!
HEEHEEHEE HEEHEEHEE
THIS IS BEYOND MY WISDOM.

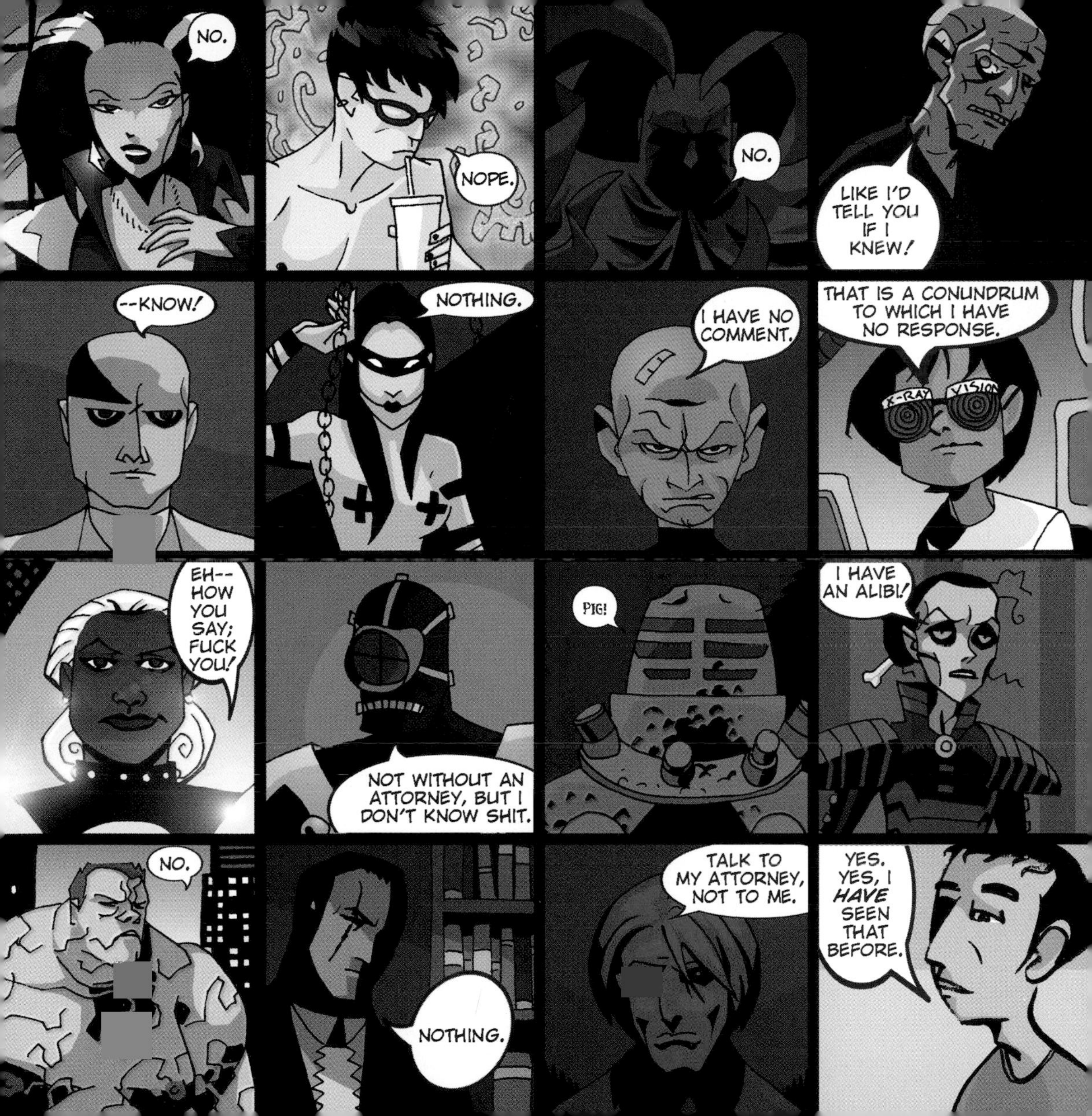
NO.
NOPE.
NO.
LIKE I'D TELL YOU IF I KNEW!
--KNOW!
NOTHING.
I HAVE NO COMMENT.
THAT IS A CONUNDRUM TO WHICH I HAVE NO RESPONSE.
X-RAY VISION
EH-- HOW YOU SAY; FUCK YOU!
NOT WITHOUT AN ATTORNEY, BUT I DON'T KNOW SHIT.
PIG!
I HAVE AN ALIBI!
NO.
NOTHING.
TALK TO MY ATTORNEY, NOT TO ME.
YES. YES, I *HAVE* SEEN THAT BEFORE.

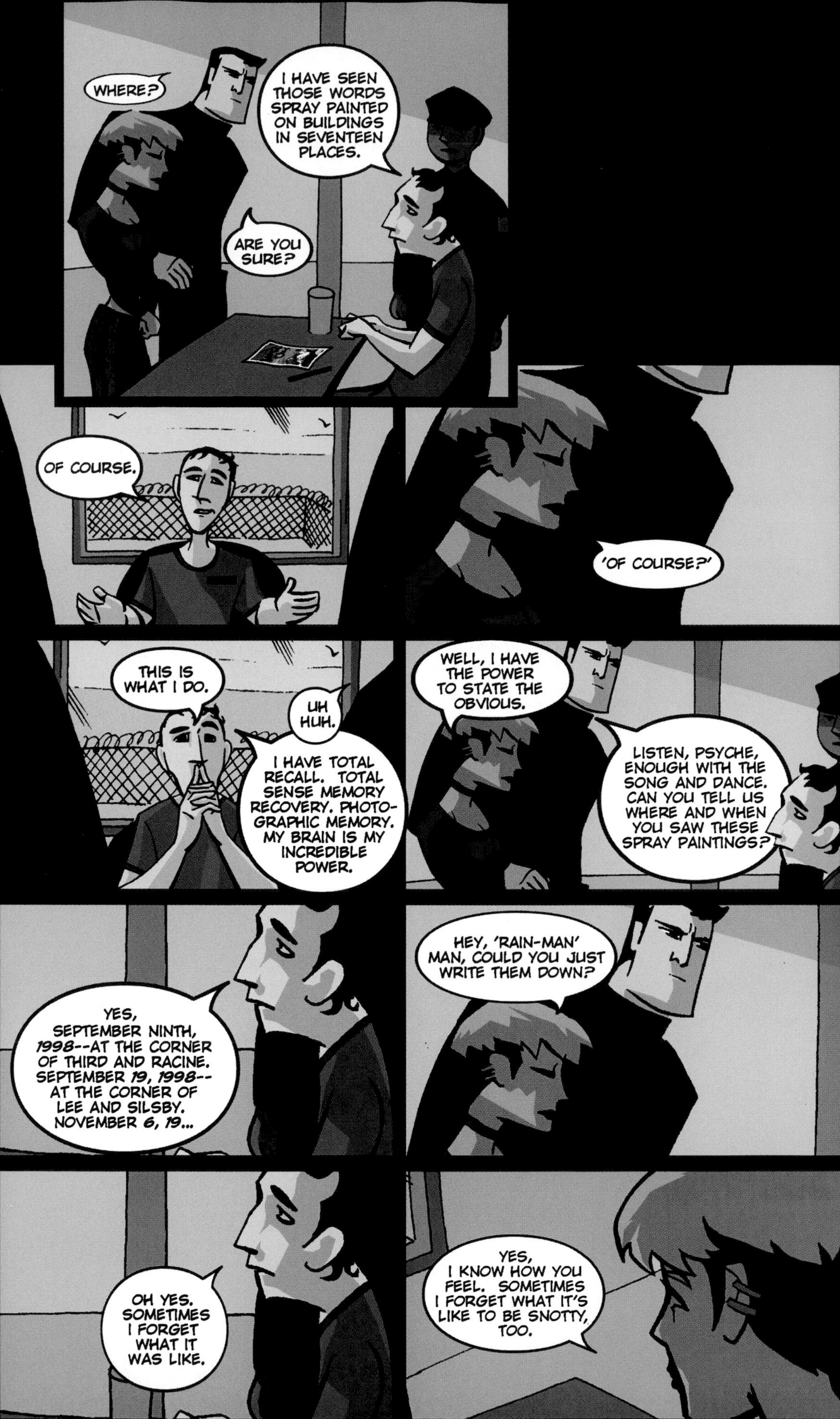
WHERE?
I HAVE SEEN THOSE WORDS SPRAY PAINTED ON BUILDINGS IN SEVENTEEN PLACES.
ARE YOU SURE?
OF COURSE.
'OF COURSE?'
THIS IS WHAT I DO.
UH HUH.
I HAVE TOTAL RECALL. TOTAL SENSE MEMORY RECOVERY. PHOTO-GRAPHIC MEMORY. MY BRAIN IS MY INCREDIBLE POWER.
WELL, I HAVE THE POWER TO STATE THE OBVIOUS.
LISTEN, PSYCHE, ENOUGH WITH THE SONG AND DANCE. CAN YOU TELL US WHERE AND WHEN YOU SAW THESE SPRAY PAINTINGS?
YES, SEPTEMBER NINTH, *1998*--AT THE CORNER OF THIRD AND RACINE. SEPTEMBER *19, 1998*--AT THE CORNER OF LEE AND SILSBY. NOVEMBER *6, 19*...
HEY, 'RAIN-MAN' MAN, COULD YOU JUST WRITE THEM DOWN?
OH YES. SOMETIMES I FORGET WHAT IT WAS LIKE.
YES, I KNOW HOW YOU FEEL. SOMETIMES I FORGET WHAT IT'S LIKE TO BE SNOTTY, TOO.

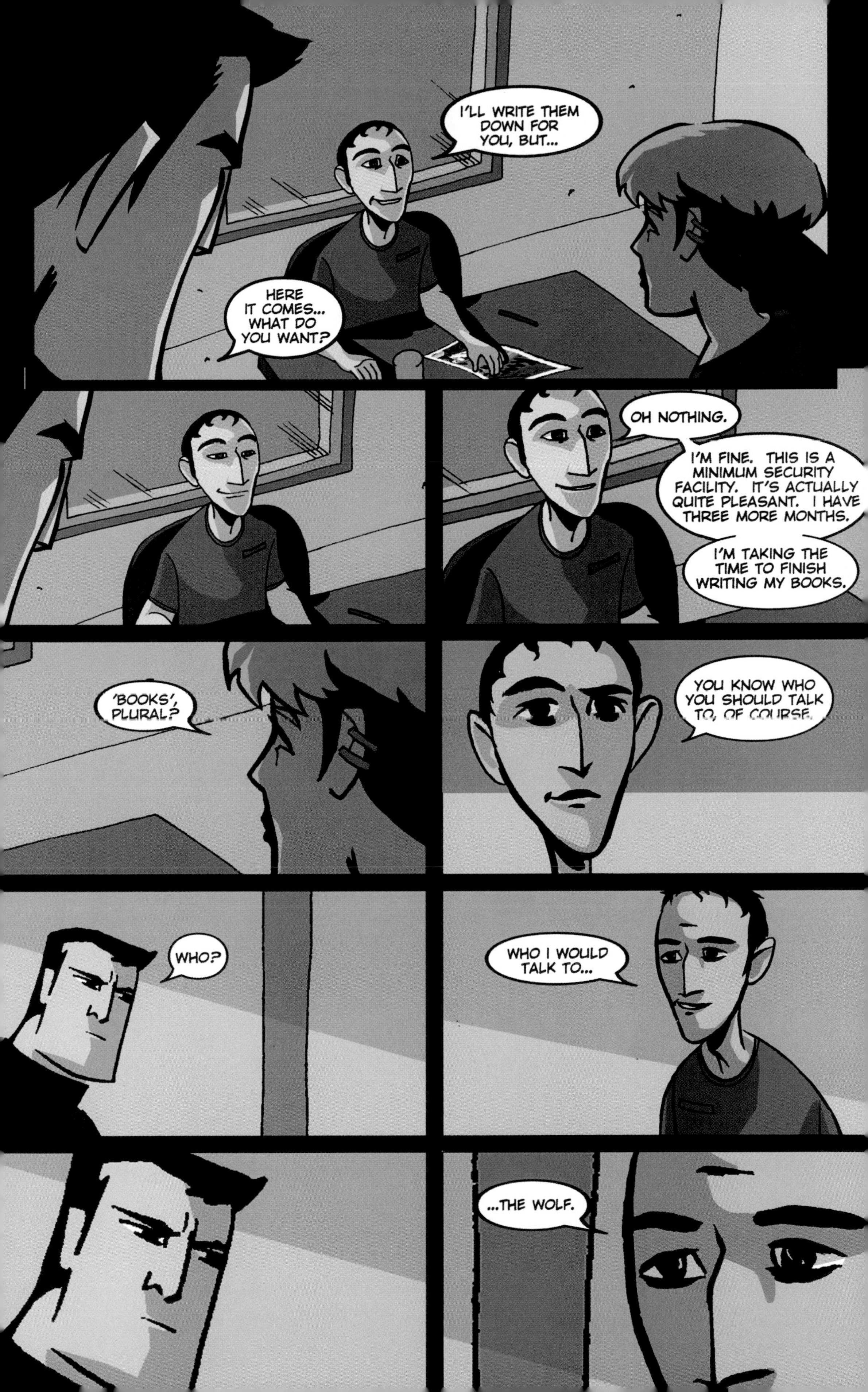
I'LL WRITE THEM DOWN FOR YOU, BUT...
HERE IT COMES... WHAT DO YOU WANT?
OH NOTHING.
I'M FINE. THIS IS A MINIMUM SECURITY FACILITY. IT'S ACTUALLY QUITE PLEASANT. I HAVE THREE MORE MONTHS.
I'M TAKING THE TIME TO FINISH WRITING MY BOOKS.
'BOOKS', PLURAL?
YOU KNOW WHO YOU SHOULD TALK TO, OF COURSE.
WHO?
WHO I WOULD TALK TO...
...THE WOLF.

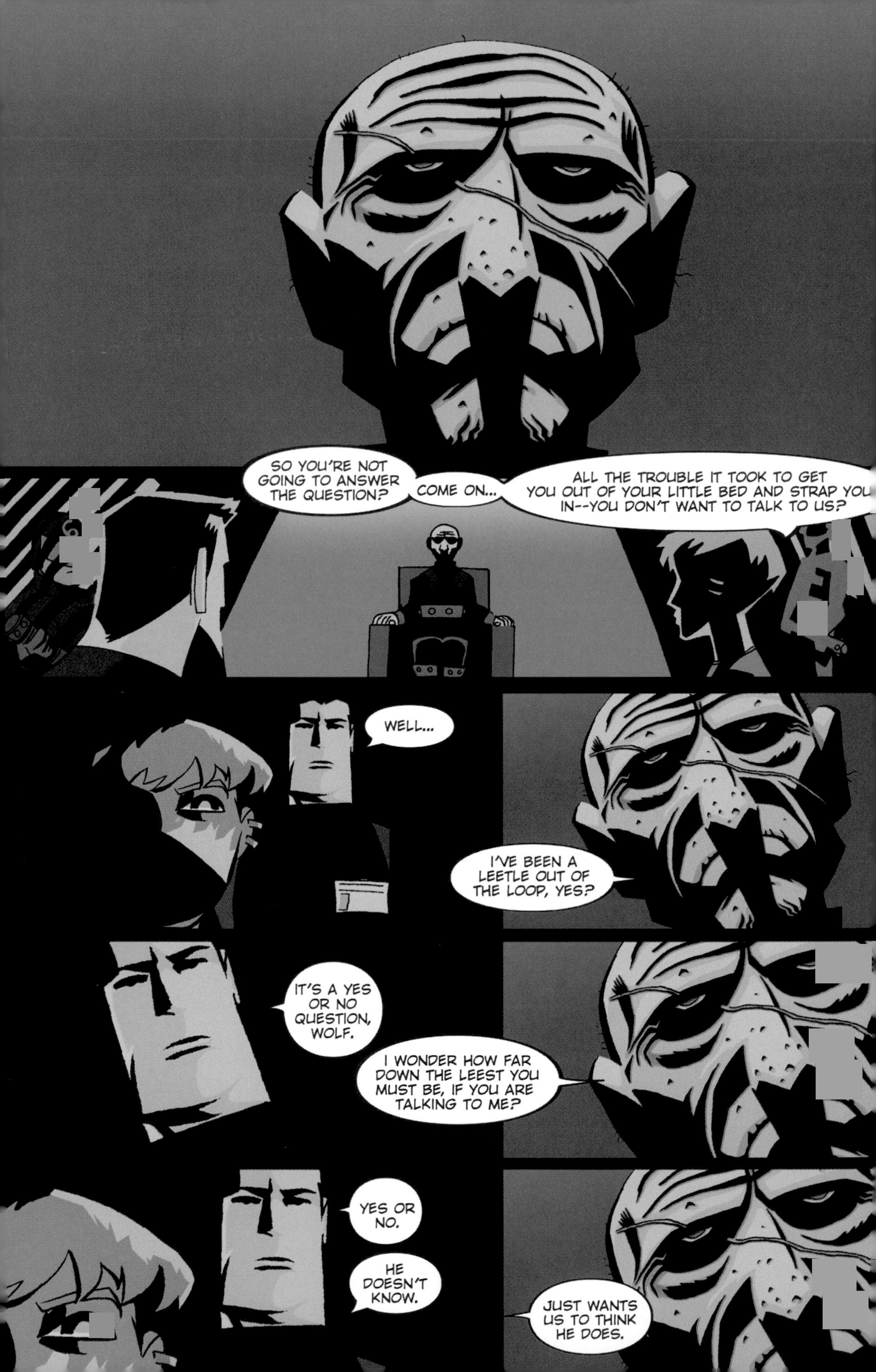
SO YOU'RE NOT GOING TO ANSWER THE QUESTION?
COME ON...
ALL THE TROUBLE IT TOOK TO GET YOU OUT OF YOUR LITTLE BED AND STRAP YOU IN--YOU DON'T WANT TO TALK TO US?
WELL...
I'VE BEEN A LEETLE OUT OF THE LOOP, YES?
IT'S A YES OR NO QUESTION, WOLF.
I WONDER HOW FAR DOWN THE LEEST YOU MUST BE, IF YOU ARE TALKING TO ME?
YES OR NO.
HE DOESN'T KNOW.
JUST WANTS US TO THINK HE DOES.

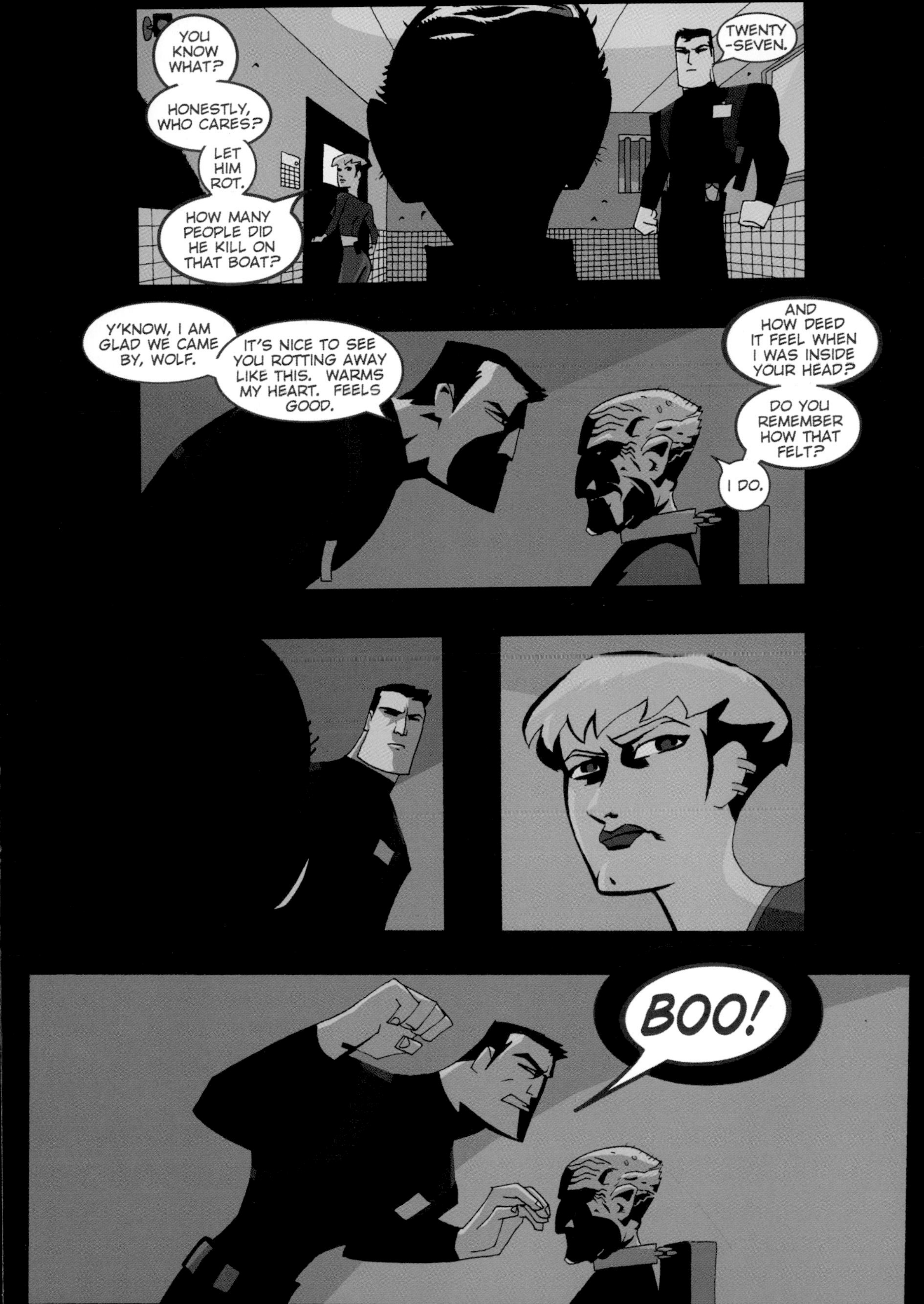
YOU KNOW WHAT?
HONESTLY, WHO CARES?
LET HIM ROT.
HOW MANY PEOPLE DID HE KILL ON THAT BOAT?
TWENTY-SEVEN.
Y'KNOW, I AM GLAD WE CAME BY, WOLF.
IT'S NICE TO SEE YOU ROTTING AWAY LIKE THIS. WARMS MY HEART. FEELS GOOD.
AND HOW DEED IT FEEL WHEN I WAS INSIDE YOUR HEAD?
DO YOU REMEMBER HOW THAT FELT?
I DO.
BOO!

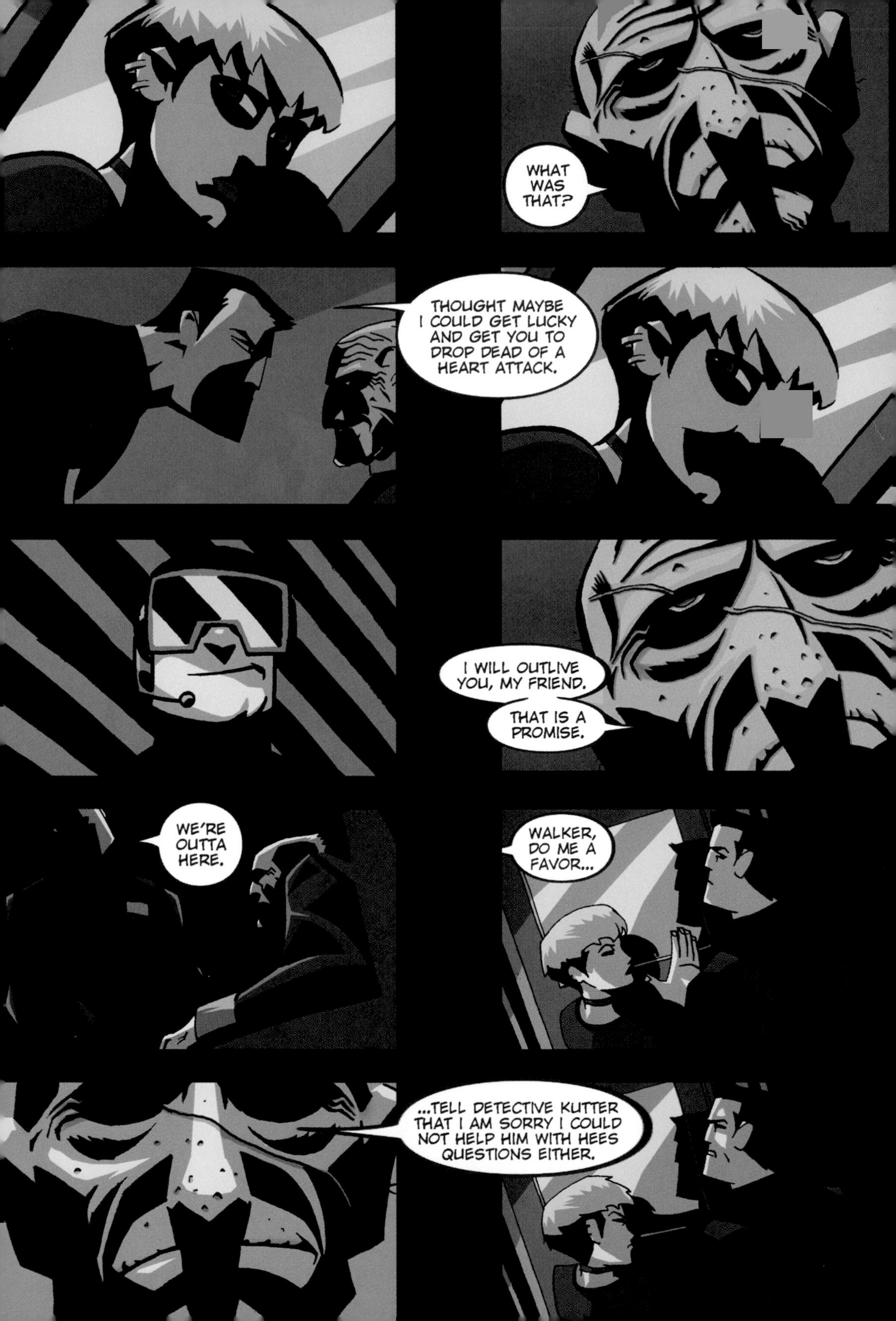
WHAT WAS THAT?
THOUGHT MAYBE I COULD GET LUCKY AND GET YOU TO DROP DEAD OF A HEART ATTACK.
I WILL OUTLIVE YOU, MY FRIEND.
THAT IS A PROMISE.
WE'RE OUTTA HERE.
WALKER, DO ME A FAVOR...
...TELL DETECTIVE KUTTER THAT I AM SORRY I COULD NOT HELP HIM WITH HEES QUESTIONS EITHER.

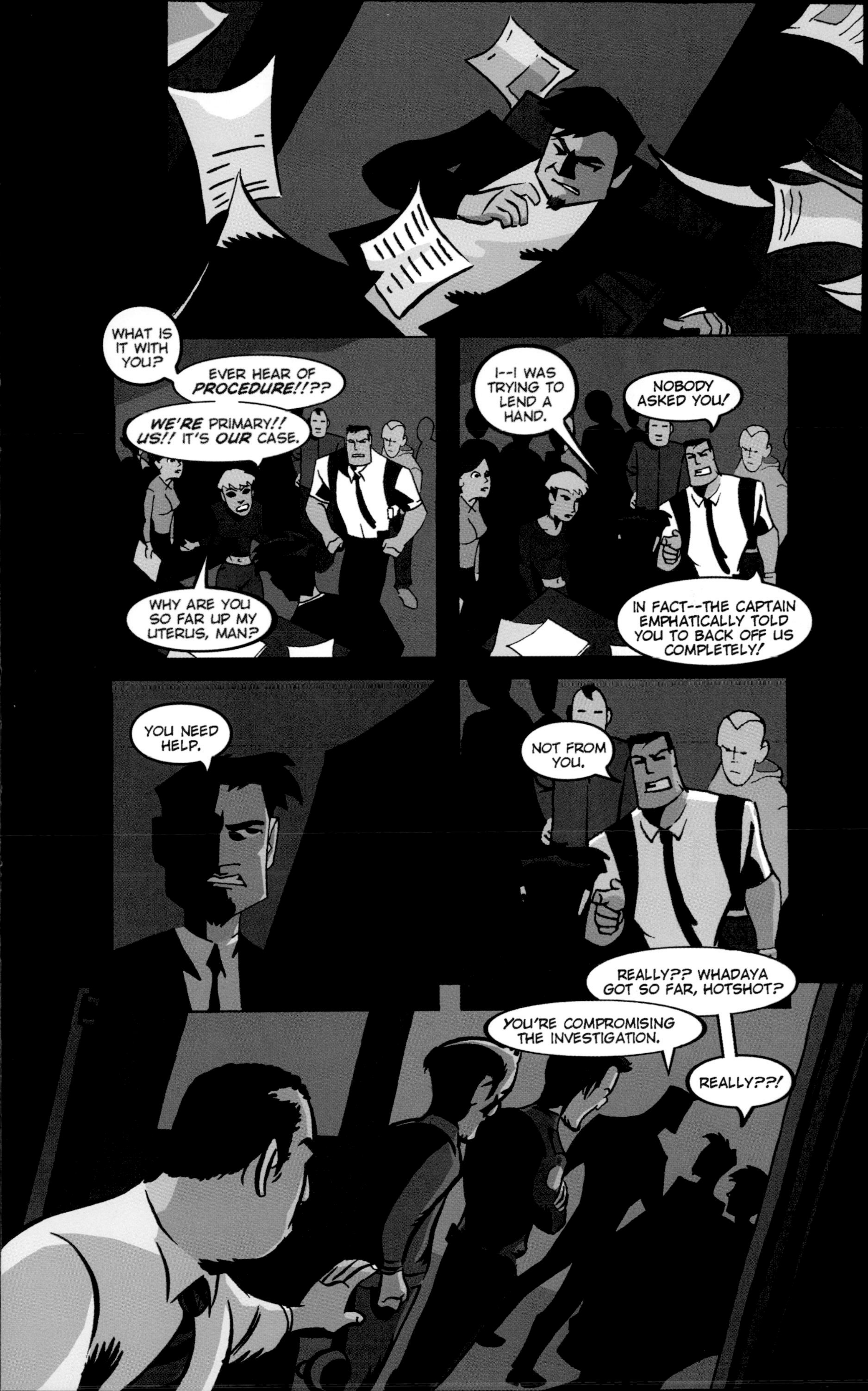
WHAT IS IT WITH YOU?
EVER HEAR OF PROCEDURE!!??
WE'RE PRIMARY!! US!! IT'S OUR CASE.
WHY ARE YOU SO FAR UP MY UTERUS, MAN?
I--I WAS TRYING TO LEND A HAND.
NOBODY ASKED YOU!
IN FACT--THE CAPTAIN EMPHATICALLY TOLD YOU TO BACK OFF US COMPLETELY!
YOU NEED HELP.
NOT FROM YOU.
REALLY?? WHADAYA GOT SO FAR, HOTSHOT?
YOU'RE COMPROMISING THE INVESTIGATION.
REALLY??!

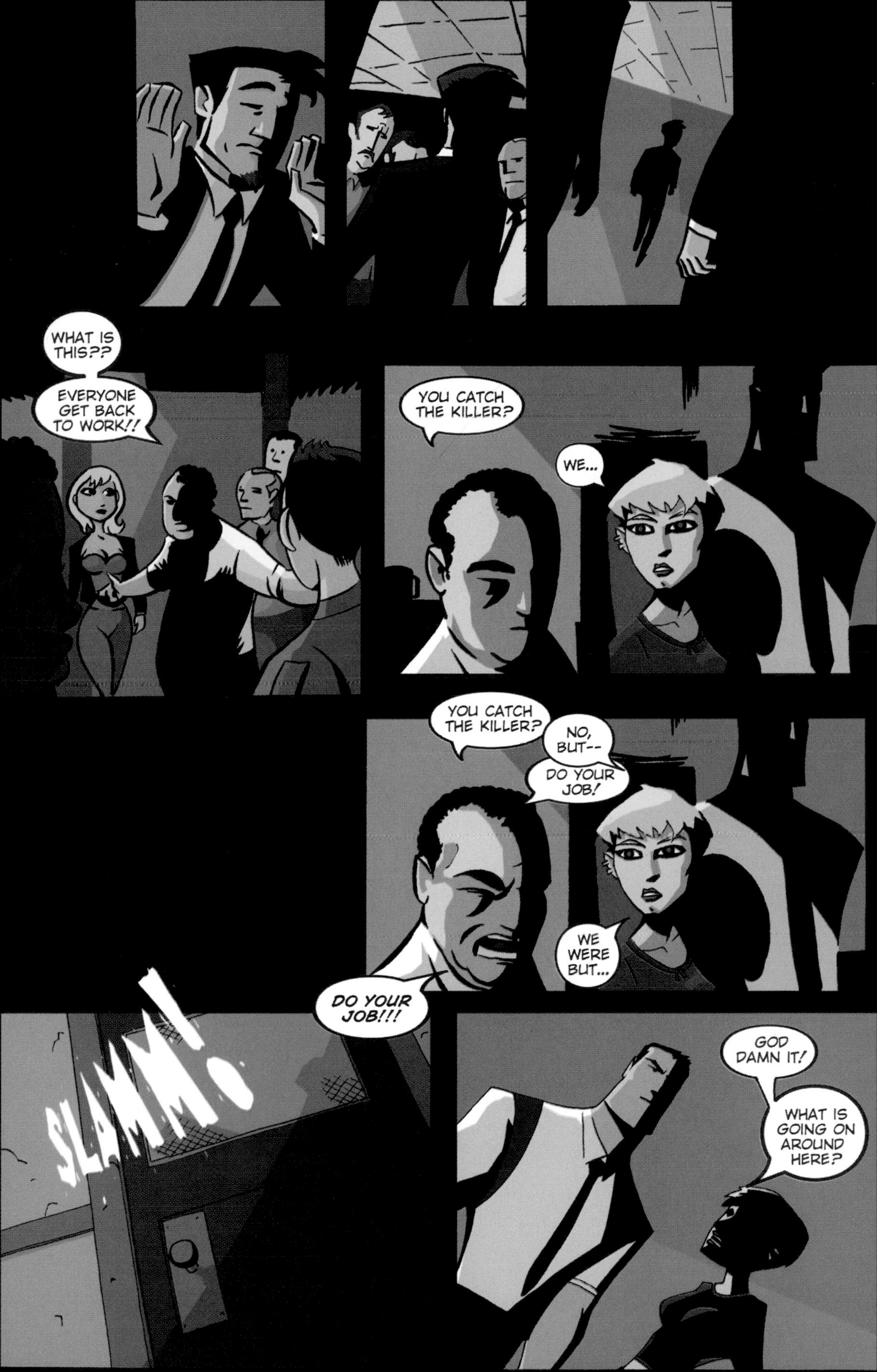
WHAT IS THIS??
EVERYONE GET BACK TO WORK!!
YOU CATCH THE KILLER?
WE...
YOU CATCH THE KILLER?
NO, BUT--
DO YOUR JOB!
WE WERE BUT...
DO YOUR JOB!!!
SLAMM!
GOD DAMN IT!
WHAT IS GOING ON AROUND HERE?

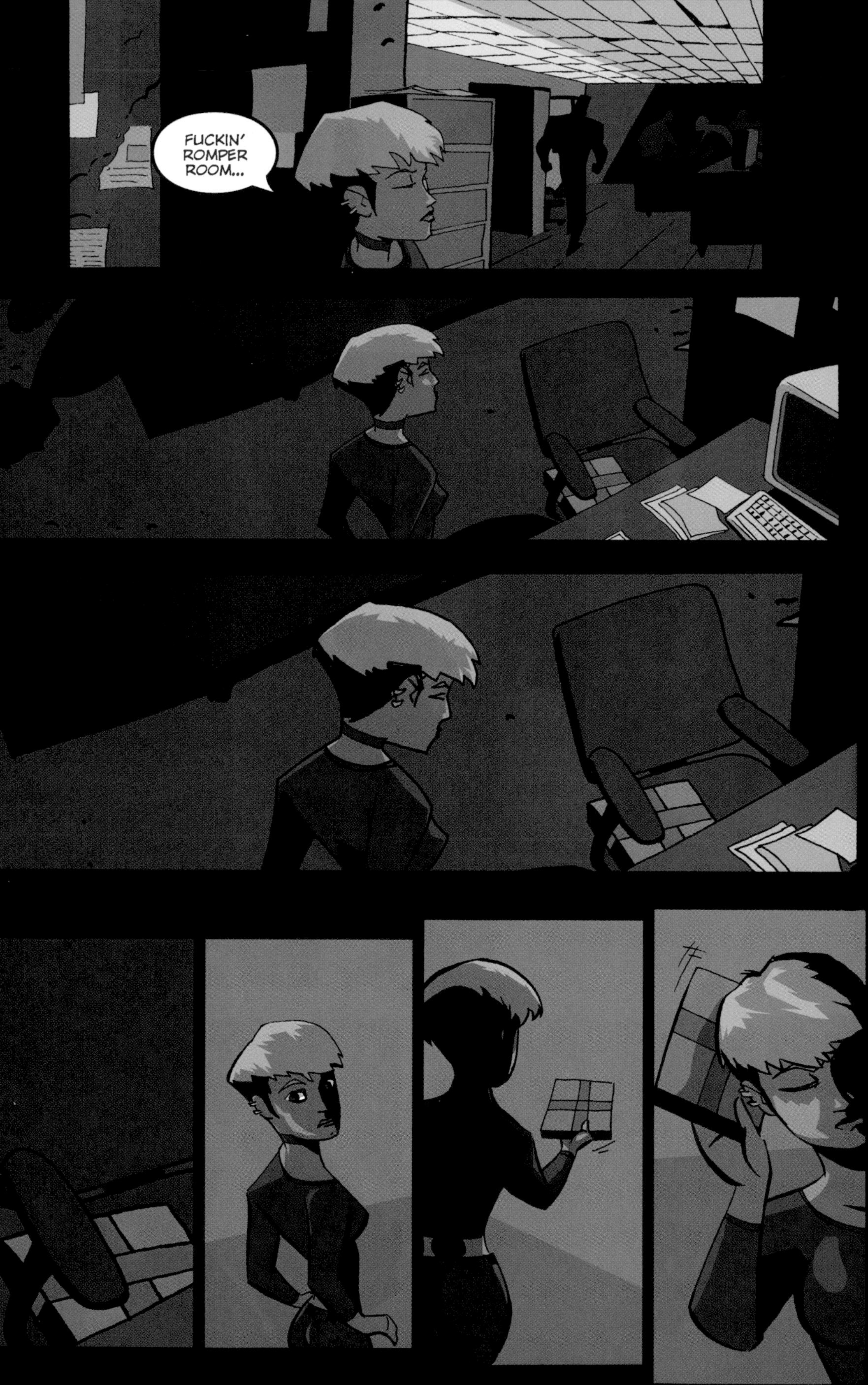
FUCKIN' ROMPER ROOM...

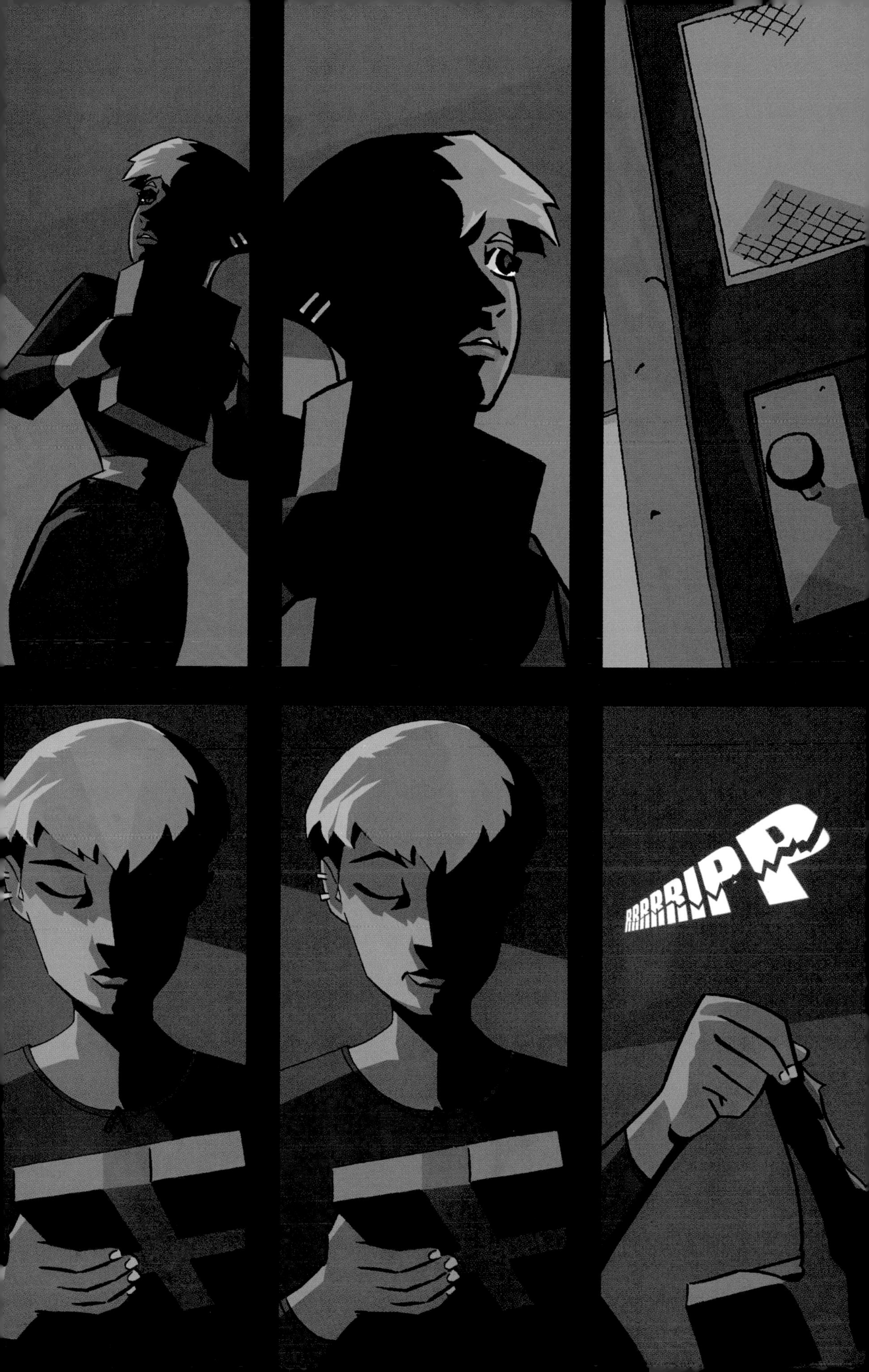
RRRRRRIPP

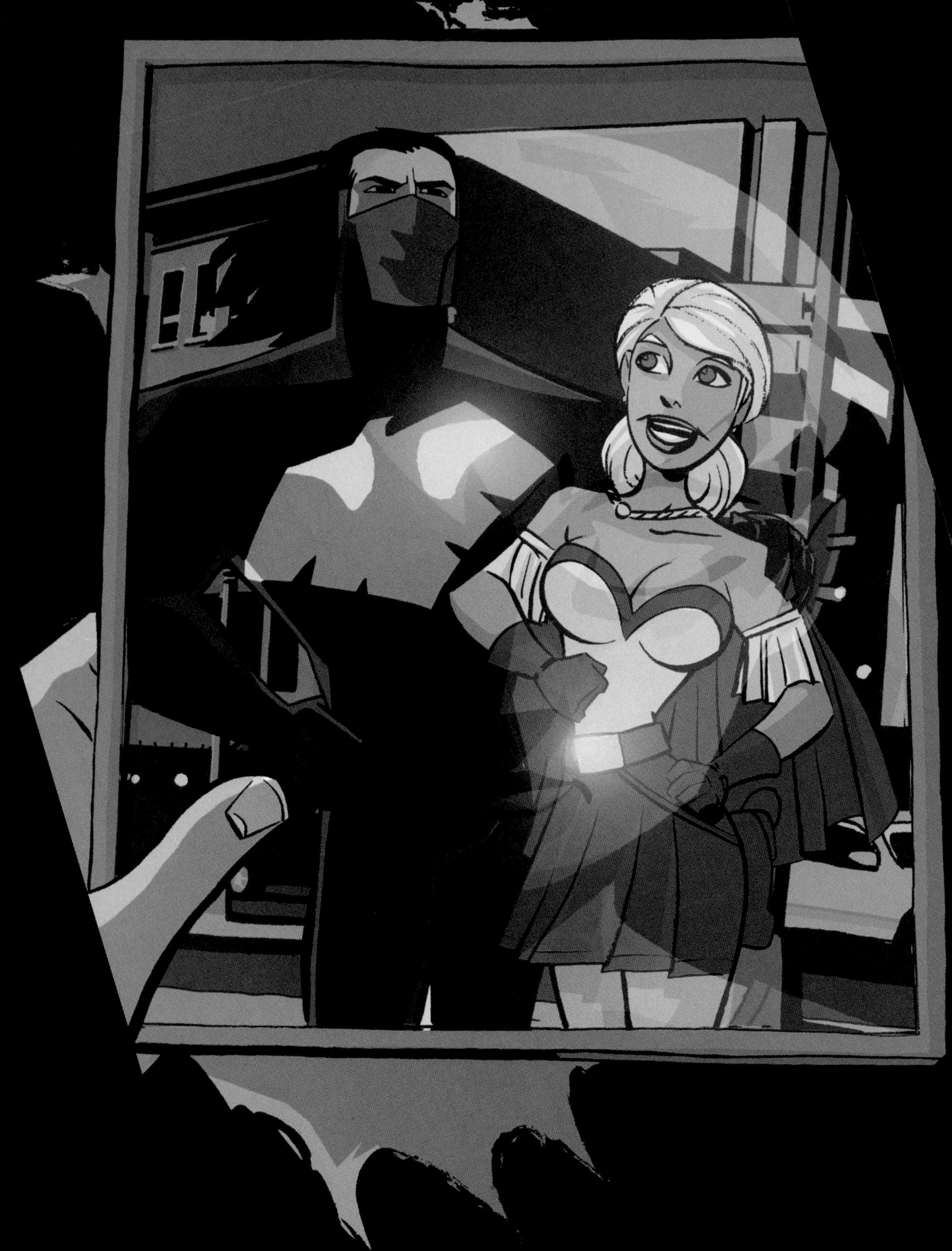

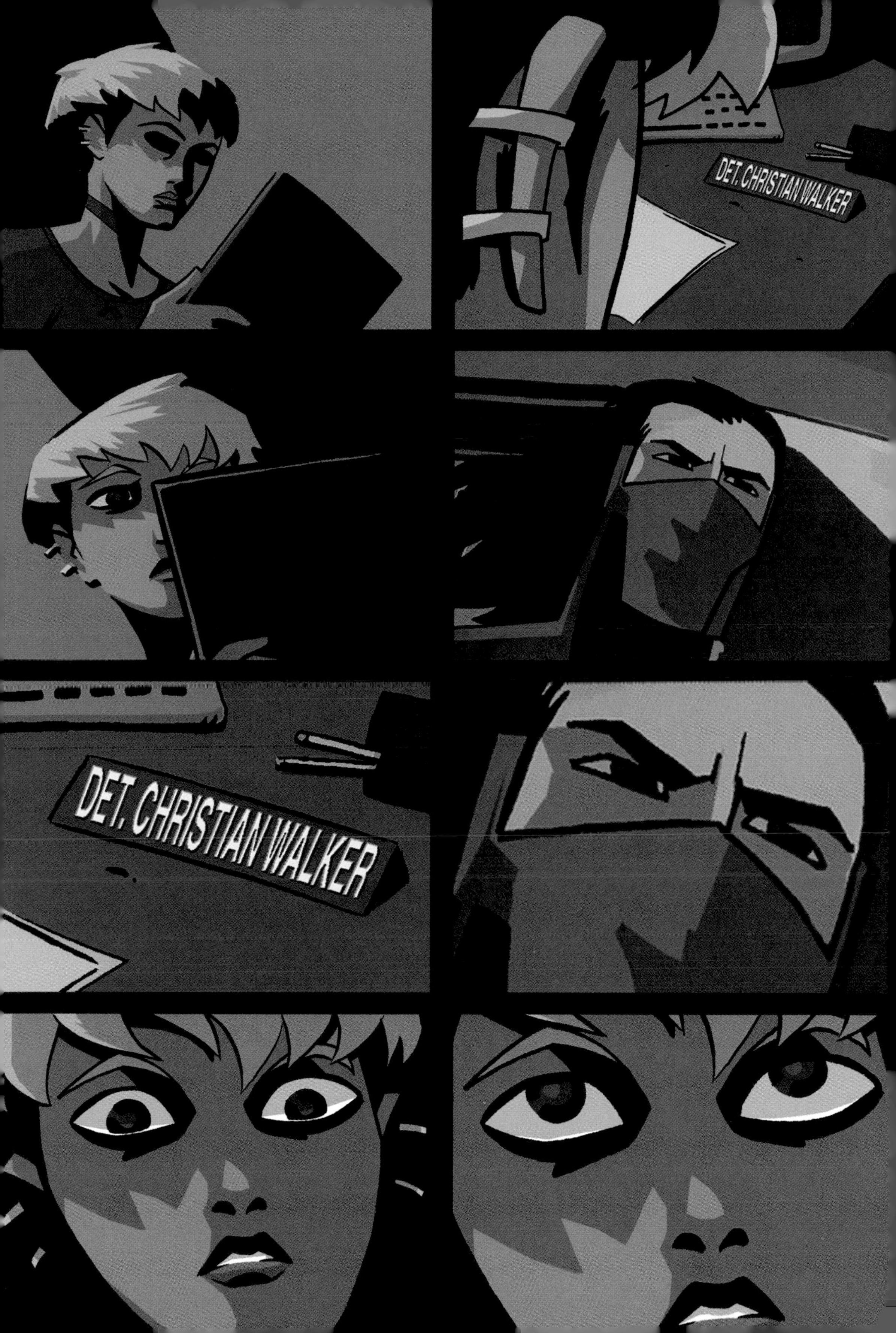
DET. CHRISTIAN WALKER
DET. CHRISTIAN WALKER

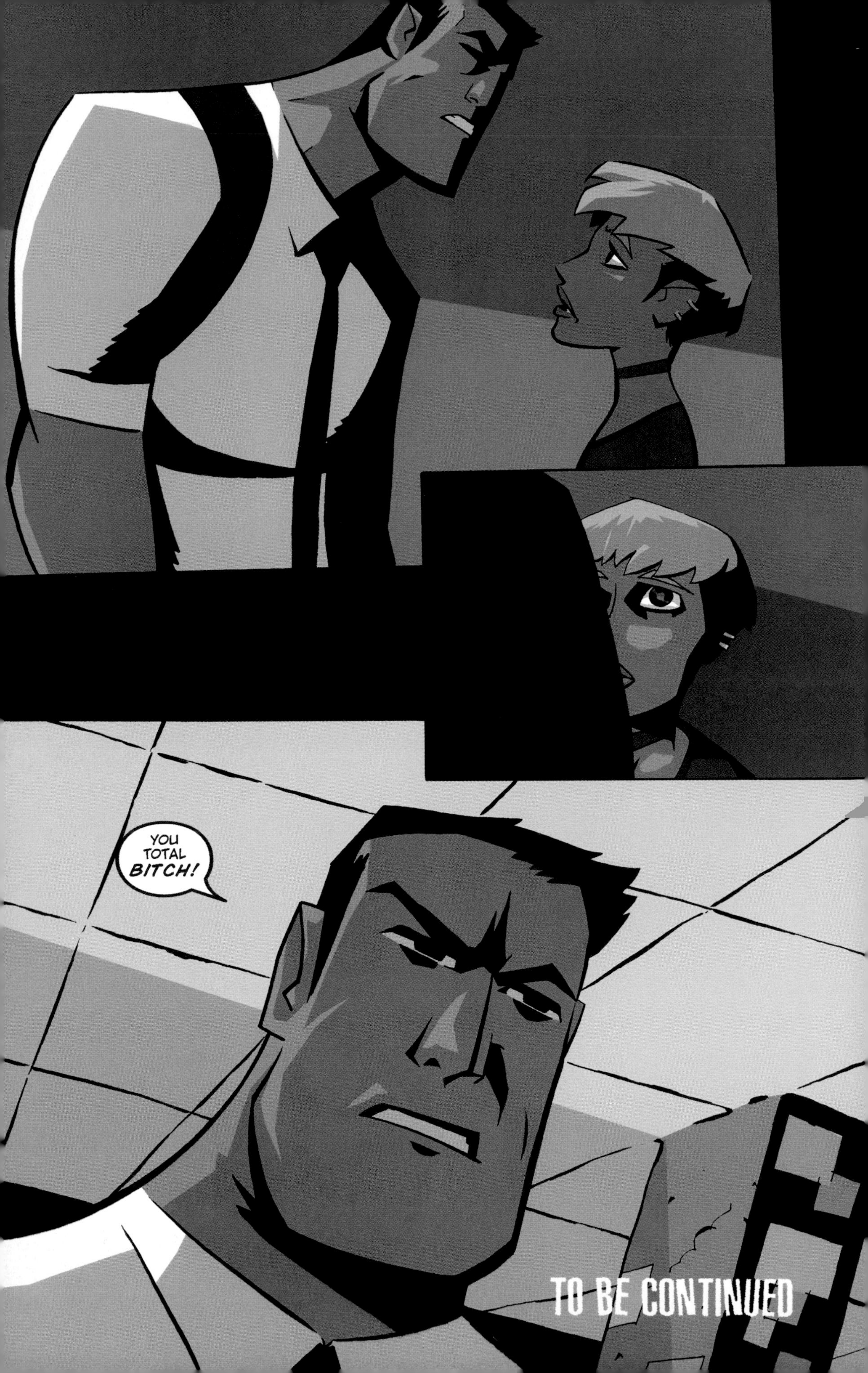
YOU TOTAL BITCH!
TO BE CONTINUED

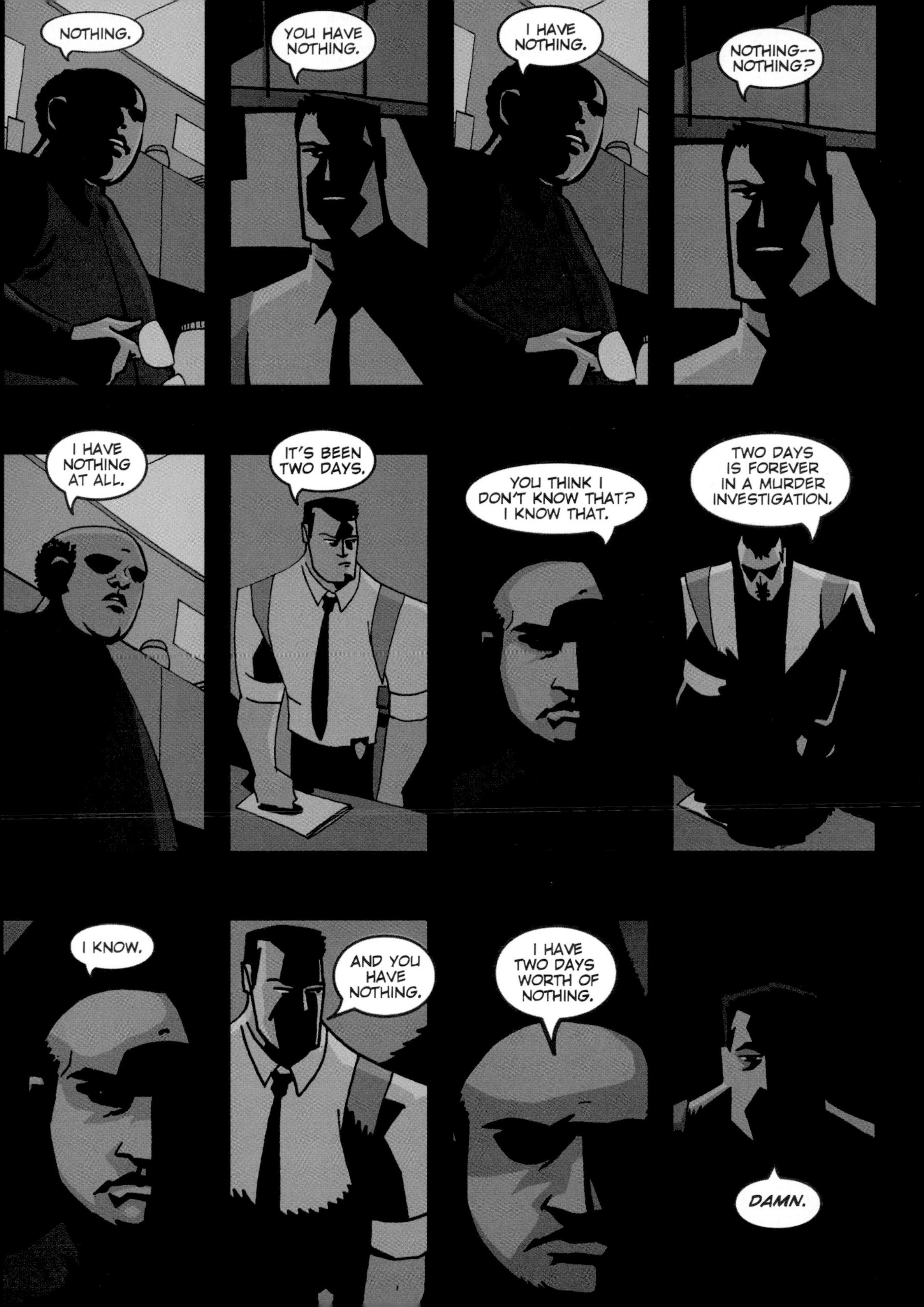
NOTHING.
YOU HAVE NOTHING.
I HAVE NOTHING.
NOTHING-- NOTHING?
I HAVE NOTHING AT ALL.
IT'S BEEN TWO DAYS.
YOU THINK I DON'T KNOW THAT? I KNOW THAT.
TWO DAYS IS FOREVER IN A MURDER INVESTIGATION.
I KNOW.
AND YOU HAVE NOTHING.
I HAVE TWO DAYS WORTH OF NOTHING.
DAMN.

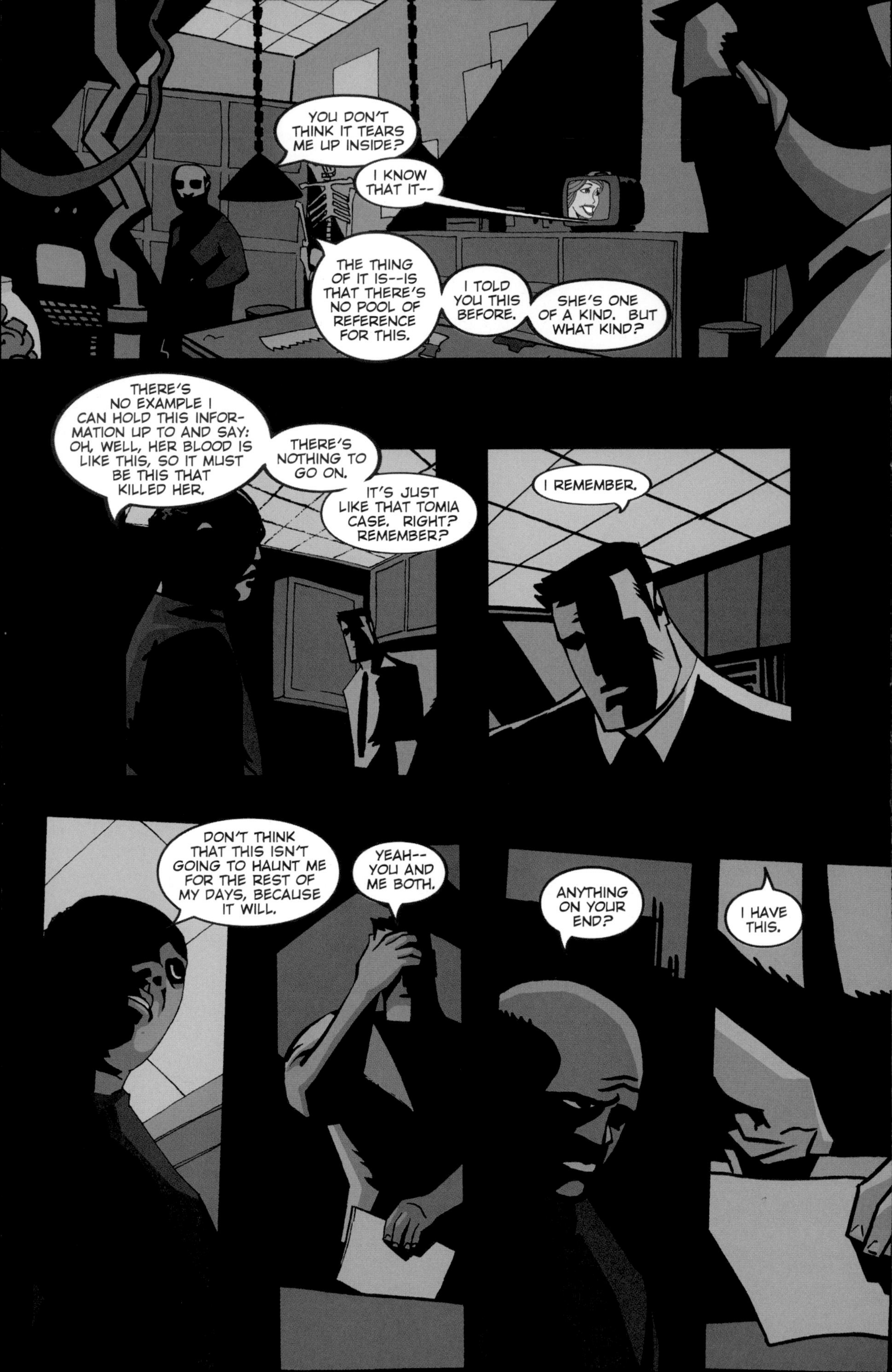
YOU DON'T THINK IT TEARS ME UP INSIDE?
I KNOW THAT IT--
THE THING OF IT IS--IS THAT THERE'S NO POOL OF REFERENCE FOR THIS.
I TOLD YOU THIS BEFORE.
SHE'S ONE OF A KIND. BUT WHAT KIND?
THERE'S NO EXAMPLE I CAN HOLD THIS INFORMATION UP TO AND SAY: OH, WELL, HER BLOOD IS LIKE THIS, SO IT MUST BE THIS THAT KILLED HER.
THERE'S NOTHING TO GO ON.
IT'S JUST LIKE THAT TOMIA CASE. RIGHT? REMEMBER?
I REMEMBER.
DON'T THINK THAT THIS ISN'T GOING TO HAUNT ME FOR THE REST OF MY DAYS, BECAUSE IT WILL.
YEAH-- YOU AND ME BOTH.
ANYTHING ON YOUR END?
I HAVE THIS.

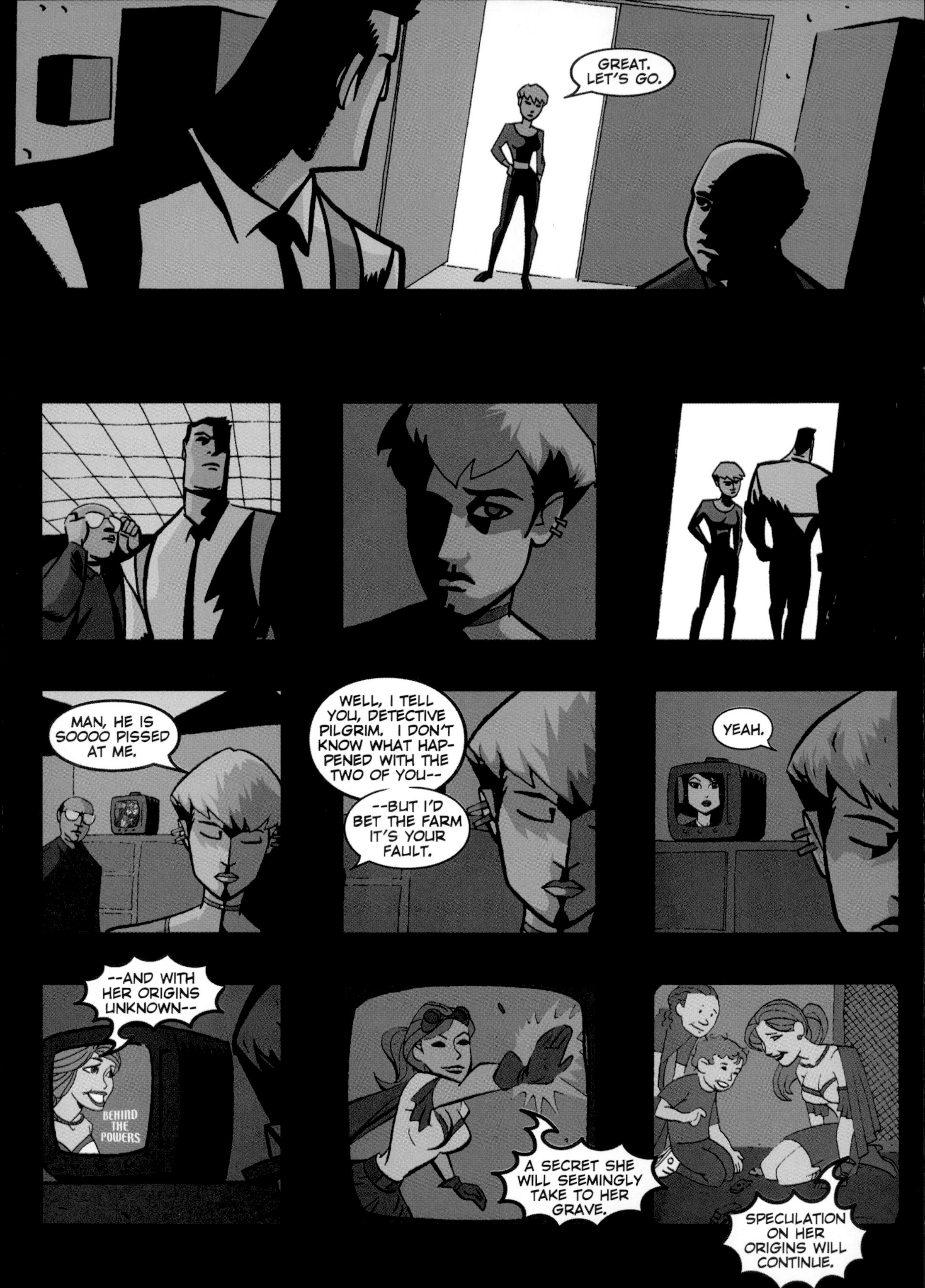
GREAT. LET'S GO.
MAN, HE IS SOOOO PISSED AT ME.
WELL, I TELL YOU, DETECTIVE PILGRIM. I DON'T KNOW WHAT HAPPENED WITH THE TWO OF YOU--
--BUT I'D BET THE FARM IT'S YOUR FAULT.
YEAH.
--AND WITH HER ORIGINS UNKNOWN--
BEHIND THE POWERS
A SECRET SHE WILL SEEMINGLY TAKE TO HER GRAVE.
SPECULATION ON HER ORIGINS WILL CONTINUE.

WHAT I'M SAYING--

--WHAT I HAVE ALWAYS BEEN SAY-ING IS THAT IT IS MY THEORY THAT WE HAVE HAD A RETRO GIRL FIGURE IN OUR LIVES SINCE THE DAWN OF MAN.

OF COURSE WE DIDN'T CALL HER RETRO GIRL. BUT THAT IS WHERE THE NAME CAME FROM. SHE HARKENS BACK TO ANOTHER TIME. A MORE INNOCENT TIME. RIGHT? SHE HAS A WORLDLY, TIMELESS BEAUTY.

BUT--BUT IF YOU LOOK AT THESE DOCUMENTS AND PICTORIALS IT'S ARGUABLE THAT THESE OTHER WOMEN HERE ARE HER SPITTING IMAGE. SEE HERE? JOAN OF ARC. CLEOPATRA.

STRONG, WORLDLY, HEROIC WOMEN THAT WE NEEDED IN THAT TIME AND THAT PLACE. WOMEN THAT ENDED UP ONLY LIVING A SHORT LIFE.

AND THESE ARE JUST THE WOMEN WHO ROSE TO A MODICUM OF FAME THOUGH CIRCUM-STANCE. WHO KNOWS HOW MANY INCARNATIONS SHE HAD THAT LIVED LIVES OF QUIET AND UNASSUMING HEROISM?

YES--YES--YES. I'VE HEARD THOSE THEORIES. IT'S--PEOPLE LIKE TO CONCOCT THESE THEORIES ON EVERYTHING. YES?

ALL OF A SUDDEN, SHE'S MOTHER NATURE?

IN MY FINDINGS. THE SIMPLEST ANSWER IS ALWAYS THE ANSWER. SHE LIVED A GOOD LIFE, AND NOW, SADLY, SHE IS DEAD. LIKE ELVIS, MARILYN, JAMES DEAN--DEAD, DEAD, DEAD.

WE INTERRUPT YOUR VIEWING OF *"BEHIND THE POWERS"* FOR AN ACTION FIVE SPECIAL REPORT.

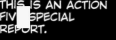

THIS IS AN ACTION FIVE SPECIAL REPORT.

WE NOW BRING YOU LIVE INSIDE THE CITY JUSTICE CENTER WHERE COLLETTE MCDANIEL IS REPORTING LIVE. COLLETTE?

THIS IS COLLETTE MCDANIEL. I AM HERE INSIDE THE HOMICIDE UNIT OF DISTRICT 55.

STANDING WITH ME IS DETECTIVE CHRISTIAN WALKER.

DETECTIVE WALKER IS THE PRIMARY DETECTIVE FOR THE RETRO GIRL MURDER INVESTI-GATION--THE HORRIBLE RETRO GIRL TRADGEDY THAT HAS GRIPPED OUR CITY IN MOURNING.

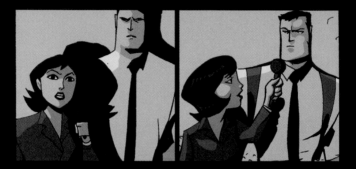

DETECTIVE, WHAT CAN YOU TELL US ABOUT YOUR PROGRESS ON THE INVESTIGATION SO FAR?

WELL, MA'AM, MOST OF THAT INFORMATION IS CLASSIFIED UNTIL THE CASE IS OFFICIALLY CLOSED, WHICH AT THIS TIME IS NOT THE CASE.

WE ARE ASKING THE PUBLIC'S HELP WITH INFORMATION IN REGARD TO THE MURDER, SPECIFICALLY TO A PIECE OF GRAFFITI THAT WE HAVE AT THE CRIME SCENE, I BELIEVE WE A--

YES, IT'S UP NOW.

ANY INFORMATION THAT ANYONE HAS ABOUT THIS OR ANYTHING THAT CAN HELP US IN OUR INVESTIGATION --ANY INFORMATION ABOUT THE MEANING OF THE WORDS OF THE PERSON OR PERSONS RESPON-SIBLE FOR THE GRAFFITI-- PLEASE CALL OUR HOTLINE AT 1-888-333-6665.

OBVIOUSLY THIS MATTER IS OF THE HIGHEST IMPORT-ANCE--ANYONE CALLING WITH PURPOSELY FALSE OR PRANK INFOR-MATION WILL BE TRACED AND PROSECUTED FOR OBSTRUCTION OF JUSTICE.

DETECTIVE, ANY WORD ON WHY JOHNNY ROYALLE WAS BROUGHT INTO THE STATION YESTERDAY?

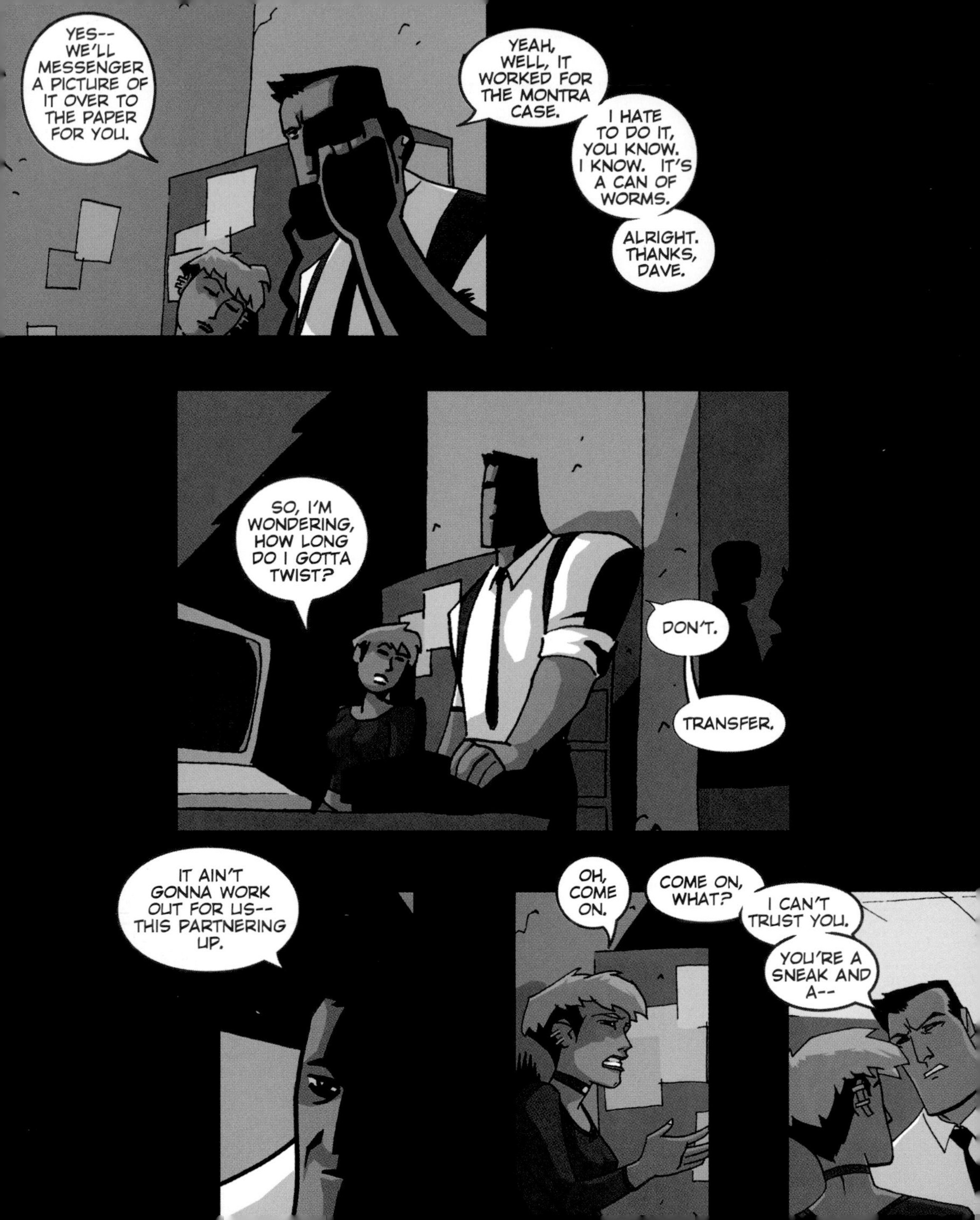
YES-- WE'LL MESSENGER A PICTURE OF IT OVER TO THE PAPER FOR YOU.
YEAH, WELL, IT WORKED FOR THE MONTRA CASE.
I HATE TO DO IT, YOU KNOW. I KNOW. IT'S A CAN OF WORMS.
ALRIGHT. THANKS, DAVE.
SO, I'M WONDERING, HOW LONG DO I GOTTA TWIST?
DON'T.
TRANSFER.
IT AIN'T GONNA WORK OUT FOR US-- THIS PARTNERING UP.
OH, COME ON.
COME ON, WHAT?
I CAN'T TRUST YOU.
YOU'RE A SNEAK AND A--

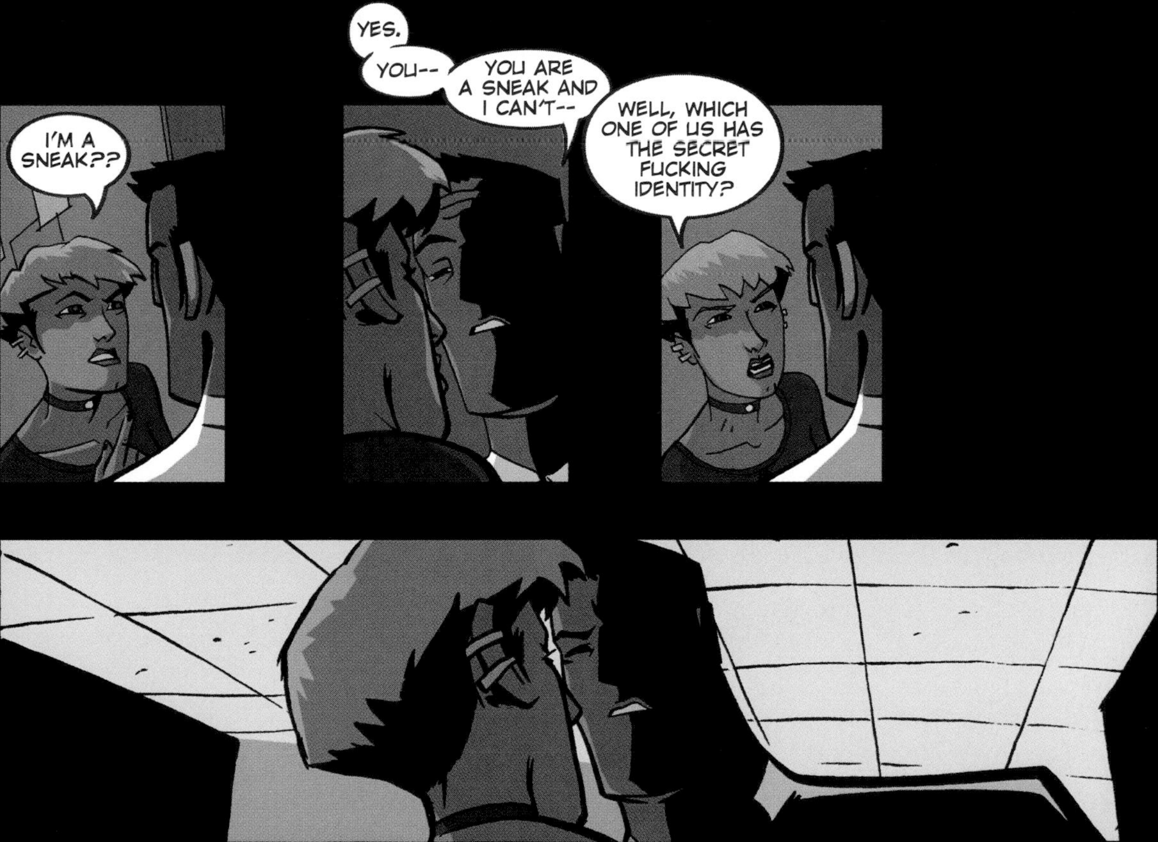
I'M A SNEAK??
YES.
YOU--
YOU ARE A SNEAK AND I CAN'T--
WELL, WHICH ONE OF US HAS THE SECRET FUCKING IDENTITY?

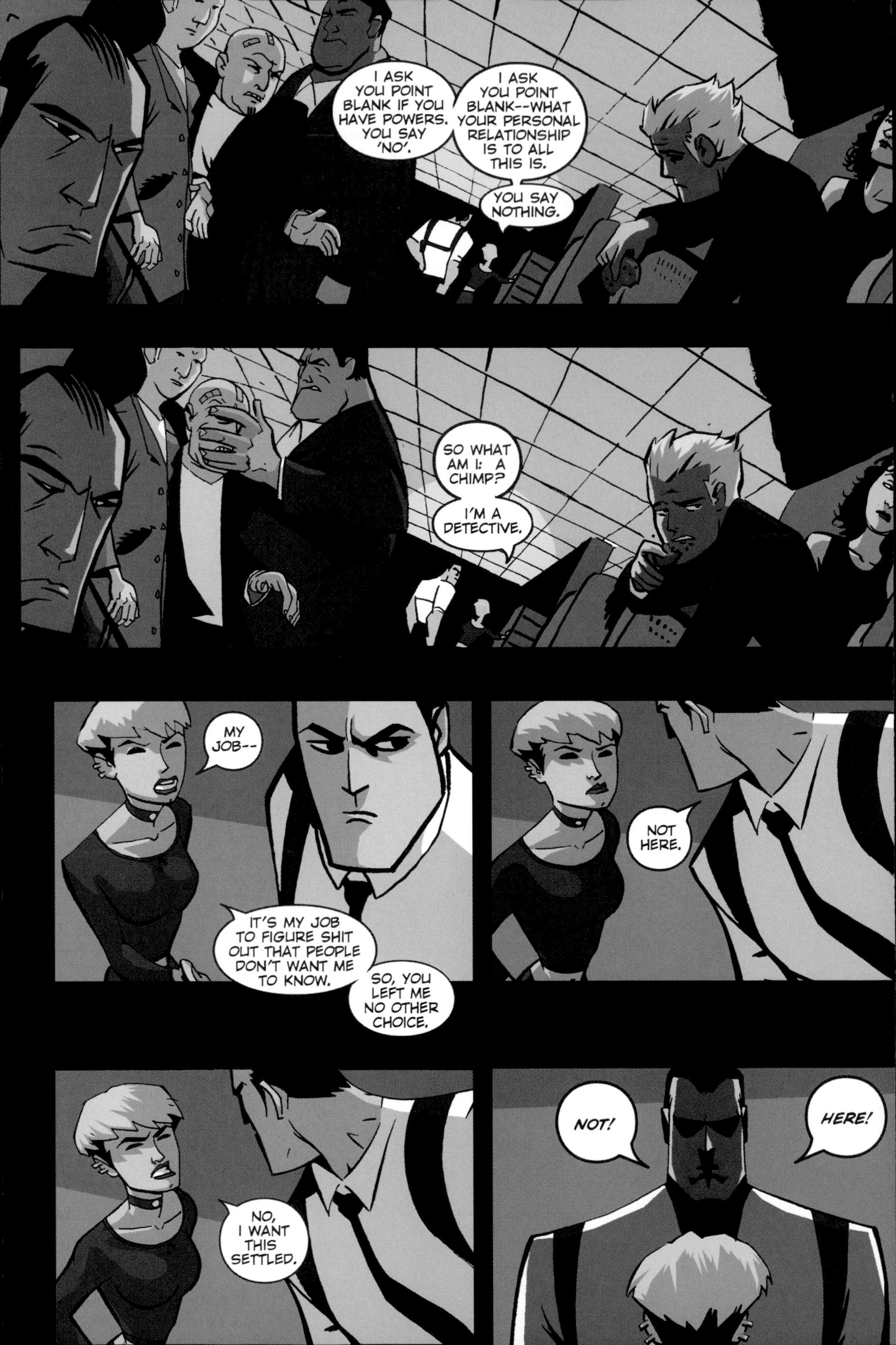
I ASK YOU POINT BLANK IF YOU HAVE POWERS. YOU SAY 'NO'.
I ASK YOU POINT BLANK--WHAT YOUR PERSONAL RELATIONSHIP IS TO ALL THIS IS.
YOU SAY NOTHING.
SO WHAT AM I: A CHIMP?
I'M A DETECTIVE.
MY JOB--
IT'S MY JOB TO FIGURE SHIT OUT THAT PEOPLE DON'T WANT ME TO KNOW.
SO, YOU LEFT ME NO OTHER CHOICE.
NOT HERE.
NO, I WANT THIS SETTLED.
NOT!
HERE!

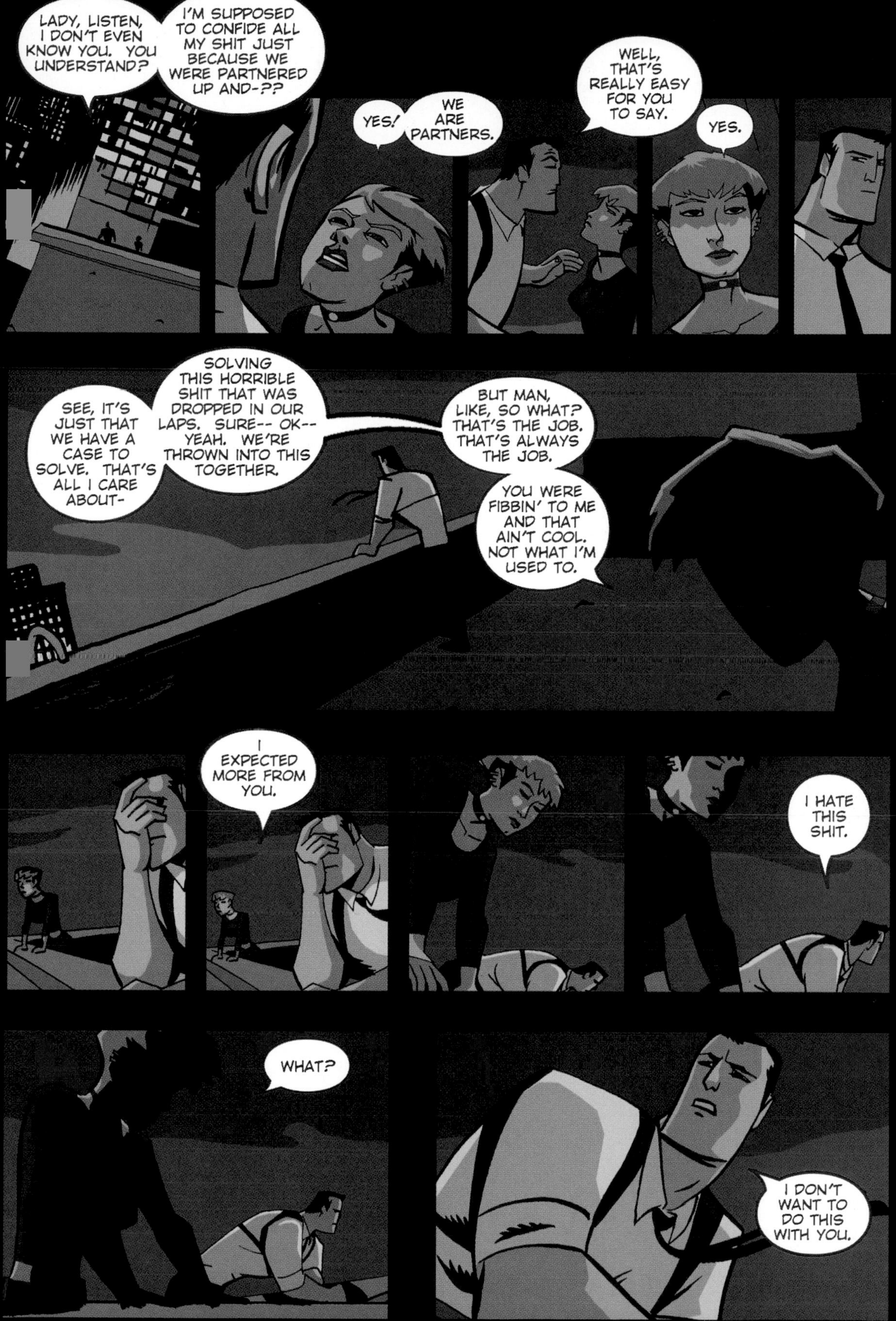
LADY, LISTEN, I DON'T EVEN KNOW YOU. YOU UNDERSTAND?
I'M SUPPOSED TO CONFIDE ALL MY SHIT JUST BECAUSE WE WERE PARTNERED UP AND-??
YES!
WE ARE PARTNERS.
WELL, THAT'S REALLY EASY FOR YOU TO SAY.
YES.
SEE, IT'S JUST THAT WE HAVE A CASE TO SOLVE. THAT'S ALL I CARE ABOUT-
SOLVING THIS HORRIBLE SHIT THAT WAS DROPPED IN OUR LAPS. SURE-- OK-- YEAH. WE'RE THROWN INTO THIS TOGETHER.
BUT MAN, LIKE, SO WHAT? THAT'S THE JOB. THAT'S ALWAYS THE JOB.
YOU WERE FIBBIN' TO ME AND THAT AIN'T COOL. NOT WHAT I'M USED TO.
I EXPECTED MORE FROM YOU.
I HATE THIS SHIT.
WHAT?
I DON'T WANT TO DO THIS WITH YOU.

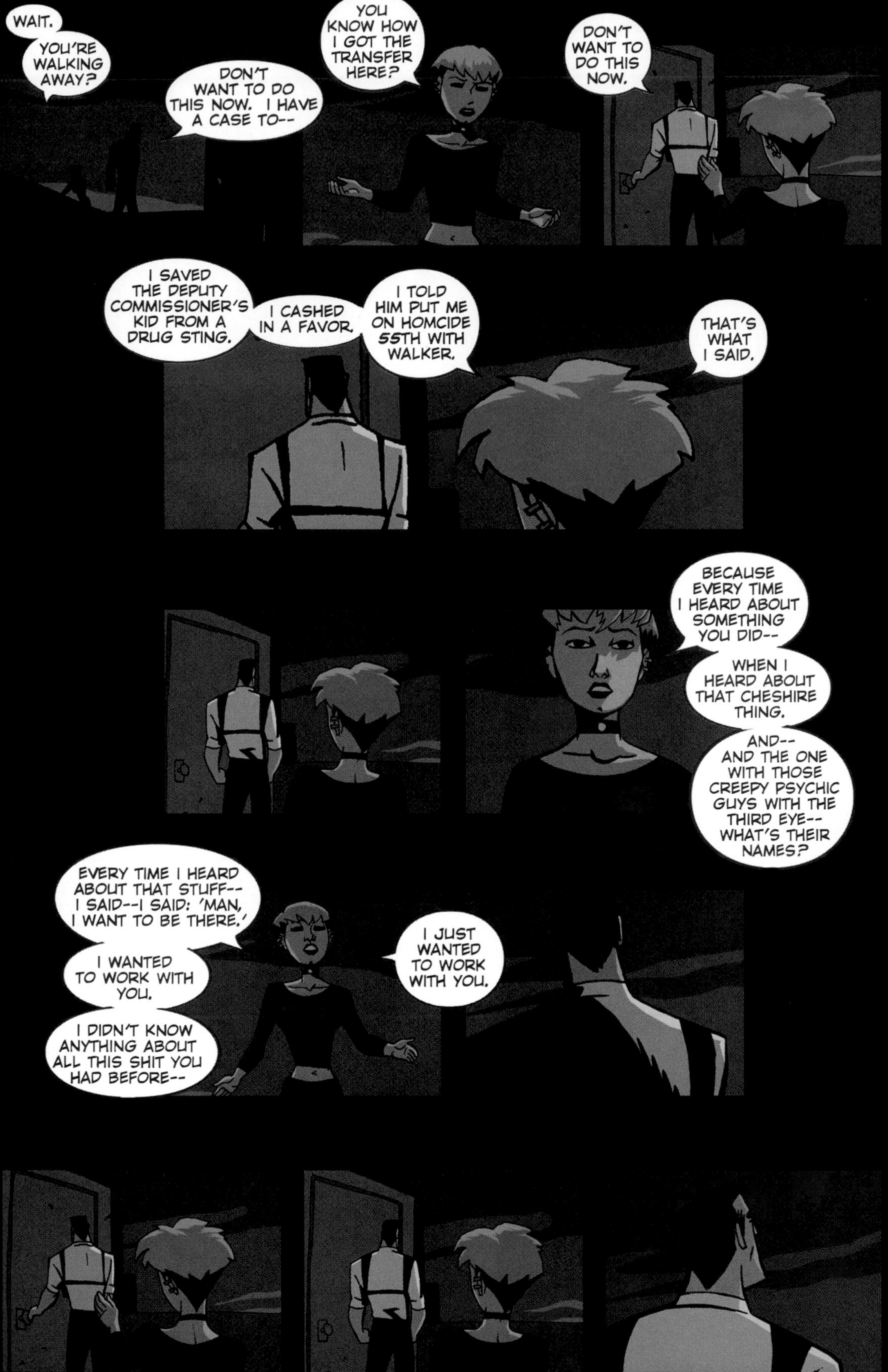
WAIT.
YOU'RE WALKING AWAY?
DON'T WANT TO DO THIS NOW. I HAVE A CASE TO--
YOU KNOW HOW I GOT THE TRANSFER HERE?
DON'T WANT TO DO THIS NOW.
I SAVED THE DEPUTY COMMISSIONER'S KID FROM A DRUG STING.
I CASHED IN A FAVOR.
I TOLD HIM PUT ME ON HOMCIDE 55TH WITH WALKER.
THAT'S WHAT I SAID.
BECAUSE EVERY TIME I HEARD ABOUT SOMETHING YOU DID--
WHEN I HEARD ABOUT THAT CHESHIRE THING.
AND-- AND THE ONE WITH THOSE CREEPY PSYCHIC GUYS WITH THE THIRD EYE-- WHAT'S THEIR NAMES?
EVERY TIME I HEARD ABOUT THAT STUFF-- I SAID--I SAID: 'MAN, I WANT TO BE THERE.'
I WANTED TO WORK WITH YOU.
I DIDN'T KNOW ANYTHING ABOUT ALL THIS SHIT YOU HAD BEFORE--
I JUST WANTED TO WORK WITH YOU.

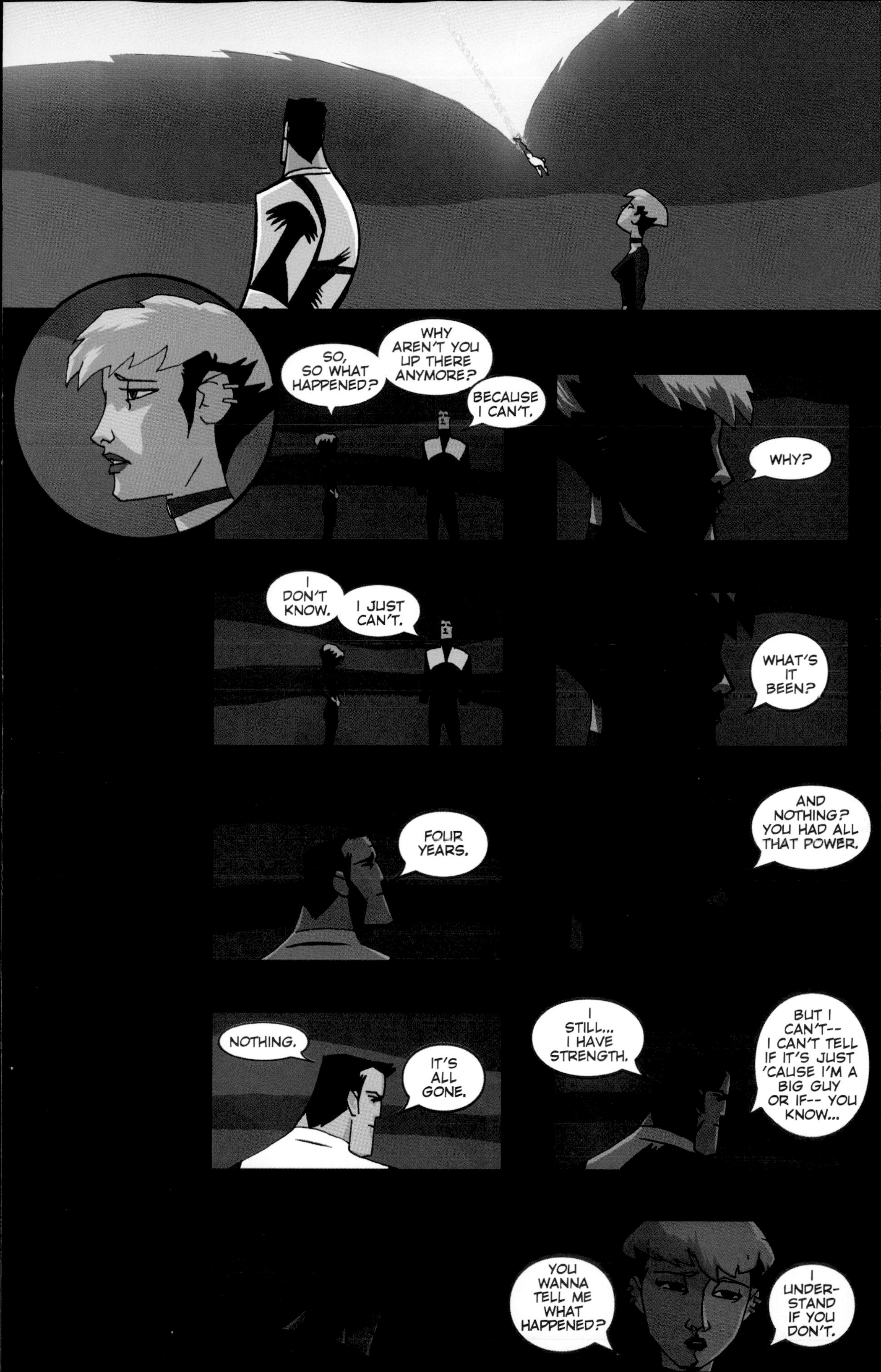
SO, SO WHAT HAPPENED?
WHY AREN'T YOU UP THERE ANYMORE?
BECAUSE I CAN'T.
WHY?
I DON'T KNOW.
I JUST CAN'T.
WHAT'S IT BEEN?
FOUR YEARS.
AND NOTHING? YOU HAD ALL THAT POWER.
NOTHING.
IT'S ALL GONE.
I STILL... I HAVE STRENGTH.
BUT I CAN'T-- I CAN'T TELL IF IT'S JUST 'CAUSE I'M A BIG GUY OR IF-- YOU KNOW...
YOU WANNA TELL ME WHAT HAPPENED?
I UNDER-STAND IF YOU DON'T.

WELL Y'SEE, I--I REALLY HAVE NO DAMN IDEA WHAT HAPPENED. JUST WHEN--IT WAS DURING THE WHOLE TERRIBLE INCIDENT WITH THE JOHNNY ROYALLE GANG.

OH YEAH--THAT'S THE LAST ANYONE EVER SAW OR HEARD FROM YOU--LIKE THAT. AS DIAMOND.

YEAH. WE WERE--WE WERE GOING AT IT PRETTY TOUGH, YOU KNOW. I MEAN--ALL THE FIGHTS ARE TOUGH--BUT THIS ONE--THIS ONE--THERE WAS SOMETHING JUST OFF ABOUT IT. IT WAS VERY CARNAL. VERY ANIMAL-LIKE. IT WAS ME AND TRIPHAMMER, WHO YOU'VE MET, AND ZORA AND RETRO GIRL AGAINST ALL THESE WACKOS. I MEAN, I DON'T EVEN REMEMBER HOW IT STARTED. SOME STUPID SCHEME OR SOMETHING.

SHIT, THAT FREAKY B.9. FOM-TOM DUDE WAS THERE.

YEAH, YEAH THAT'S RIGHT. AND CHESHIRE, AND TWILIGHT, BUT I WAS FIGHTING SSAZZ. AGAIN. HE'S SOME KIND OF MUTATION OR SOMETHING. ONE OF THOSE GENETIC MISHAPS WITH A HARD-ON FOR EVERYTHING. AND HE SMELLS SO--SO BAD. WE HAD FOUGHT BEFORE, Y'SEE, AND OF COURSE I BEAT THE HOLY CRAP OUT OF HIM. BUT THIS TIME HE HAD SOME KIND OF--SOME KIND OF ENHANCEMENT ON HIM OR SOMETHING.

LIKE A POWER ENHANCER?

YEAH.

I READ ABOUT THOSE IN SCIENTIFIC AMERI--

AND--AND I'M DOING EVERYTHING I CAN JUST TO END THE FIGHT. JUST END THE FIGHTING. JUST STOP IT. I GET, LIKE, THIS SUDDEN BURST OF ADRENALINE OR WHATNOT. LIKE A BURST OF ENERGY. NEVER HAPPENED BEFORE. BUT, WHAM!, AND I WAS WINNING THE DAY. AND THEN--AND THEN--*POOF!*

POOF?

POOF.

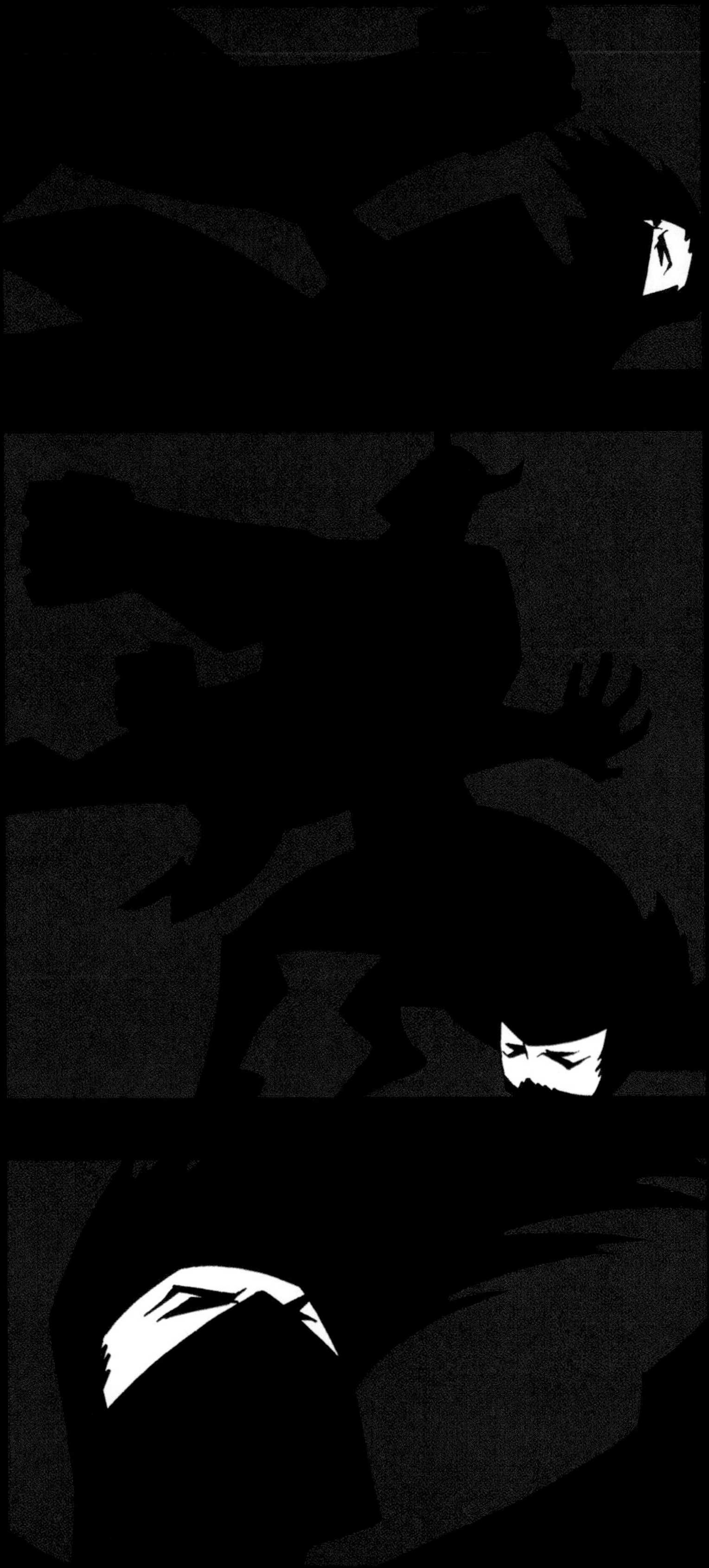

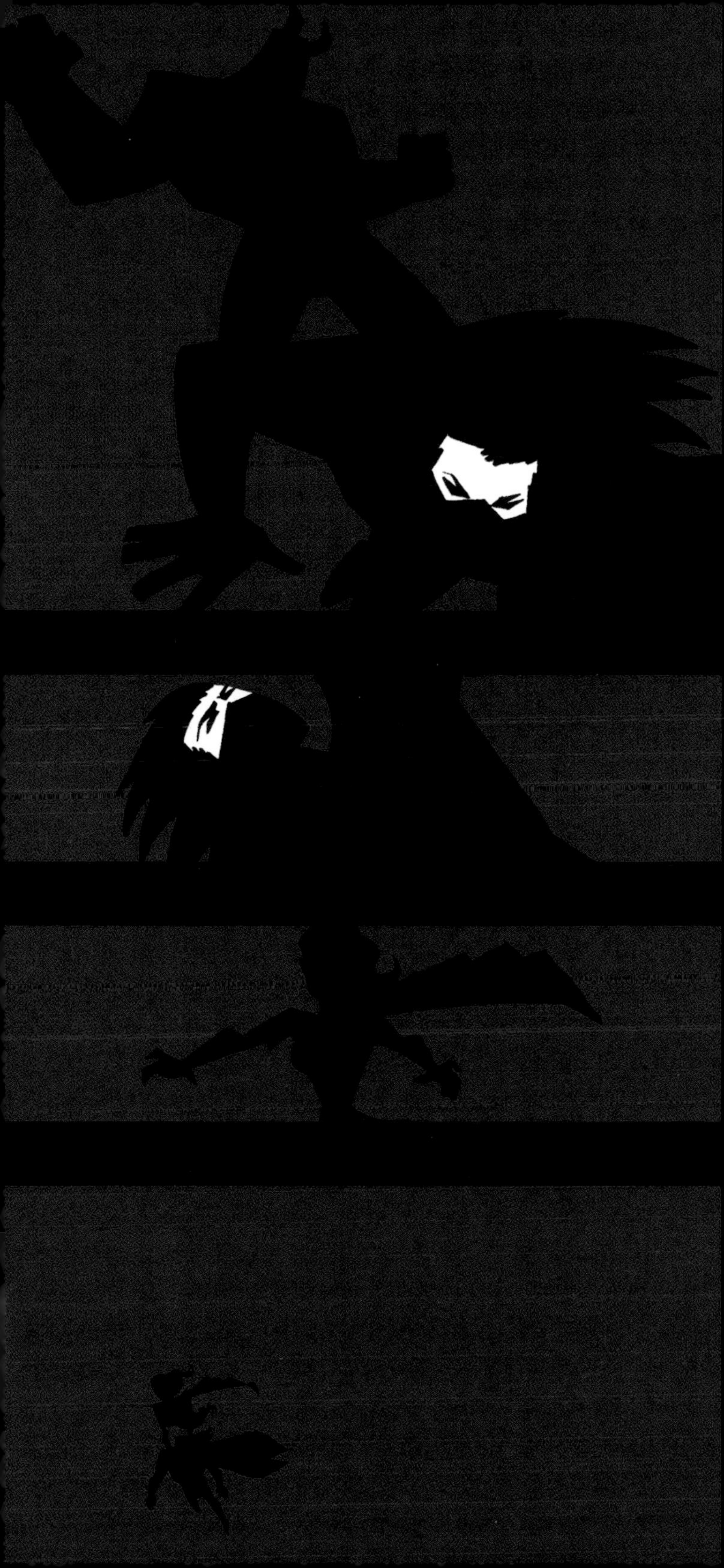

THAT'S IT?

THAT'S IT. BUT I WAS RIGHT IN THE MIDDLE OF THE FRAY. Y'SEE? I MEAN. HERE I AM--AND NOW I'M JUST A GUY IN AN OUTFIT AND ON TOP OF IT, I'M CONFUSED AND DISORIENTED. AND I HAVE NO WAY TO DEFEND MYSELF AND I DON'T KNOW WHAT THE FUCK HAS HAPPENED TO ME.

DO YOU THINK IT'S SOMETHING THAT SSAZZ GUY DID TO YOU?

NO, ACTUALLY. BECAUSE WHEN GUYS LIKE THAT DO SOMETHING LIKE THAT--THEY NEVER SHUT UP ABOUT IT. I DON'T THINK HE EVEN FIGURED IT OUT. JUST THOUGHT HE WAS PUTTING A BEATING ON ME.

HOW'D YOU GET OUT OF THERE?

WELL, I WAS GETTING BEATEN ON PRETTY BAD. AND SSAZZ--HE WAS ABOUT TO BASICALLY ELECTROCUTE ME WHEN--WHEN JANIS--***RETRO GIRL***--SHE SAVED MY LIFE. SHE FLEW ME OUT OF THERE.

SHE STOPPED--***HA***--SHE STOPPED TO KISS THE BOO BOO I HAD ON MY FOREHEAD. AND SHE FLEW BACK TO FINISH THE FIGHT. THAT'S ACTUALLY THE LAST TIME I EVER SAW HER.

BUT WEREN'T YOU GUYS FRIENDS?

SEE, YOU KEEP MISSING THE POINT ON THAT.

WERE YOU OR WEREN'T YOU?

WELL, YES AND NO. WE--WE WORKED TOGETHER ON OCCASION IS A[illegible]WE--WE DIDN'T MAKE A HABIT OF GETTING INTO EACH OTHER'S PERSONAL LIVES. WE DIDN'T HAVE A CLUB HOUSE. JUST--

WE UNDERSTOOD THIS--IT WAS AN UNWRITTEN RULE TO SUPPORT EACH OTHER IN PUBLIC AND NOT TO GET INTO EACH OTHER'S BUSINESS.

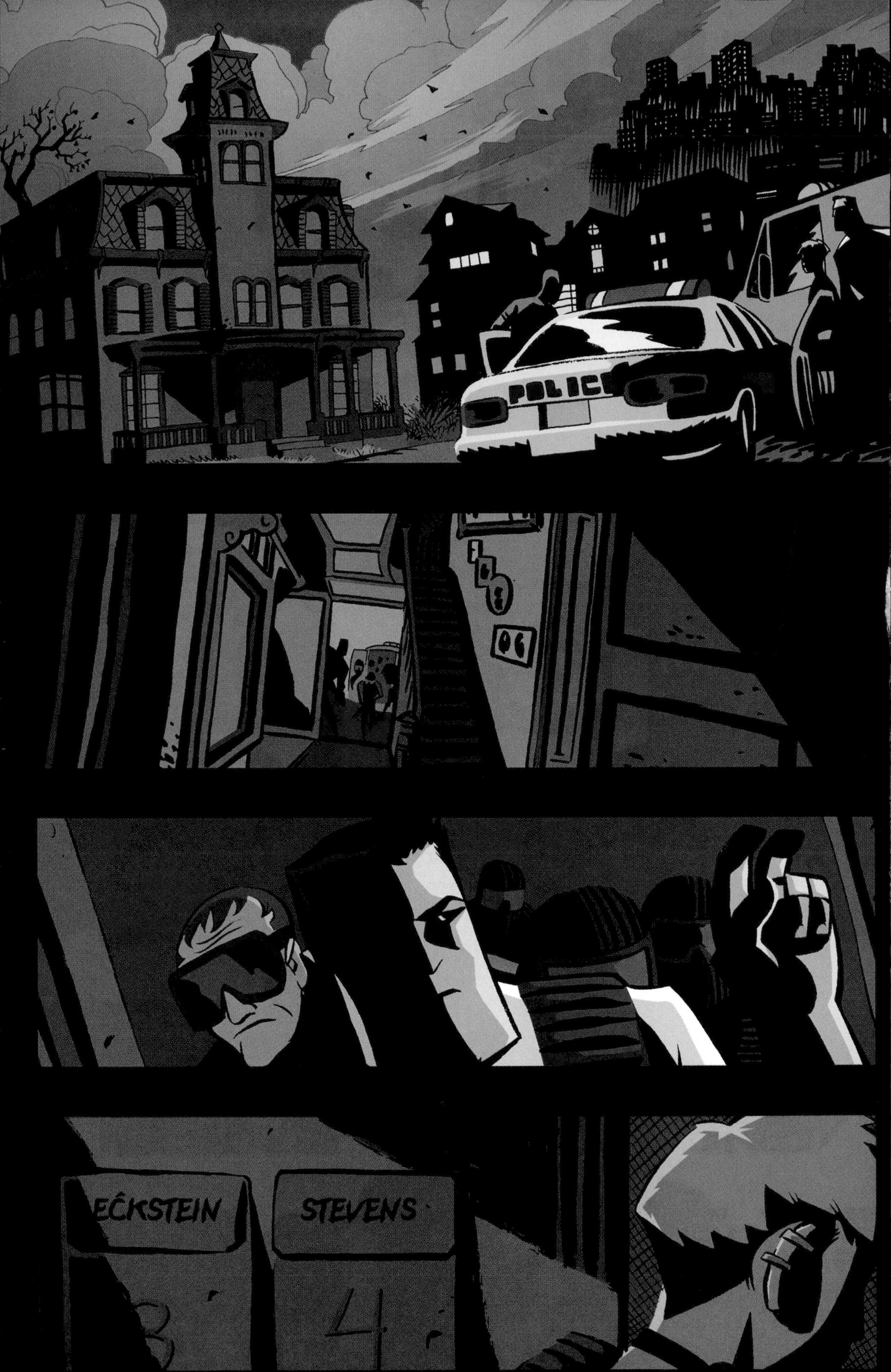
POLICE
ECKSTEIN
STEVENS
3
4

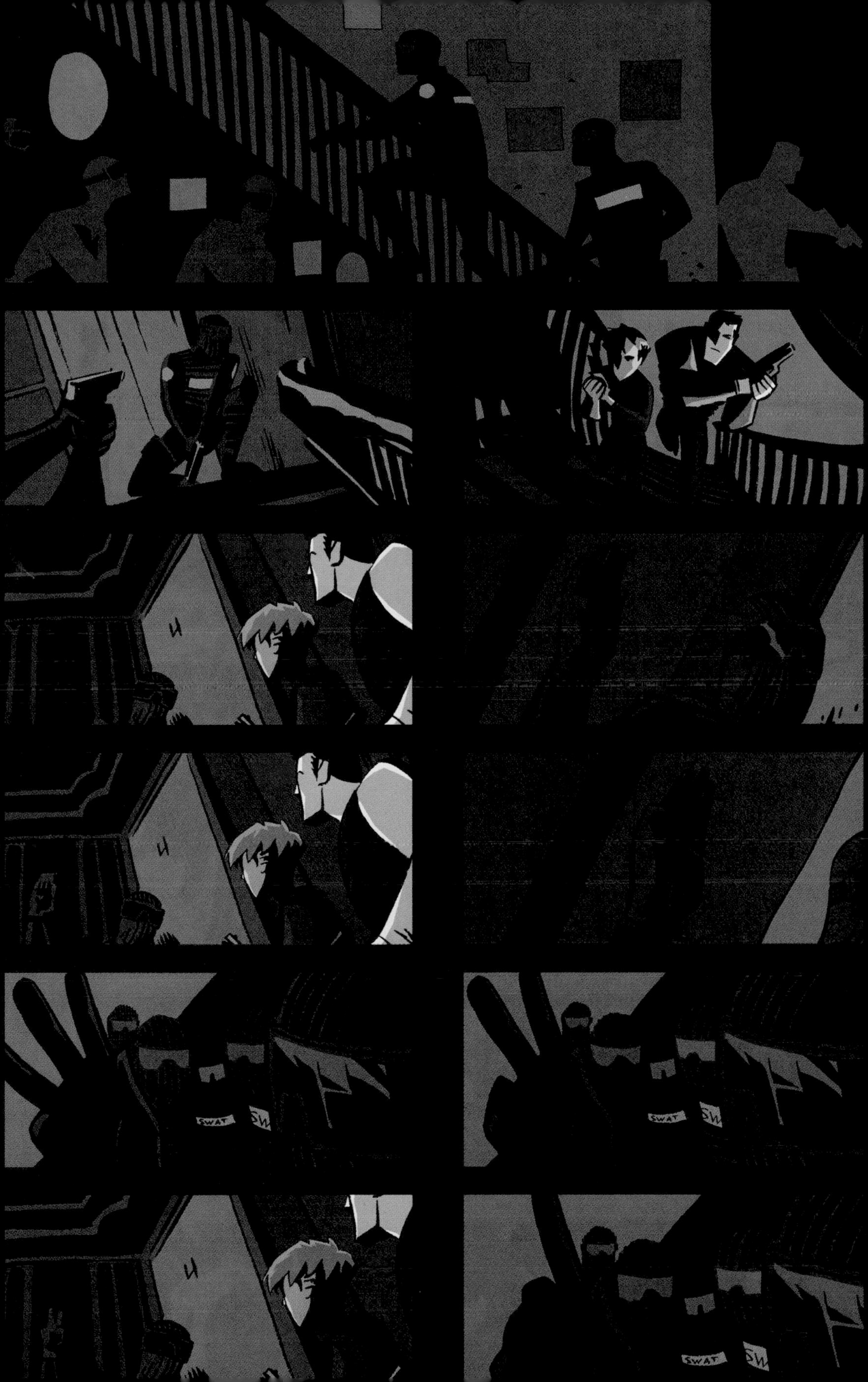
SWAT
SWAT
SWAT

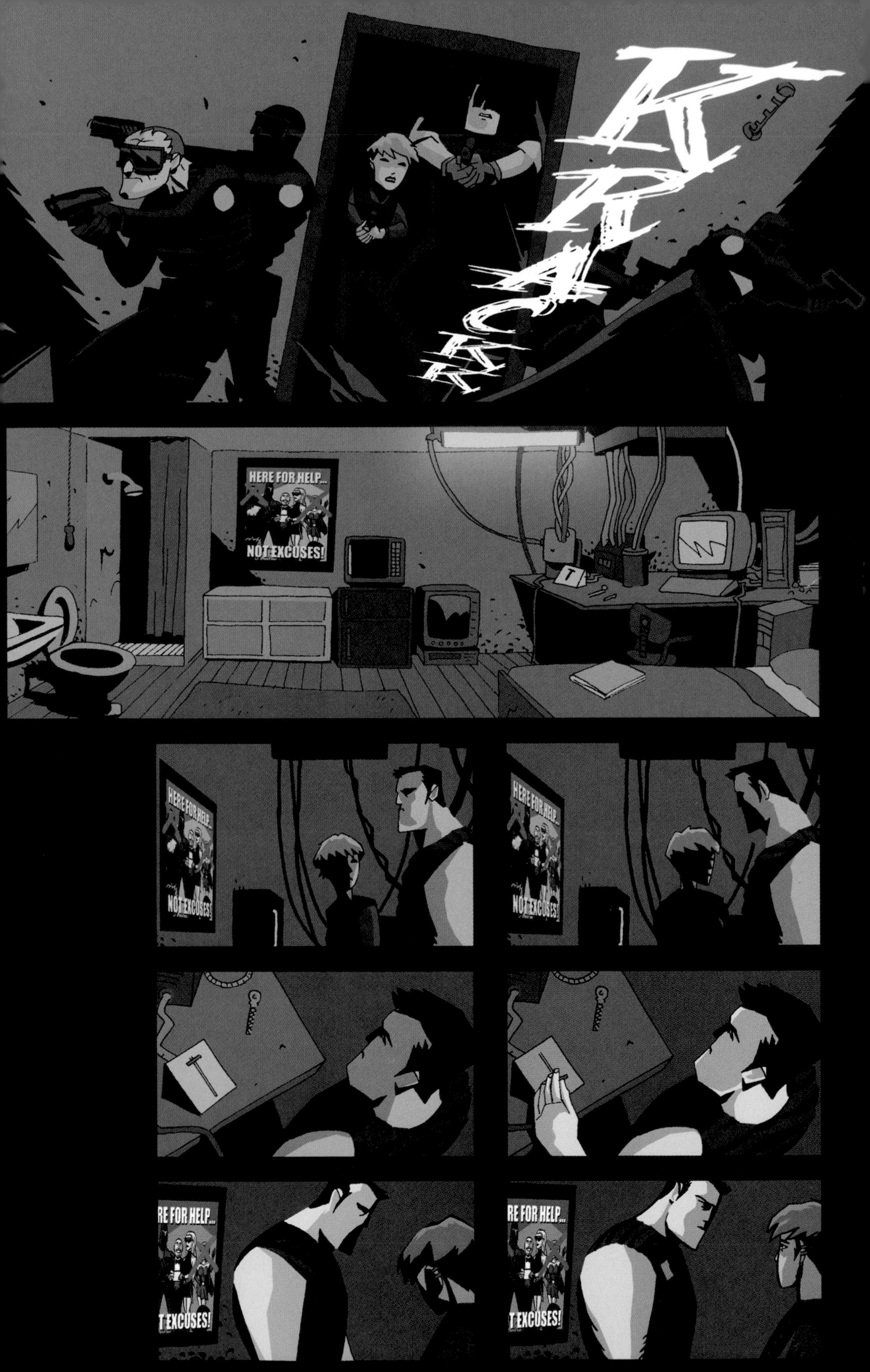
KRACK
HERE FOR HELP...
NOT EXCUSES!

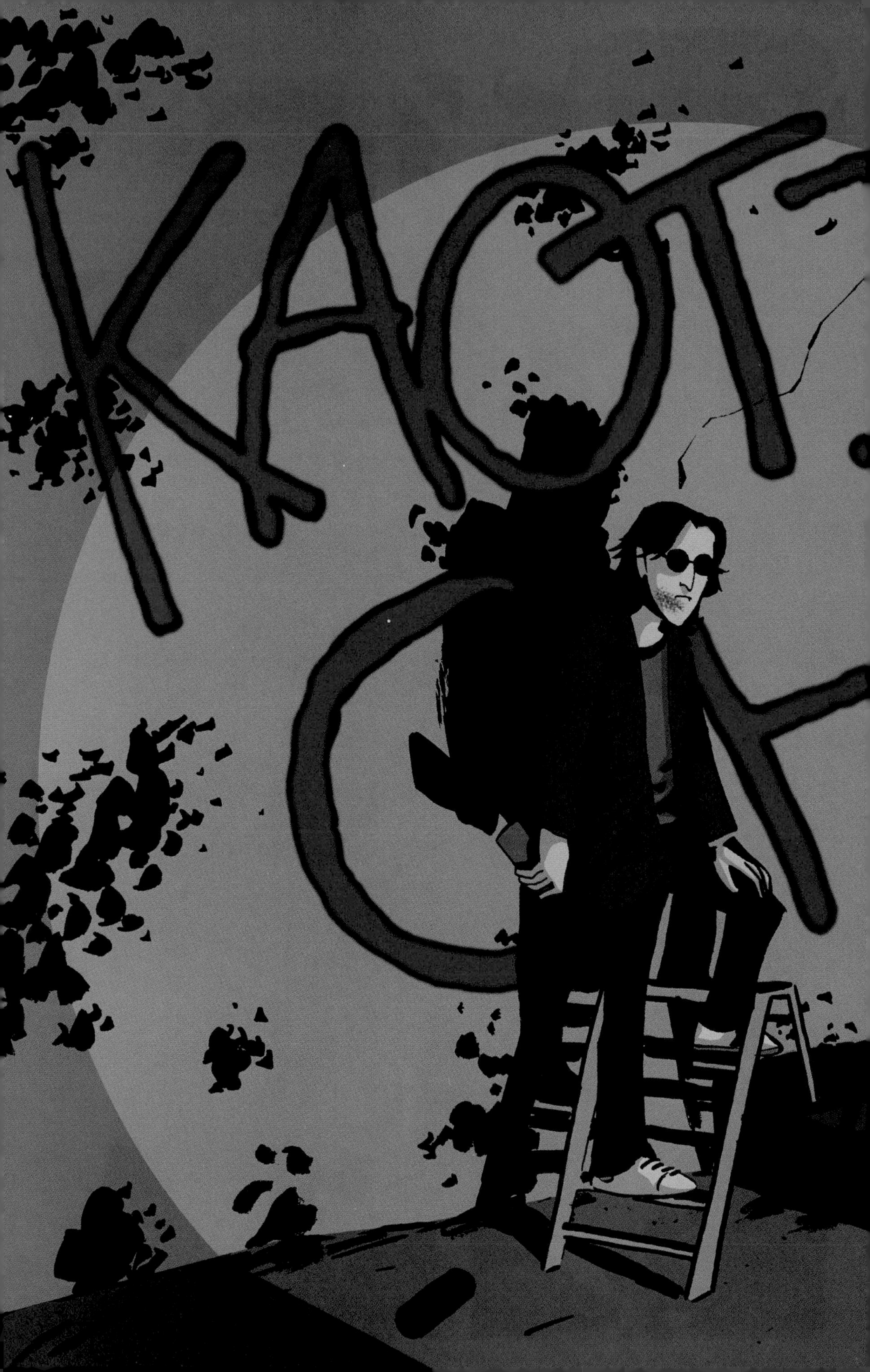

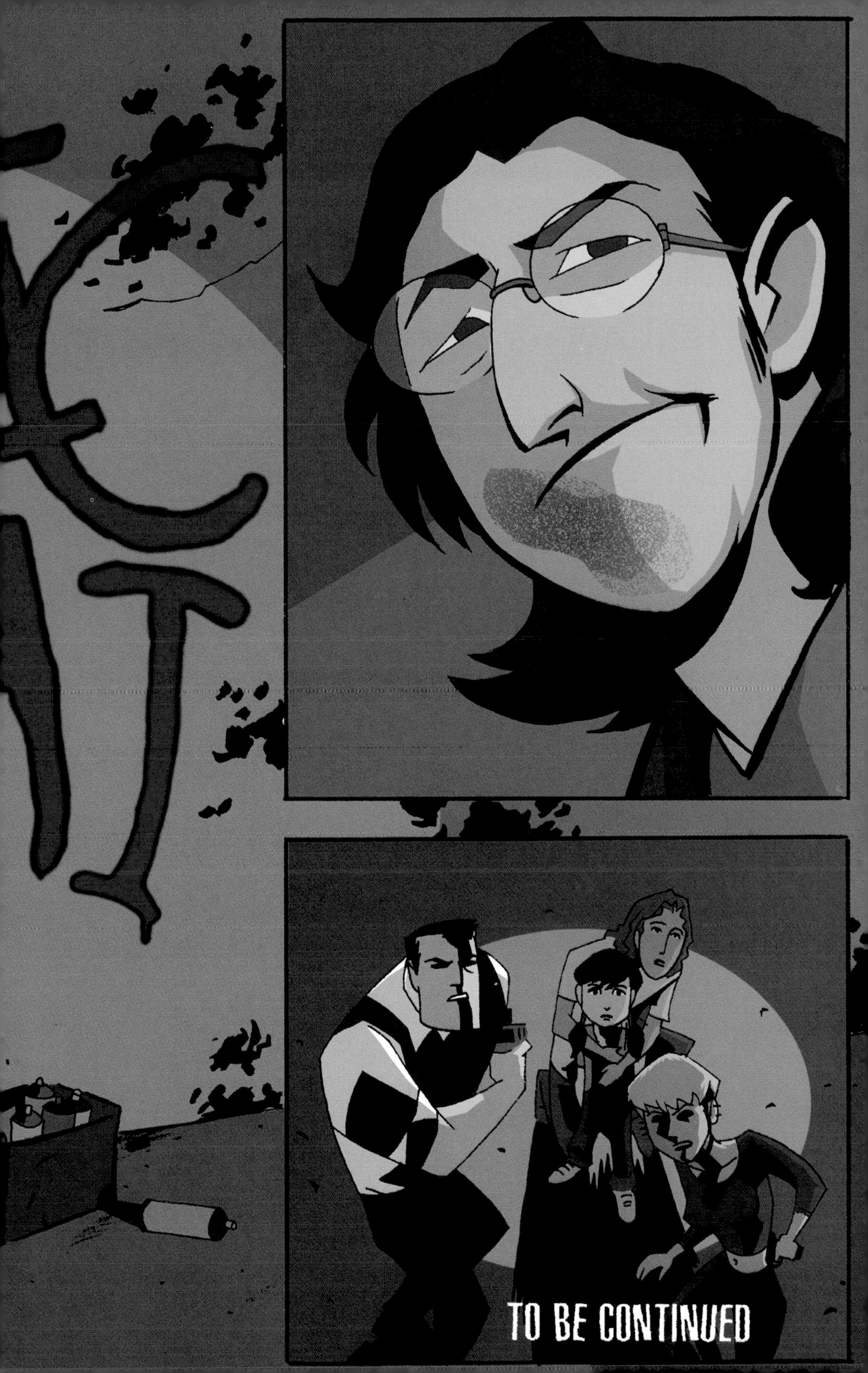
TO BE CONTINUED

AM I ON?
WELL, HOW LONG
WILL IT--?
HELLO??

OH MY! AHEM--
THIS IS COLLETTE
MCDANIEL. IT WAS
RIGHT HERE ON THE
SOUTH SIDE OF THE
POLICE DEPARTMENT
ENTRANCE AT THE
THE DOWNTOWN
JUSTICE CENTER.

THAT--
JUST MOMENTS
AGO--DETECTIVE
CHRISTIAN WALKER
AND RELATIVE
NEWCOMER TO
THE HOMICIDE
DEPARTMENT
DETECTIVE
DEENA PILGRIM
BROUGHT AN
UNKNOWN
MAN INTO
CUSTODY.

THE MAN WAS APPREHENDED WHILE DEFACING POLICE PROPERTY WITH THIS GRAFFITI, JUST A FEW FEET AND AROUND THE CORNER FROM THE VERITABLE THRONG OF MEDIA THAT HAS BEEN CAMPED OUT HERE SINCE THIS TRAGEDY BEGAN.

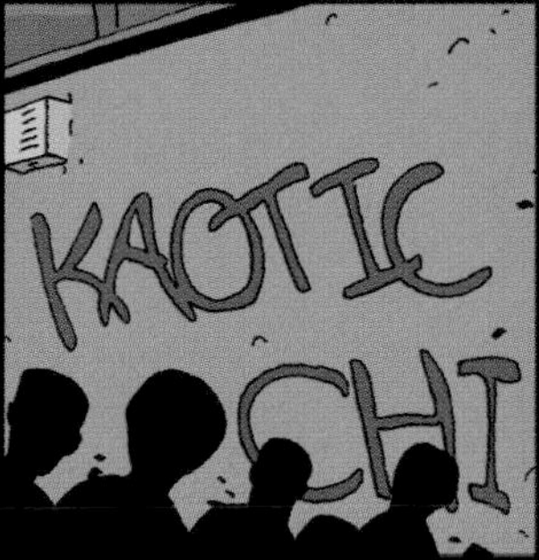
KAOTIC
CHI

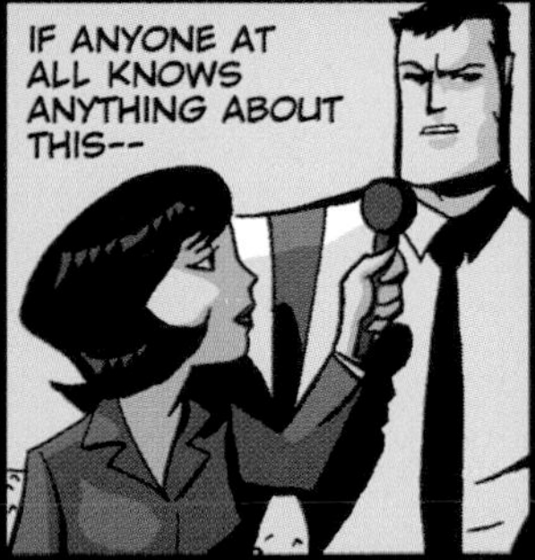
IF ANYONE AT ALL KNOWS ANYTHING ABOUT THIS--

KAOTIC CHIC-- THIS ODD GRAFFITI MATCHES THE GRAFFITI FOUND AT THE ***RETRO GIRL*** CRIME SCENE. IT WAS RIGHT HERE ON ***LIVE AT FIVE,*** EARLIER TODAY, THAT DETECTIVE WALKER PLEADED WITH OUR VIEWERSHIP FOR INFORMATION RELATED TO THE CRYPTIC MESSAGE.

OUR CAMERAS CAUGHT ONLY A GLIMPSE OF THE MAN. THERE HAS BEEN NO WORD AS YET TO THE IDENTITY OF THE MAN OR IF HE HAS IN FACT BEEN CHARGED IN THE RETRO GIRL MURDER.

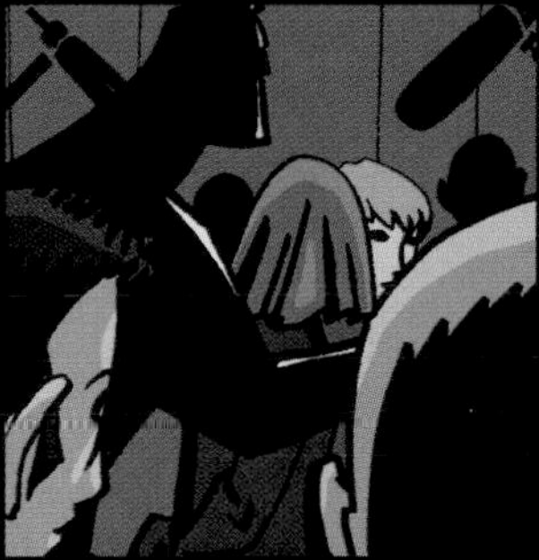

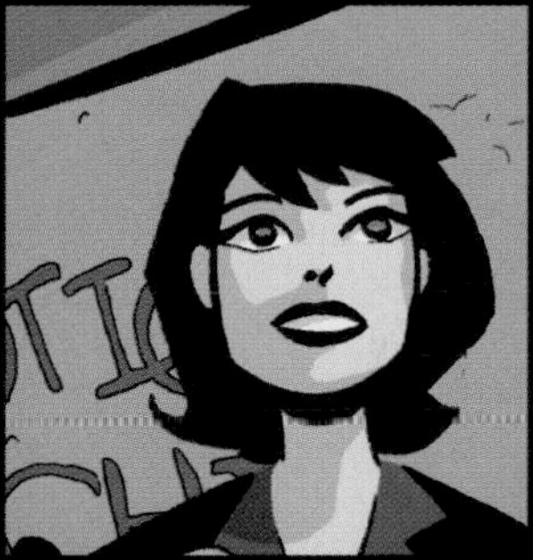

WE WILL STAY ON THE AIR WITH ROUND-THE-CLOCK COVERAGE UNTIL THE BLUE CODE OF SILENCE LIFTS HERE AT POLICE HEADQUARTERS.

WE CAN ONLY WAIT AND HOPE THAT THIS HORRIBLE TRAGEDY IS NEAR AN END.

BACK TO YOU IN THE STUDIO.

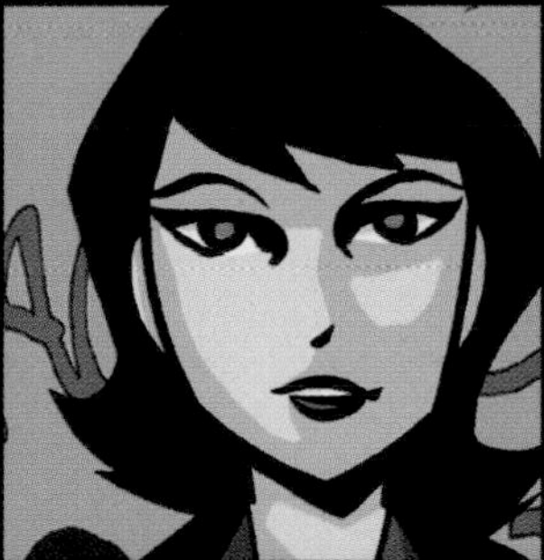

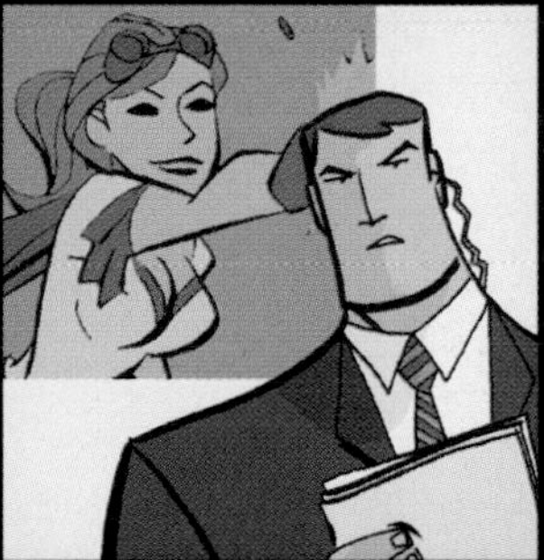

THANK YOU, COLLETTE.

FOR THOSE JUST JOINING US, THIS IS DAY TWO IN OUR WALL-TO-WALL LIVE COVERAGE OF... ***THE MURDER OF RETRO GIRL.***

WE'LL BE RIGHT BACK AFTER THIS STATION IDENTIFICATION.

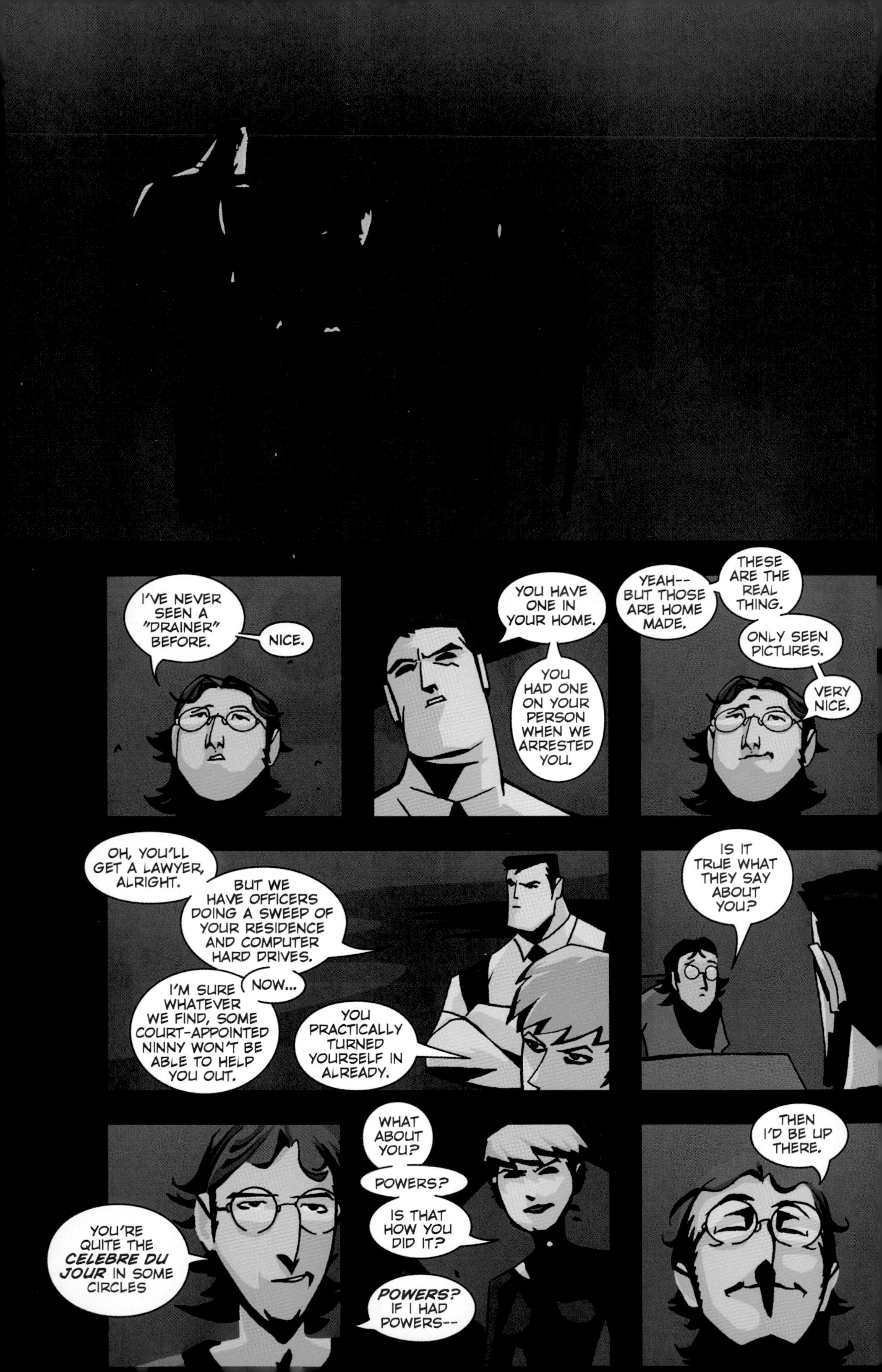
I'VE NEVER SEEN A "DRAINER" BEFORE.
NICE.
YOU HAVE ONE IN YOUR HOME.
YOU HAD ONE ON YOUR PERSON WHEN WE ARRESTED YOU.
YEAH-- BUT THOSE ARE HOME MADE.
THESE ARE THE REAL THING.
ONLY SEEN PICTURES.
VERY NICE.
OH, YOU'LL GET A LAWYER, ALRIGHT.
BUT WE HAVE OFFICERS DOING A SWEEP OF YOUR RESIDENCE AND COMPUTER HARD DRIVES.
NOW...
I'M SURE WHATEVER WE FIND, SOME COURT-APPOINTED NINNY WON'T BE ABLE TO HELP YOU OUT.
YOU PRACTICALLY TURNED YOURSELF IN ALREADY.
IS IT TRUE WHAT THEY SAY ABOUT YOU?
YOU'RE QUITE THE *CELEBRE DU JOUR* IN SOME CIRCLES
WHAT ABOUT YOU?
POWERS?
IS THAT HOW YOU DID IT?
POWERS? IF I HAD POWERS--
THEN I'D BE UP THERE.

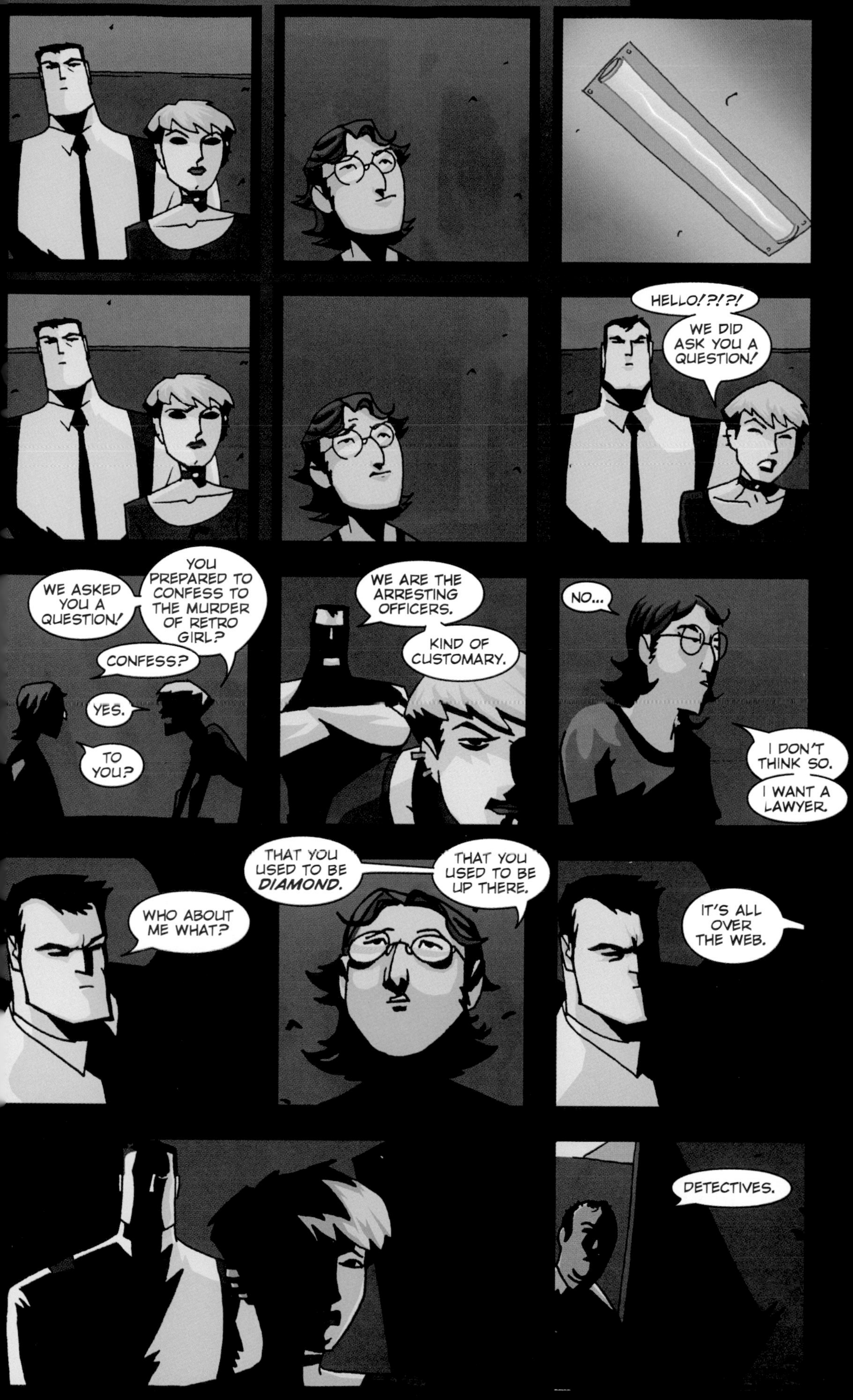
HELLO!?!?!
WE DID ASK YOU A QUESTION!
WE ASKED YOU A QUESTION!
YOU PREPARED TO CONFESS TO THE MURDER OF RETRO GIRL?
CONFESS?
YES.
TO YOU?
WE ARE THE ARRESTING OFFICERS.
KIND OF CUSTOMARY.
NO...
I DON'T THINK SO.
I WANT A LAWYER.
WHO ABOUT ME WHAT?
THAT YOU USED TO BE UP THERE.
THAT YOU USED TO BE DIAMOND.
IT'S ALL OVER THE WEB.
DETECTIVES.

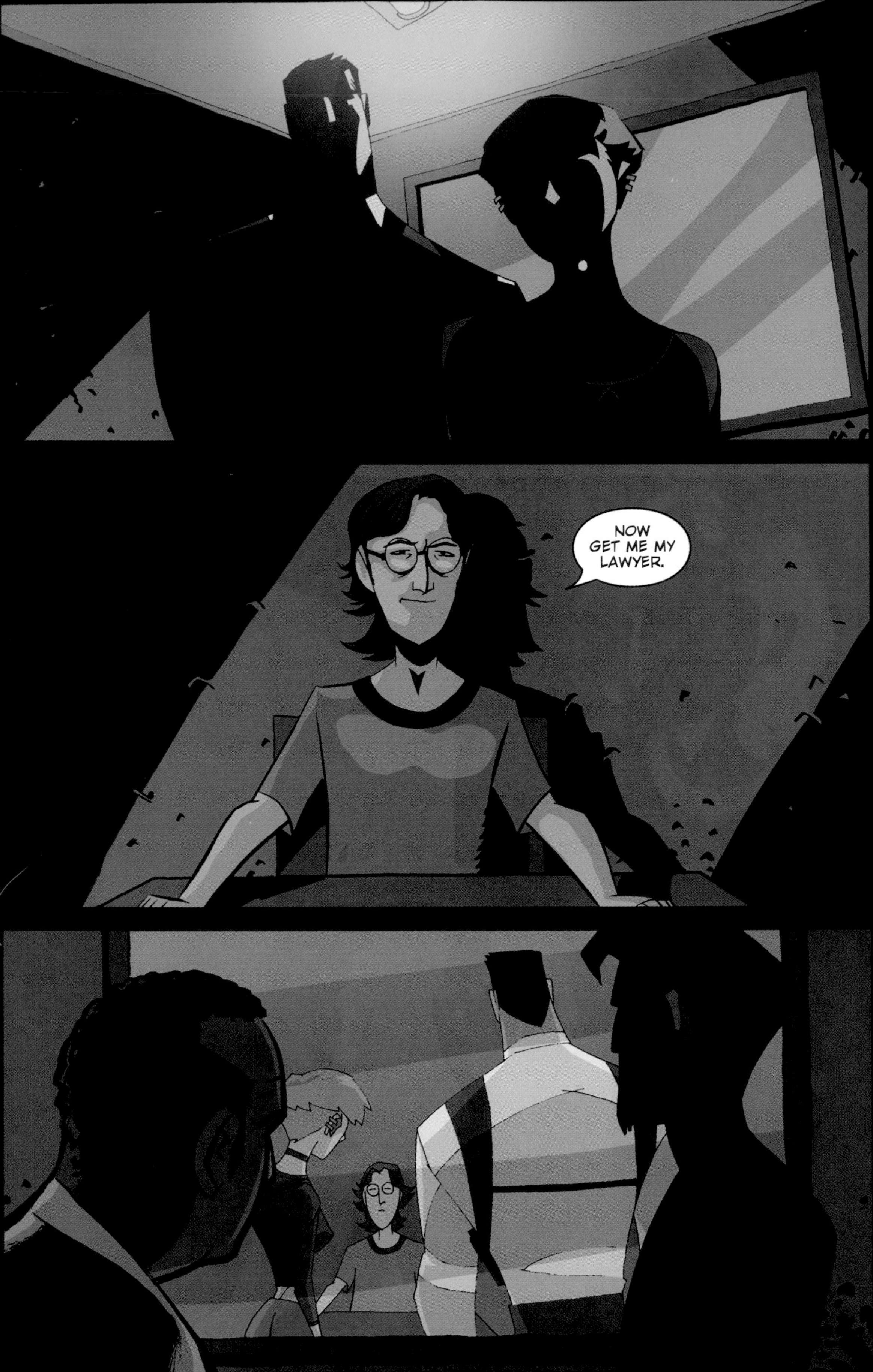
NOW GET ME MY LAWYER.

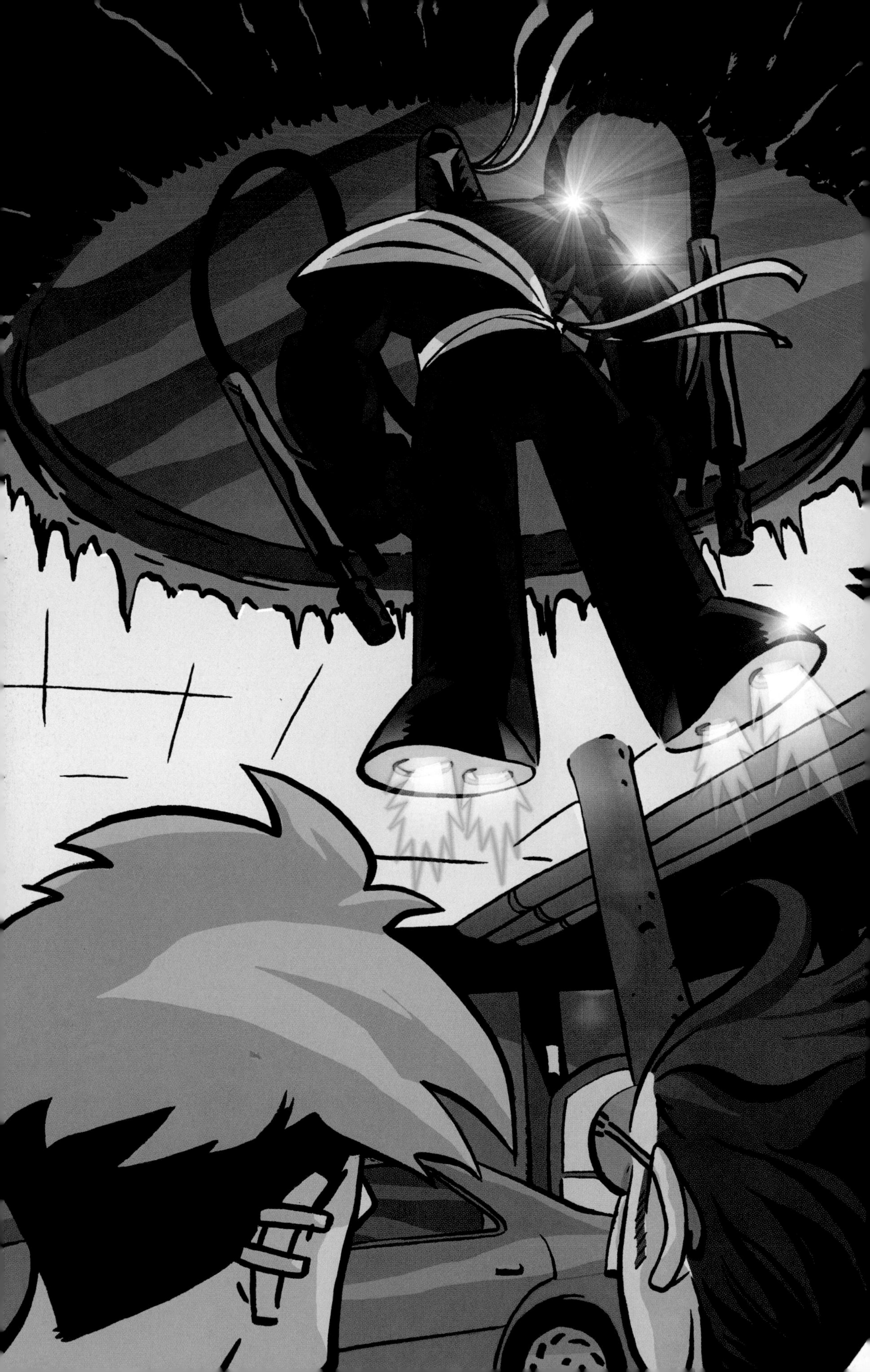

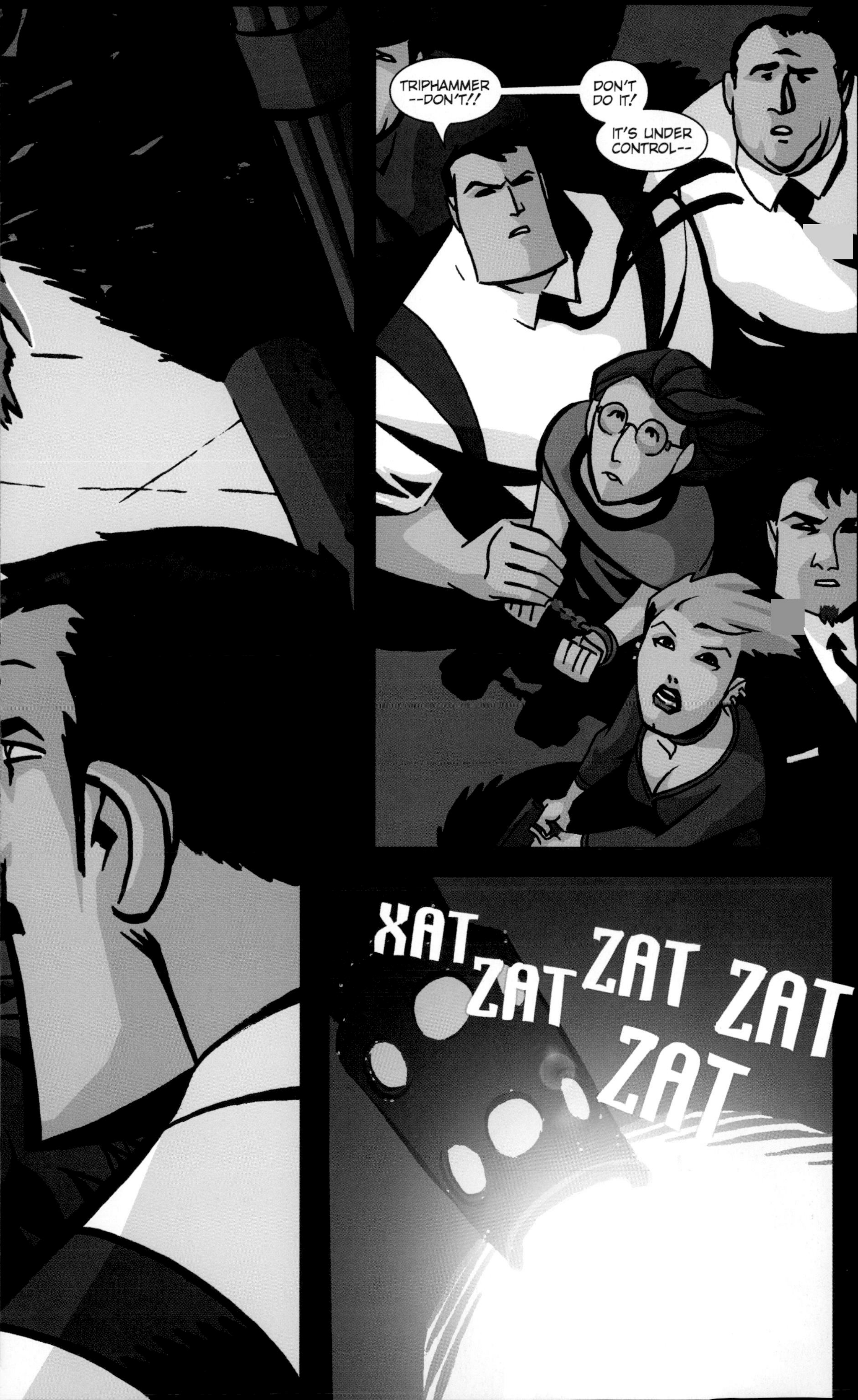
TRIPHAMMER
--DON'T!!
DON'T
DO IT!
IT'S UNDER
CONTROL--
XAT
ZAT
ZAT
ZAT
ZAT

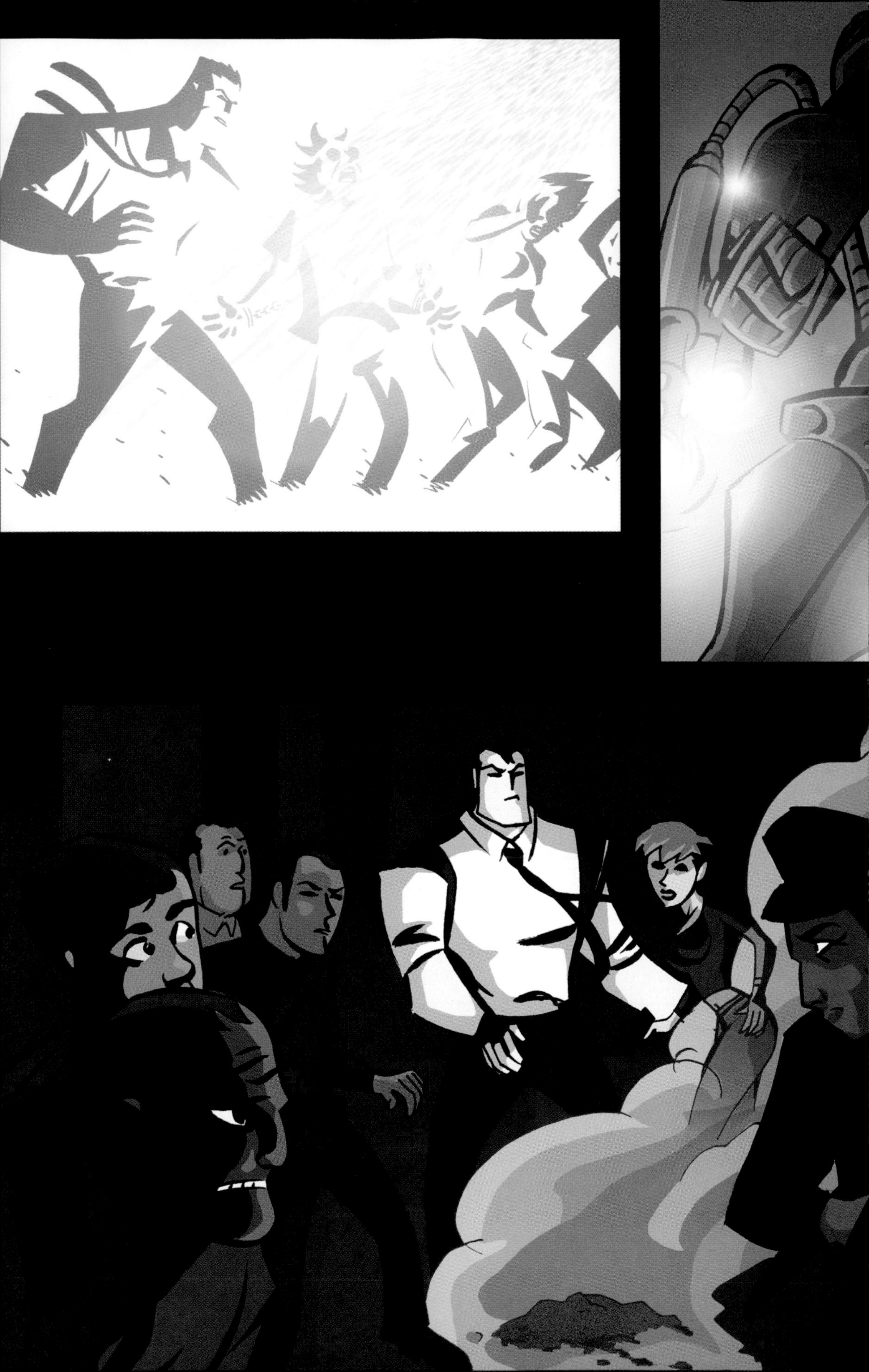

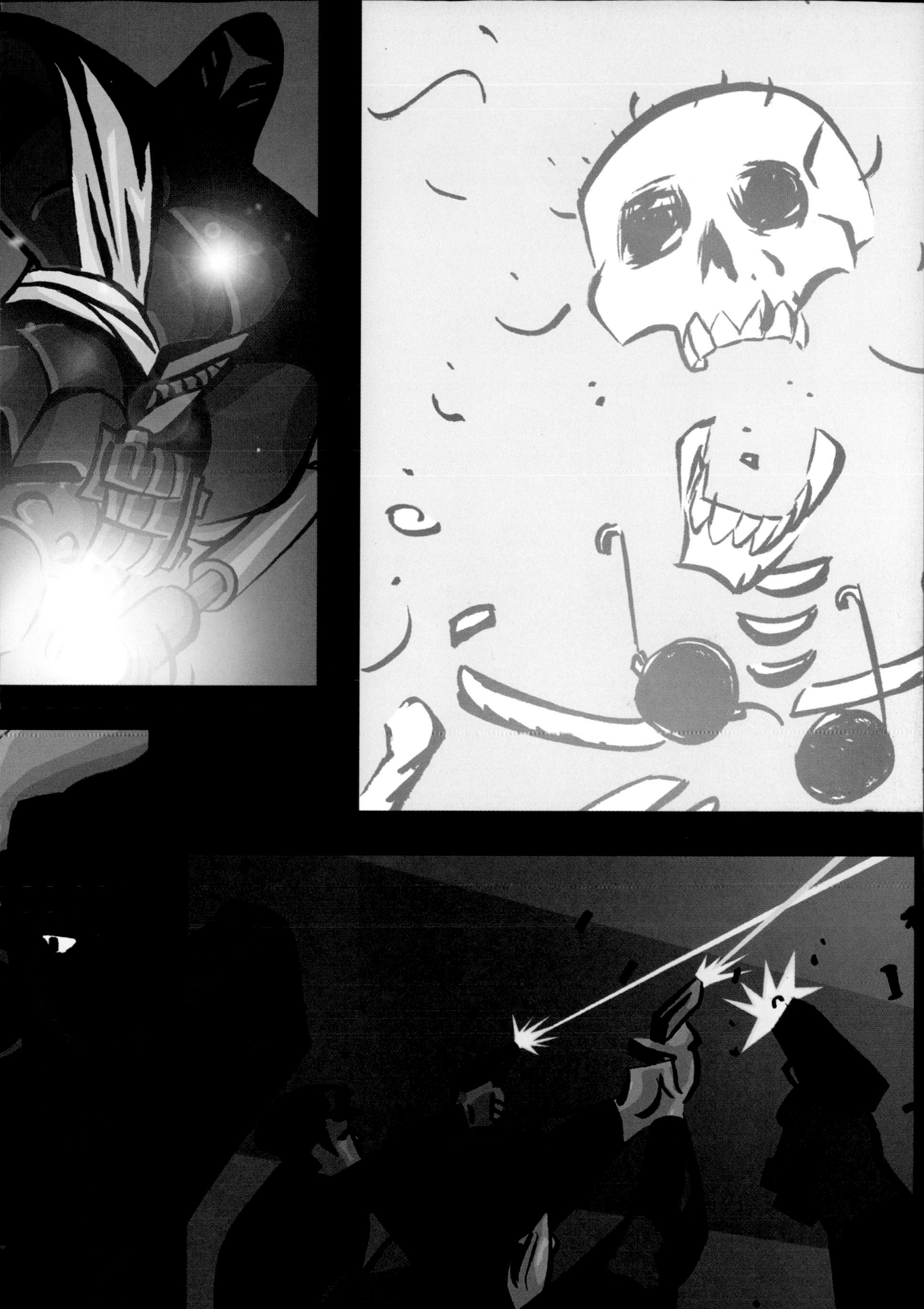

GLAD I DON'T HAVE TO DO THE PAPER WORK.

...AFTERWARDS, OFFICERS WERE DISPATCHED TO HARLEY COHEN'S--A.K.A. TRIPHAMMER'S--KNOWN RESIDENCE.

IT HAD, IN FACT, BEEN ABANDONED.

THE FBI AND OTHER AGENCIES HAVE BEEN NOTIFIED OF THE CRIME.

TRIPHAMMER'S WHEREABOUTS ARE OUT OF OUR JURISDICTION, IT SEEMS, AND THAT ENDS OUR INVOLVEMENT.

WITH A TAPED CONFESSION TO THE MURDER OF THE WOMAN KNOWN AS RETRO GIRL BY JON JACKSON STEVENS, AND THE PHYSICAL EVIDENCE FOUND AT HIS RESIDENCE--WE CAN ANNOUNCE TO YOU, THE PEOPLE OF THE CITY, THAT THIS CASE IS CLOSED.

IF I MAY TAKE THIS OPPORTUNITY TO PUBLICLY ACKNOWLEDGE THE TIRELESS EFFORTS OF DETECTIVES CHRISTIAN WALKER AND DEENA PILGRIM--

--FOR CLOSING THIS CASE SO PROFESSIONALLY BEFORE THE TRAGIC EVENTS THAT ENDED THE LIFE OF--

SO, LIKE, IS THIS KAOTIC CHIC THING ALL DONE?

GOOD, GOOD.

SO--UH--I GUESS NOW THAT ALL THIS IS OVER-- I GUESS TOMORROW WE'RE GOING TO TRY TO FIND YOU A PLACE TO LIVE AND A COOL SCHOOL TO GO TO.

IT'S ALL DONE.

YEAH, I HAD A DREAM.

I HAD A DREAM, AND THE GIRL IN THE DREAM TOLD ME THIS STORY--WITH STUFF IN IT--SHE TOLD ME THAT IT WAS, LIKE, THE OLDEST STORY EVER--

--IT WAS A LONG, LONG TIME AGO AND THERE WAS A GIRL--

--AND THE GIRL SAID THAT SHE WAS GOING TO BE THE BEST GIRL EVER, LIKE A PRINCESS OR SOMETHING.

FOREVER AND EVER, NO MATTER WHAT. THE BEST GIRL.

--SHE SAID SHE ALWAYS FINDS A WAY TO GO ON.

AND THEN SHE TOLD ME THAT EVERY ONCE IN A WHILE SOMEONE STOPS THE GIRL FROM BEING THE BEST GIRL.

BUT SHE SAID--

SHE SAID THAT ONCE YOU FIGURED OUT WHAT THE WORDS MEANT--

--THE WORDS ON THE WALL--THAT I COULD HELP HER.

I ASKED HER--I ASKED: HEY, WHY ME?

SHE SAID SHE TOLD YOU THIS ONCE--

AND SHE SAID: THAT'S HOW IT WORKED. THAT IS HOW IT HAS WORKED ALWAYS AND ALWAYS.

--BUT THAT YOU PROBABLY FORGOT BECAUSE SHE TOLD YOU TO FORGET.

SHE SAID THAT EVERTHING THAT HAPPENS TO US HAPPENS FOR A REASON.

AND THAT'S WHY I GOT TO HANG OUT WITH YOU--AND WHY YOU GOT TO DO ALL THE STUFF YOU DO.

SHE SAID THAT YOU WERE A GREAT GUY AND WOULD WORRY ABOUT ME--

--BUT IF I TOLD YOU NOT TO NICELY...

YOU WOULDN'T.

DON'T WORRY ABOUT ME, CHRISTIAN.

VOLUME IIIIIIIIII

--IMAGE YOU ARE SEEING IS LIVE IN CHAYKIN PARK. AN IMPROMPTU CANDLELIGHT VIGIL.

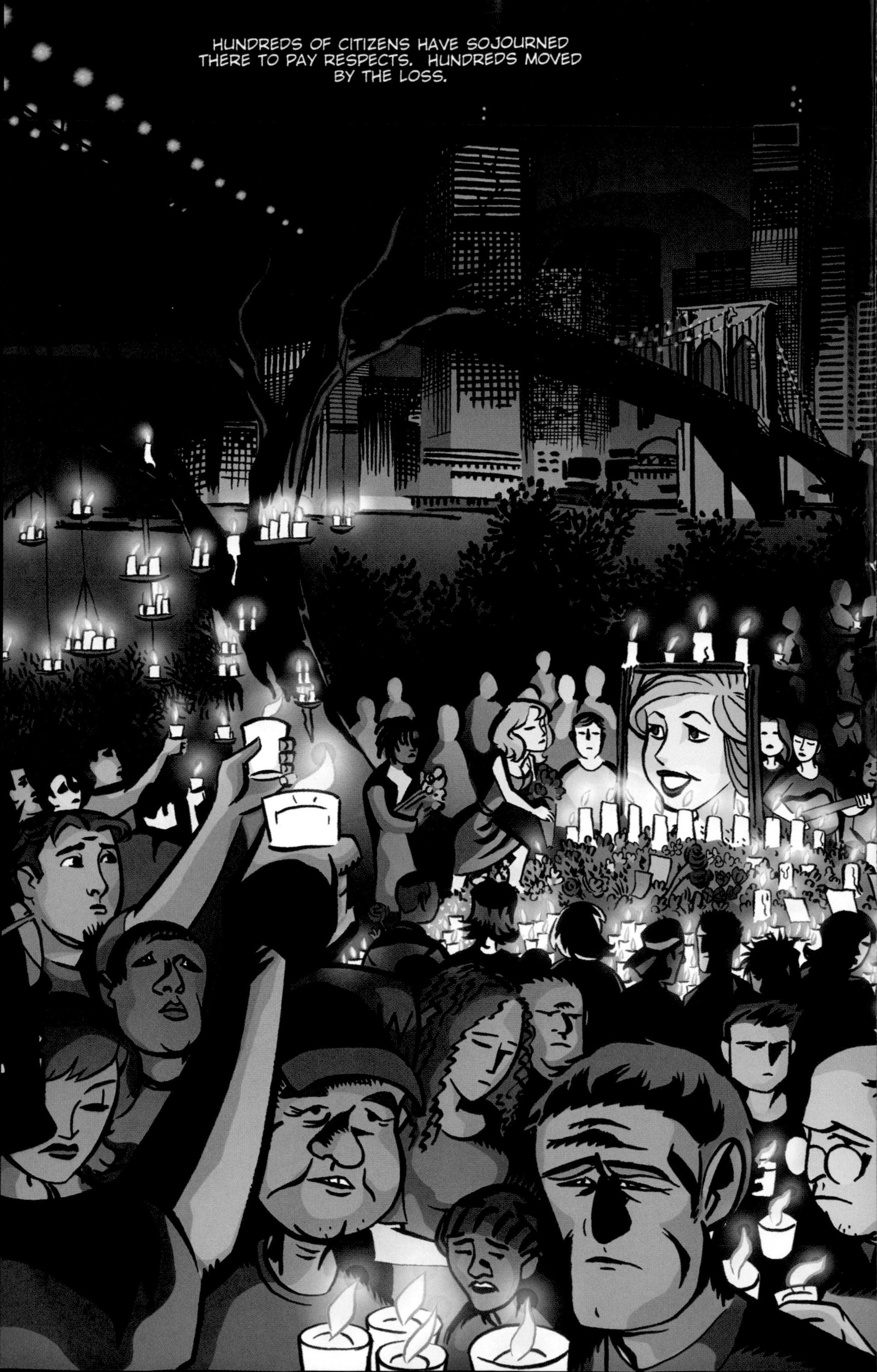
HUNDREDS OF CITIZENS HAVE SOJOURNED THERE TO PAY RESPECTS. HUNDREDS MOVED BY THE LOSS.

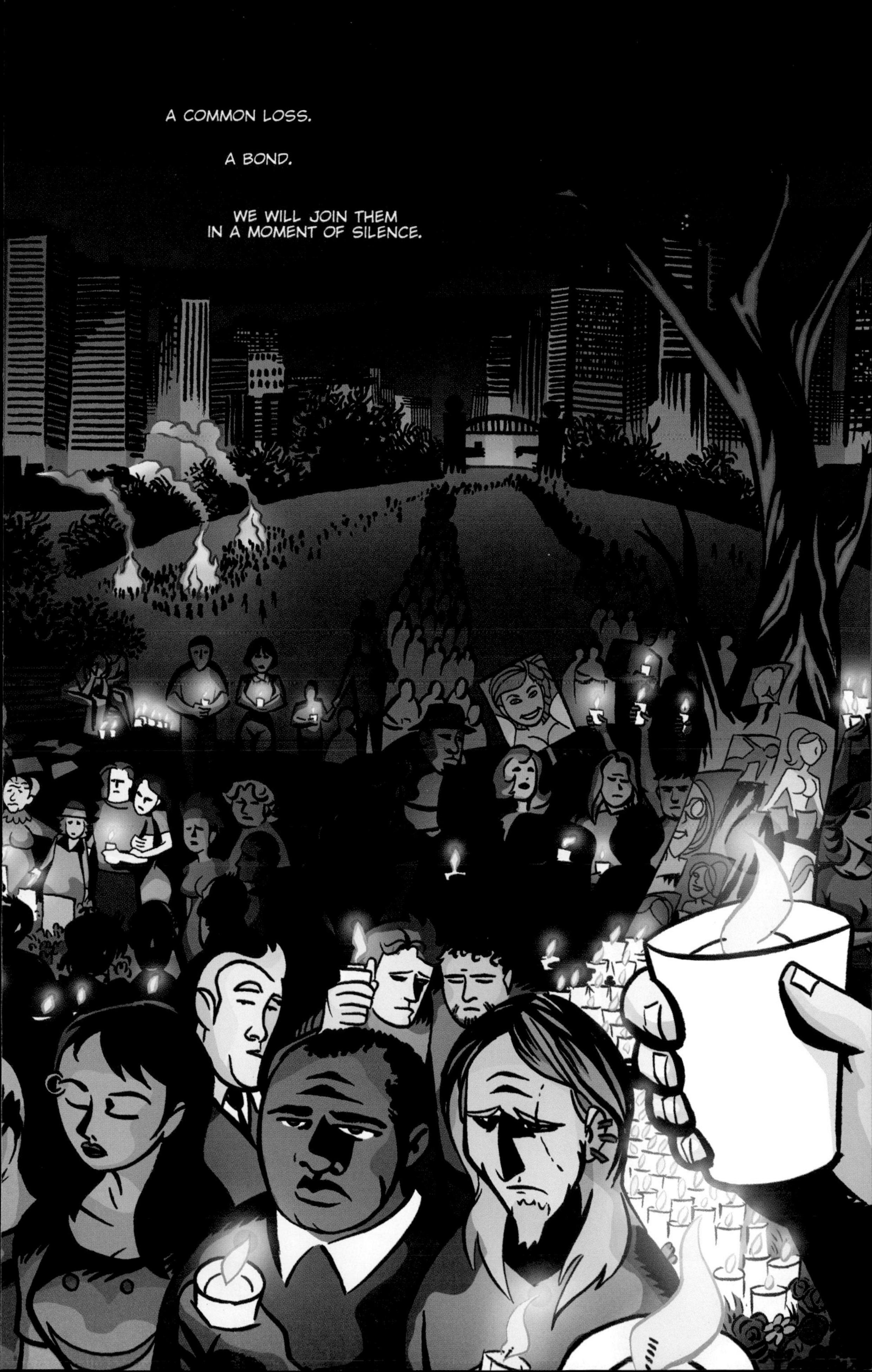
A COMMON LOSS.
A BOND.
WE WILL JOIN THEM IN A MOMENT OF SILENCE.

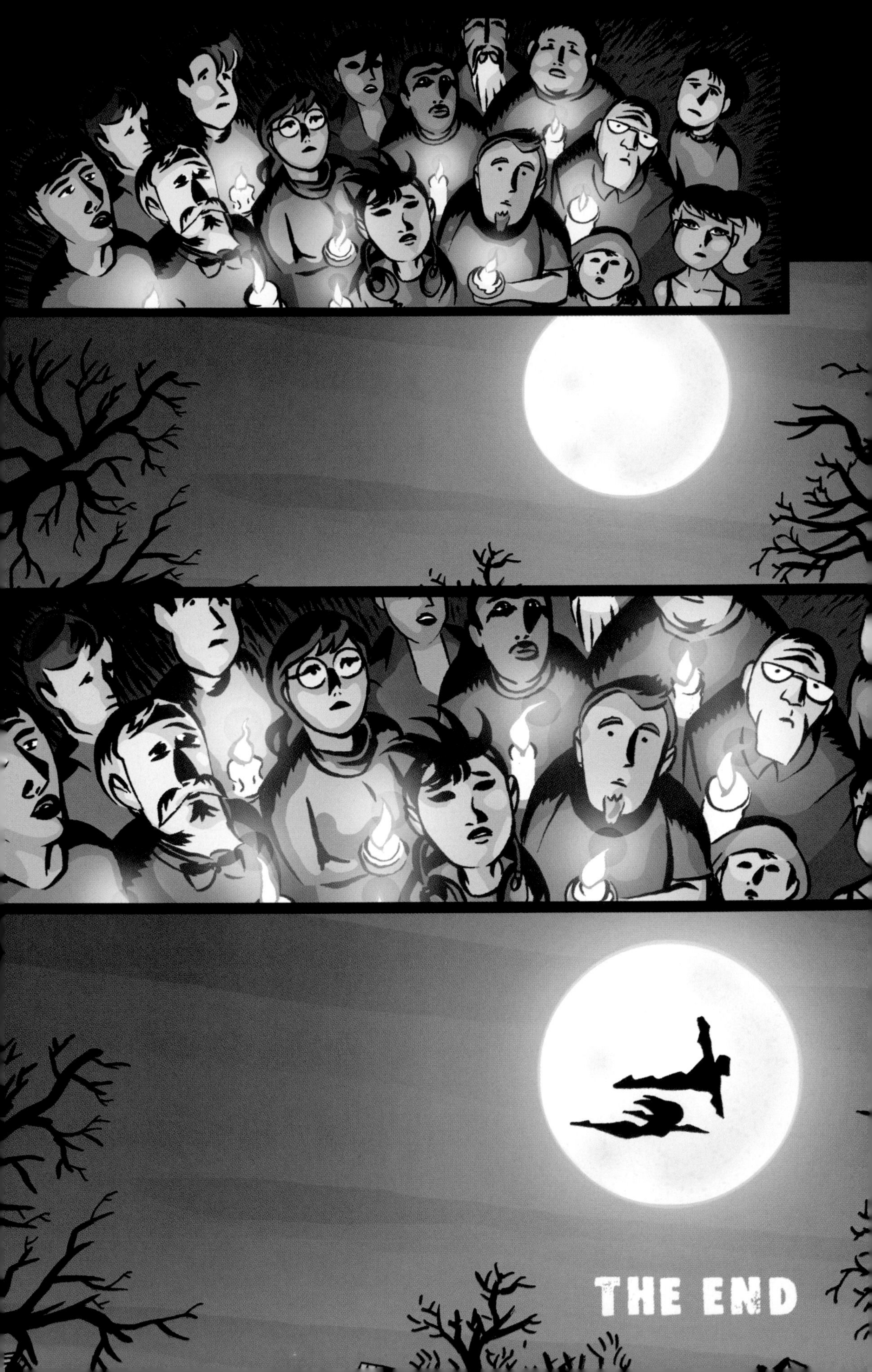
THE END

POWERS SUPPLEMENTAL MATERIAL

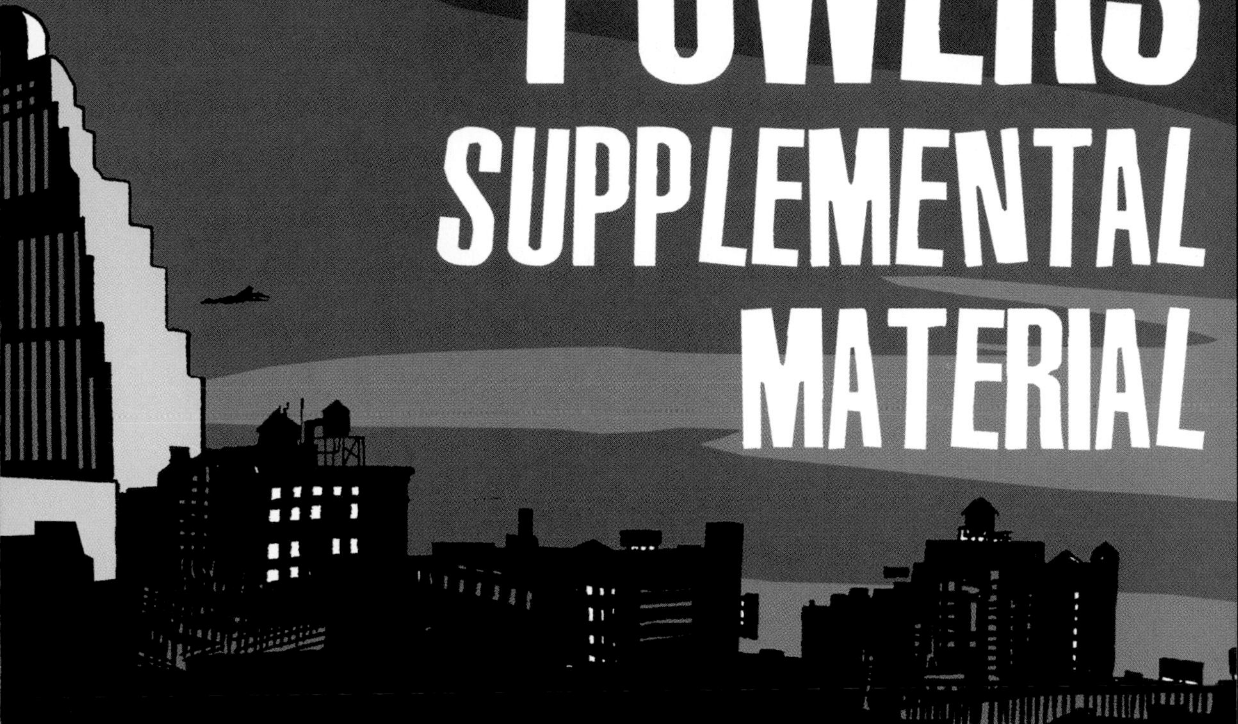

Hi! Powers writer Brian Michael Bendis with you.

Let me be your tour guide through this bonus material section, which has been prepared specifically for this collection.

Creating this work has turned into one of the most creatively vibrant times of our lives and you may view this section as a diary of this experience.

THE POWERS COMIC SHOP NEWS STRIPS

Cliff Biggers and Ward Batty, long time supporters of my career, were kind enough to offer us the opportunity to preview our new series in strips that ran in the pages of their excellent periodical Comic Shop News.

This is the first time these strips have been printed in any comic book publication. The coloring and lettering were done by me because this was pre- Pat.

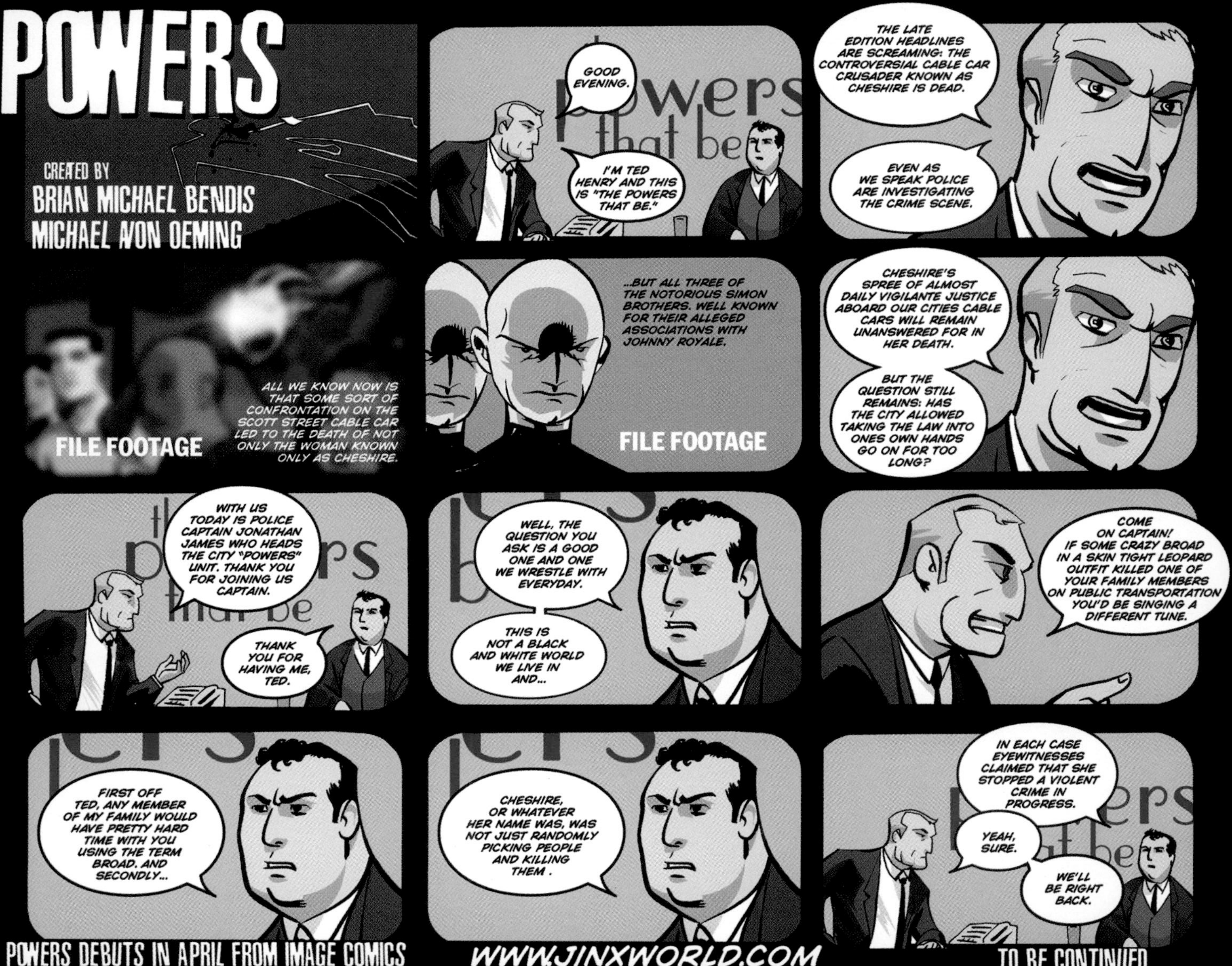

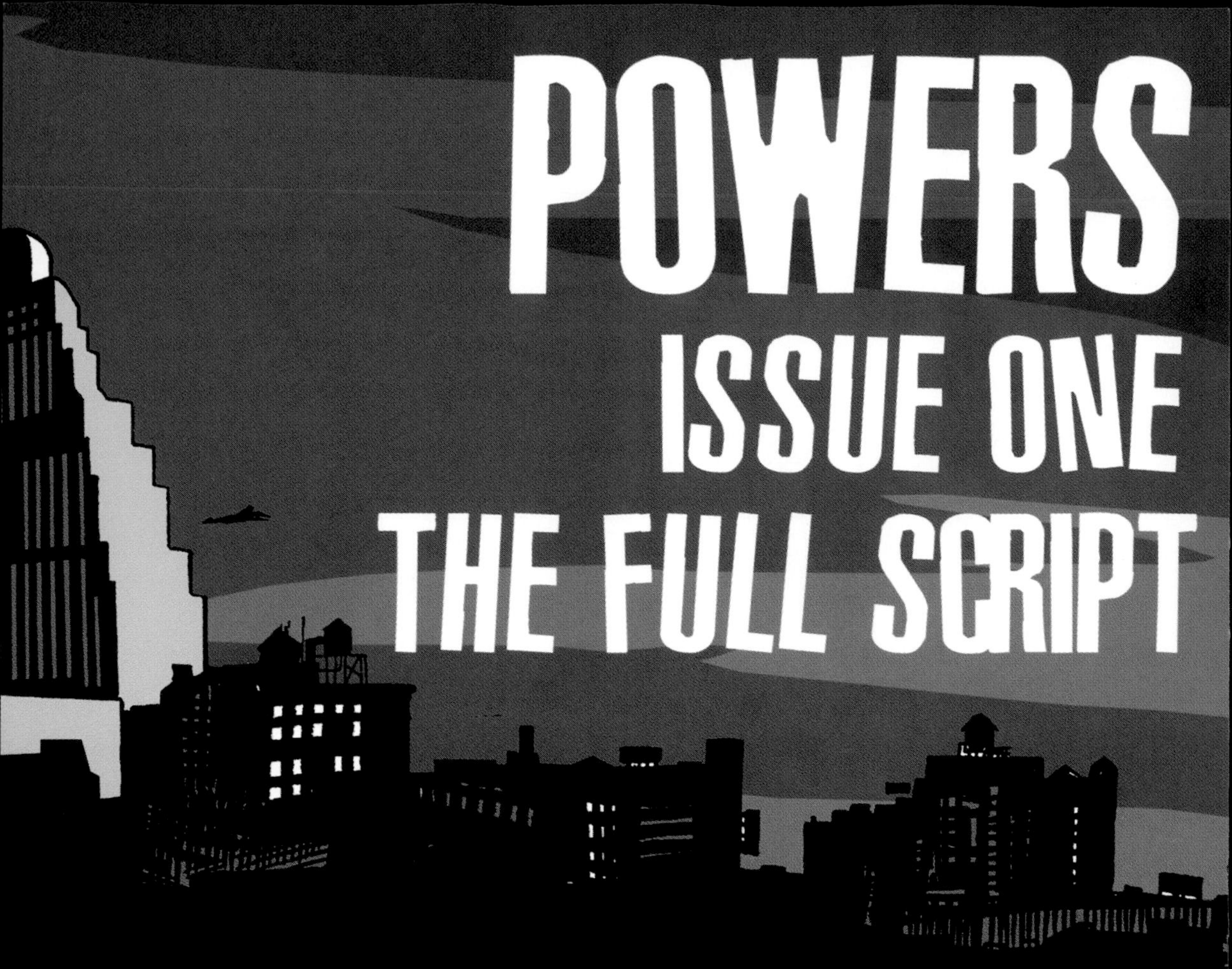
POWERS
ISSUE ONE
THE FULL SCRIPT

By popular demand, (well, someone asked me at a convention once) we present to you the full script of the very first issue of Powers. I have not copy edited or corrected this in any way in an attempt to show it to you exactly the way Mike first saw it.

For aspiring writers: this is not proper script format. This is the format I use when writing books I own.

This was prepared using the Final Draft screenwriting program.

Enjoy!

POWERS

WHO KILLED RETRO GIRL?

ISSUE ONE

BY BRIAN MICHAEL BENDIS FOR MIKE AVON OEMING

PAGE IFC & 1-

THREE EQUAL SIZED PAGE LONG PANELS.

PANEL 1- THE SKY LINE OF OUR NAMELESS CITY. SILHOUETTE TOWERS PIERCE A GRAY BLUE NIGHT SKY.

MIKE: THIS IS OUR WORLD AND WE MAKE THE RULES , BUT WHATEVER RULES WE MAKE HERE WE HAVE TO STICK TO.

THIS CITY IS AN EQUAL CHARACTER TO EVERY LEAD IN THE BOOK. IT HAS TO SMELL AND BREATHE AND TASTE LIKE IT.

2- TIGHTER ON A INDISCRIMINATE BLOCK OF BUILDINGS. EACH HAS ITS OWN DISTINCT CHARACTERS.

3- A SLIGHT WORM'S EYE OF A CITY STREET CORNER BELOW. IT'S A HOSTAGE CRIME SCENE OUTSIDE A SEMI- RUNDOWN APARTMENT BUILDING. GO AHEAD AND FIND PHOTO REFERENCE FOR IT.

POLICE CARS, EMERGENCY VEHICLES. YELLOW POLICE TAPE IS UP KEEPING THE CASUAL SMATTERING OF A CROWD AT BAY.

A COUPLE OF NEWS VANS ARE PARKED AS CLOSE AS THEY CAN GET.

COPS MILL ABOUT. THIS HAS BEEN GOING ON FOR QUITE A WHILE.

A NONDESCRIPT WHITE CAR HAS MADE ITS WAY TO THE FRONT OF THE SCENE.

PAGE 2-

FIVE EQUAL SIZED PAGE LONG PANELS.

EACH PANEL IS THE SAME SHOT- ITS THE SAME CRIME SCENE THE SAME MOMENT AS THE LAST PANEL, BUT FROM THE TOP OF THE STAIRS OF THE APARTMENT BUILDING LOOKING DOWN ONTO THE STREET.

(CONTINUED

CONTINUED:

1- THE WHITE CAR HAS STOPPED DEAD-CENTER OF THE PANEL.
GETTING OUT OF THE CAR IS DETECTIVE CHRISTIAN WALKER WHO IS
IMMEDIATELY SURROUNDED BY THE TOP COPS WHO WERE ALREADY ON
THE SCENE.

THEY FOLLOW HIM AS THEY TALK.

                    CAPTAIN
          WALKER.

                    WALKER
          CAPTAIN...

                    CAPTAIN
          WE BEEN CALLING...

                    WALKER
          I WAS AT THE MOVIES.

                    CAPTAIN
          WE BEEN CALLING IS ALL...

                    WALKER
          YEAH, WELL--
          WHAT IS THIS?
          I'M HOMICIDE.

                    CAPTAIN
          YOU'RE A COP,
          AND THE GUY INSIDE WANTS YOU.

                    WALKER
          WHO? WILLIAMS?

                    WILLIAMS
               (THE NEGOTIATOR)
          NO- HEY WALKER- NO, I SCREWED THE POOCH.

                    CAPTAIN
          YOU COULDN'T NEGOTIATE SUPER-SIZING A
          HAPPY MEAL, YOU PIECE OF--!!!

                    WILLIAMS
          COME ON...

                    CAPTAIN
          I'M GOING TO DEAL WITH YOUR INCOMPETENT
          ASS LATER.

          NO, THE GUY HOLDING THE PLACE, HE ASKED
          FOR YOU.

                                        (CONTINUED

CONTINUED: (2)

                    WALKER
          THE GUY INSIDE?

          HE ASKED FOR ME?

                    CAPTAIN
          AND YOU ONLY?

                    WALKER
          HE ASKED FOR ME? WHO IS IT?

                    CAPTAIN
          SOME SHMUCK...

          GOES BY THE NAME OF- OF FINCH.

          FINCH.

                    WALKER
          FINCH?

                    CAPTAIN
          FINCH. WEARS A GREEN THING WITH A THING
          ON HIS BACK.

                    WALKER
          FINCH?

                    CAPTAIN
          HE'S GOT A LITTLE GIRL IN THERE.
          USED TO DATE THE MOM.

          HE CAME OVER THEY GOT INTO A DOMESTIC...

          HE THREW HER OUT THE SECOND STORY WINDOW
          AND BOARDED HIMSELF UP IN THERE.

                    WALKER
          THE WOMAN? THE MOM?

                    CAPTAIN
          TOOK HER DOWN TO MERCY? SHE WAS ALERT
          ENOUGH TO CALL US.

                    WALKER
          FINCH? I DON'T KNOW A FINCH.

                    CAPTAIN
          THEN THE DOCTORS AT THE HOSPITAL LEFT HER
          ALONE FOR SOMETHING LIKE TWO SECONDS AND
          SHE VANISHED.

                                        (CONTINUED

CONTINUED: (3)

                    WALKER
        VANISHED?

                    CAPTAIN
        NO ONE SAW, NO ONE KNOWS.

        THE GUY INSIDE- THE GUYS GOT ONE OF THOSE
        BACK PACK THINGS. GOT PINCHED ON A COUPLE
        OF DEPARTMENT STORE HOLD UPS...

                    WALKER
        DOESN'T HELP ME...

                    CAPTAIN
        WELL, HE KNOWS YOU AND HE'S GOT A GOD
        DAMN SEVEN YEAR OLD GIRL IN THERE.

        GUYS BEEN CRYING LIKE A BABY FOR OVER AND
        HOUR.

                    WALKER
        THE GIRL OR THE GUY?

                    CAPTAIN
        THE GUY.

        AND I'M NOT GOING TO HAVE THIS LOSER
        PSYCHO POP A GIRL ON THE SIX O CLOCK!!
        NOT TODAY. NOT ANY DAY.

                    WALKER
        YEAH...WELL, COULD YA-

        LET'S TRY TO MODULATE THE VOLUME, OK?

PAGE 3-

1-WALKER IS AT THE DOOR TO THE APARTMENT WITH HIS GUN OUT OF
THE HOLSTER. THERE ARE SWAT GUYS ALL AROUND. ONE IN
PARTICULAR IS HUGGING THE OTHER SIDE OF THE DOOR.

VARIANTS OF THIS SHOT IS REPEATED OVER AND OVER UNTIL THE
SCENE IS OVER.

                    SETZER
        HEY WALKER...

(CONTINUED

CONTINUED: (4)

> WALKER
> HEY, OH HEY SETZER. WHAT'S GOING ON?

> SETZER
> WHERE YOU BEEN?

> WALKER
> MOVIES.

> SETZER
> WHAT YOU SEE?

> WALKER
> THE TRAILERS.

> SETZER
> WELL THIS SUCKS, THIS GUY IN HERE SUCKS.
> FUCK THIS GUY.

> GUY'S GOING TO DO THE DUTCH IS ALL.

> THE KID'S WATCHING CARTOONS.
> HE KEEPS CRYIN' LIKE A...

> WALKER
> --LIKE A BABY. I HEARD.

2- PAUSE AS THEY LISTEN TO THE GUYS FAINT RAMBLING.

3-

> WALKER (CONT'D)
> (TO THE DOOR)
> FINCH. IT'S DETECTIVE WALKER.

4- PAUSE.

5-

> WALKER (CONT'D)
> FINCH? WHAT DID YOU CALL ME DOWN HERE
> FOR?

> FLINCH
> OOOOOH!!! EFF YOU WEAR YOU LIVE, WALKER!!
> YOU SHITHEEL!!!

> WALKER
> DO I KNOW YOU?

> FLINCH
> ITS FLINCH!! NOT FINCH, FLINCH!!! YOU
> EFFIN' ASSHOLES!!!

(CONTINUED

CONTINUED: (5)

                    WALKER
       OH!!! FLINCH!!! DUDE! I'M SORRY MAN.

       THESE ASSHOLES DON'T KNOW ANYTHING OUT
       HERE.

PAGE 4-

1- SETZER LOOKS TO HIM AS IF TO SAY: "YOU KNOW THIS GUY."

WALKER LOOKS BACK AS IF TO SAY: "I HAVE NO FUCKING IDEA WHO
THIS IS."

                    FLINCH
       YEAH, WELL. I'VE HAD TO LISTEN TO THEIR
       BULLSHIT ALL DAY!!! STUPID, STUPID
       BULLSHIT!!

                    WALKER
       YEAH WELL, EVERYONE'S SORTA OUTTA SORTS
       TODAY-- SEEING AS YOU GOT A KID IN THERE.

2- PAUSE.

3-

                    WALKER (CONT'D)
       NO MORE BULLSHIT, FLINCH. THIS IS THE
       GOODS-- IF YOU SEND THE KID OUT OF THERE
       WE CAN HAVE A TALK.

                    FLINCH
       MOTHER'S A BITCH!!!

                    WALKER
       PROBABLY IS FLINCH, DOESN'T HAVE A THING
       TO DO WITH THE KID.

4- PAUSE

5-

                    WALKER (CONT'D)
       RIGHT?

                    FLINCH
       BITCH TOOK ALL MY MONEY!!

                              (CONTINUED

CONTINUED: (6)

                    WALKER
          SHE DID?

                    FLINCH
          I WAS SAVING THAT MONEY TO FINISH MY GOD
          DAMN PROJECT AND NOW I'M GOING
          TO....AAAARRGGHH!!!

          IT'S ALL RUINED. DO YOU KNOW WALKER? DO
          YOU KNOW? YOU DON'T KNOW.

                    WALKER
          I KNOW THAT THE GIRL IN THERE IS NOT THE
          ANSWER TO YOUR PROBLEMS.

          AND I CAN'T EVEN THINK ABOUT HELPING YOU
          UNTIL YOU GIVE ME THE GIRL AND START
          TALKING TO ME MAN TO MAN.

          FACE TO FACE.

PAGE 5-

1- PAUSE.

2- SAME SHOT, BUT IT IS GETTING SLIGHTLY TIGHTER ON WALKER

                    WALKER (CONT'D)
          TODAY'S A SHIT DAY, FLINCH.

          I SWEAR TO YOU- I SWEAR TO YOU I KNOW
          THAT KIND OF DAY.

          BUT YOU GOTTA LOOK AT IT ANOTHER WAY. A
          DAY LIKE THIS- A DAY LIKE THIS IS WHEN
          YOU FIND OUT WHAT YOUR MADE OF. RIGHT?

          ANY ASSHOLE CAN KEEP THEIR SHIT TOGETHER
          ON THE GOOD DAYS.

          BUT THE SHIT DAY?

          THAT'S WHEN YOU SHOW YOUR CHARACTER.
          TODAY'S THE DAY YOU SHOW EVERYONE WHAT
          YOU'RE REALLY MADE OF.

3- SAME BUT EVEN TIGHTER.

CONTINUED: (7)

                        WALKER (CONT'D)
            AND I DAMN WELL KNOW YOU'RE MADE OF
            BETTER THAN THIS, RIGHT FLINCH?

            YOU'RE GONNA LET A GIRL DRIVE YOU NUTS
            LIKE THIS?

            ROLL IT OFF AND BE A MAN.

            ALL YOU DONE IN YOUR LIFE- ALL THE STUFF
            THAT MADE YOU, YOU--

            --AND YOU WANNA BE REMEMBERED AS SOME
            SHMUCK HELD A LITTLE GIRL?

            HELL, NO. AM I RIGHT? THIS IS SILLY SHIT.

            I SAY- I SAY WE FORGET THIS SILLY SHIT
            TODAY, YOU OPEN THE DOOR, THEN ME AND
            YOU, WHAT ARE WE GONNA DO?

            WE'LL FIND THAT BITCH AND GET YOUR MONEY
            BACK IS WHAT.

4- PAUSE. SAME EVEN TIGHTER

5- SAME EVEN TIGHTER. THIS IS NOW A CLOSE UP ON WALKERS
DETERMINED FACE. JUST ONE BEAD OF SWEAT.

                        FLINCH
            AH DAMN IT... THIS IS JUST...

                        WALKER
            YEAH, LET'S JUST OPEN THE DOOR AND...

PAGE 6-

1- BIG PANEL- HALF A PAGE

SPX: BOOM!!

WIDER SHOT OF HALLWAY. THE NOISE KNOCKS WALKER AND THE SWAT
TEAM OFF THEIR FEET FOR A SECOND.

2- IN A FURY OF ACTIVITY, LIKE A WELL OILED MACHINE, POWERS
DIVES OUT OF THE WAY SO THE SWAT TEAM CAN BURST THE DOOR
DOWN.

                                        (CONTINUED

CONTINUED: (8)

SPX: CRACK!!

3- FROM POWERS P.O.V. POWER'S GUN IS OUT IN THE FOREGROUND.
IN THE LIVING ROOM OF A TYPICAL CHEAP APARTMENT. RUBBLE IS
FALLING DOWN IN THE CENTER OF THE ROOM. SWAT TEAM IS RUNNING
ALL OVER THE APARTMENT.

4- HE POINTS HIS GUN TO A GIANT HOLE IN THE CEILING.

5- THEN POINTS DOWN TO THE FLOOR WHERE THE FALLING RUBBLE
LANDS.

6- THEN POINTS TO THE RIGHT, NOTHING BUT HALLWAY AND SWAT.

7- THEN TO THE LEFT, A CUTE SEVEN YEAR OLD GIRL, CALISTA IS
EATING PEANUT BUTTER OUT OF A JAR AND WATCHING A CARTOON
TAPE. SHE IS JUST NOW, BROKEN FROM HER INTENSE TELEVISION
WATCHING TO SEE THE LARGE GROUP OF MEN COMING INTO THE ROOM.

8- SAME. TIGHT ON WALKER LOOKING AT THE GIRL. SHES OK.

PAGE 7-

2 EQUAL HALF PAGE PANELS

1- WALKER AND A COUPLE OF SWAT LOOK UP THROUGH THE HOLE IN
THE CEILING. ALL WE CAN SEE IS A DOT WITH A SMOKE TRAIL.

2- A HIGH BIRD'S EYE LOOK DOWN AT WALKER AND A COUPLE OF SWAT
STARING UP AT THE SKY. THEY LOOK LIKE LITTLE KIDS LOOKING UP
AT A KITE.

                    SETZER
          TOTAL ASSHOLE!

                    WALKER
          WELL, HE FOUND ANOTHER WAY OUT.

                    SETZER
          HE COULDN'T DO THAT THREE HOURS AGO? I
          MISSED THE GAME.

(CONTINUED

CONTINUED: (9)

PAGES 8- 9

DOUBLE PAGE SPREAD

PANELS 1-3 ARE PAGE LONG SLANTED SHOTS.

A STREET LEVEL WORM'S EYE VIEW OF WALKER AND SOME OF THE SWAT
TEAM COMING OUT THE FRONT DOOR OF THE APARTMENT BUILDING.
THEY ARE LOOKING UP TOWARDS THE DOT AND SMOKE TRAIL THAT
POPPED OUT OF THE ROOF OF THE APARTMENT. IT IS A LITTLE
BIGGER NOW.

3- SAME. WE ARE FOLLOWING WALKER AND THE COPS AS THEY FOLLOW
FLINCH LIKE HE IS A KITE IN THE AIR. THEY ARE NOW DOWN THE
STAIRS IN THE MIDDLE OF THE STREET.

THERE ARE MANY GUNS TRAINED ON THE DOT AND TRAIL AS IT IS NOW
COMING TOWARDS THEM. WALKER HAS TURNED TOWARDS THE READER BUT
IS LOOKING ANNOYED AT THE OTHER COPS.

> WALKER
> WHOAH WHOAH WHOAH!
> DO NOT SHOOT!!

> SETZER
> WHAT?

> WALKER
> WHO KNOWS WHAT HE- HE COULD HAVE A
> NUCLEAR DEVISE STRAPPED TO HIS BACK FOR
> ALL WE KNOW!! CHRIST SAKE!!

4- SAME. THE GUNS ARE STILL TRAINED ON FLINCH, WHO WE CAN
CLEARLY SEE. HE IS HEADING TOWARDS THE GROUND. FEET FIRST.

FLINCH IS A SKINNY LOSER IN A GREEN JUMP SUIT WITH A CRAPPY
VERSION OF THE ROCKETEER BACK PACK STRAPPED TO HIS BACK.

HIS BACK PACK IS PUTTING...

SPX:PUT PUT PUT

THIS IS SLOWING FLINCH'S DESCENT DOWN, BUT HE ISN'T IN
CONTROL OF HIS LANDING.

> FLINCH
> OW...OW...OW...OH NO...

5- WORM'S EYE VIEW OF WALKER, THE COPS AND THE PRESS. THEY
ALL FLINCH AS FLINCH HITS THE GROUND WITH A THUD.

SPX: THUD.

(CONTINUED

CONTINUED: (10)

6- THE BILL MURRAY I HAVE BEEN SLIMED SHOT FROM GHOSTBUSTERS.
FLINCH IS LAYING ON HIS BACK PACK, IN PAIN

                    FLINCH (CONT'D)
          SERIOUSLY...OW.

PAGE 10-

1- THE EDDIE MURPHY "IS THERE A PROBLEM OFFICER'S?" SHOT FROM
TRADING PLACES. TIGHT ON FLINCH'S FACE WHICH NOW HAS EIGHT
GUNS TO IT.

2- WIDE SHOT. THE STREET IS A CHAOS OF ACTIVITY. IN THE
FOREGROUND FLINCH IS BEING PUT INTO AN AMBULANCE. WALKER HAS
CAUGHT UP JUST BEFORE THEY SLIDE HIM IN. IN THE BACKGROUND WE
CAN SEE A COUPLE OF SPECIAL SWAT TEAM MEMBERS PUTTING HIS
BACK PACK INTO A TRANSPARENT HIGH TECH CONTAINER. THE PRESS
IS EATING IT ALL UP.

                    WALKER
          HOLD ON. HOLD ON.

3- TWO SHOT OF WALKER. HE IS IN FLINCH'S FACE.

                    WALKER (CONT'D)
          HEY ASSHOLE, WHAT'S WITH YOU, MAN?

                    FLINCH
          WHAT?

                    WALKER
          I'VE NEVER SEEN YOU BEFORE IN MY LIFE?
          WHAT IS WITH YOU CALLING ME DOWN HERE TO
          DEAL WITH ALL YOUR BULLSHIT?

4- TIGHT ON FLINCH, IN PAIN AND A LITTLE SCARED. WALKER IS
CASTING A SHADOW OVER HIM.

                    FLINCH
          IT WAS- IT WAS WOLFE...HE...

5- WALKER FROM FLINCH'S P.O.V.

                    WALKER
          WHAT?

6- SAME AS FOUR.

                                        (CONTINUED

CONTINUED: (11)

                        FLINCH
          IT WAS WOLFE HE- HE SAID...WHEN I WAS
          HOLD UP IN BLAIR GREEN WITH WOLFE AND
          THOSE GUYS...

          HE SAID- HE SAID IF THE SHIT EVER GOT TO
          THICK WE SHOULD ALWAYS ASK FOR YOU-D-D-D-
          DETECTIVE CHRISTIAN WALKER...

7- SAME AS FIVE.

                        WALKER
          WHY?

8- SAME AS FOUR.

                        FLINCH
          HE SAID YOU WERE SOFT- SOFT ON GUYS WITH
          POWERS.

9- SAME AS FIVE. WALKER IS REALLY MIFFED AT THIS.

PAGE 11-

1- SAME AS PANEL 2 OF LAST PAGE. A TWO SHOT OF FLINCH AND
WALKER. BUT WALKER IS GRABBING FLINCH BY THE COLLAR AND IS
READY TO HIT HIM. THE OTHER PEOPLE REACT, TRYING TO STOP HIM.

                        WALKER
          WELL, YOU TELL WOLFE THAT WHEN HE'S UP
          FOR PAROLE IN 4 YEARS AND 3 MONTHS!!

          YOU TELL HIM THAT I'LL BE THERE AT THE
          HEARING AND HE'LL SEE HOW SOFT I AM!!

                        FLINCH
          PLEASE- NO DON'T.

                        AMBULANCE DRIVER
          DETECTIVE PLEASE!!

                        CAPTAIN
          WHAT'S GOING ON HERE?

2- MID SHOT OF WALKER. HE HAS COMPOSED HIMSELF AND NOW HE IS
A LITTLE ASHAMED OF HIMSELF. HIS CAPTAIN IS STANDING BEHIND
HIM.

                                        (CONTINUED

CONTINUED: (12)

                              CAPTAIN (CONT'D)
               WALKER, WHAT'S WRONG WITH YOU?

               THE PRESS IS ALL OVER THIS.

                              WALKER
               IT'S DONE. LET'S NOT MAKE A THING OF IT.

                              CAPTAIN
               A THING? I'LL SEE YOU BACK AT THE
               STATION.

3- WALKER IS WATCHING HIS CAPTAIN KISS THE MEDIA'S ASS AS HE
GOES TO LEAVE THE OTHER COPS TO CLEAN UP THE MESS.

IN THE BACKGROUND IS THE FRONT OF THE APARTMENT BUILDING. A
SWAT TEAM MEMBER IS HOLDING THE GIRL.

                              SWAT 1
               WALKER...

4- THE SWAT TEAM MEMBER HOLDING THE GIRL COMES UP TO WALKER.

                              SWAT 1 (CONT'D)
               HAPPY BIRTHDAY!

                              WALKER
               WHAT IS THIS?

                              SWAT 1
               LIEUTENANT SAYS SHE'S YOURS...

                              WALKER
               HOW SO?

                              SWAT 1
               YOUR COLLAR. DEMS THE RULES...

5- TIGHT ON CALISTA'S ADORABLE FACE. SHE IS SAD AND CONFUSED.

6- HER POINT OF VIEW, WALKER LOOKS DOWN AT HER.

                                            (CONTINUED

CONTINUED: (13)

PAGE 12-

1- EXTERIOR SHOT OF THE POLICE STATION. AN OLD FASHIONED
BUILDING ON THE OUTSIDE. SOMETHING OUT OF A 50'S CRIME MOVIE.
THE LIT BALL LIGHT OUTSIDE THAT SAYS POLICE STATION.

                    WALKER
          YES HELLO? I'VE BEEN ON HOLD FOR--

          LISTEN THIS IS DETECTIVE CHRISTIAN
          WALKER... HOMI- HOMICIDE. YES.

          WHAT? NO, I NEED YOUR HELP. I- WHAT? NO.
          IS THIS SOCIAL SERVICES? WELL, I HAVE A
          YOUNG-- WHAT?

          NO. NO I DIDN'T HEAR. NO.

2- THE INSIDE OF A THE HOMICIDE SQUAD ROOM. ITS A HUSTLE AND
A BUSTLE. ITS A TYPICAL STATION HOUSE, GO GET YOUR PHOT
REFERENCE YOU LAZY FUCKER.

PEOPLE HUSTLE ABOUT, BUT....

BIG BUT.

THERE IS SOMETHING A LITTLE OFF ABOUT IT. WE CAN TELL THAT
PEOPLE WITH SUPERPOWERS EFFECT EVERY PART OF THE STATION.

THERE ARE BULLETPROOF GLASS CAGES AND SOME PEOPLE HAVE WEIRD
ARMOR ON. THERE ARE POSTERS ON THE WALL. ONE OF THEM IS RETRO
GIRL SAYING TO BUCKLE YOUR SEAT BELT. THIS BROUGHT TO YOU BY
RETRO GIRL INC. AND CITY COUNCIL FOR A BETTER TOMORROW.

I DON'T WANT THIS TO BE A HIGH TECH PLACE OR FILLED WITH
SUPERPOWERED PEOPLE. THAT WOULD BE SILLY AND ITS BEEN DONE,
THIS IS MORE SUBTLE.

WANTED POSTERS AND A SPECIAL WEAPONS WALL IS ENOUGH.

THINK THE SQUAD ROOM OF HOMICIDE LIFE ON THE STREET...
PLAYING EVERY NIGHT ON COURT TV.

                    WALKER (CONT'D)
          WHEN DID THIS HAPPEN? NO, I HAVEN'T SEEN
          THE NEWS. NO, I DIDN'T-- WERE PEOPLE
          HURT?

          GONE, GONE?

          THE BUILDING IS JUST- ITS GONE.

                    (MORE)

(CONTINUED

CONTINUED: (14)

                        WALKER (CONT'D)
        FIREBALL? FIREBALL- GOOD LORD! YEAH, I
        THOUGHT THAT GUY WAS...NO.

        OK. WELL, I AM REALLY SORRY TO- THAT'S
        HORRIBLE. IT...

        WELL, I HAVE THIS LITTLE GIRL AND...

        HOW IS THAT GOING TO? WELL, I CAN'T. I
        UNDERSTAND THERE'S NOBODY THERE.

         YES, I UNDERSTAND THAT THERE IS NO THERE
        ANYMORE.

        HEY, I SAID I- YES I DO.

        I AM A HOMICIDE DETECTIVE AND I AM IN THE
        MIDDLE OF FIFTEEN OPEN- NO I CAN'T.

3- TIGHTER ON WALKER. HE IS LOSING HIS BATTLE ON THE PHONE.

                        WALKER (CONT'D)
        NO- NO I CAN'T.

        'CAUSE YOU'RE SUPPOSED TO- CAN'T YOU SEE
        I AM TRYING TO DO THE BEST THING FOR THE--

        DAMN.

4- THE CONVERSATION HAS OBVIOUSLY ENDED.

5- RUBBING HIS FACE IN FRUSTRATION WITH ONE HAND, WALKER
DANGLES THE PHONE OVER THE RECEIVER.

6- THEN HANGS IT UP.

7- TIGHT ON THE GIRL LOOKING AT THE PHONE

8- THEN AT WALKER.

9- WALKER IS INTERNALLY CONFUSED AS TO WHAT TO DO NOW.

                                            (CONTINUED

CONTINUED: (15)

PAGE 13-

1- HE LOOKS AT THE GIRL.

2- SHE LOOKS BACK. INNOCENT EYES. CHILDLIKE EXPRESSION OF CURIOSITY.

>   CALISTA
>   WHAT'S A CLITORIS?

3- WALKER JUST STARES AT HER BLANKLY.

4- SAME.

>   WALKER
>   UH- I DON'T KNOW.

5- CALISTA LOOKING AT THE FLOOR. TALKING TO HERSELF.

>   CALISTA
>   HOW COME NOBODY KNOWS THAT?
>
>   I ASK EVERYONE AND NOBODY HAS A CLUE.

PAGE 14-15

DOUBLE PAGE SPREAD.

A ROW OF LITTLE PANELS ON TOP. A LONG DOUBLE PAGE SPREAD OF THE ROOM IN THE MIDDLE AND A ANOTHER ROW OF LITTLE PANELS ON THE BOTTOM.

1- WALKER.

>   WALKER
>   YOU HUNGRY?

2- WALKER REACHES INTO HIS DESK AND PULLS OUT A BOWL.

>   CALISTA
>   TOTALLY. LAST NIGHT MY MOM MADE THESE
>   PORK CHOPS LIKE SHE SAW ON THE FOOD
>   CHANNEL,

3- THEN ANOTHER. THEN SILVERWARE.

(CONTINUED

CONTINUED: (16)

                    CALISTA (CONT'D)
         BUT SHE LIKE TOTALLY BURNED THE SHIT OUT
         OF THEM. AND I HATE PEAS. YOU LIKE PEAS?

4- THEN A BIG BOX OF FRUITY CHOCO CRUNCHIES SERIAL.

                    WALKER
         I DO NOT LIKE PEAS.

5- CALISTA AMAZED.

                    CALISTA
         YOU KEEP CEREAL IN YOUR DESK?

6- WALKER OPENS THE BOX AND POURS THE DRY CEREAL IN.

                    WALKER
              YEP.

7- CALISTA IMPRESSED.

                    CALISTA
         THAT IS THE COOLEST THING I'VE EVER SEEN
         IN MY LIFE.

8- WALKER HANDS HER BOWL OF DRY CEREAL AND HOLDS HIS.

                    WALKER
         WELL, YOU'RE YOUNG.

9- BIG PANEL!!- WALKER AND THE GIRL WALK THROUGH HOMICIDE
DEPARTMENT. A WAIST LEVEL LOOK AROUND THIS UNIQUE DEPARTMENT.

                    CALISTA
         HEY, YOU KNOW WHAT?

                    WALKER
              WHAT?

                    CALISTA
         MY MOMMY SAYS THAT I CAN EXPRENTIATE
         MYSELF ANY WAY I WANT.

                    WALKER
         EXPRENTIATE?

                    CALISTA
         SHE SAYS HER DADDY- HE USED TO LIKE SMACK
         HER EVERY TIME SHE TALKED AND THAT I CAN
         TALK ABOUT WHATEVER I WANT BECAUSE SHE
         SAID HE WAS AN ASSHOLE.

                                        (CONTINUED

CONTINUED: (17)

                WALKER
      YOU DON'T SAY?

                CALISTA
      DO YOU KNOW HIM?

                WALKER
      WHO?

LITTLE PANELS.

10- WALKER AND CALISTA AT THE VENDING MACHINES.

                CALISTA
      MY MOM'S DAD?

                WALKER
      DO I KNOW HIM? NO.

                CALISTA
      OH. I THINK HE KILLED SOMEBODY OR
      SOMETHING,

      THAT'S WHY I ASKED IS ALL.

11- WALKER LOOKS DOWN PUZZLED AT HER. HE HAS A MILK.

                WALKER
      HE DID?

                CALISTA
      I THINK. OR SOMEBODY KILLED HIM OR
      SOMETHING, I DON'T KNOW.

                WALKER
      YOU'RE TOO LITTLE TO BE THINKING ABOUT
      THINGS LIKE THAT.

12- CALISTA LOOKS AT HER BOWL OF DRY CEREAL.

                CALISTA
      YOU WATCH CARTOONS?

                WALKER
      USED TO.

13- CALISTA LOOKS UP.

(CONTINUED

CONTINUED: (18)

             CALISTA
        DO YOU SEE THIS THING THAT SOMETIMES THE
        BACKGROUNDS AND THE PEOPLE DON'T LOOK
        RIGHT?

14- WALKER IS LOOKING ACROSS THE STATION HOUSE. THERE IS
COMMOTION.

PAGE 16-

ALL THE KUTTER SHOTS ARE WIDE. FROM WALKER'S POV.

KUTTER, 20'S, IS A YOUNG, SEVERELY AMBITIOUS ROOKIE DETECTIVE
WHOSE IDEALS AND ALLEGIANCES MAY OR MAY NOT BE ON THE UP AND
UP.

HE LOOKS JUST LIKE BENJAMIN BRATT FROM LAW AND ORDER

1- HE HAS BROUGHT IN A VILLAIN...YOUR CHOICE MIKE.

             VILLAIN
        YOU ONLY THINK YOU CAN HOLD ME!! DO YOU
        UNDERSTAND? DO YOU? YOUR PLAIN OF
        EXISTENCE IS ONLY ONE OF...

             KUTTER
        CALM DOWN BIG TIME!

        IT'S OVER. YOU KNOW IT'S OVER. I KNOW ITS
        OVER. EVERYBODY KNOWS IT'S OVER. SUCK IT
        UP.

2- WALKER IS WATCHING.

             WALKER
        HOW SO?

             CALISTA
        SOMETIMES THE BACKGROUNDS ARE ALL COOL
        LOOKING AND NICELY COLORED IN OR
        SOMETHING. BUT THE PEOPLE AREN'T. THEY-
        THEY ARE JUST FLAT LOOKING. SUCKY.

3- THE VILLAIN TRIES TO ESCAPE AND THEY HIT HIM WITH
SOMETHING THAT IS SIMILAR TO A CATTLEPROD.

                                        (CONTINUED

CONTINUED: (19)

                    VILLAIN
          YOU WILL NEVER LEARN!! YOU WILL
          NEVER...!!

4- WALKER IS WATCHING THIS AND NOT THE GIRL.

                    WALKER
          NEVER NOTICED.

5- THEY THROW HIM IN THE TANK.

                    CALISTA
          NEVER NOTICED? IT DRIVES ME UP THE DAMN
          WALL IS ALL. WHY DO THEY DO THAT?? WHY
          CAN'T THEY PAINT THE PEOPLE AS NICE AS
          THEY PAINT THE SKY?

                    COP
          KUTTER, CAN YOU KEEP IT UNDER CONTROL
          OVER THERE, I'M TRYING TO READ!!

                    KUTTER
          GOOD LUCK, HOT SHOT.

6- KUTTER SEES THAT WALKER IS WATCHING HIM.

                    WALKER
          YEAH, I DON'T - I DON'T KNOW.

7- KUTTER SMILES THERE IS SOMETHING BAD BETWEEN THE TWO.

PAGE 17-

1- WALKER IS FOCUSED BACK ON THE GIRL. THEY ARE WALKING BACK
TO THE DESK.

                    WALKER (CONT'D)
          HEY, WHY DO YOU HAVE TO SWEAR EVERY
          THIRTY SECONDS?

                    CALISTA
          SWEAR?

                    WALKER
          YOU KNOW...

                                        (CONTINUED

CONTINUED: (20)

> CALISTA
> I TOLD YOU, MY MOM...

> WALKER
> YOUR MOM DOESN'T LET YOU TALK THAT WAY,
> YOU AIN'T FOOLIN' ME.

2- THEY ARE BACK AT THE DESK. CALISTA SITTING IN HER LITTLE CHAIR.

> CALISTA
> SHE AIN'T COMIN BACK TO GET ME IS SHE?

3- WALKER IN HIS SEAT. SERIOUS.

> WALKER
> I DON'T KNOW.

4- SHE LOOKS AT HER CEREAL.

> CALISTA
> DAMN SUCKY CARTOONS.

5- TIGHT ON THE BOWL FULL OF LITTLE 'R'S FLOATING IN MILK.

PAGE 18-

SIX PAGE LONG PANELS

A VERY TIGHT CLOSE UP OF DEENA PILGRIM. SHE IS TELLING AN ANECDOTE.

THE SHOT EVENTUALLY PULLS OUT TO A WIDE SHOT OF THE CAPTAIN'S OFFICE. HE LISTENS INTENTLY.

1-

> DEENA
> HA! YEAH--THAT'S A FUNNY STORY ACTUALLY.
>
> I WAS ON SWAT FOR I DON'T KNOW- LIKE A WEEK.
>
> THERE WAS THIS GUY HOLD- HE HOLD HIMSELF UP IN SOME GOVERNMENT OFFICE.

(CONTINUED

CONTINUED: (21)

                      CAPTAIN
DID HE HAVE..?

                      DEENA
WHAT? NO. JUST A GUY.

GUY WITH A BEEF. GUY WITH A SCREW LOOSE
HOLDS HIMSELF UP IN A BUILDING. HIS MOMMY
DIDN'T SPANK HIM ENOUGH AS A KID, I DON'T
KNOW.

BUT HE HOLDS HIMSELF UP IN THERE SO LONG
WE HAD TO BE RELIEVED FOR A SECOND SHIFT.

                      CAPTAIN
THAT'S A LONG..

                      DEENA
TOTALLY. SO, THE SHIFTS OVER. WE DROP OUR
GEAR IN THE VAN AND WE ALL HEAD OVER TO
THIS THAI PLACE THAT WE HAD BEEN STARING
AT FROM ACROSS THE STREET FOR THE LAST
BILLION HOURS STRAIGHT.

2-

                   DEENA (CONT'D)
NOW THE WHOLE RESTAURANT IS FILLED WITH
SWAT TEAM GUYS. SO WE'RE EATIN' OUR
APPETIZERS AND KICKIN' BACK WHEN MY
PARTNER DAVE...

HE POINTS OUT THE WINDOW TO THE PAYPHONE.

THE GUY- THE GUY WE WERE WAITIN' ON-

THE GUY THE NEGOTIATOR HAD SPENT LIKE A
BILLION HOURS TRYING TO TALK OUT OF THE
BUILDING UNTIL HE STOPPED TALKING...

THE GUY IS RIGHT THERE MAKIN' A PHONE
CALL.

                      CAPTAIN
YOU RECOGNIZED THE GUY?

                      DEENA
WELL, WE ALL DID ONCE WE SEEN HIM.

THEY HAD A PIC THEY PASSED AROUND SO WE
KNEW WHO TO TAKE DOWN IF IT CAME TO THAT.

                  (MORE)

(CONTINUED

CONTINUED: (22)

                    DEENA (cont'd)
SO LIKE- LIKE THE WHOLE RESTAURANT JUST
STARES AT HIM IN DISBELIEF AND THEN ALL
AT ONCE- LIKE ALL AT THE SAME TIME...WE
POUR OUT-

THE WHOLE RESTAURANT POURS OUT ONTO THE
STREET AND CIRCLES THE PHONE BOOTH.

3-

                    DEENA (CONT'D)
WE ALL HAVE OUR GUNS OUT. WE'RE READY.
WE'RE READY FOR FREDDY.

THE GUY- THE GUY DOESN'T EVEN NOTICE US.
HE JUST KEEPS ON TALKING.

FIFTY GUNS AT HIS HEAD HE'S TOTALLY
OBLIVIOUS.

                    CAPTAIN
'S FUNNY...

                    DEENA
NOT THE END OF IT.

SO ONE OF THE GUYS, JOEY, HE LIGHTLY TAPS
ON THE GLASS TO GET HIS ATTENTION.

THE GUY DOES ONE OF THESE MOVES WHERE HE
JUST TURNS AWAY FROM THE DOOR HOLDING HIS
HAND TO HIS EAR.

SO JOEY TAPS ON THE GLASS AGAIN, NOW THE
PERP TURNS REAL SHARP AND BARKS: "DO YOU
SEE I'M ON THE...."

AND NOW HE SEES WHAT'S WHAT. SO FUCKING
FUNNY. THE GUY SHAT HIMSELF I SWEAR
TOO...PRICELESS.

                    CAPTAIN
GOOD ONE...

4-

                    DEENA
YEAH...

SO THE GUY HE - HE GOES FOR IT.

                    CAPTAIN
NO...

                                        (CONTINUED

CONTINUED: (23)

                    DEENA
          YEAH.

                    CAPTAIN
          SO...

                    DEENA
          SO, HE'S RIDDLED IN A SECOND. DOWN FOR
          THE COUNT. ITS OVER. POPPED.

                    CAPTAIN
          JEEZ...

                    DEENA
          THAT'S THE WAY IT WENT DOWN.

          BUT THE PHONE- BUT THE PHONE IS STILL
          DANGING OFF THE HOOK.

          STILL IN ONE PIECE.

          WHOEVER WAS ON THE OTHER LINE, THEY HEARD
          THE WHOLE THING. CAN YOU IMAGINE?

          SO- SO DAVE HE- HE PICKS UP THE PHONE AND
          HE SAYS INTO THE RECEIVER:

          "I'M SORRY, YOUR FRIEND HERE HAS BEEN
          DISCONNECTED."

          AND WE- WE COULDN'T HELP IT, WE ALL BURST
          OUT LAUGHING AT THIS CRAZY FUCKING THING
          HE JUST SAID.

6-

                    CAPTAIN
          HE SAID THAT? THAT'S...

                    DEENA
          YEAH, THING OF IT IS THOUGH...THE PERSON
          ON THE OTHER END WAS THE GUY'S MOM.

                    CAPTAIN
          OY..

                    DEENA
          CAN YOU IMAGINE?

          SO - SO THAT'S WHAT HAPPENED TO MY OLD
          PARTNER.

                    (MORE)

(CONTINUED

CONTINUED: (24)

                        DEENA (cont'd)
            I THINK HE'S WORKING AT BORDERS NOW
            SOMEONE TOLD ME.

PAGE 19-

1- SAME AS SIX FROM LAST PAGE. WALKER BARGES IN.

                        WALKER
            RED ALERT.

                        CAPTAIN
            WALKER...

                        WALKER
            I GOT SIDELINED WITH THE LITTLE GIRL FROM
            THIS AFTERNOON'S BULLSHIT--
                    (TO DEENA)
            HI
                    (TO CAPTAIN)
            AND SOCIAL SERVICES...

                        CAPTAIN
            IS NO MORE. I KNOW.

                        WALKER
            I DIDN'T. I CAN'T - I DON'T KNOW WHAT TO
            DO WITH...

2- SAME BUT TIGHTER. WALKER IS A LITTLE FRAZZED COMPARED TO
THE OTHER TWO'S LAID BACK MEETING.

                        DEENA
            WHAT HAPPENED TO SOCIAL SERVICES?

                        CAPTAIN
            A BLAST I HEARD...

                        WALKER
            FIREBALL IS WHAT...

                        CAPTAIN
            I'LL PUT IN A CALL TO GEAUGA COUNTY BUT
            FOR THE MEANTIME YOU'RE GOING TO HAVE TO
            BABY-SIT, I...

                        WALKER
            BUT I HAVE CASES.

                                            (CONTINUED

CONTINUED: (25)

> CAPTAIN
> THIS IS TRUE.

> WALKER
> I HAVE CASES.

> CAPTAIN
> WE ALL HAVE CASES.

> WALKER
> BUT I HAVE CASES.

> CAPTAIN
> AND THAT'S WHY WE HAVE DAY CARE.
>
> DROP HER OFF WITH BABS FOR THE SHIFT AND
> WE WILL SEE WHAT WE CAN DO.

3- SAME BUT TIGHTER ONTO DEENA AND WALKER.

> DEENA
> HOW OLD IS SHE?

> WALKER
> WHAT? I DON'T I- I DON'T KNOW SIX OR- HOW
> CAN YOU TELL?

> DEENA
> YOU COULD ASK.

> WALKER
> YEAH, WELL IT'S A- I'M SORRY, WHO ARE...?

> DEENA
> OH, I'M DEENA PILGRIM. I'VE JUST BEEN
> REASSIGNED.

> WALKER
> OH- UH- CONGRATS I GUESS. PULL THE SHORT
> END OF THE...

> DEENA
> NOPE, REQUESTED.

> WALKER
> SERIOUSLY?

> DEENA
> TOTALLY.

> WALKER
> HUH.

(CONTINUED

CONTINUED: (26)

                    DEENA
            SO DID YOU, RIGHT?

4- WALKER JUST STARES AT HER.

5- WALKER BACK TO THE CAPTAIN

                    WALKER
                (TO CAPTAIN)
            SO, WHAT FLOOR IS DAY CARE?

                    CAPTAIN
            THIRD. 309. TAKE YOUR NEW PARTNER WITH
            YOU.

6- WALKER JUST STARES AT HER AGAIN.

                    WALKER
            HUH.

                    DEENA
            HUH, YOURSELF.

                    WALKER
            NO I...

                    DEENA
            COME ON.

PAGE 20-

1- CALISTA LOOKING AROUND THE SQUAD ROOM. SHE SEES A COUPLE
OF COPS ARGUING.

                    COP 1
            HOW COULD YOU EVEN SAY THAT, THE GUY HAD
            A...

                    COP 2
            YOU KNOW!! YOU KNOW WHAT HE WAS GOING
            TO....

                    COP 1
            IT'S A 314. WHAT DO YOU DO IN A 314?

                                        (CONTINUED

CONTINUED: (27)

2- CALISTA WATCHES A COP PICK UP THE PHONE.

                    COP 3
          HOMICIDE. 4TH. THIS IS BERMAN...

3- CALISTA LOOKS TO THE PHONE ON WALKER'S DESK AS IT RINGS.

4- AND RINGS.

5- AND RINGS, CALISTA IS LOOKING TO SEE IF SOMEONE IS GOING
TO PICK IT UP.

6- CALISTA PICKS IT UP.

                    CALISTA
          HOMICIDE. 4TH. THIS IS CALISTA.

          WHAT?

          EEWW!!

          THAT'S SO GROSS- WHAT?

7- BIGGER PANEL. WALKER, PILGRIM BEHIND HIM, GRABS THE PHONE
AWAY FROM HER.

                    WALKER
          HOMICIDE, WAL- WHAT?

8- WALKER LOOKS LIKE HE SAW A GHOST.

9- DEENA LOOKS AT HIS REACTION.

                    DEENA
          WE ON THE MOVE?

10- SAME AS 8

                    WALKER
          WE'RE ON THE MOVE.

PAGE 21-

1- BIG PANEL. WALKER AND PILGRIM PULL UP TO A CRIME SCENE.

THIS ONE IS A BARRICADED ALLY. THE COPS ARE FENDING OFF AN
EXTREMELY LARGE GATHERING CROWD.

                                        (CONTINUED

CONTINUED: (28)

THE PRESS BEAT THEM TO IT BUT CAN'T GET NEAR THE SCENE.

2- DEENA AND WALKER IN THE CAR.

                    DEENA
          WELL- WELL, THIS IS A FUCKING CIRCUS.

                    WALKER
          THREE RING. GET USED TO IT.

3- THESE SHOTS ARE FROM THE P.O.V. OF THE CORPSE WE ARE
LOOKING UP AT WALKER AND PILGRIM AND A UNIFORM YOUNG
POLICEMAN.

BUILDING TOWER INTO PERSPECTIVE IN THE BACKGROUND

                    WALKER (CONT'D)
          WHO CALLED IT IN?

                    COP
          ANONYMOUS.

                    WALKER
          IT'S A LONG SHOT- BUT RUN A TAP ANYHOW.

                    DEENA
          COULD IT BE? THERE'S NO WAY IT'S HER.

                    WALKER
          IT'S HER.

                    DEENA
          COULD BE A LOOK-A-LIKE...

5- SAME, WALKER IS VERY SERIOUS.

                    WALKER
          COULD BE. BUT IT ISN'T.

                    DEENA
          BUT- HOW DO YOU KNOW?

                    WALKER
          MET HER.

                    DEENA
          STILL...

                    WALKER
          TRUST ME.

          SHES NOT-

                                        (CONTINUED

CONTINUED: (29)

6- WALKER

                    WALKER (CONT'D)
          YOU DON'T FORGET HER.

          IT'S HER.

PAGE 22-

BIG PAGE SHOT OVER THEIR SHOULDERS DOWN TO THE GROUND OF THE
ALLEY.

IT IS A DEAD GIRL IN A HIP AND TASTEFUL WONDER GIRL STYLE
SUPERHERO OUTFIT AND SHORT SKIRT AND GO- GO BOOTS.

ITS RETRO GIRL.

AND SHE IS DEAD. HER THROAT CUT. A POOL OF ALMOST BLACK
BLOOD.

ON THE ALLEY WALL. MORE GRAFFITI LIKE IN THE FIRST SCENE.

THE PHRASE KAOTIC CHIC IS SPRAY PAINTED ON THE WALL WITH SOME
OTHER STUFF.

                    DEENA
          BUT SHE'S- SHE'S...

                    WALKER
          WHO COULD HAVE KILLED RETRO GIRL?

                    DEENA
          SHIT OL' MIGHTY, CAN I PICK EM.

NEXT ISSUE: WHO KILLED RETRO GIRL?

POWERS
THE SKETCHBOOK

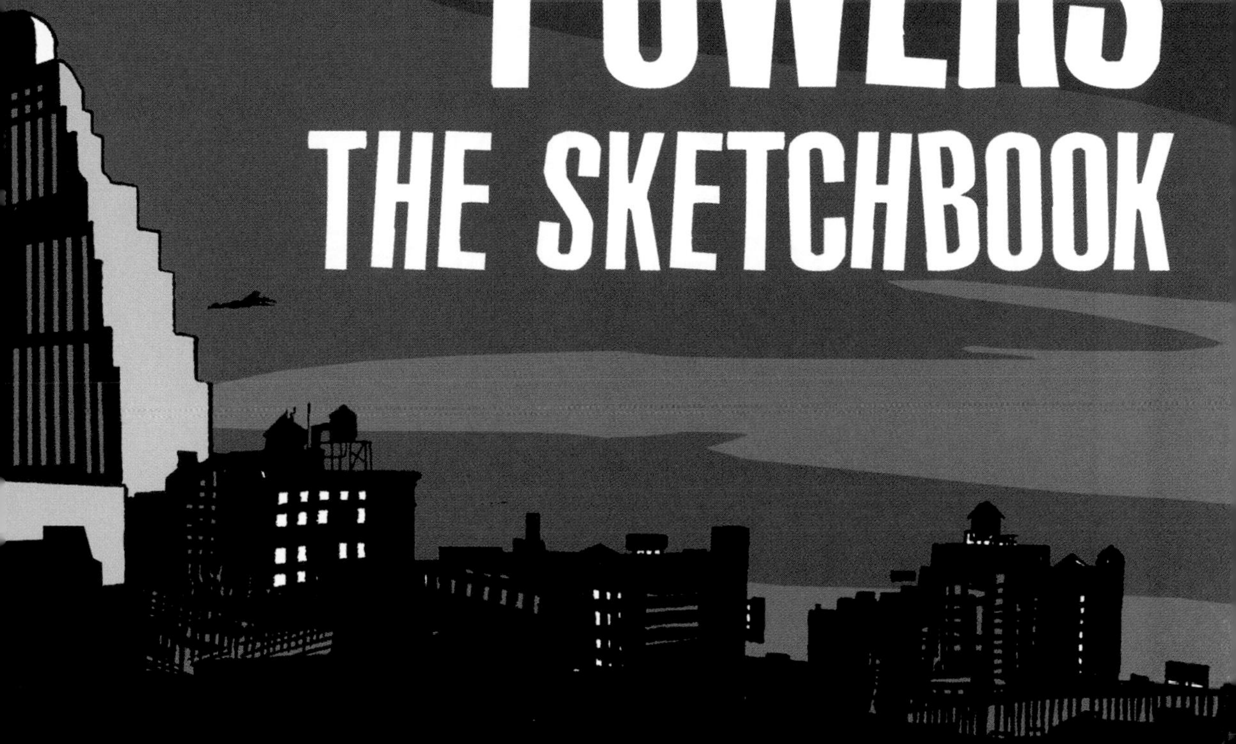

In this section you will see one of Michael Avon Oeming's true strengths as an artist. Every gesture, every character design, every brushstroke looks so simple- so effortless- but in reality it is a laborious process. This is an intense decision making process that defines everything about the book.

For every sketch revealed here, there are literally dozens more. Mike is a fountain of ideas and images. For months prior to working on the actual pages I would receive daily faxes of these ideas and images. What a rush.

I hope you get even half the thrill from these that I do.

THE CHARACTERS

Here is a smattering of images that explore how many ways any of the characters could have gone

WALKER

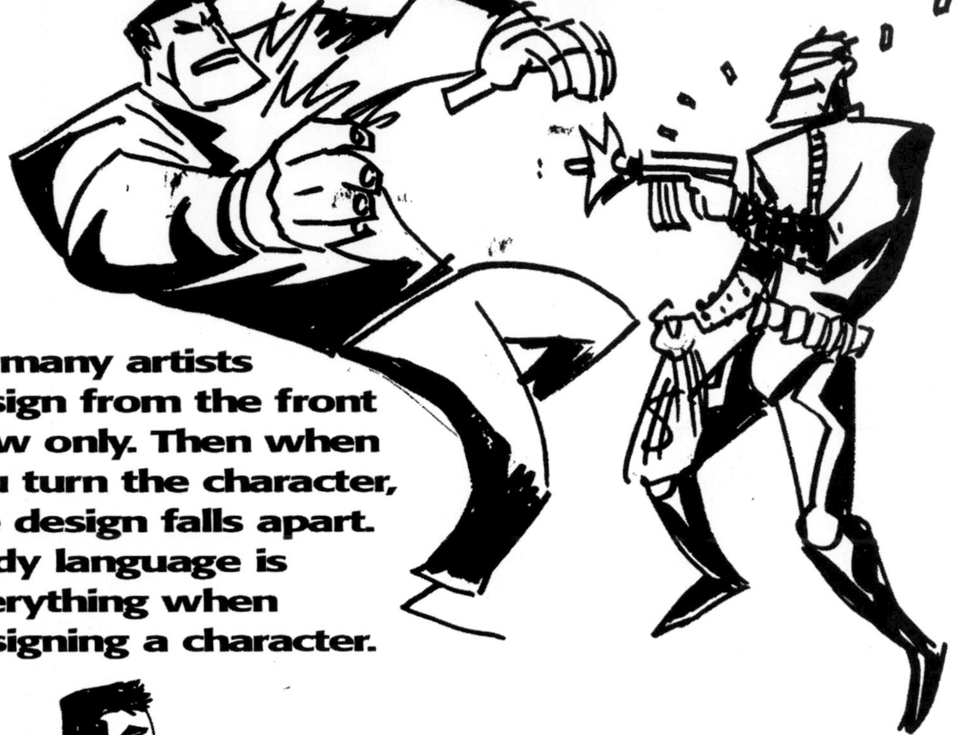

So many artists design from the front view only. Then when you turn the character, the design falls apart. Body language is everything when designing a character.

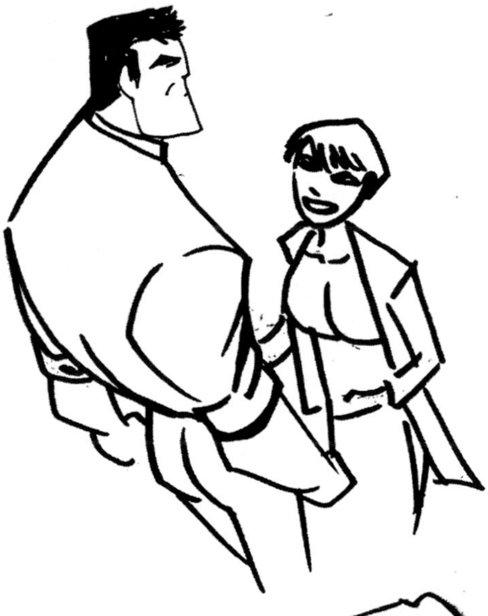

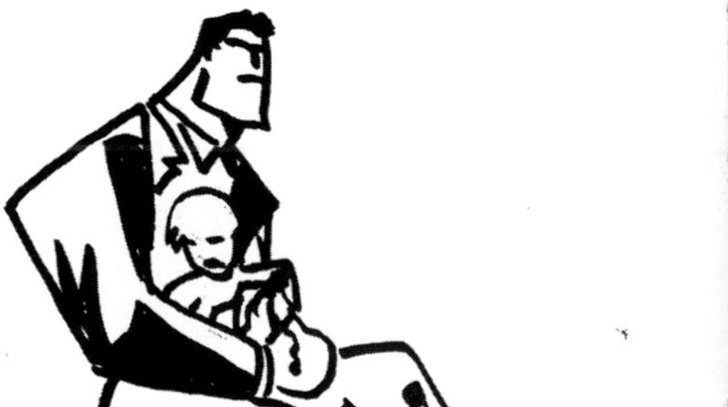

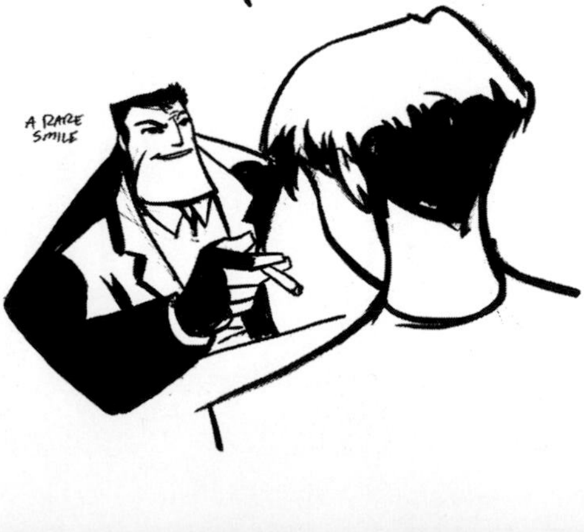
A RARE SMILE

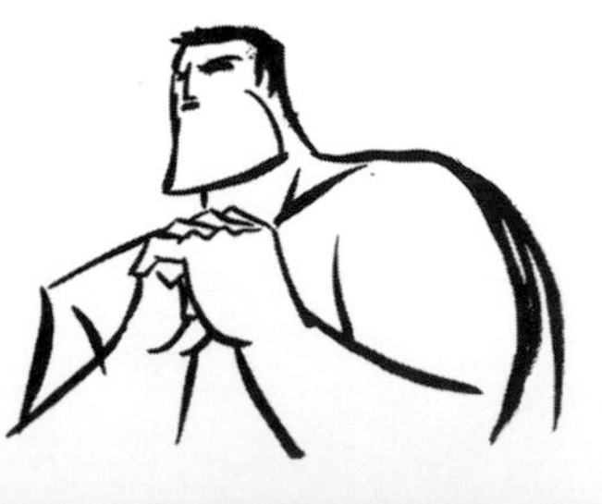

6- IF ~~WE~~ WE GO COLOR AT IMAGE ~WE NEED TO SUSTAIN HIGHER NUMBERS-
DO YOU THINK USING MY _SECONDARY_ ANIMATION STYLE (THE ~~OLD~~ NEWER STUFF
I'VE BEEN FAXING WITH ALL THE LINES) WOULD GRAB US LARGER NUMBERS?
THE MORE SIMPLE "TIMM" STUFF IS FINE FOR A 2-3,000 B+W AUDIENCE,
BUT MIGHT SCARE FOLKS AWAY AS COLOR. LOOK AT HOW MANY DON'T
READ "LEAVE IT TO CHANCE" OR THE ADVENTURES BOOKS BECAUSE
THEY THINK ITS TOO "CARTOONS" OR SIMPLE. - WHAT ARE YOUR THOUGHTS

This is an extremely early stab at Walker that came with a hilarious note from Mike (which is being reprinted with his permission.)

-THIS STUFF IS LOOSE - ABOUT 85% THERE, ENOUGH TO GIVE AN IDEA.

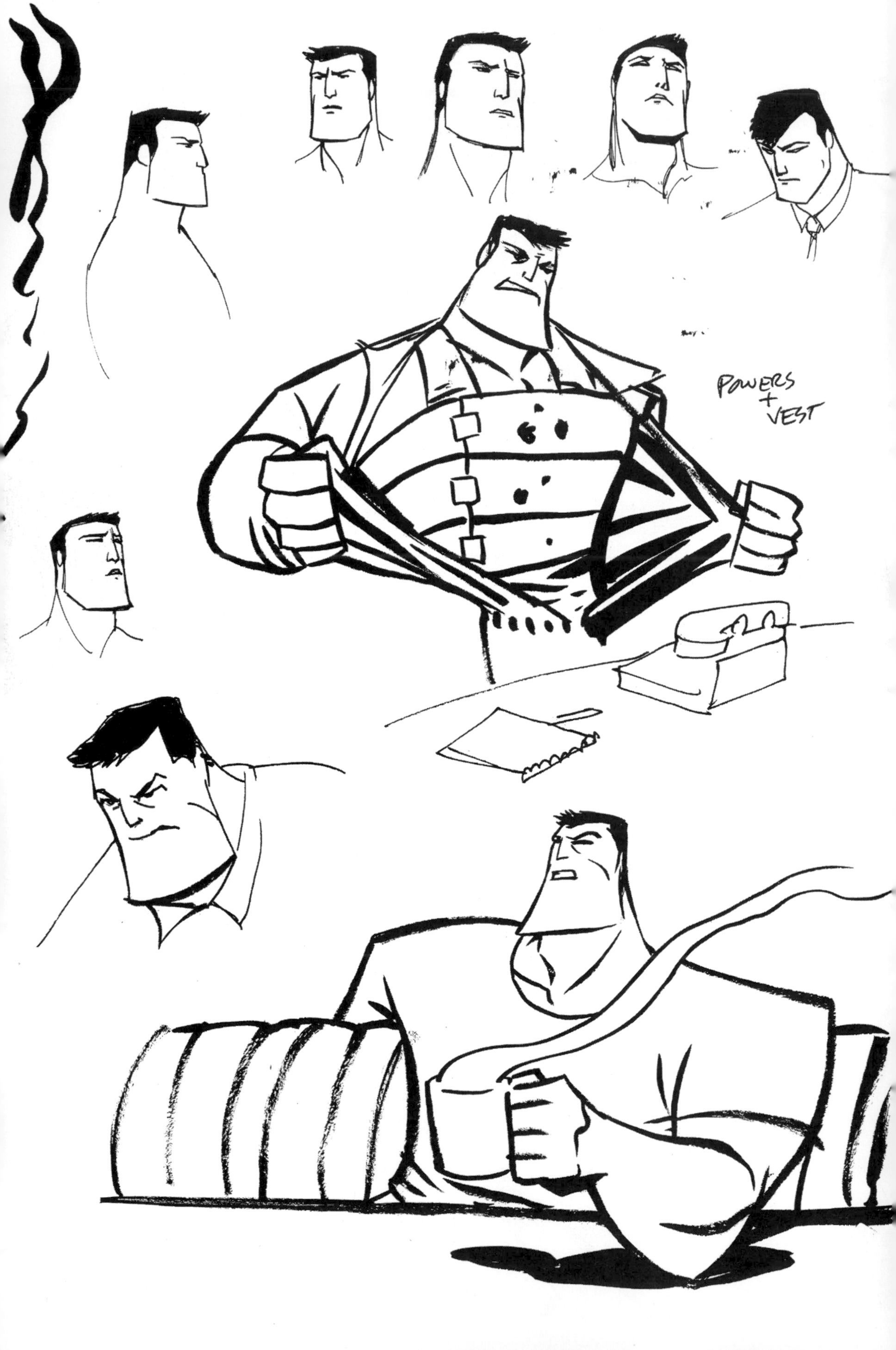
POWERS
+
VEST

Below: early model sheets for Walker and Pilgrim. Notice that funky Leno chin.

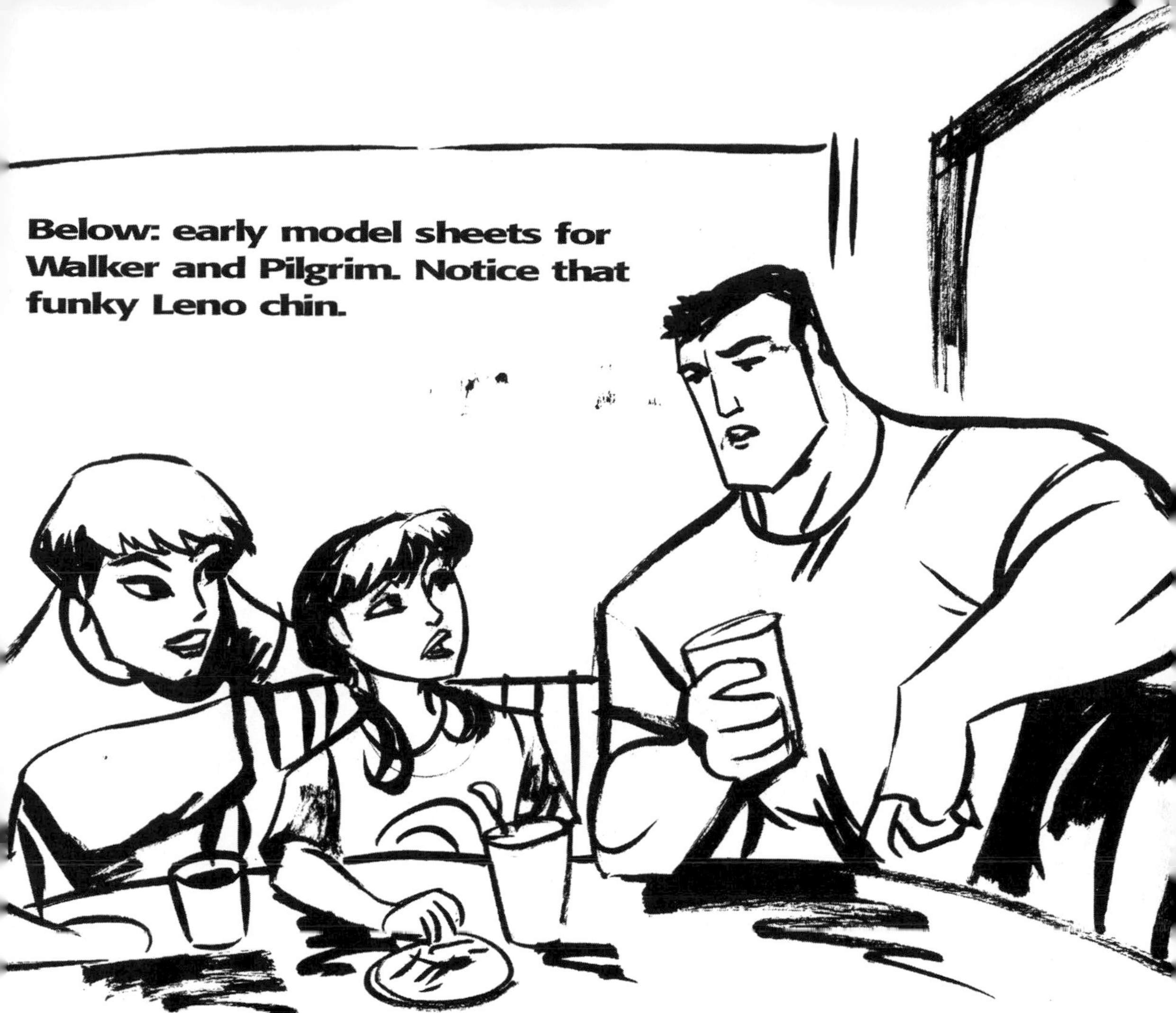

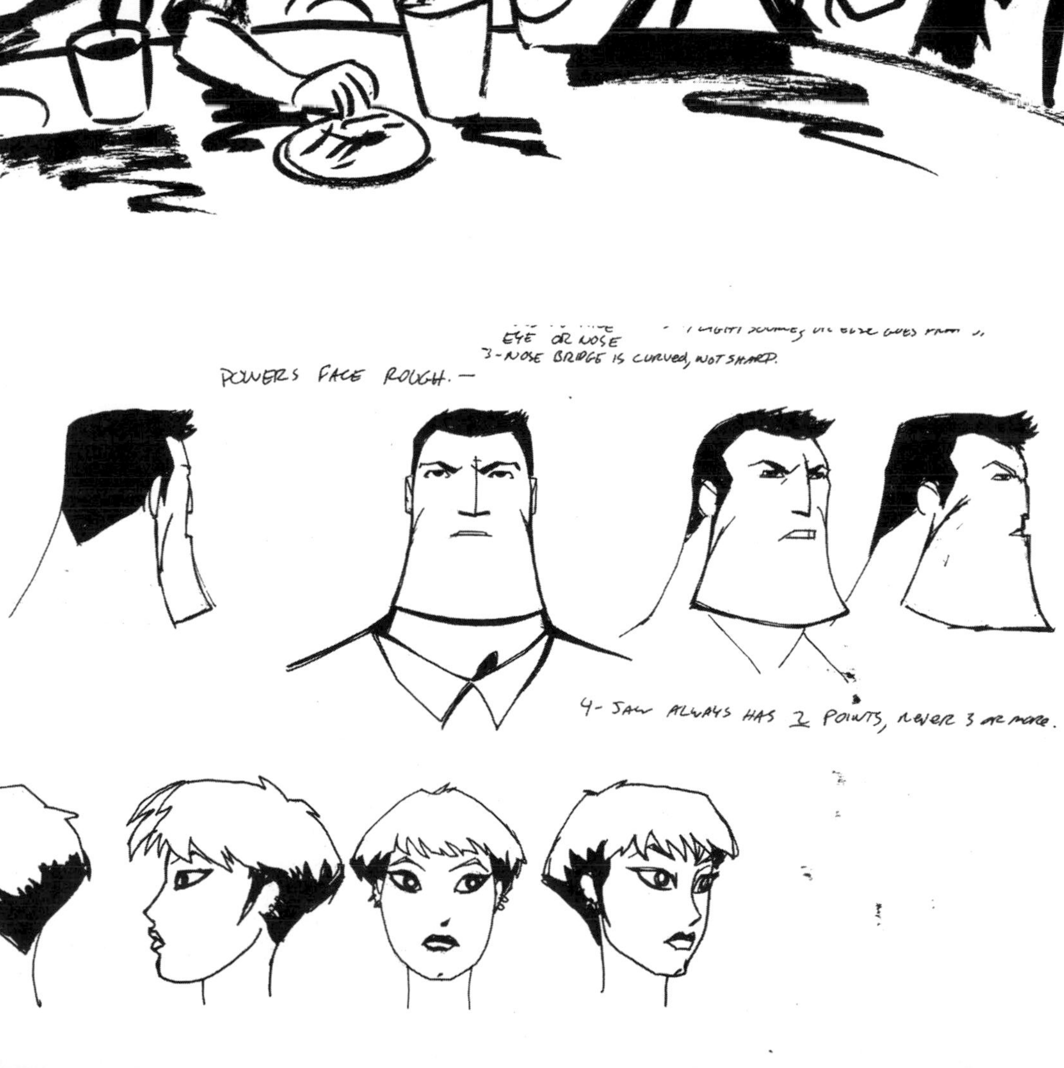

EYE OR NOSE
3-NOSE BRIDGE IS CURVED, NOT SHARP.
POWERS FACE ROUGH.–
4- JAW ALWAYS HAS 2 POINTS, NEVER 3 OR MORE.

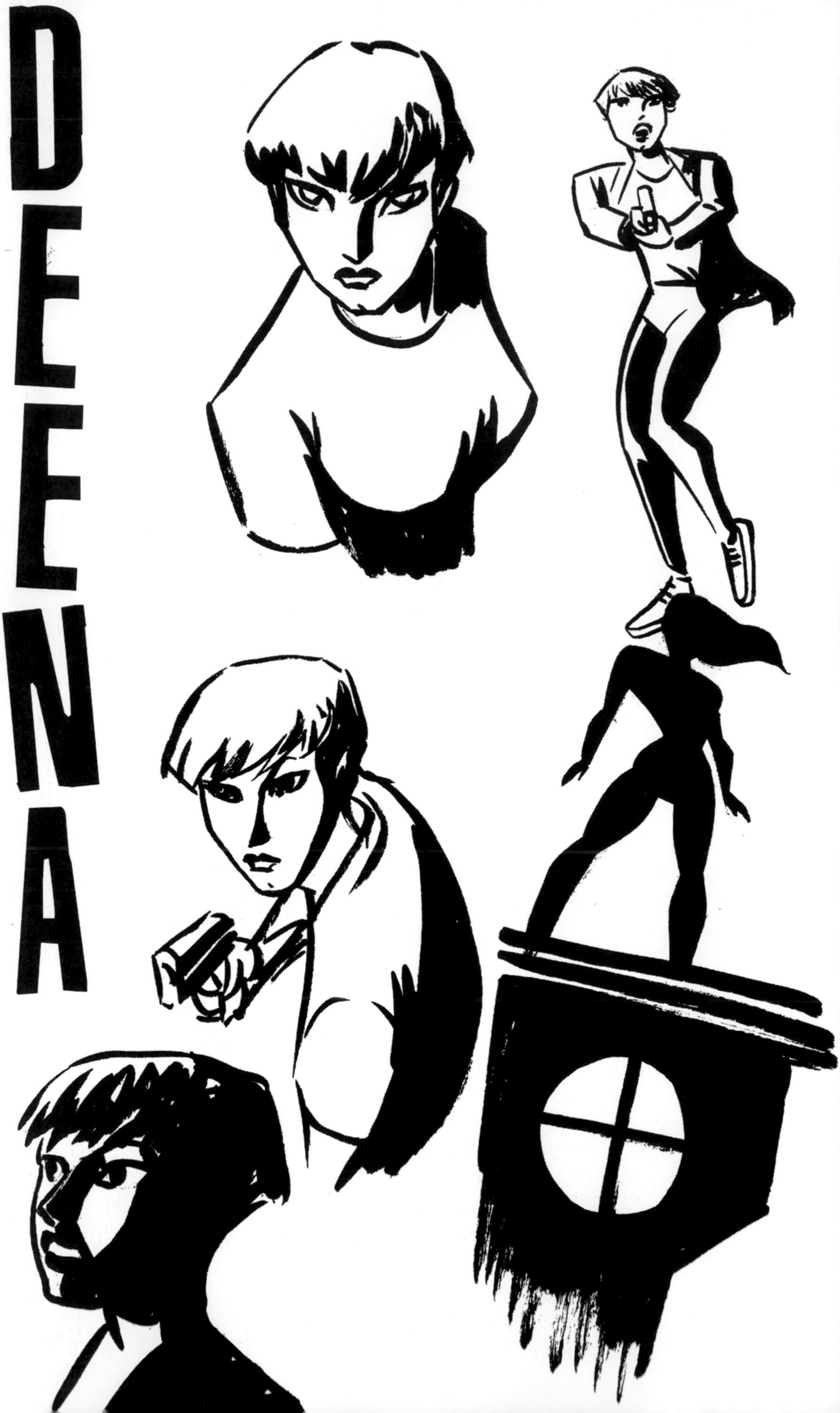
DEENA

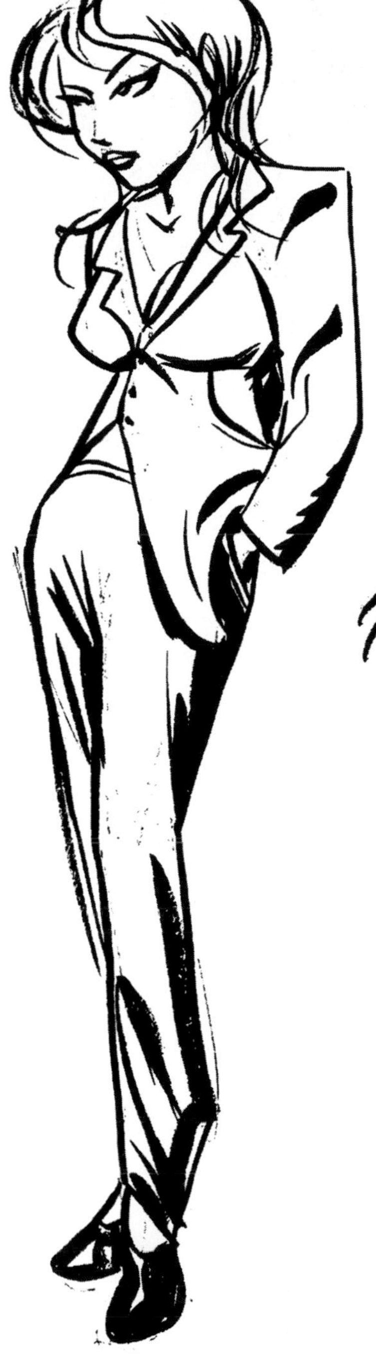

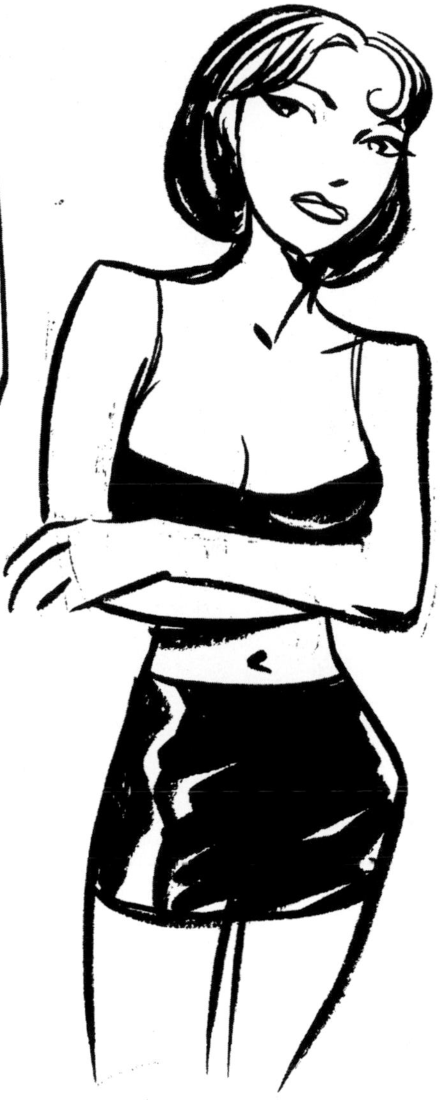

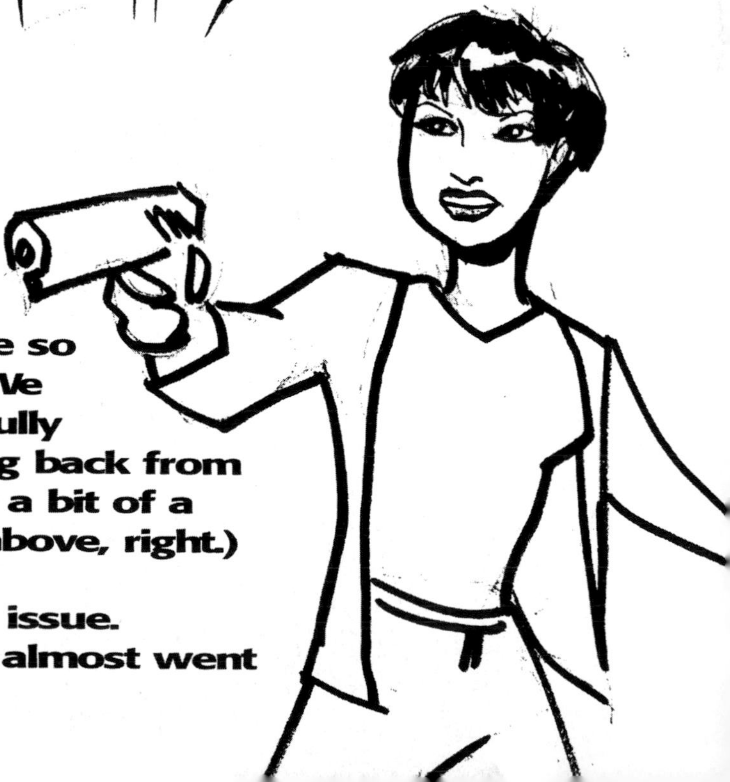

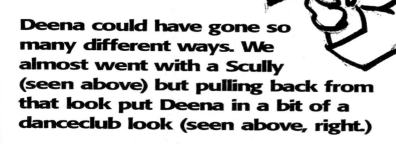

Deena could have gone so many different ways. We almost went with a Scully (seen above) but pulling back from that look put Deena in a bit of a danceclub look (seen above, right.)

Even hair color was an issue. A brunette Deena? We almost went that way. (See right.)

CALISTA

Little Calista. What age do we make Calista? We resisted the cute little kid look, but really when it came down to it...she's a cute little kid.

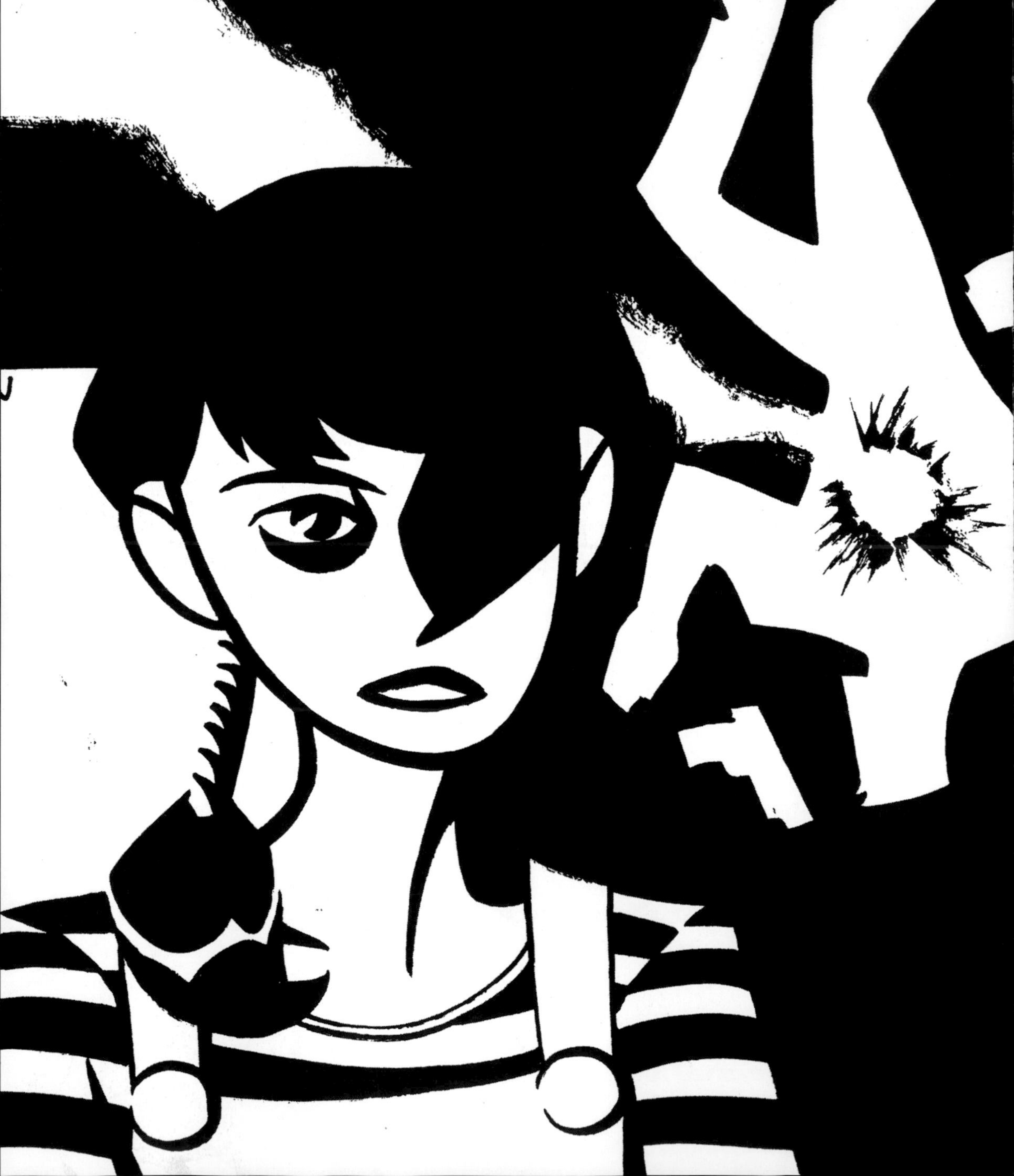

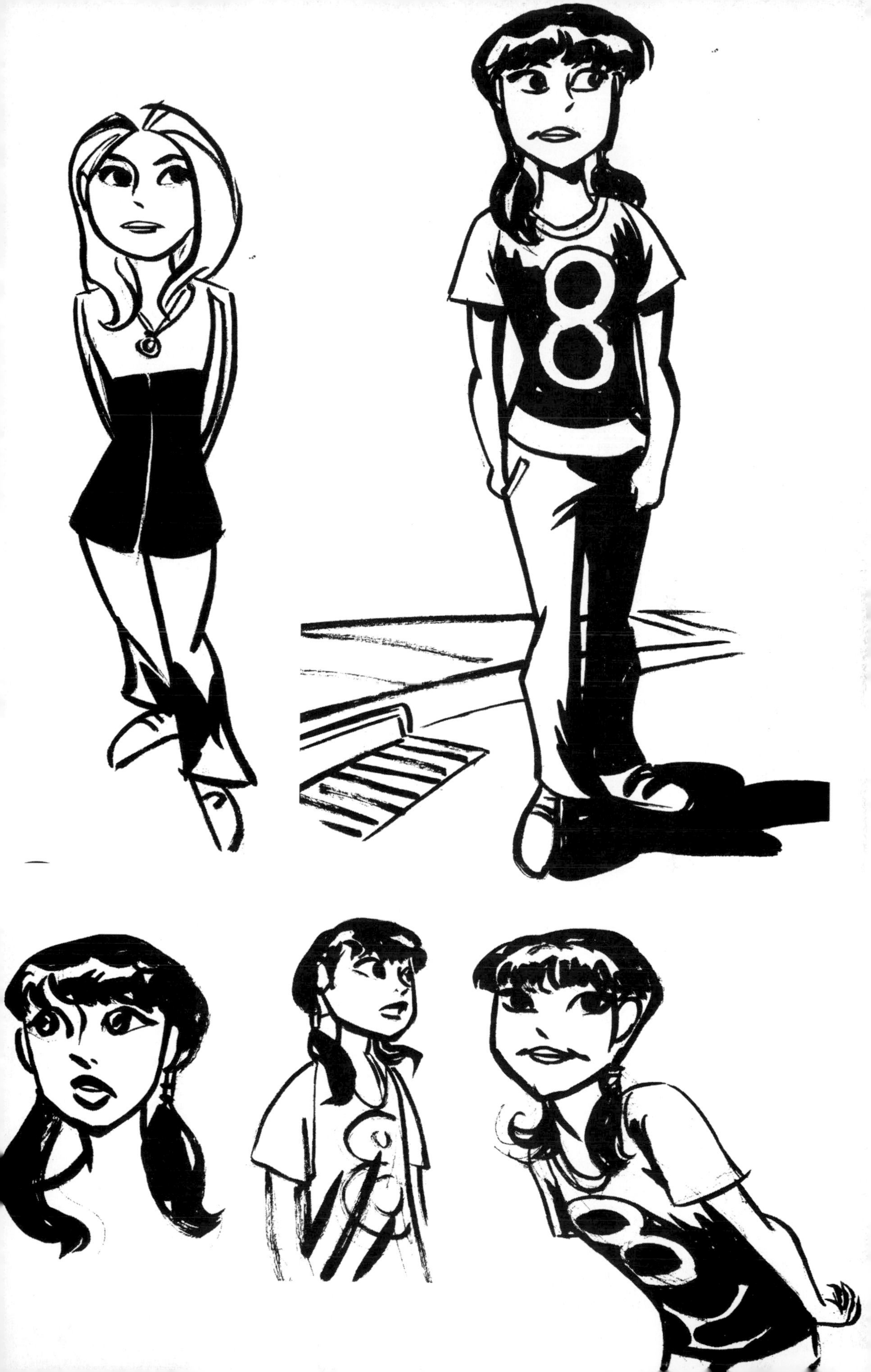
8

The sketch on the left is by far my all time favorite. I just adore it.

Retro Girl is probably the single most important character design. The design has to say everything about the character. It has to give across all of her traits and attributes. It has to tell her entire story on a subliminal level without coming off as silly or trite. And I think these do.

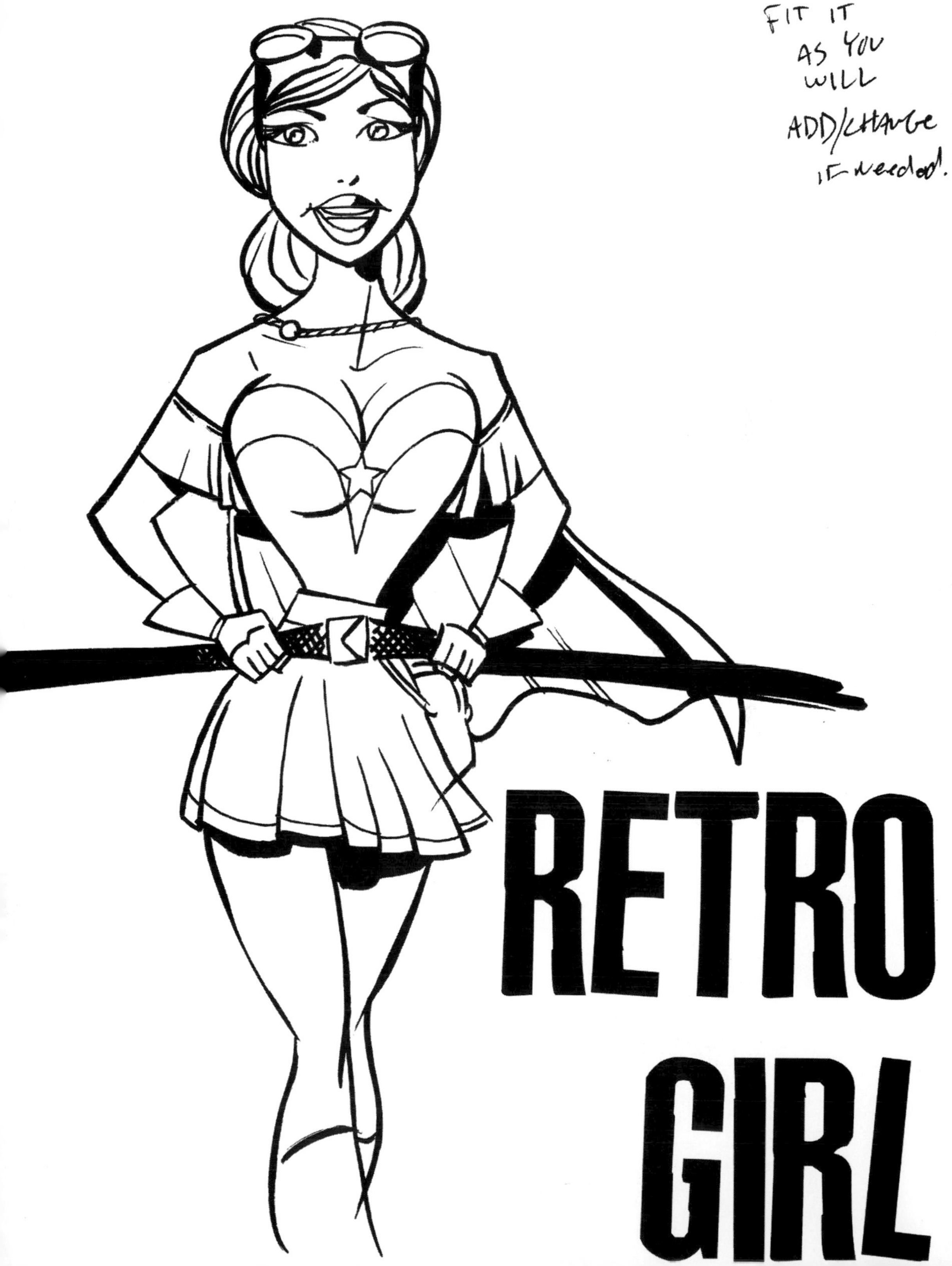
FIT IT AS YOU WILL
ADD/CHANGE IF needed!
RETRO GIRL

RETRO - FIRST TRY -

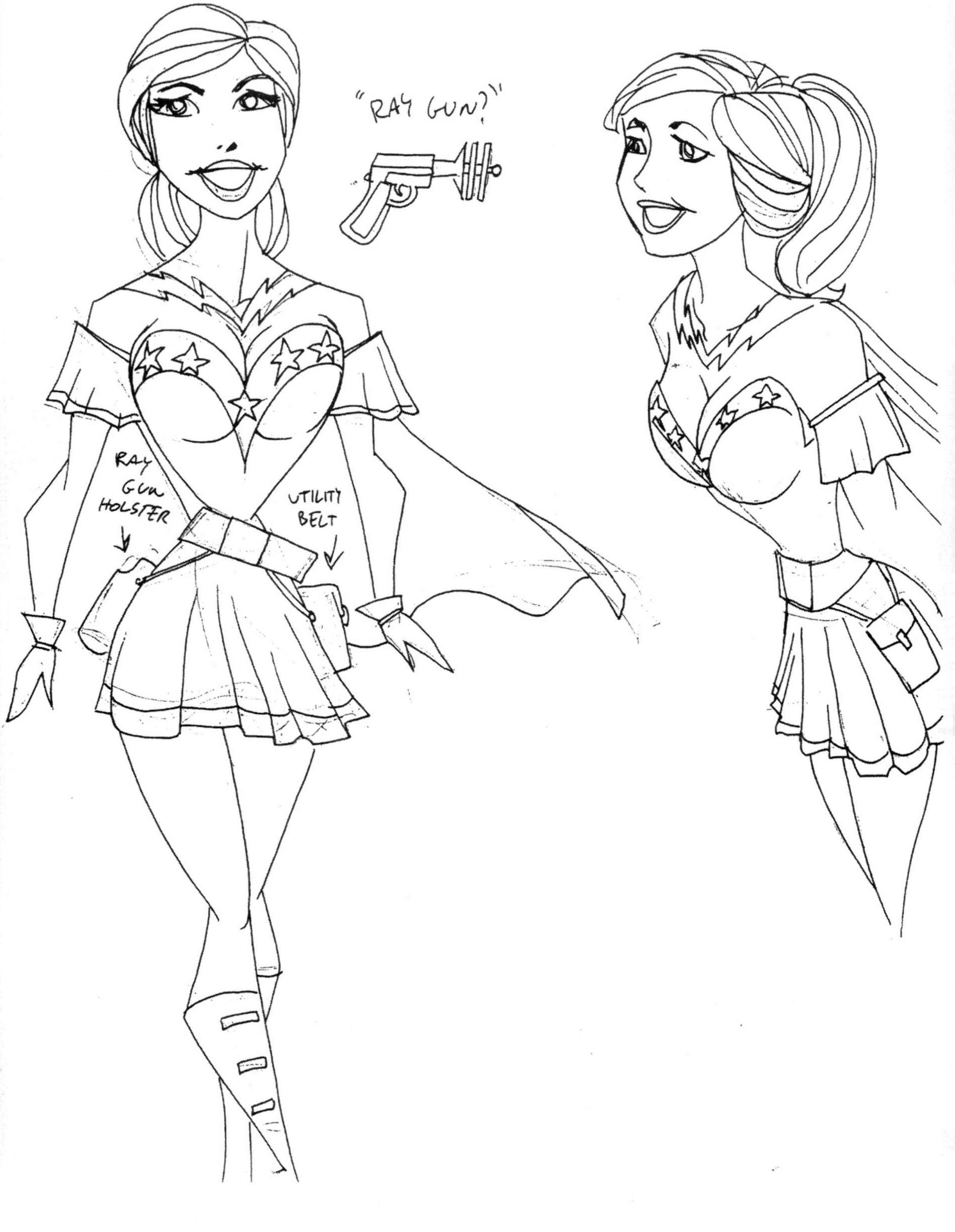

"RAY GUN?"
RAY GUN HOLSTER
UTILITY BELT

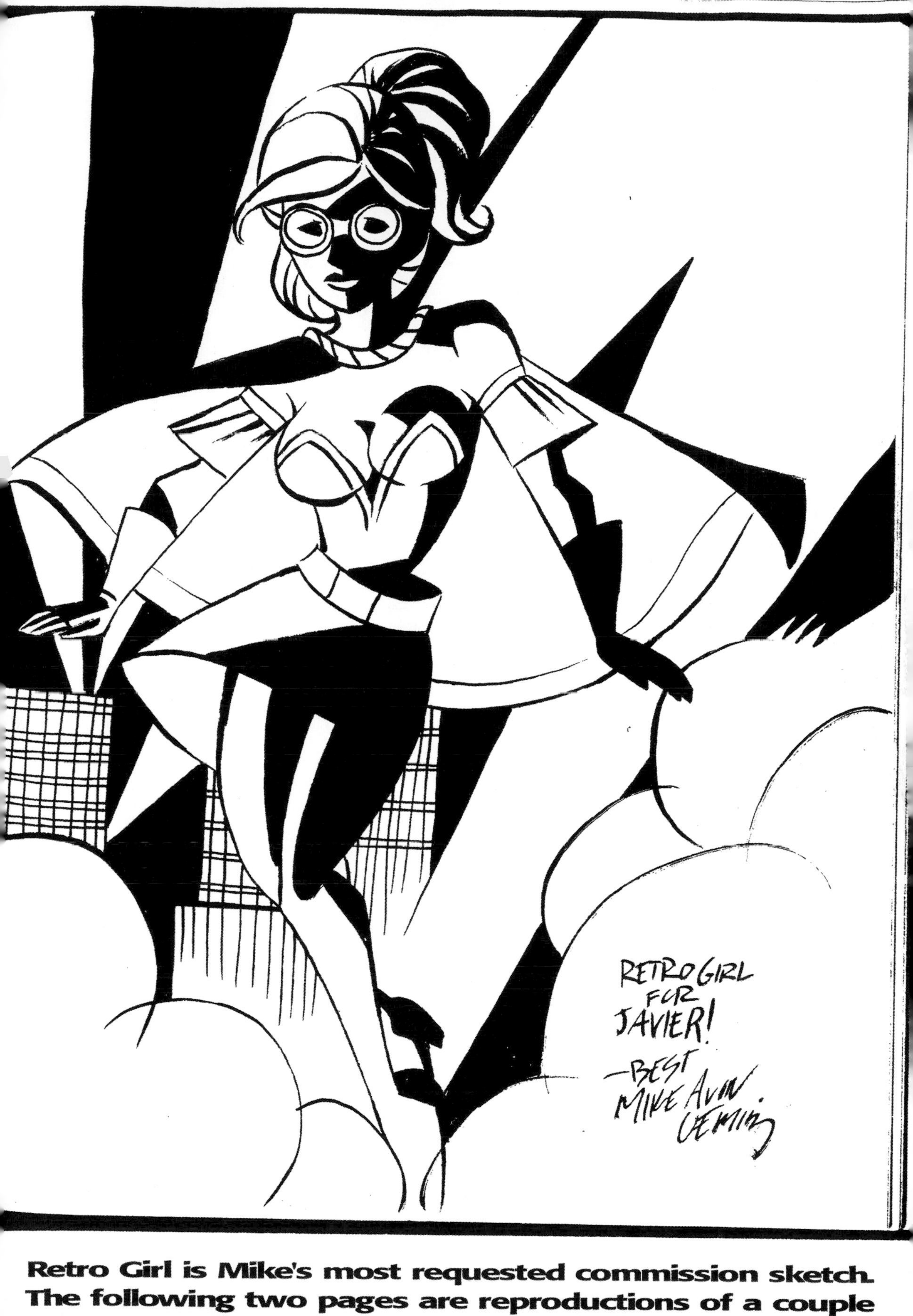
RETRO GIRL
FOR
JAVIER!
—BEST
MIKE AVON
OEMING

Retro Girl is Mike's most requested commission sketch. The following two pages are reproductions of a couple of my favorite pieces that Mike has done for a couple of lucky readers of the monthly book.

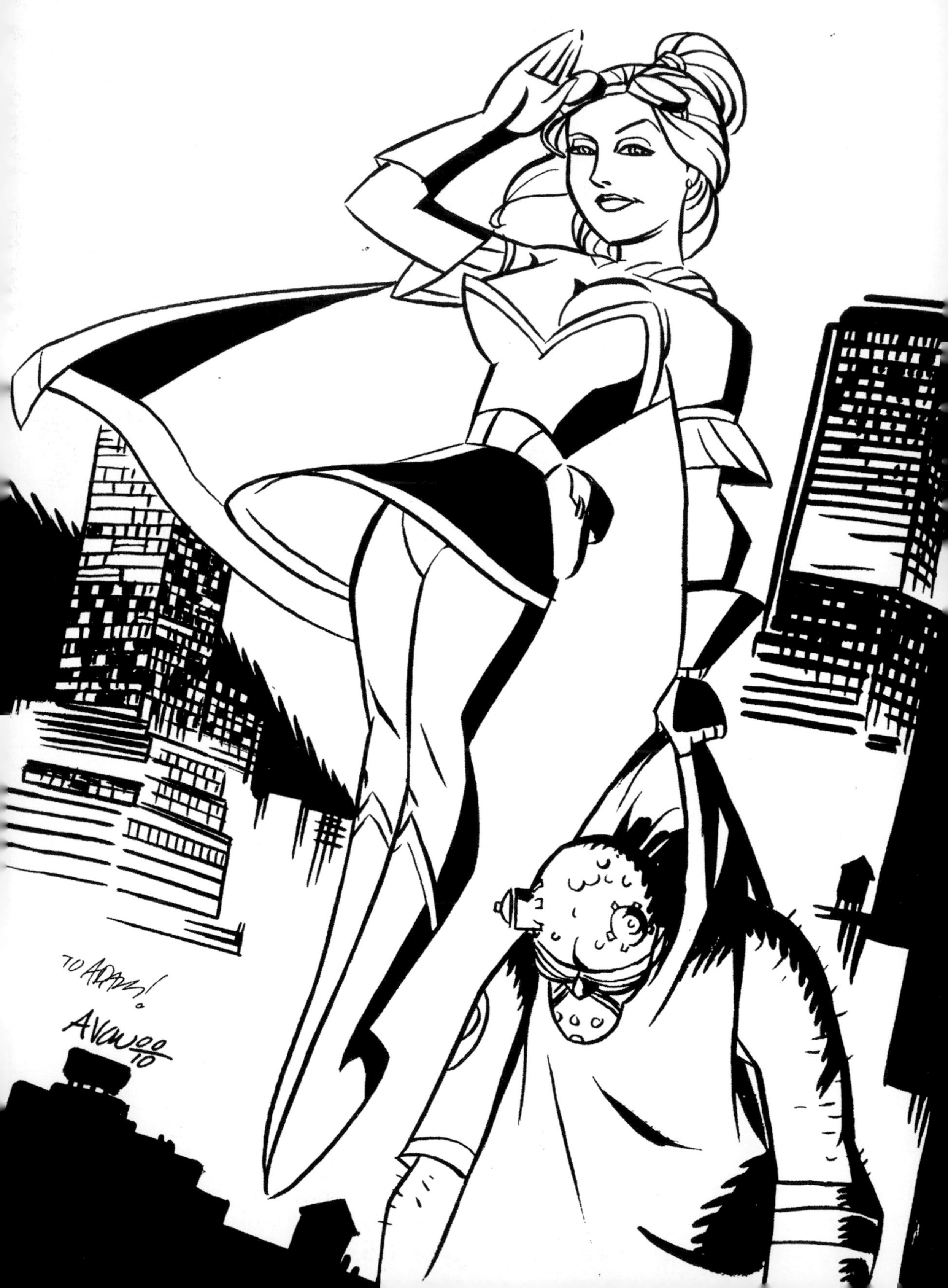

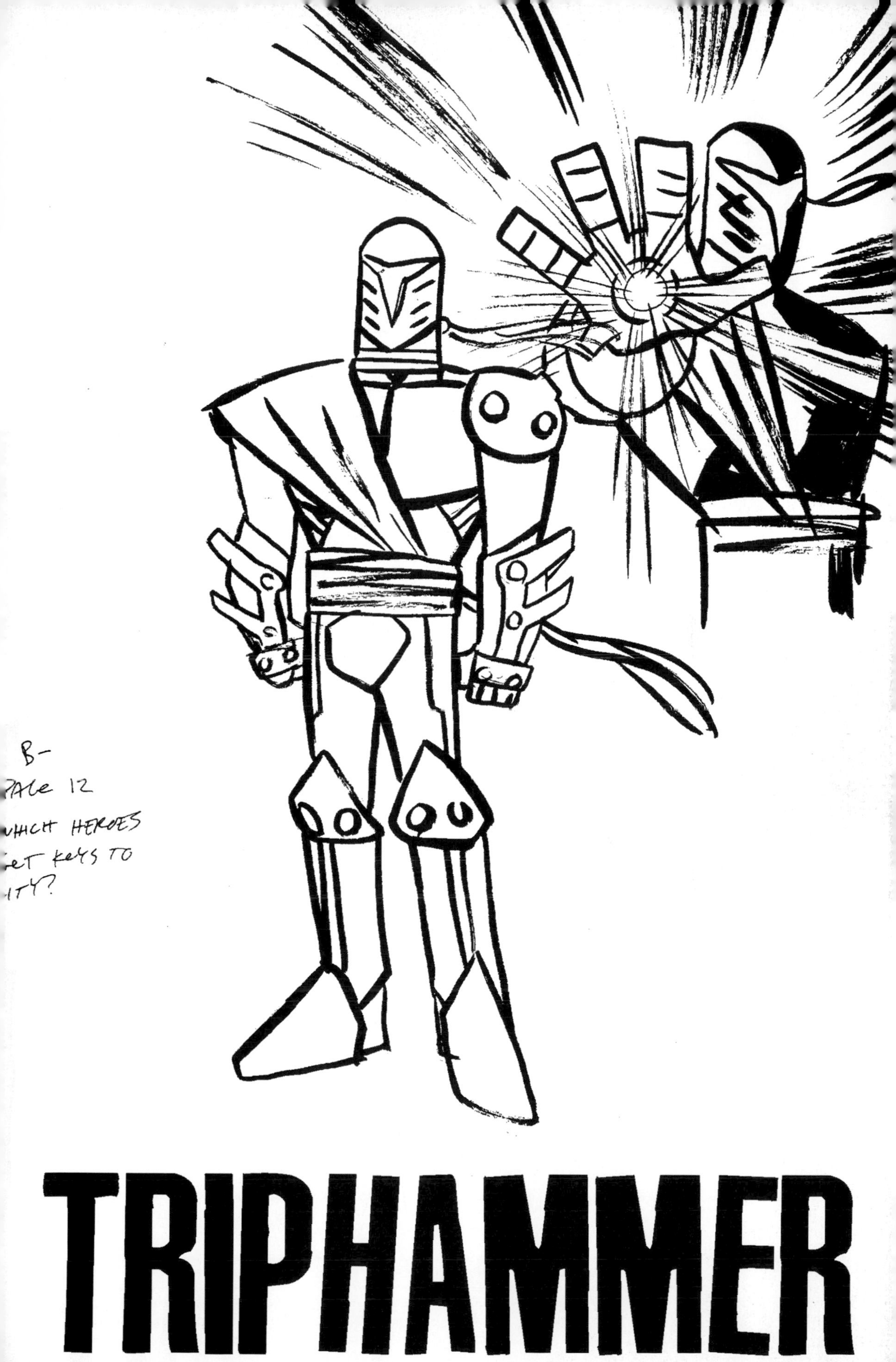

B-
PAGE 12
WHICH HEROES
GET KEYS TO
CITY?

TRIPHAMMER

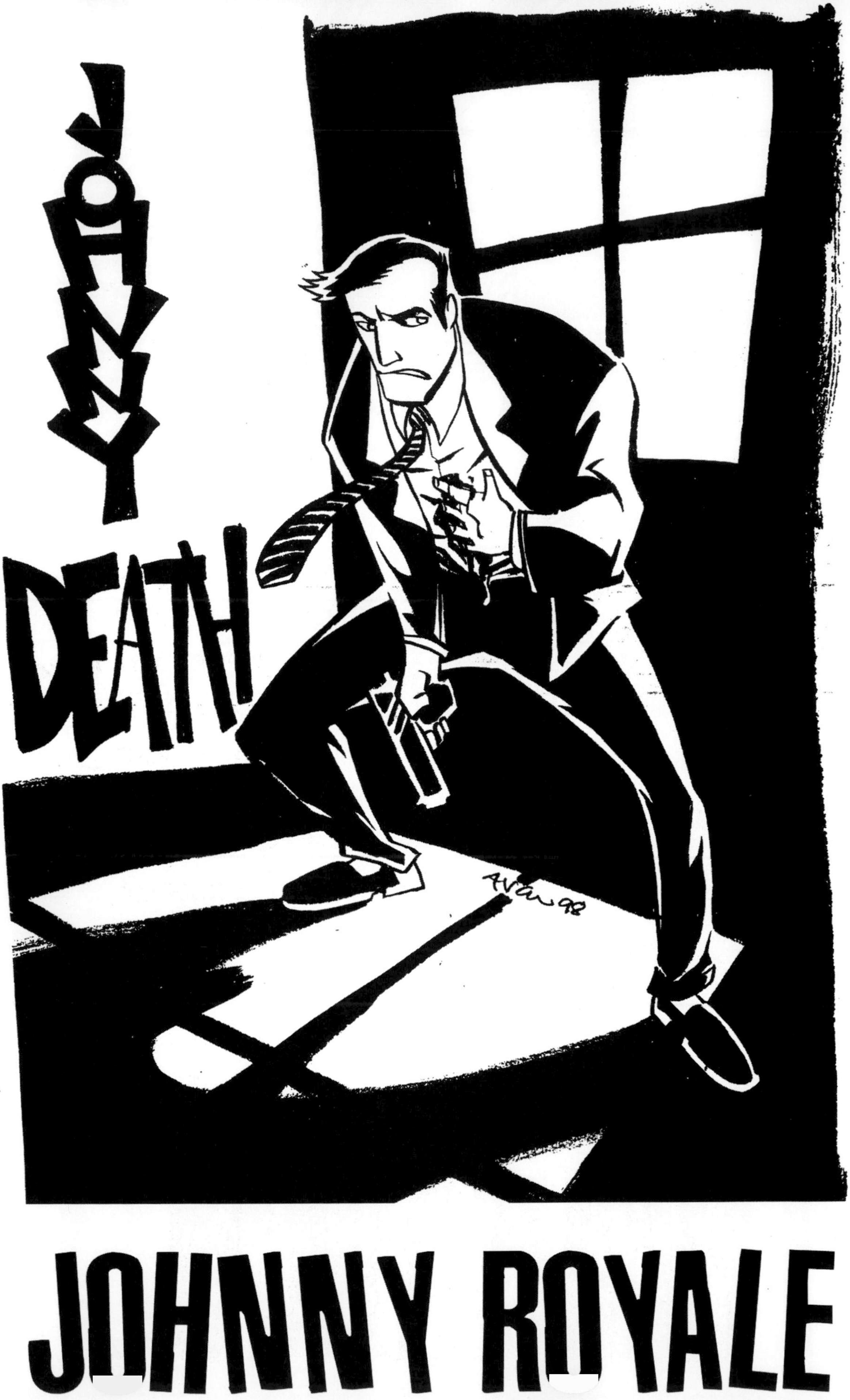
JOHNNY
DEATH
AVON 98

JOHNNY ROYALE

A.

B.

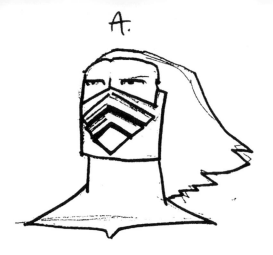

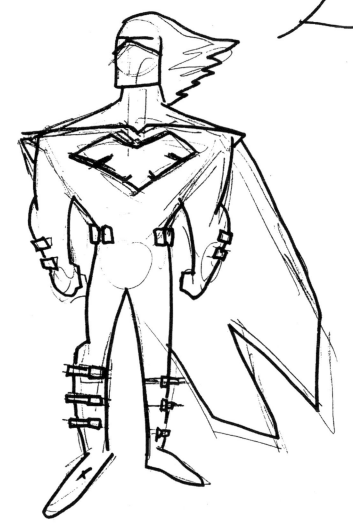

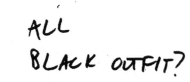

ALL
BLACK OUTFIT?

- IM SURE YOU HAVE
HIS WHOLE "SCHTICK"
DOWN - BUT I
HAVE SOME IDEAS
IF YOUR NOT
SETTLED.

OTHER HEROES/VILLAINS
NEED TO BE SETTLED
TOO

DIAMOND

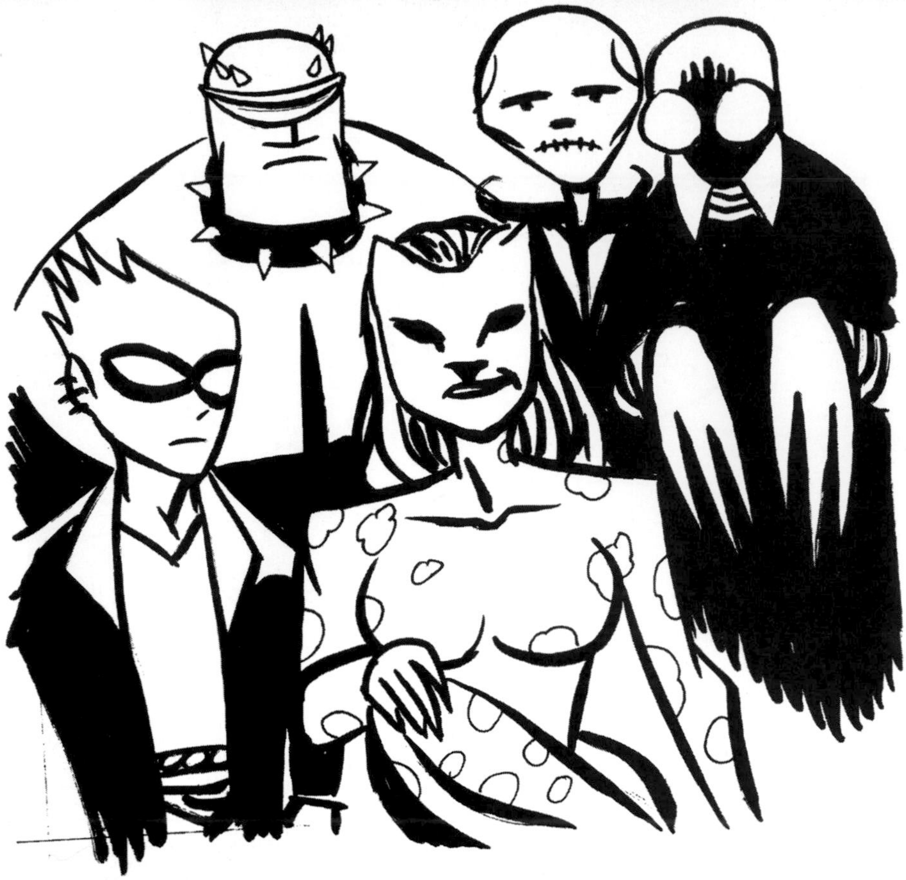

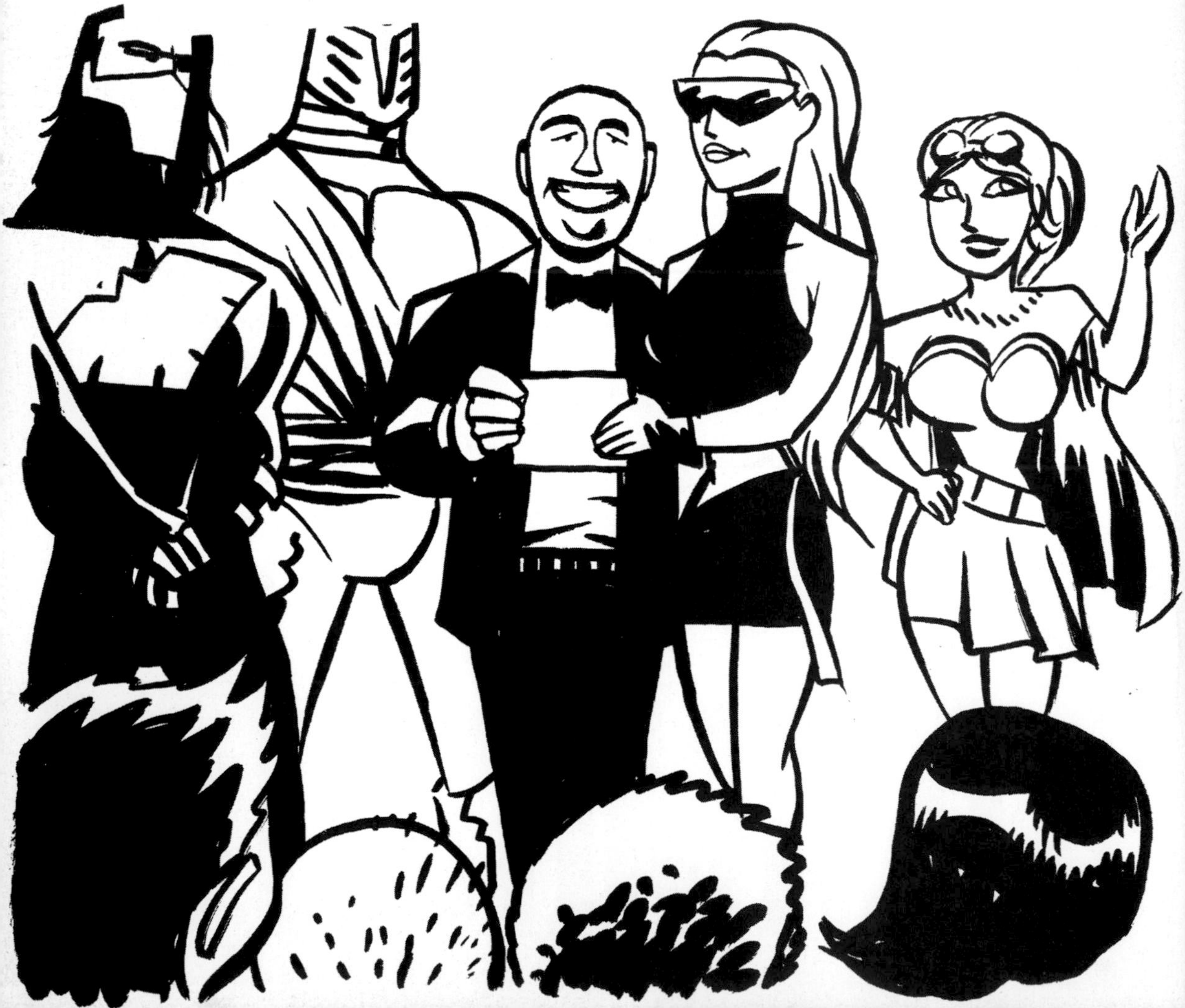

POWERS
THE SKETCHBOOK

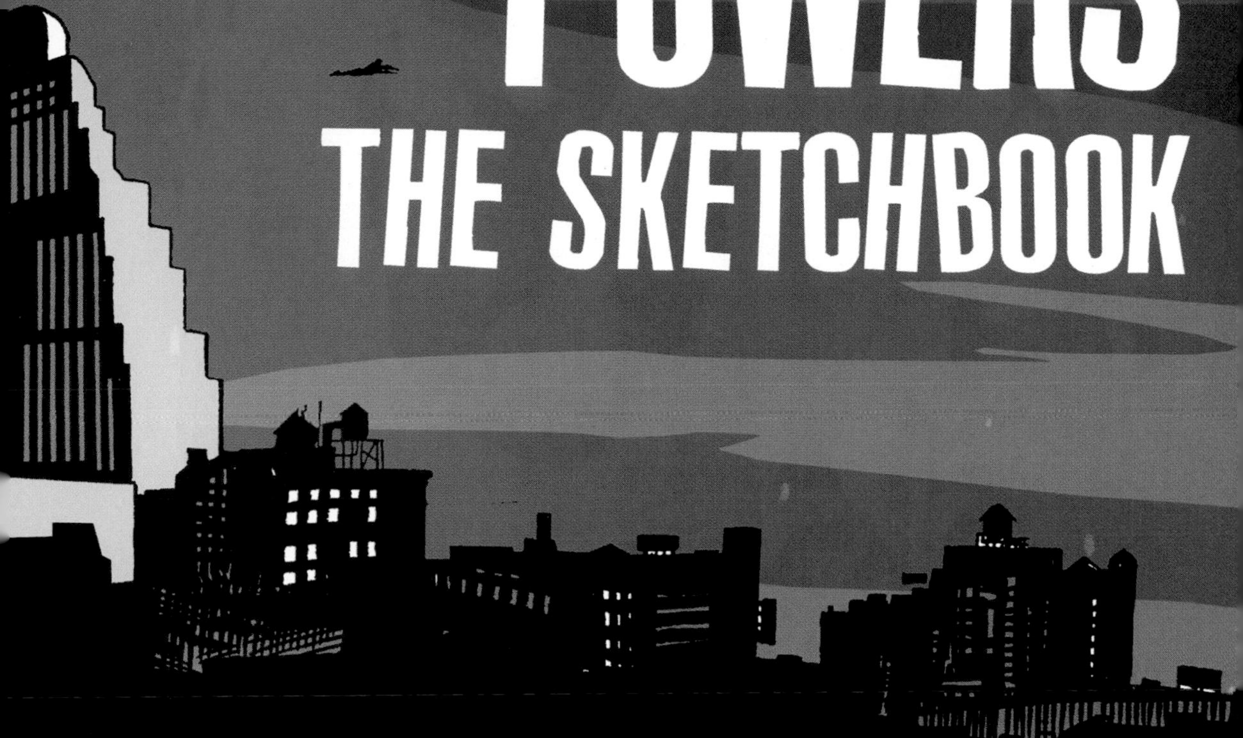

THE WORLD OF POWERS

They say that one of the rules of film noir is that the city itself should be considered a lead character in the story. The look, the smells, the taste should all be distinct. The following drawings were the direct result on our conversations on this subject.

I made Mike watch the amazing documentary "Visions of Light." This is an amazing documentary made by the American Cinematographers Institute about the art of lighting in film. In my opinion, it is is also a great film on the making of comic books.

Using the theories in that documentary, and other sources, these images started just pouring out of Mike.

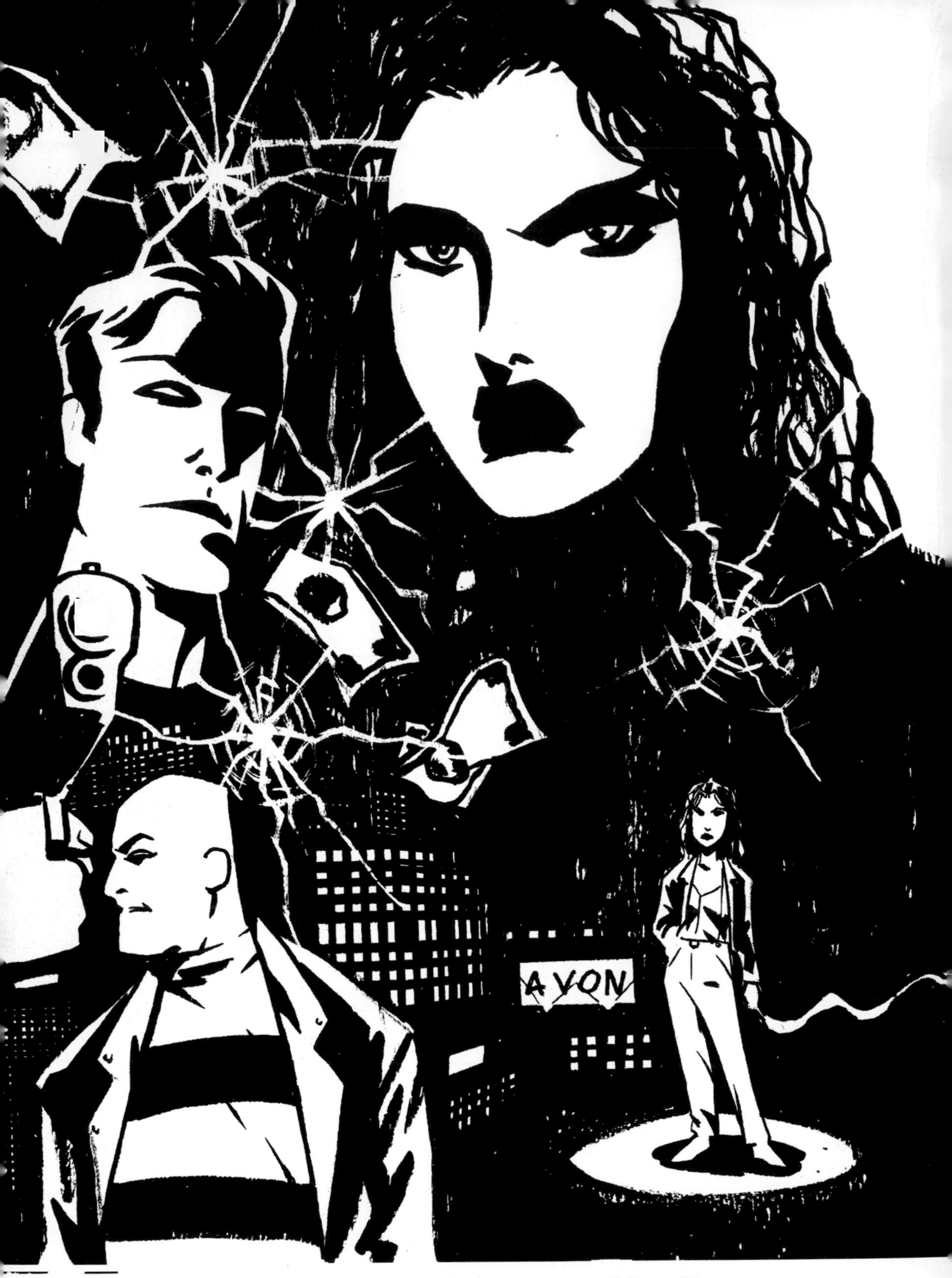
AVON

The image that started it all.

Years ago, Mike, did a pin up of my comic book series Jinx (above) and one of David Mack's comic book series Kabuki in a style he was working with... just for fun. It is now referred to as his Powers' style. This single image inspired everything in this book.

Even before there was a script, Mike started doing practice pages so he could get a handle on how this style would feel "in use."

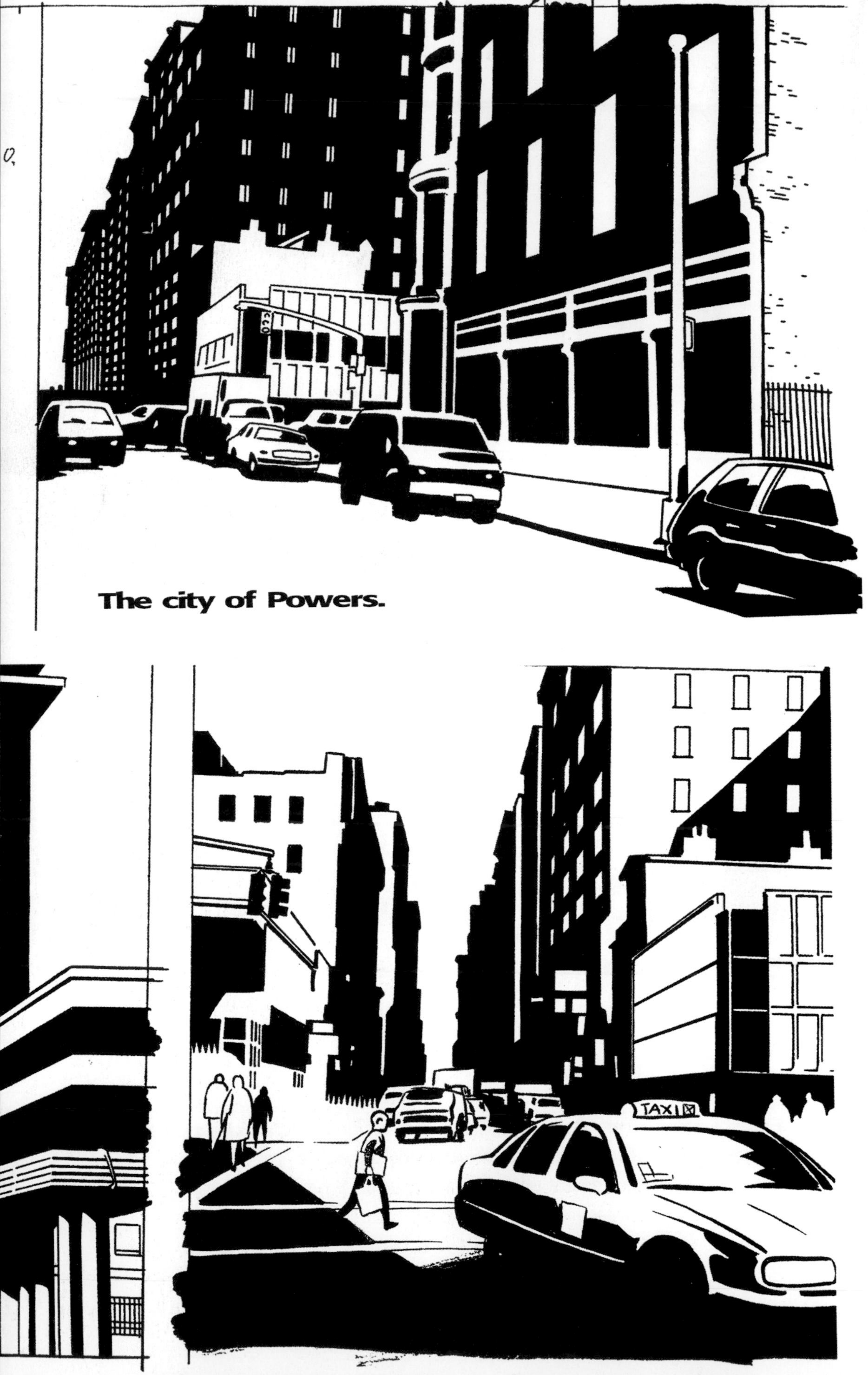
The city of Powers.
TAXI

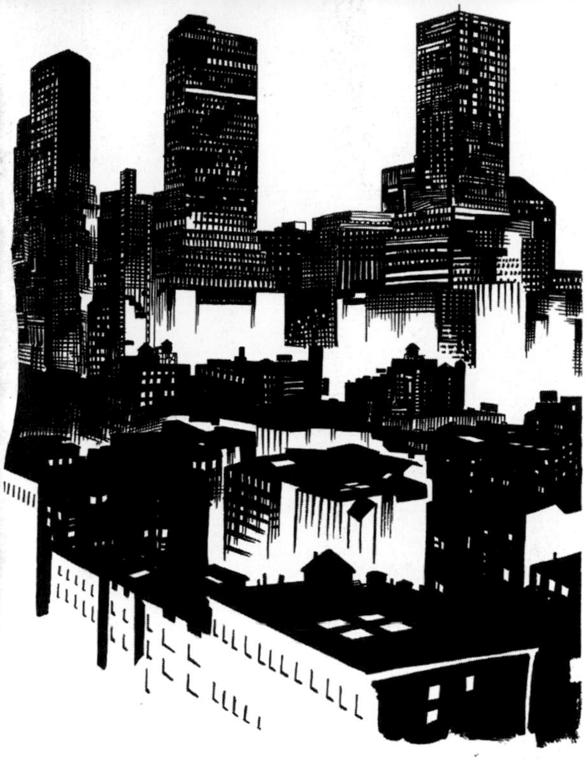

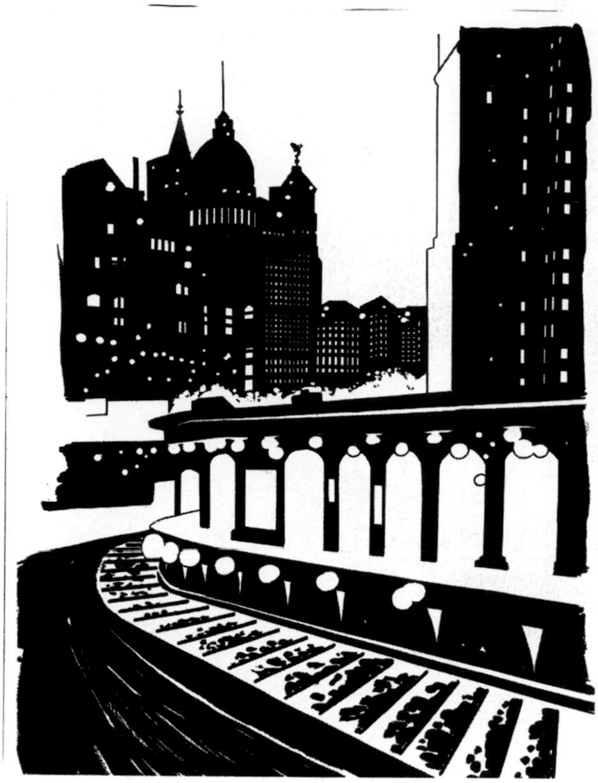

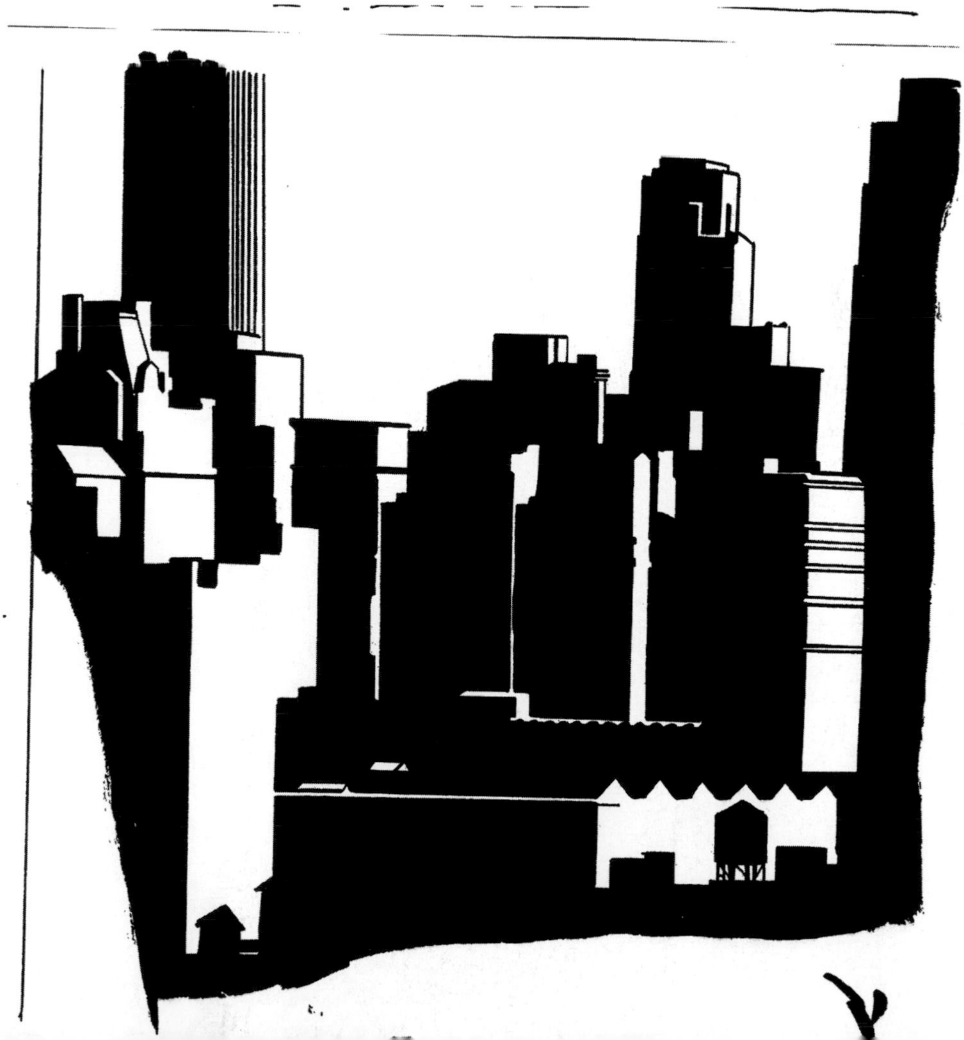

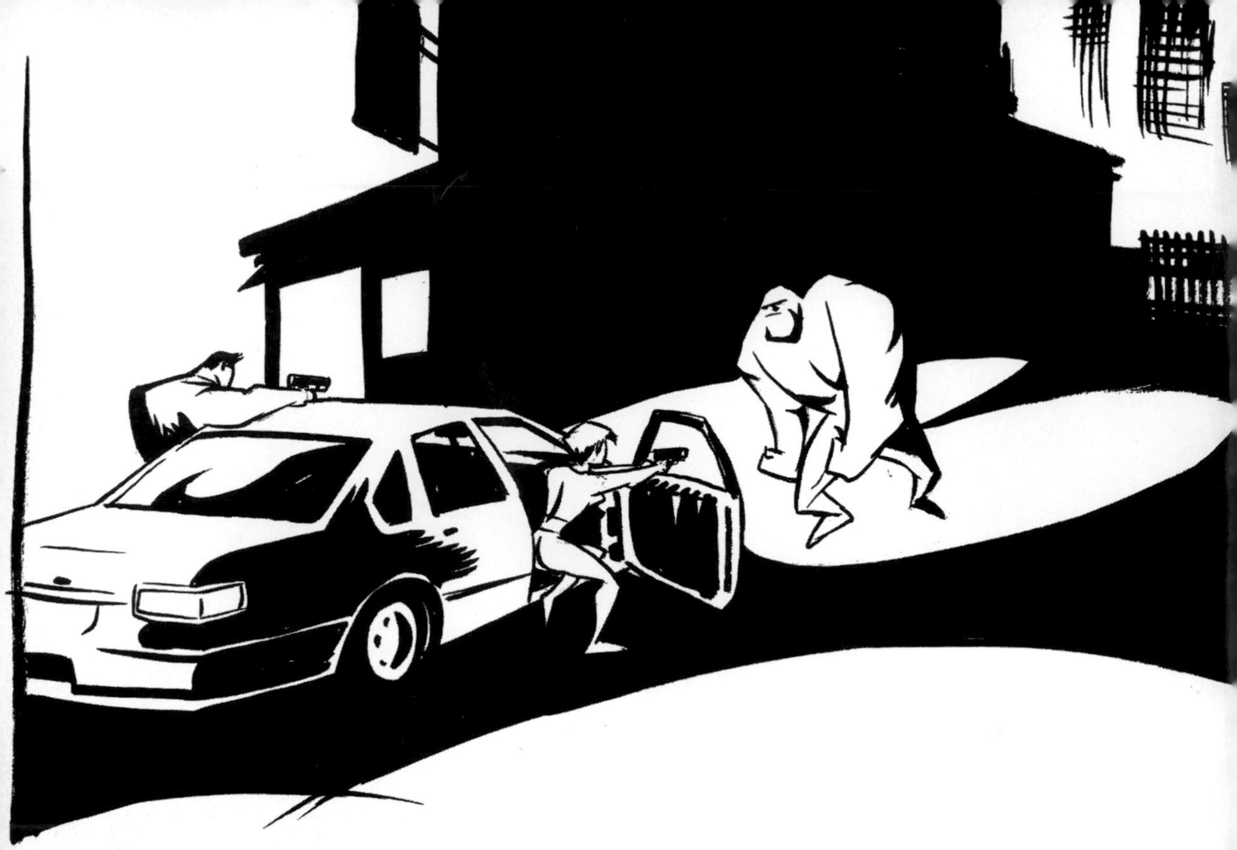

One of the key elements to the visuals of Powers is the juxtaposition of noir and superhero images. These are some of the ideas Mike was toying with while thinking about this juxtaposition.

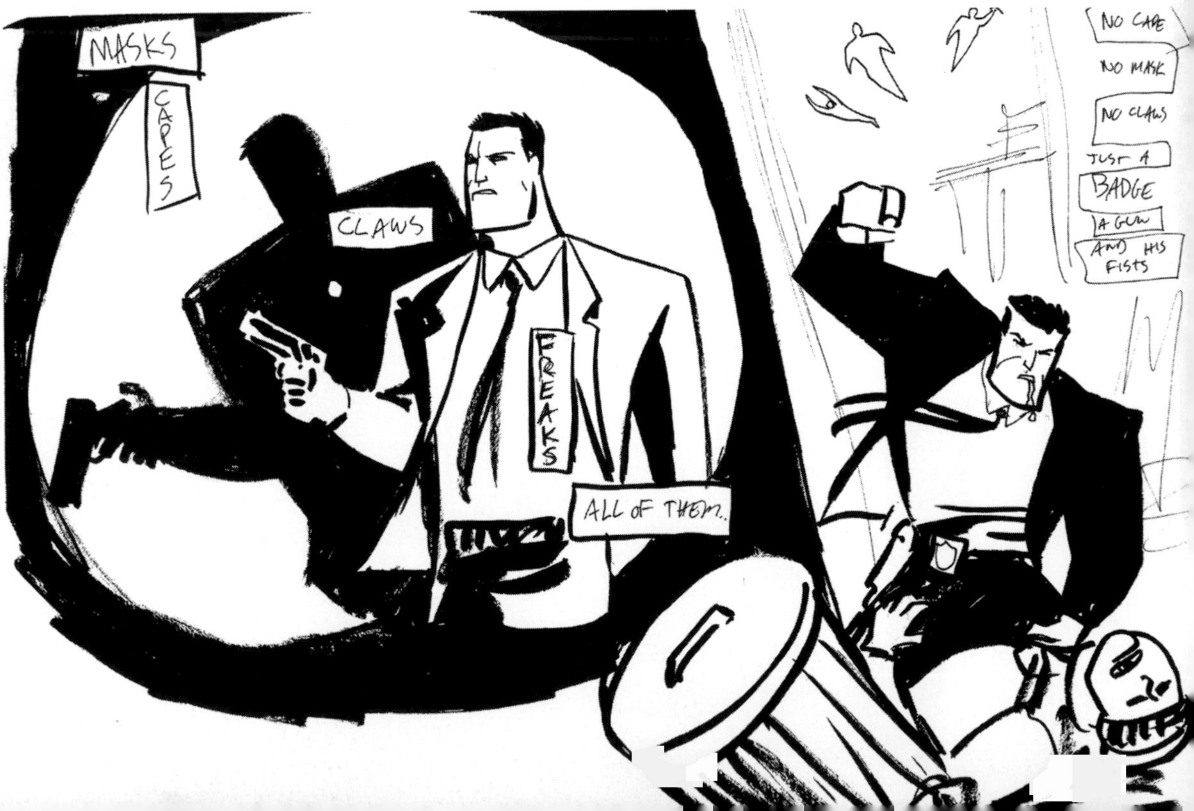
MASKS
CAPES
CLAWS
FREAKS
ALL OF THEM..
NO CAPE
NO MASK
NO CLAWS
JUST A
BADGE
A GUN
AND HIS FISTS

POWERS COVER GALLERY

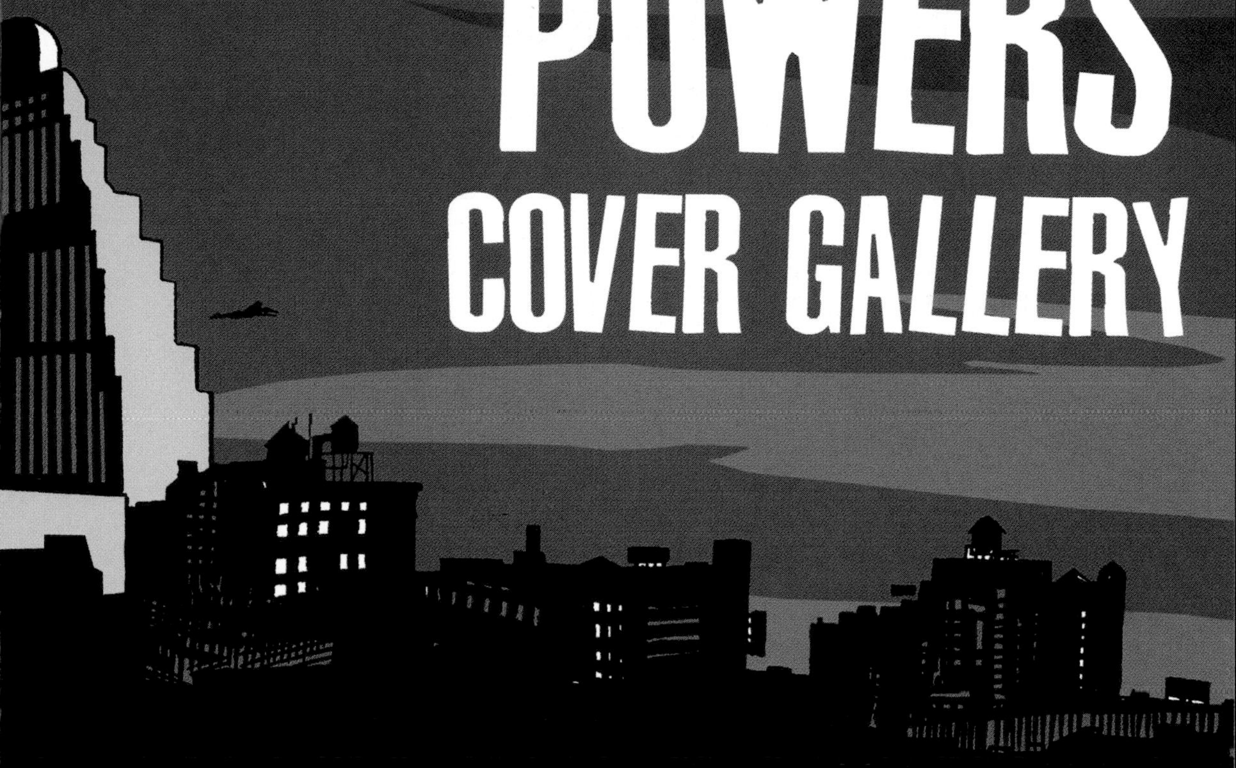

This section is a comprehensive look at the creation of the covers for the monthly series.

We have included original sketch work or ink work that Mike sent for discussion before he committed to the final art. The colors on these covers were done by yours truly for completely selfish purposes. I just wanted to be part of the process.

Also included here are a smattering of unused covers and promotional images. Among these rejects are some of our favorites, but we just did not feel they fit the issue at hand.

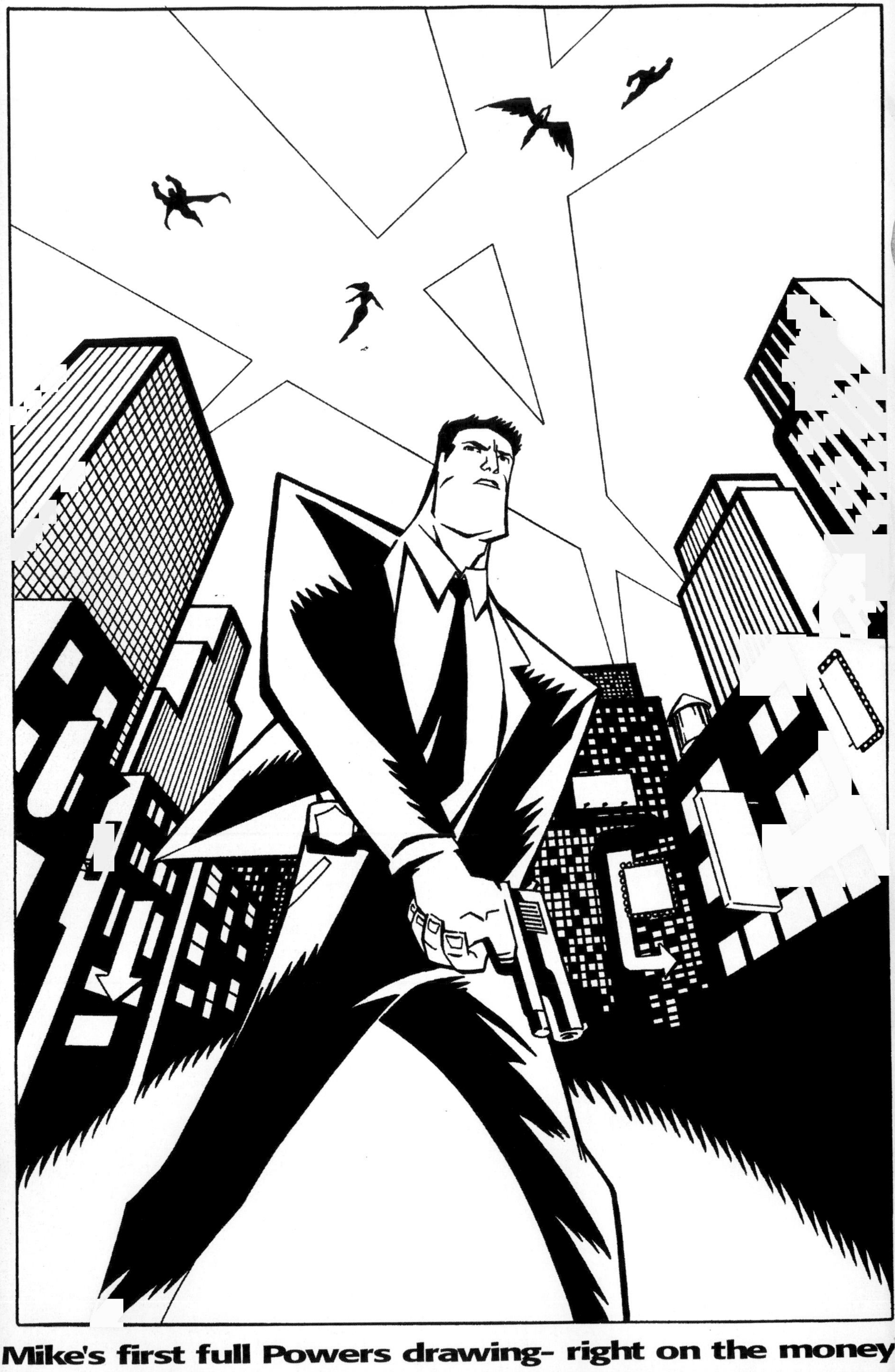

Mike's first full Powers drawing- right on the money.

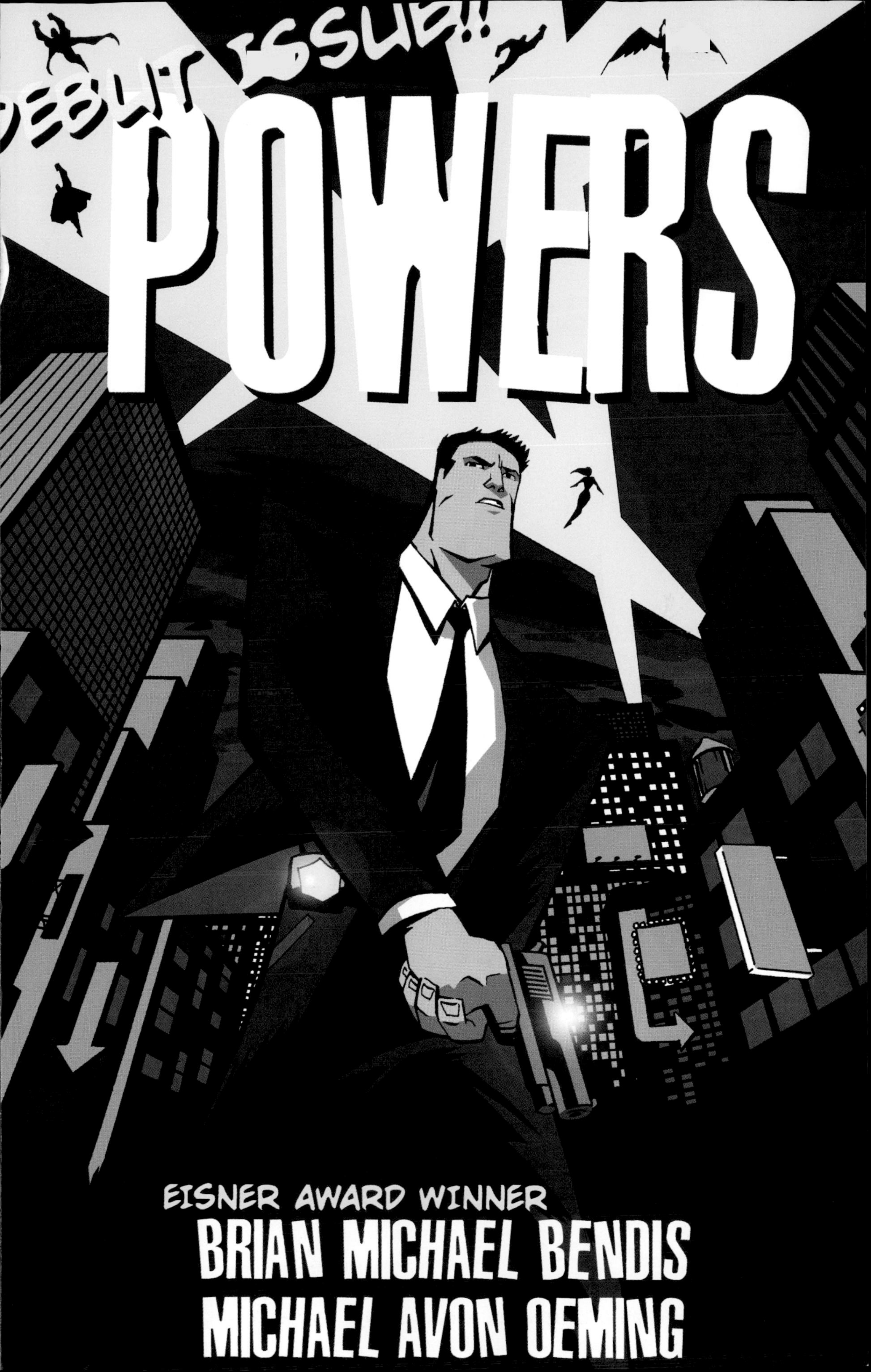
DEBUT ISSUE!!
POWERS
EISNER AWARD WINNER
BRIAN MICHAEL BENDIS
MICHAEL AVON OEMING

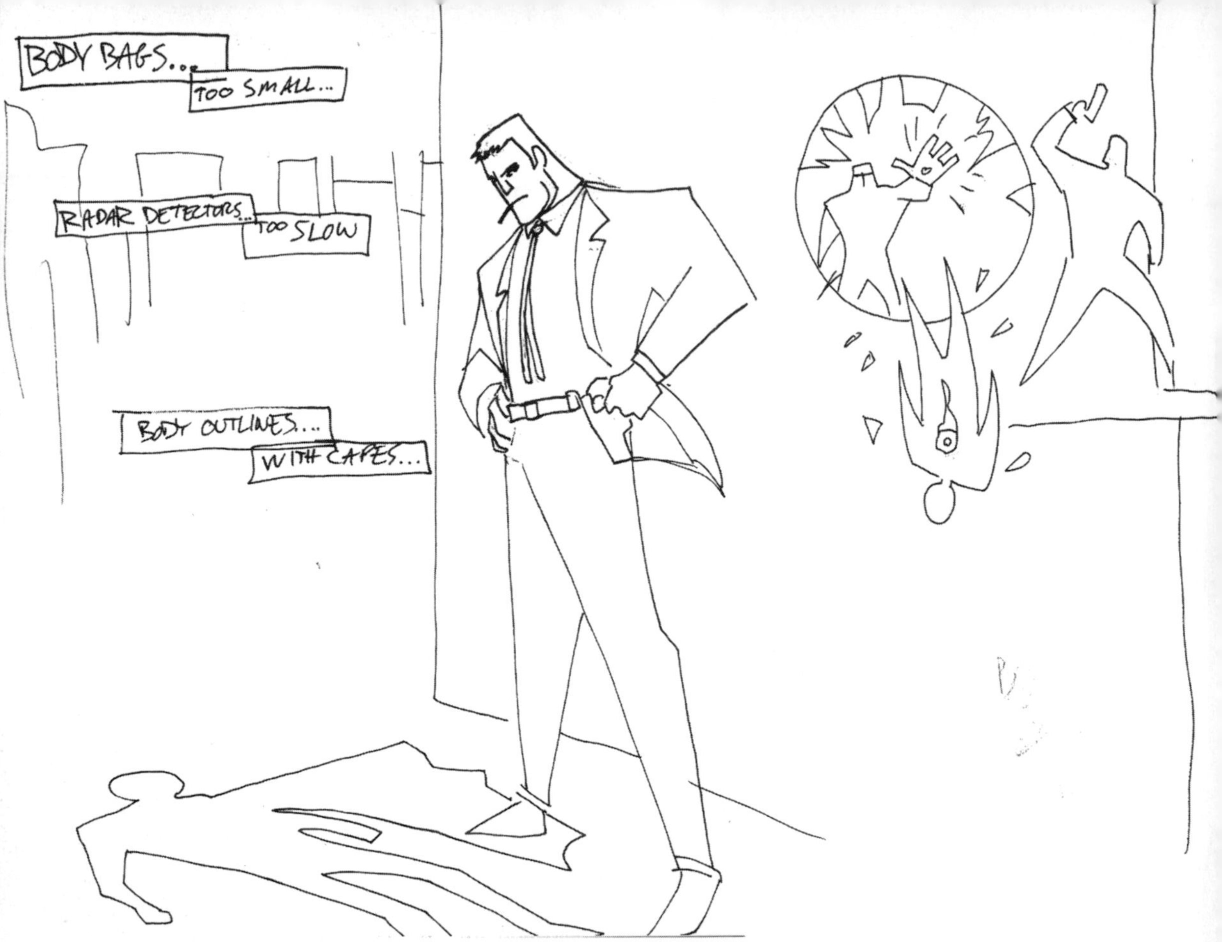
BODY BAGS...
TOO SMALL...
RADAR DETECTORS...
TOO SLOW
BODY OUTLINES...
WITH CAPES...

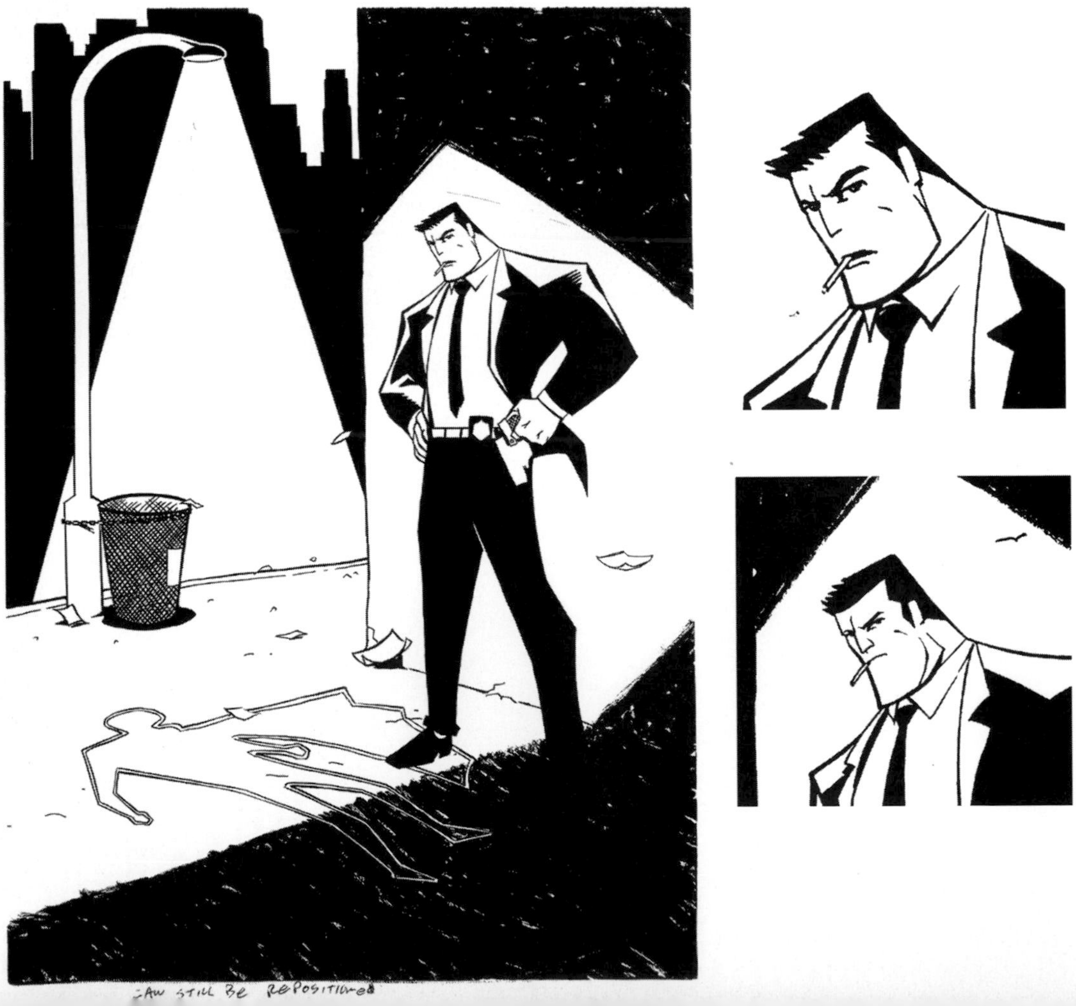
CAN STILL BE REPOSITIONED

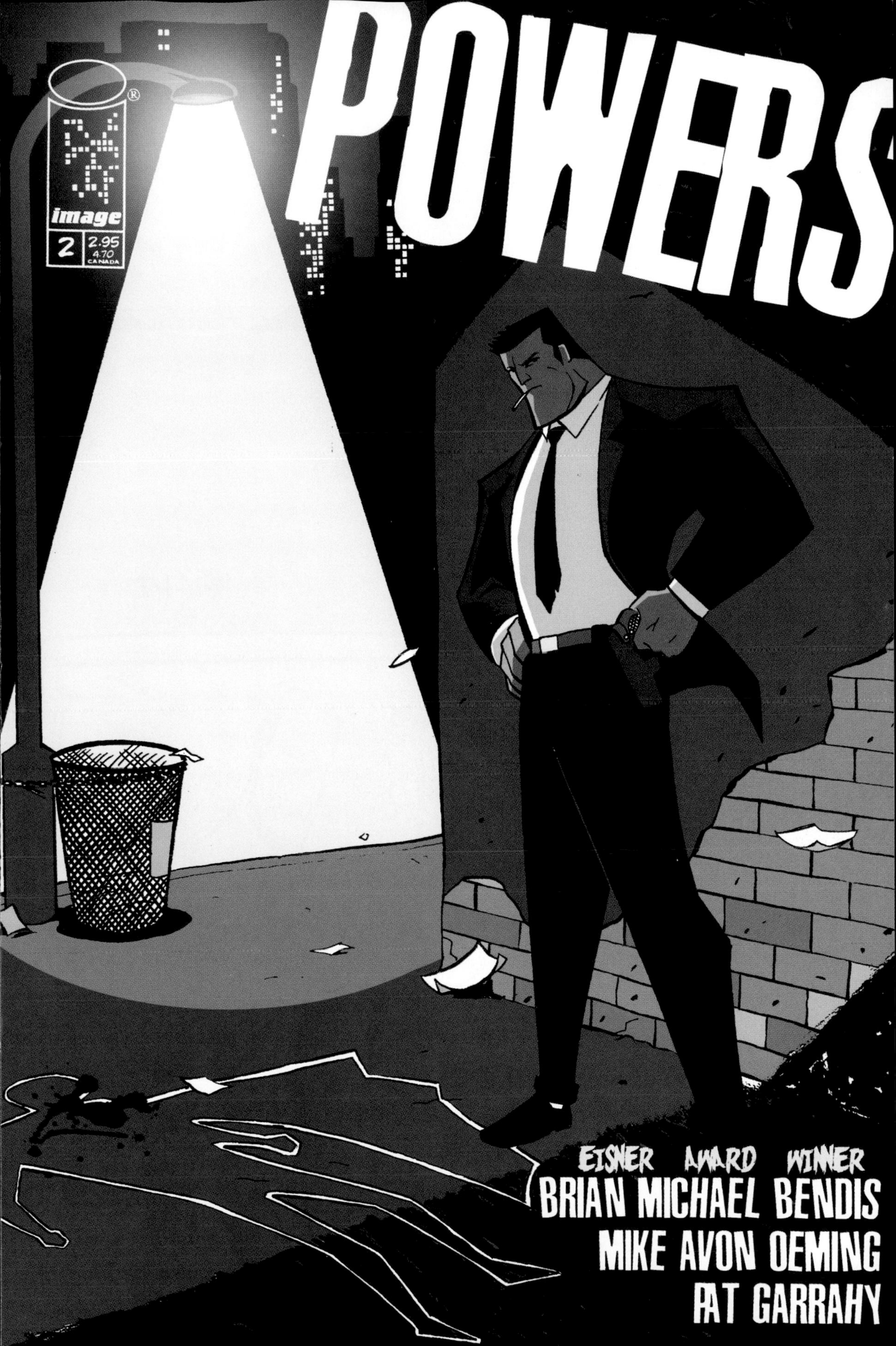
image
2
2.95
4.70 CANADA
POWERS
EISNER AWARD WINNER
BRIAN MICHAEL BENDIS
MIKE AVON OEMING
PAT GARRAHY

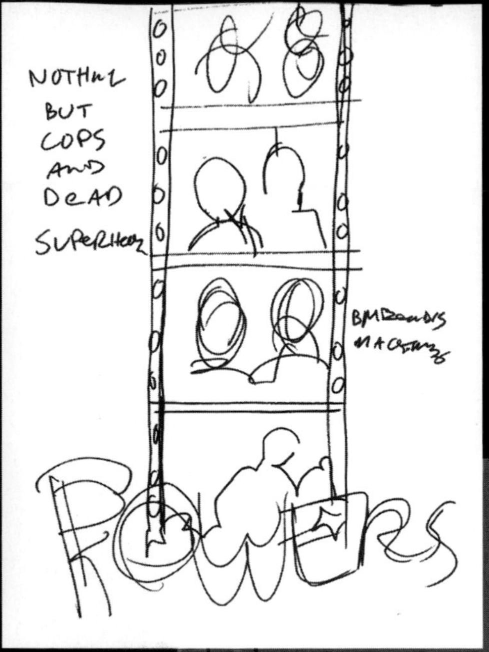
NOTHIN' BUT COPS AND DEAD SUPERHEROES
POWERS

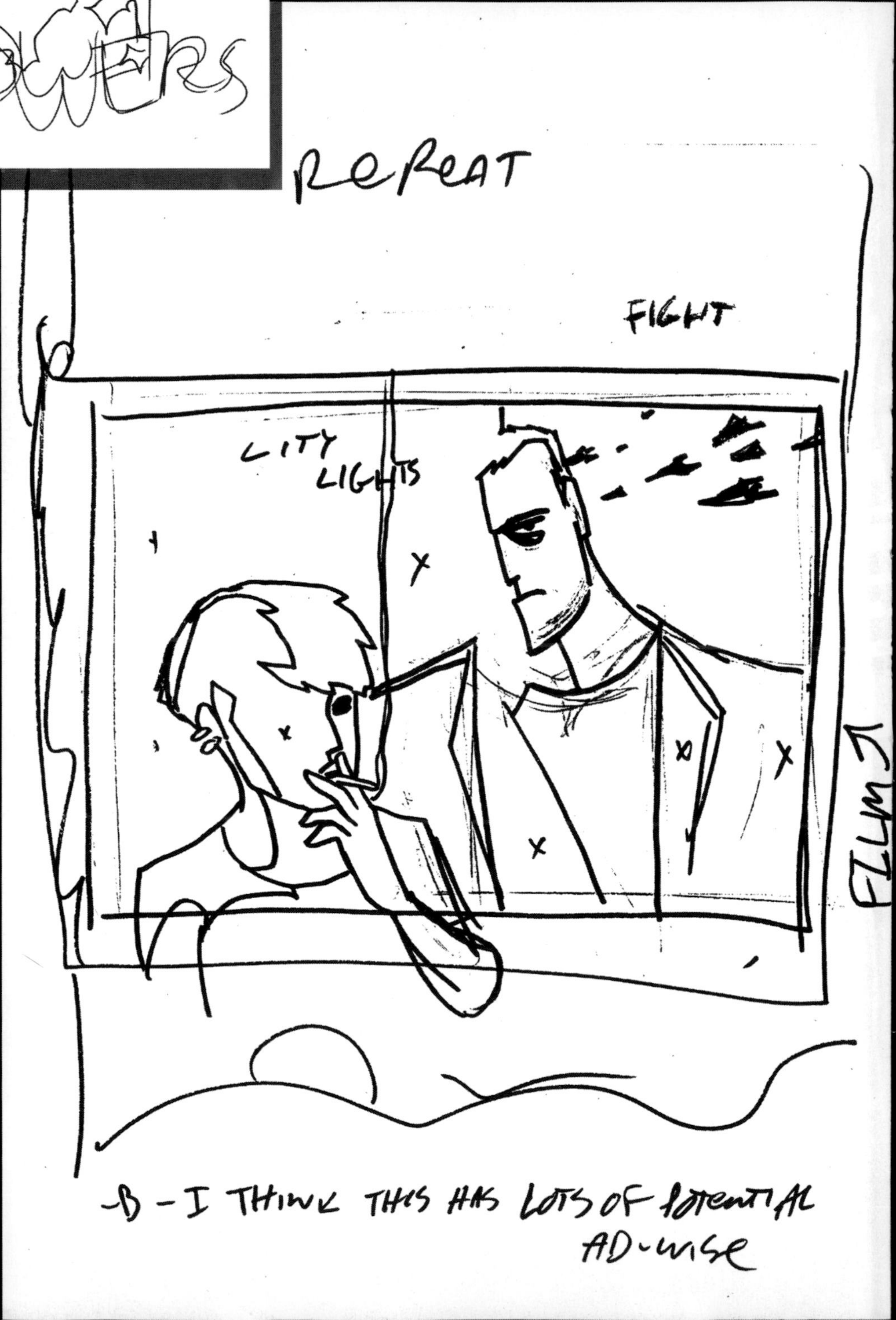
REPEAT
FIGHT
CITY LIGHTS
FILM
-B- I THINK THIS HAS LOTS OF POTENTIAL AD-WISE

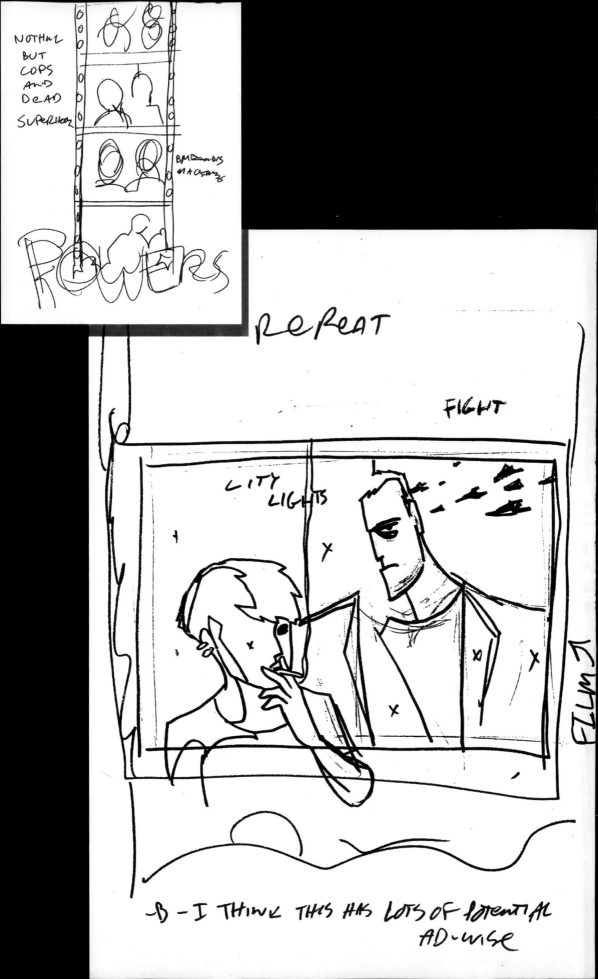

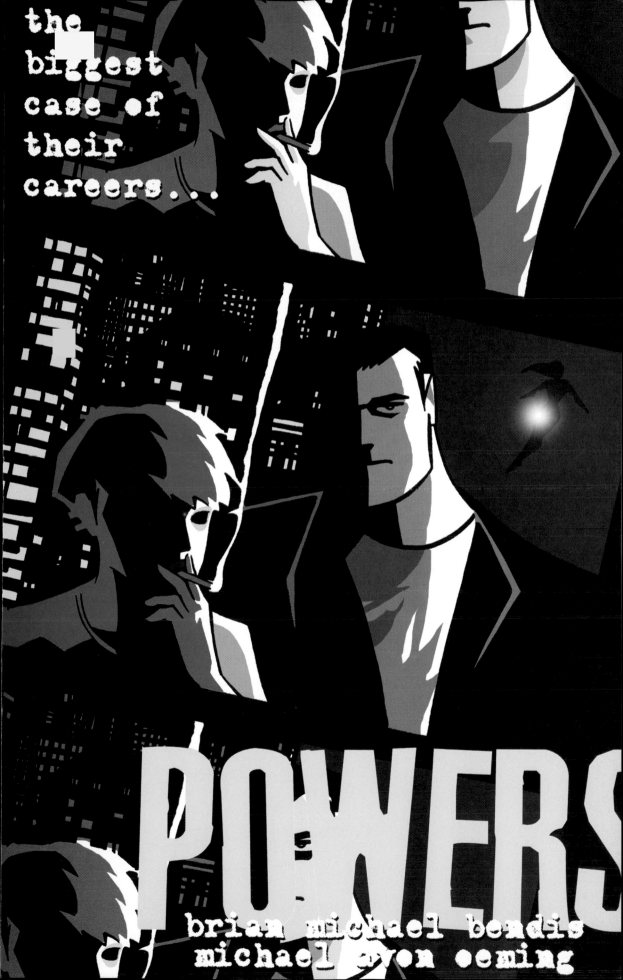

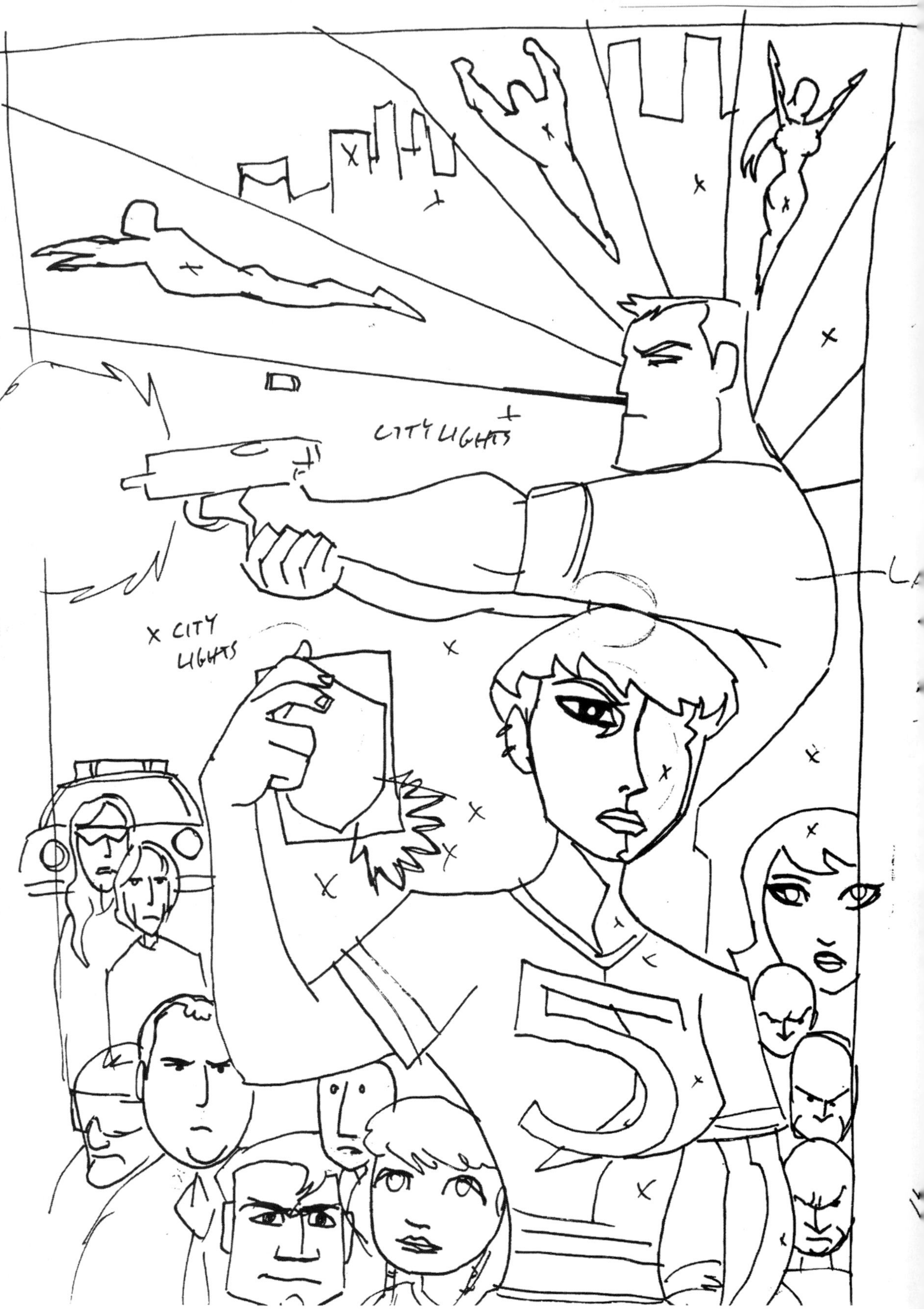

CITY LIGHTS
X CITY LIGHTS
5

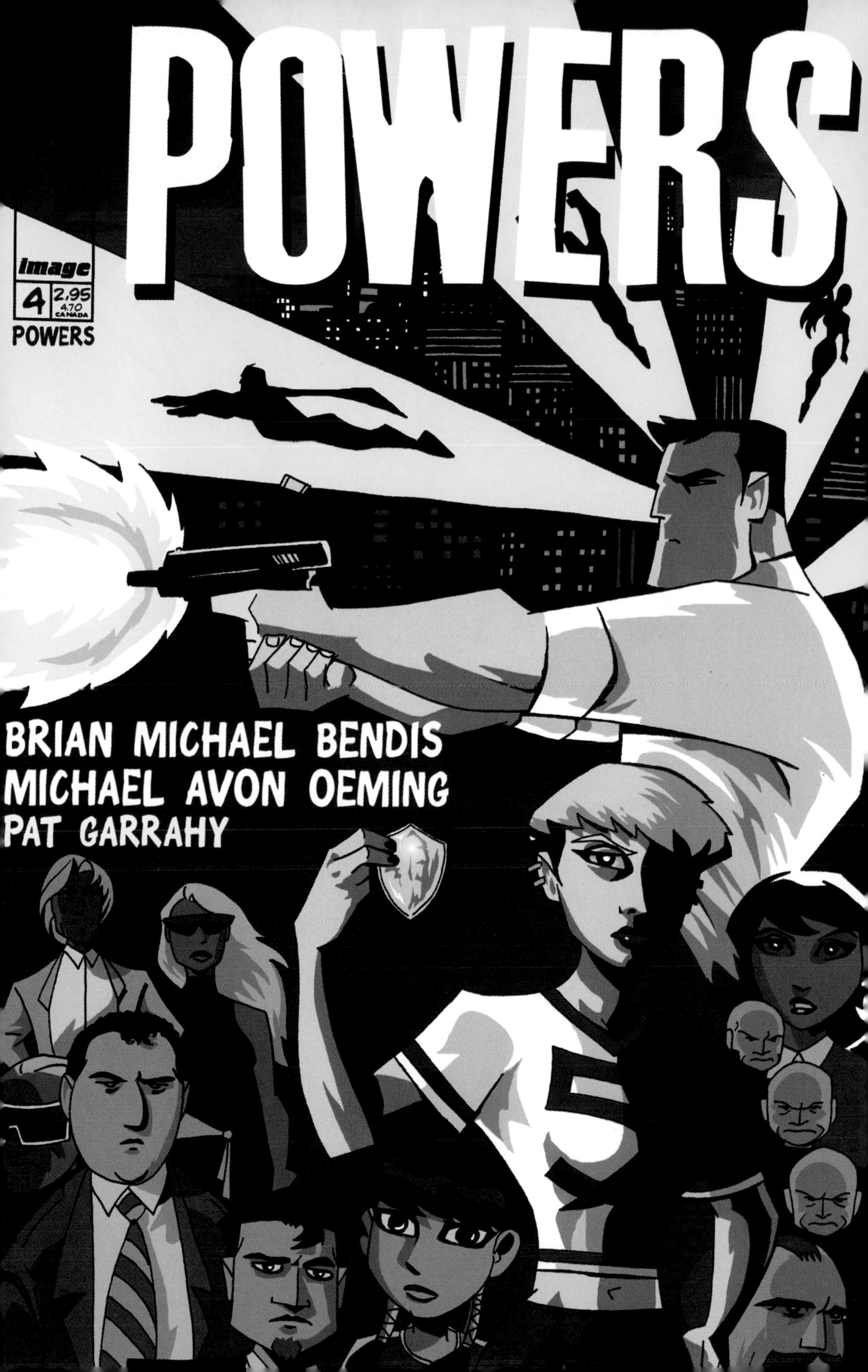
POWERS
image
4
2.95
4.70 CANADA
POWERS
BRIAN MICHAEL BENDIS
MICHAEL AVON OEMING
PAT GARRAHY

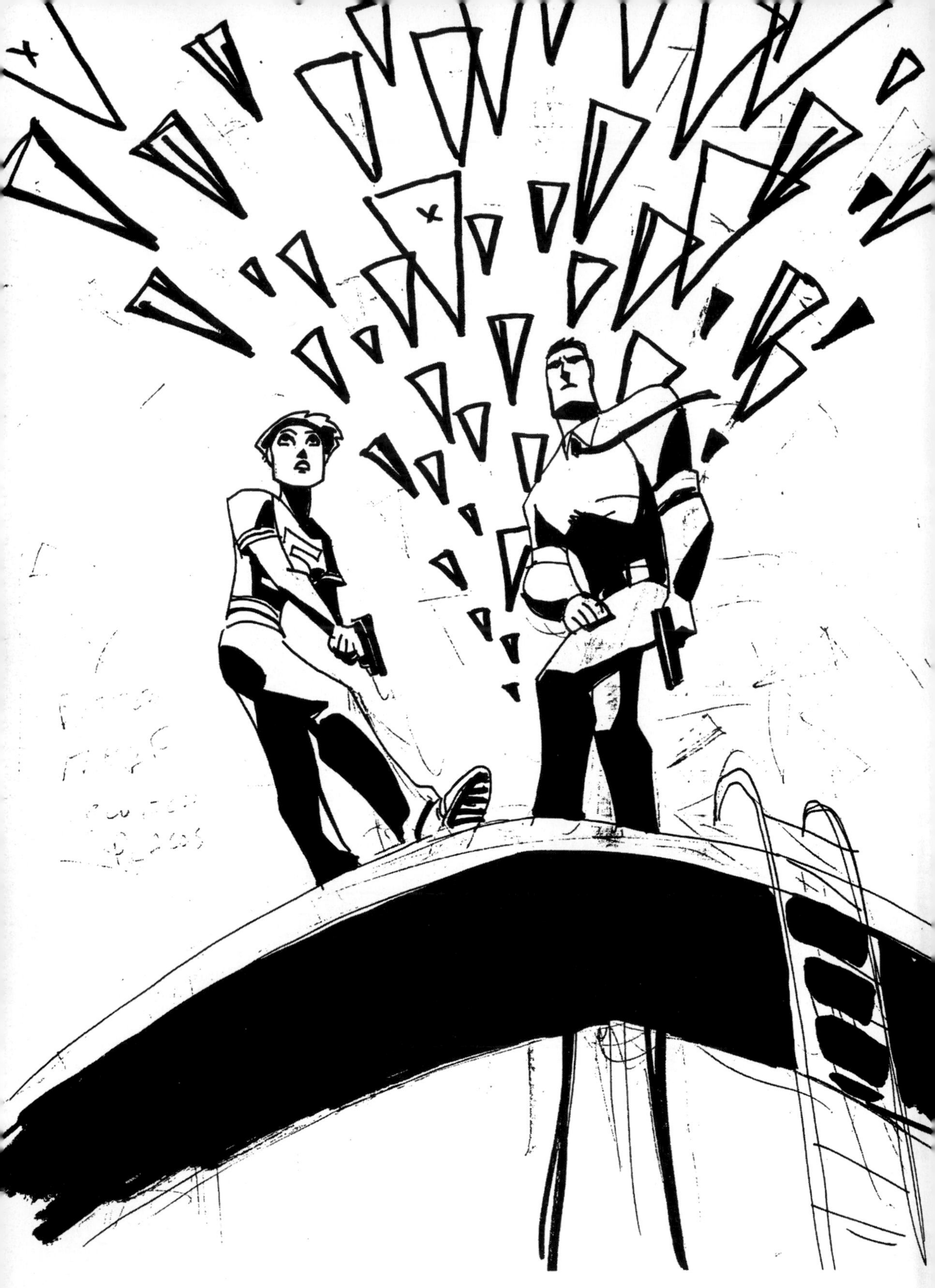

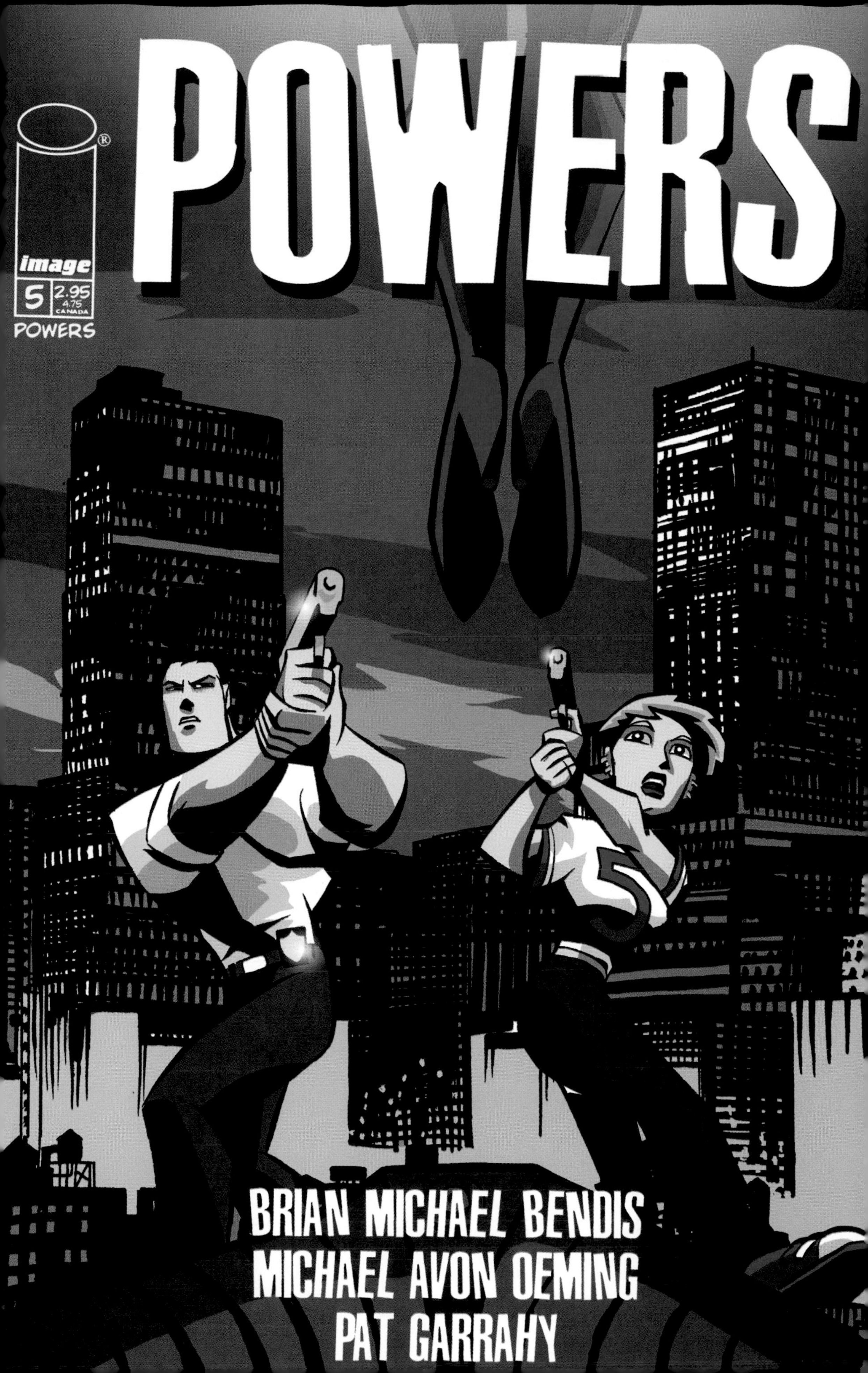
POWERS
image
5 2.95 4.75 CANADA
POWERS
BRIAN MICHAEL BENDIS
MICHAEL AVON OEMING
PAT GARRAHY

Unused layout and cover for issue six.

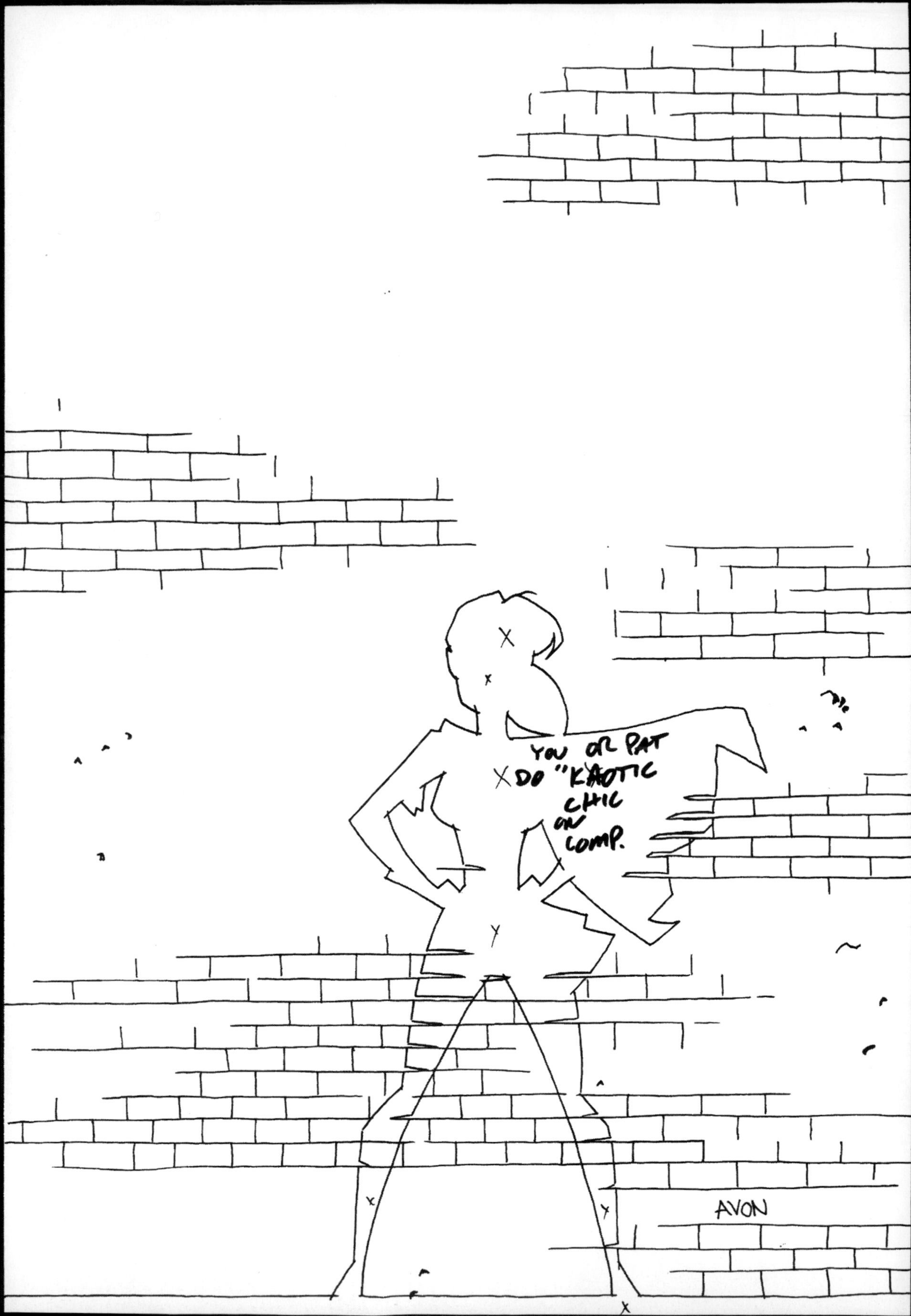
YOU OR PAT
DO "KAOTIC
CHIC
ON
COMP.
AVON

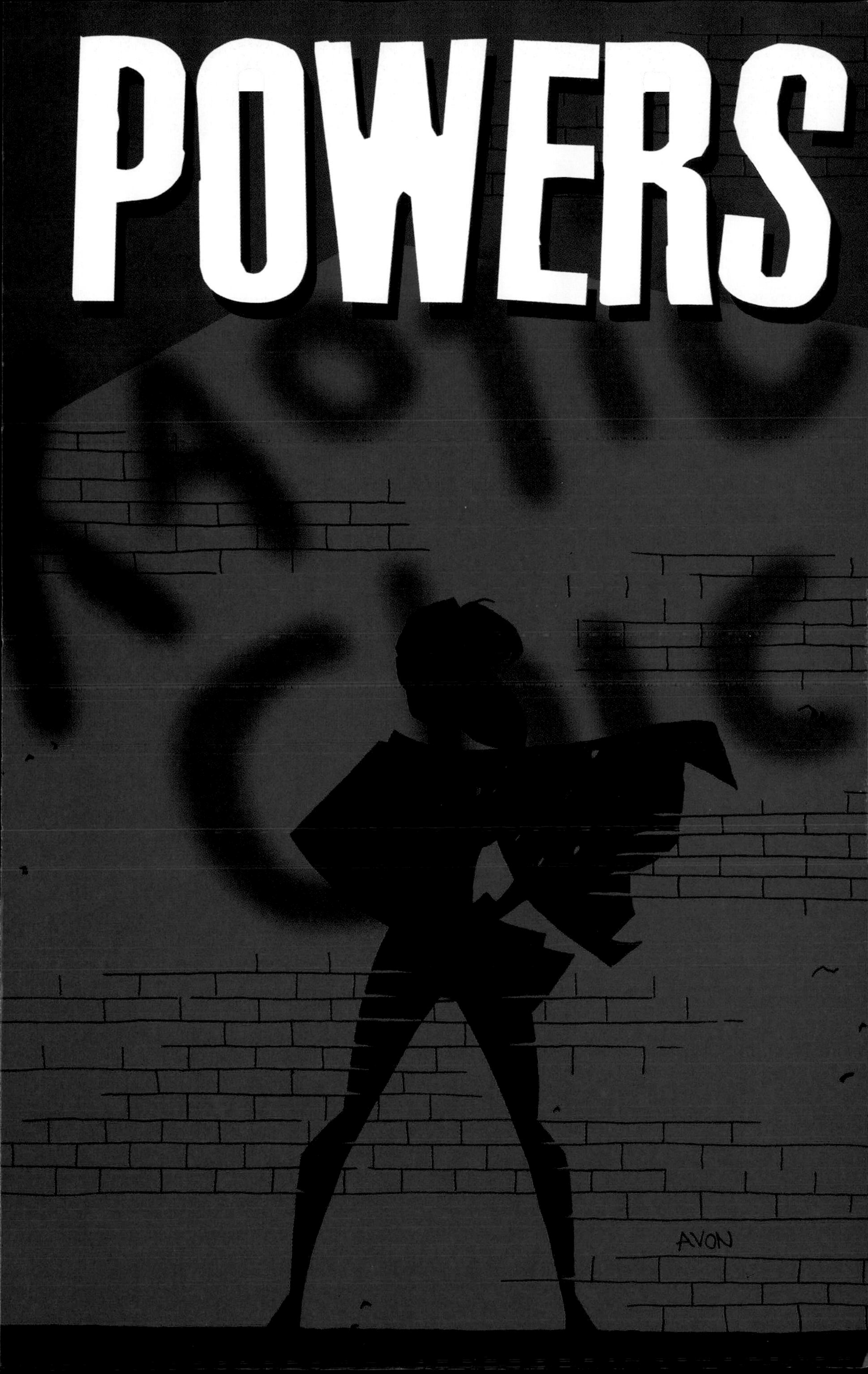
POWERS
AVON

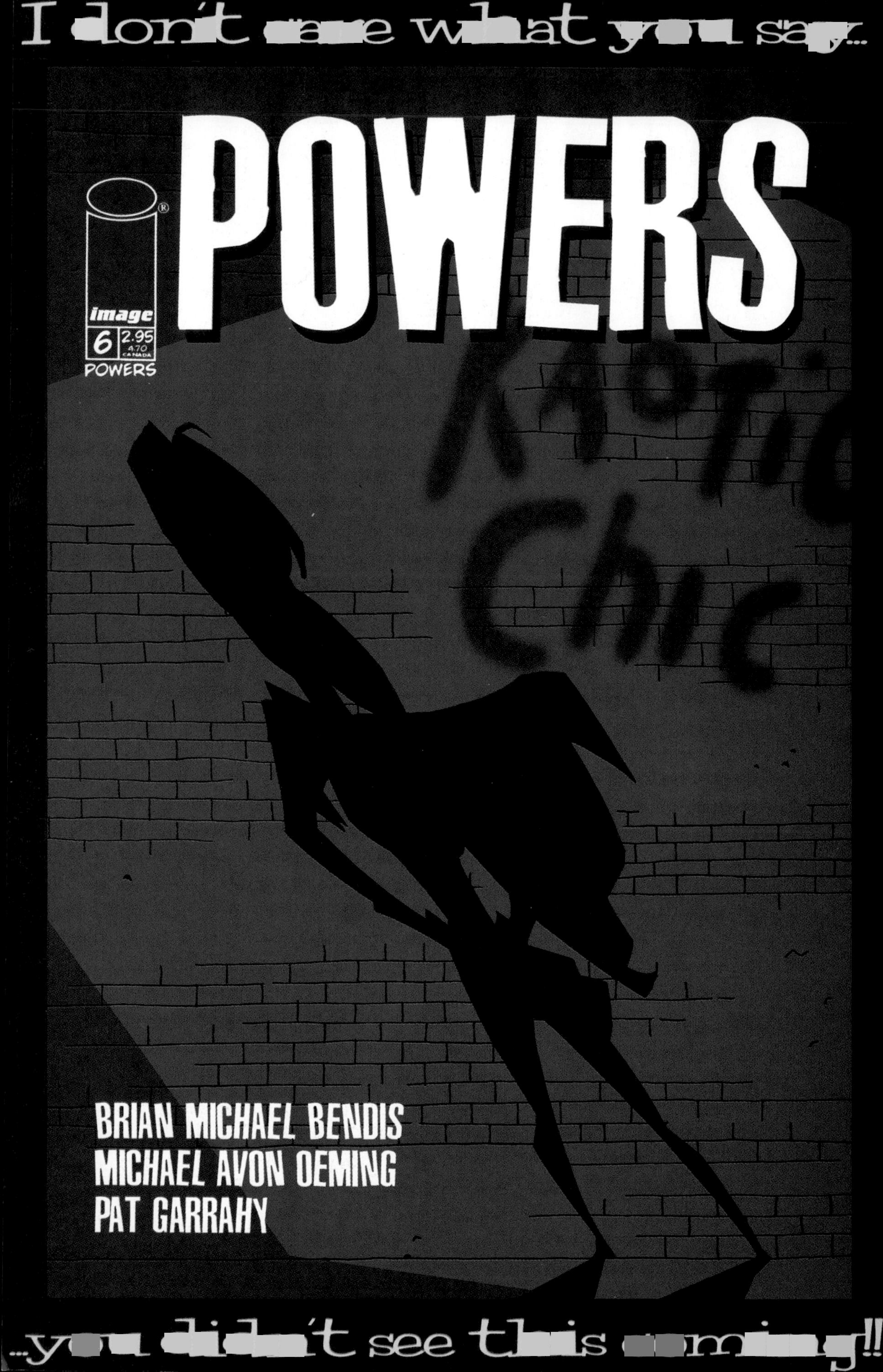
POWERS
image
6
2.95
4.70 CANADA
POWERS
KAOTIC Chic
BRIAN MICHAEL BENDIS
MICHAEL AVON OEMING
PAT GARRAHY

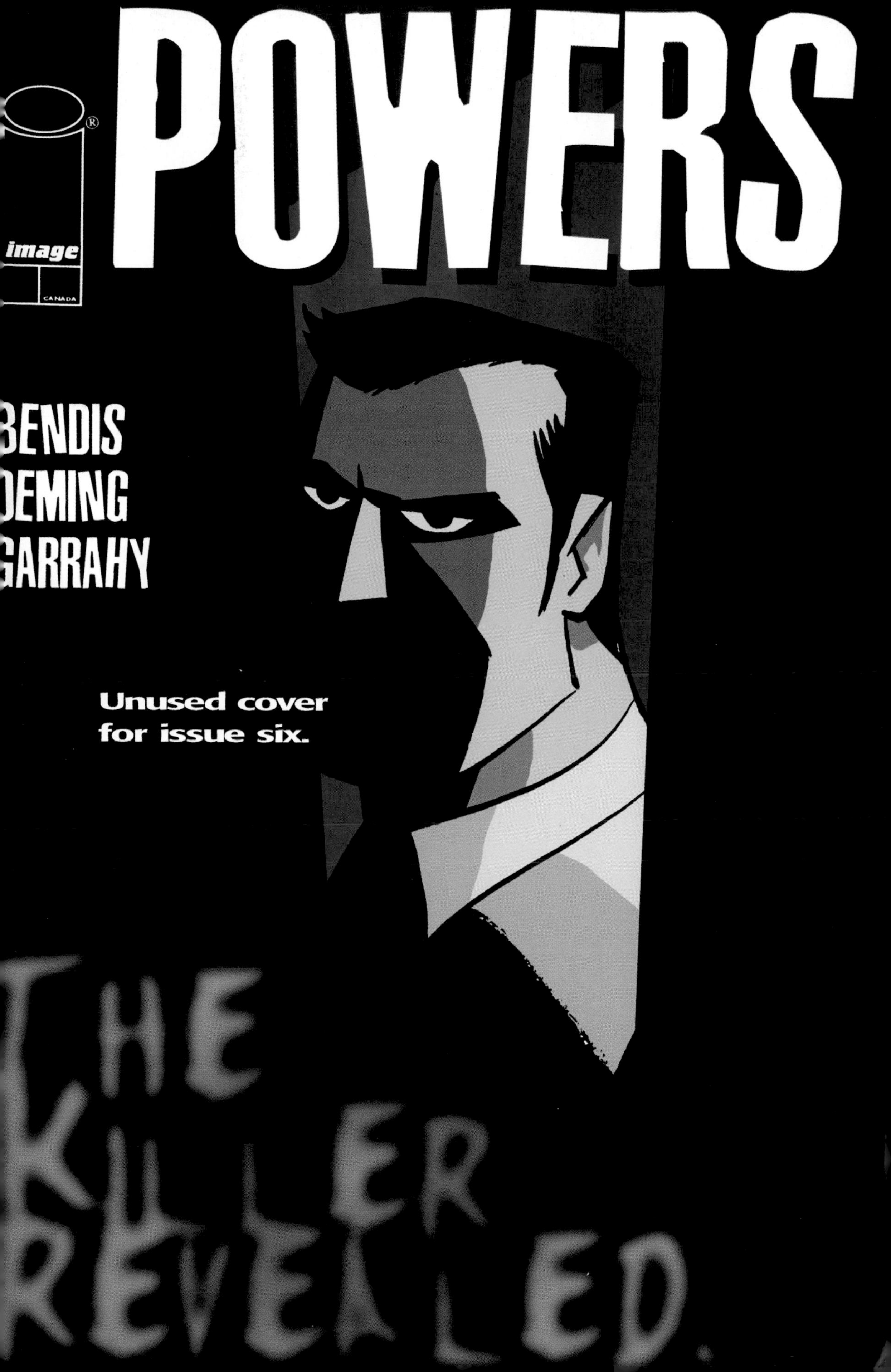
POWERS
image
CANADA
BENDIS
DEMING
GARRAHY
THE KILLER REVEALED.

Unused cover for issue six.

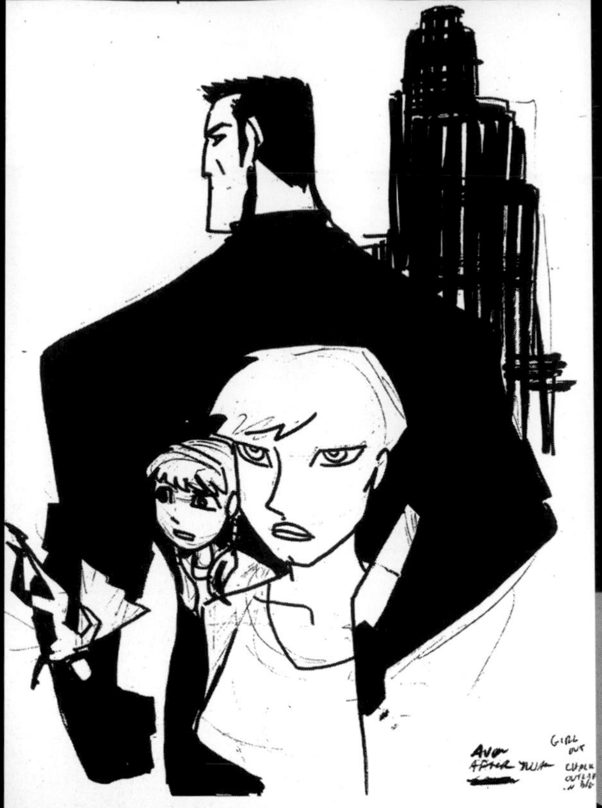
AVON
GIRL OUT

Unused layout and cover for issue three.

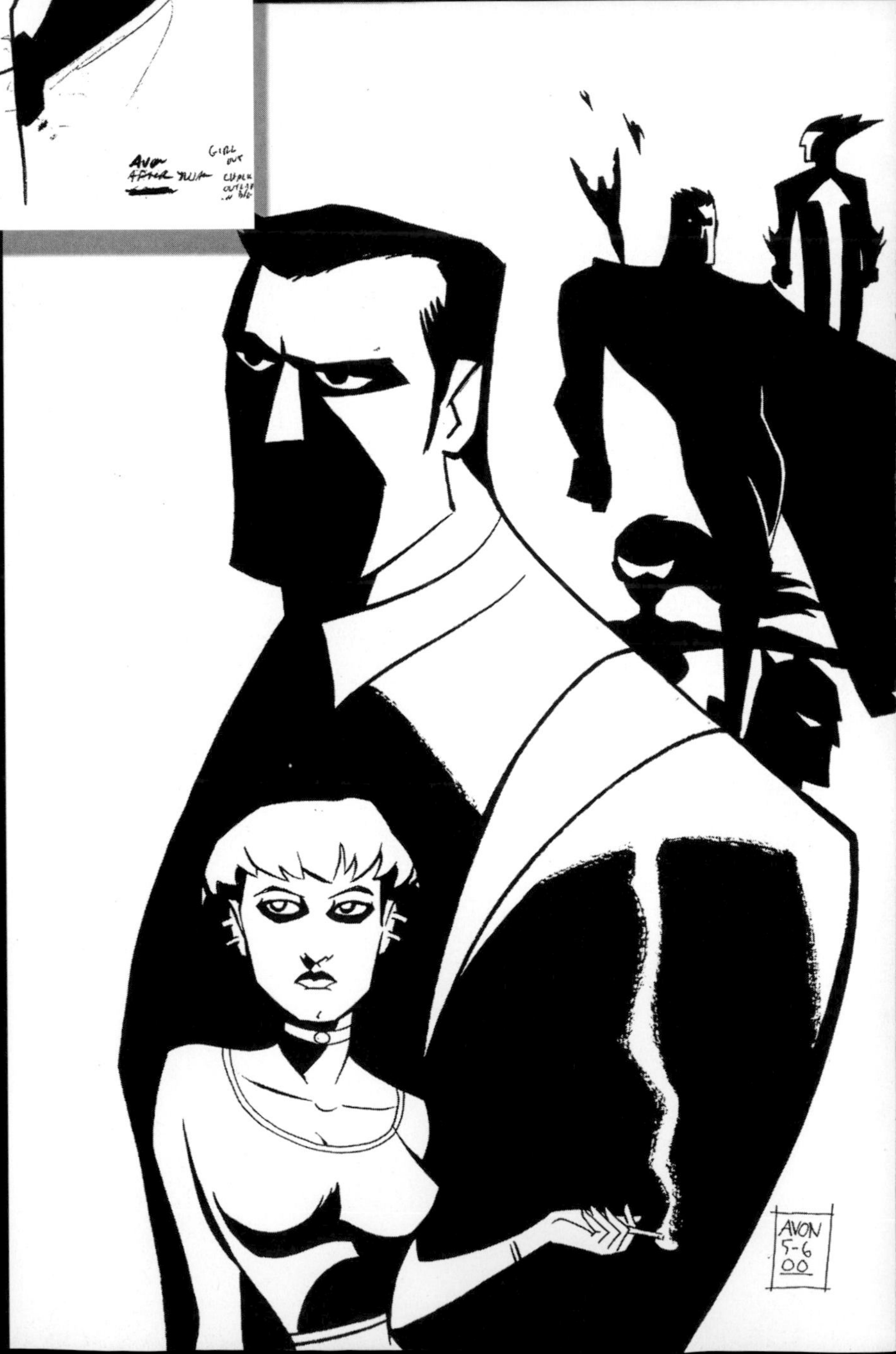
AVON 5-6 00

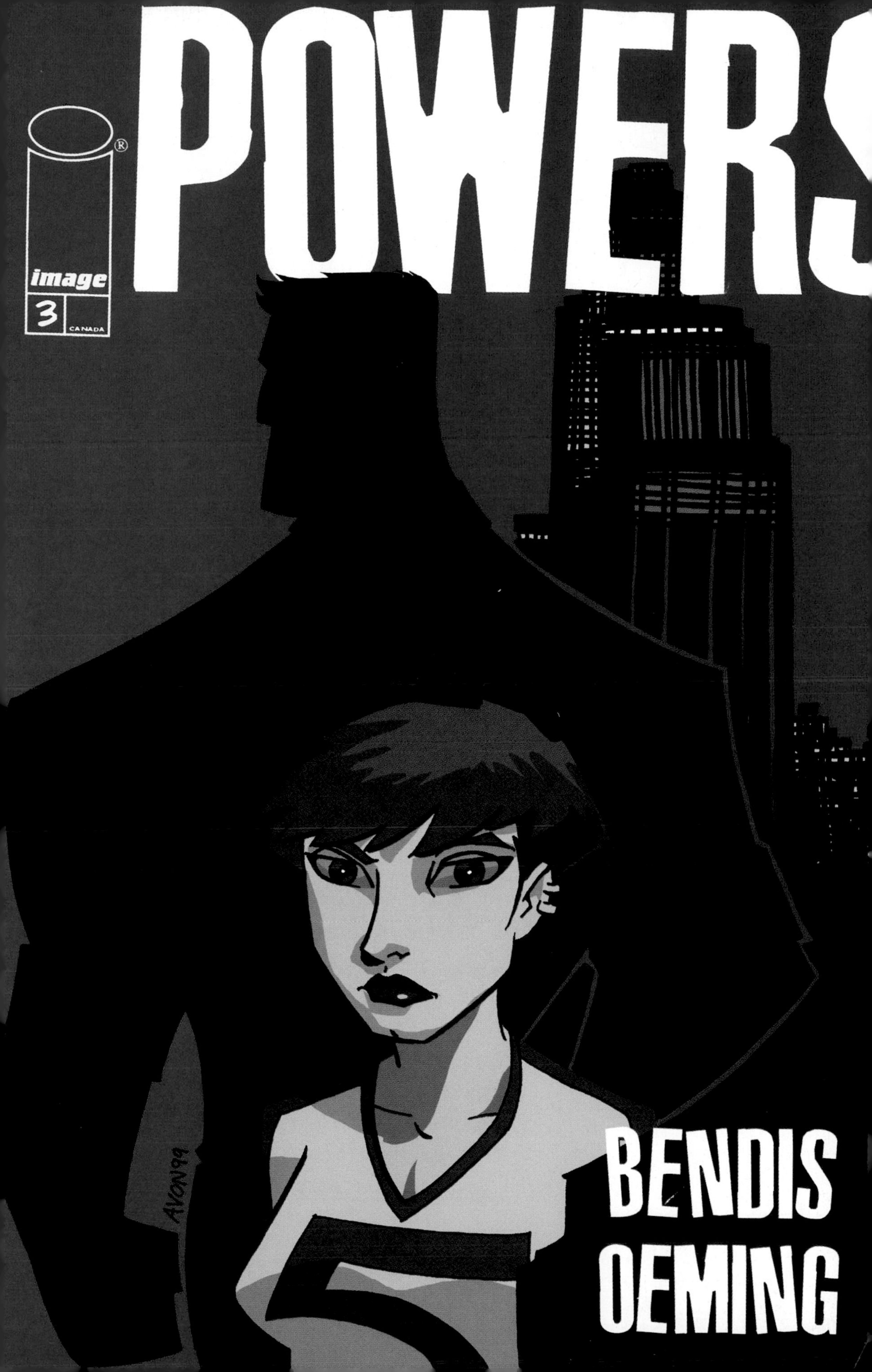
POWERS
image
3
CANADA
AVON99
BENDIS
OEMING

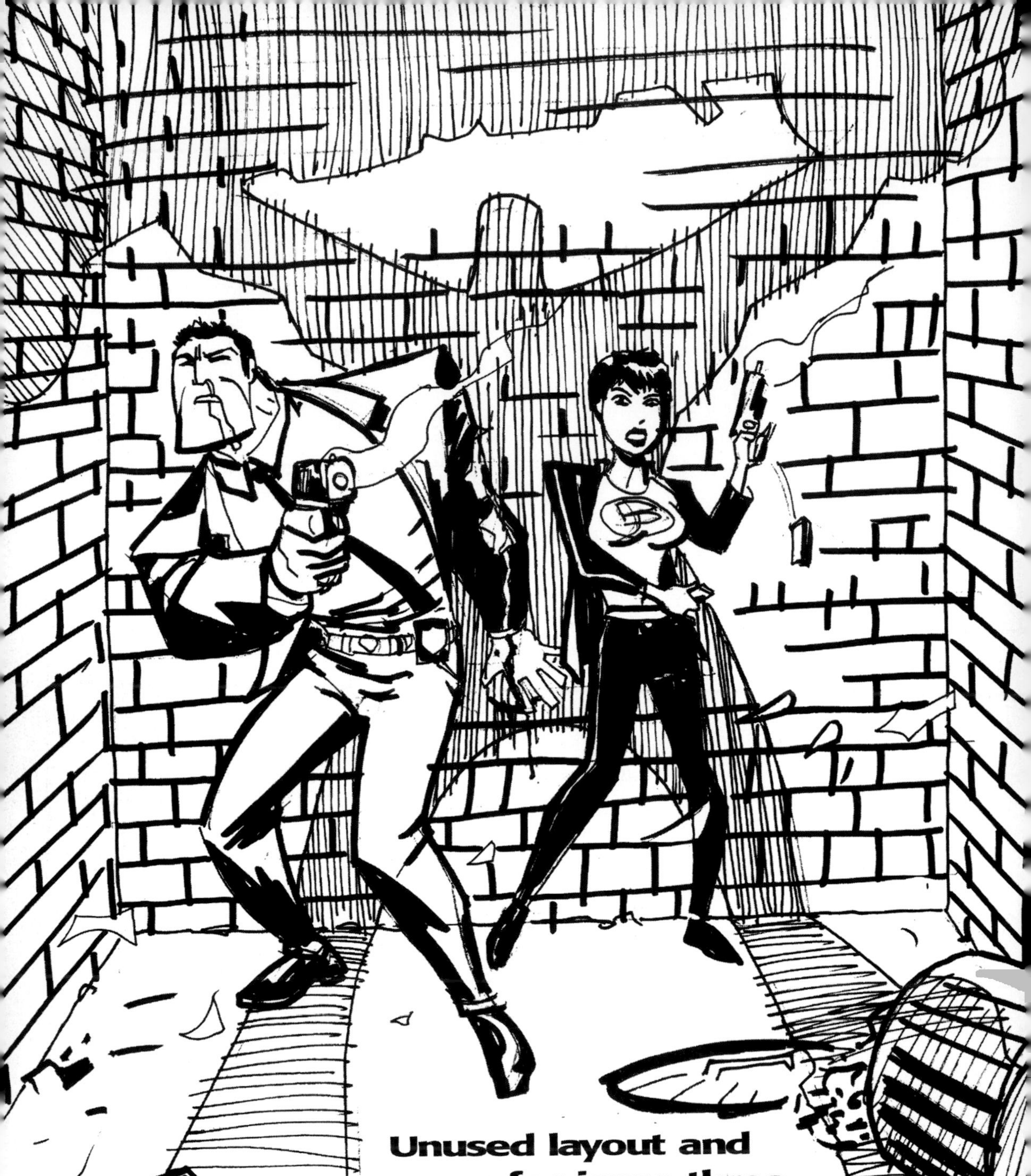

Unused layout and cover for issue three.

It ended up being the cover to the Mid-Ohio Convention program book.

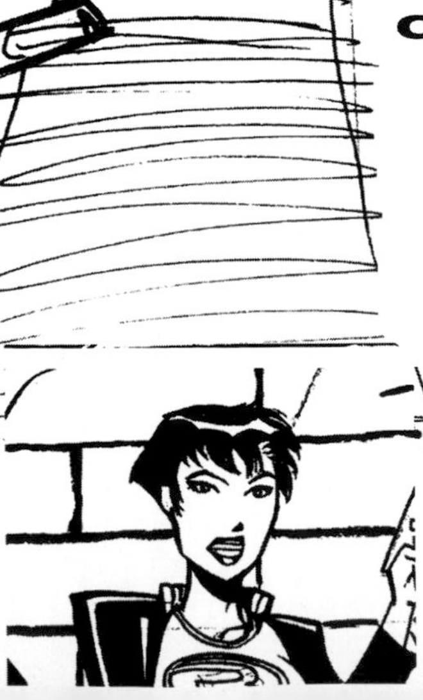

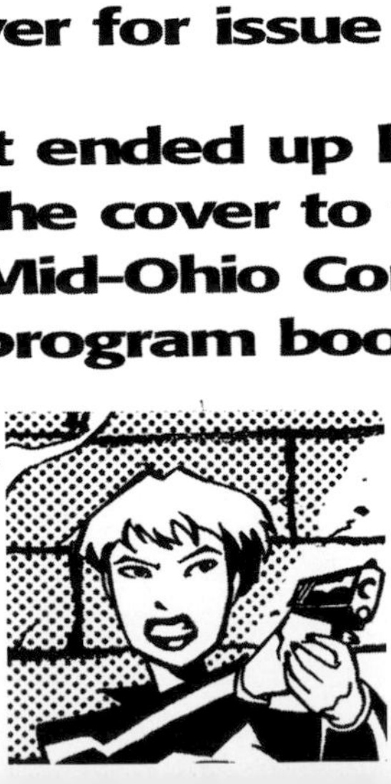

The ongoing saga of Deena's hair.

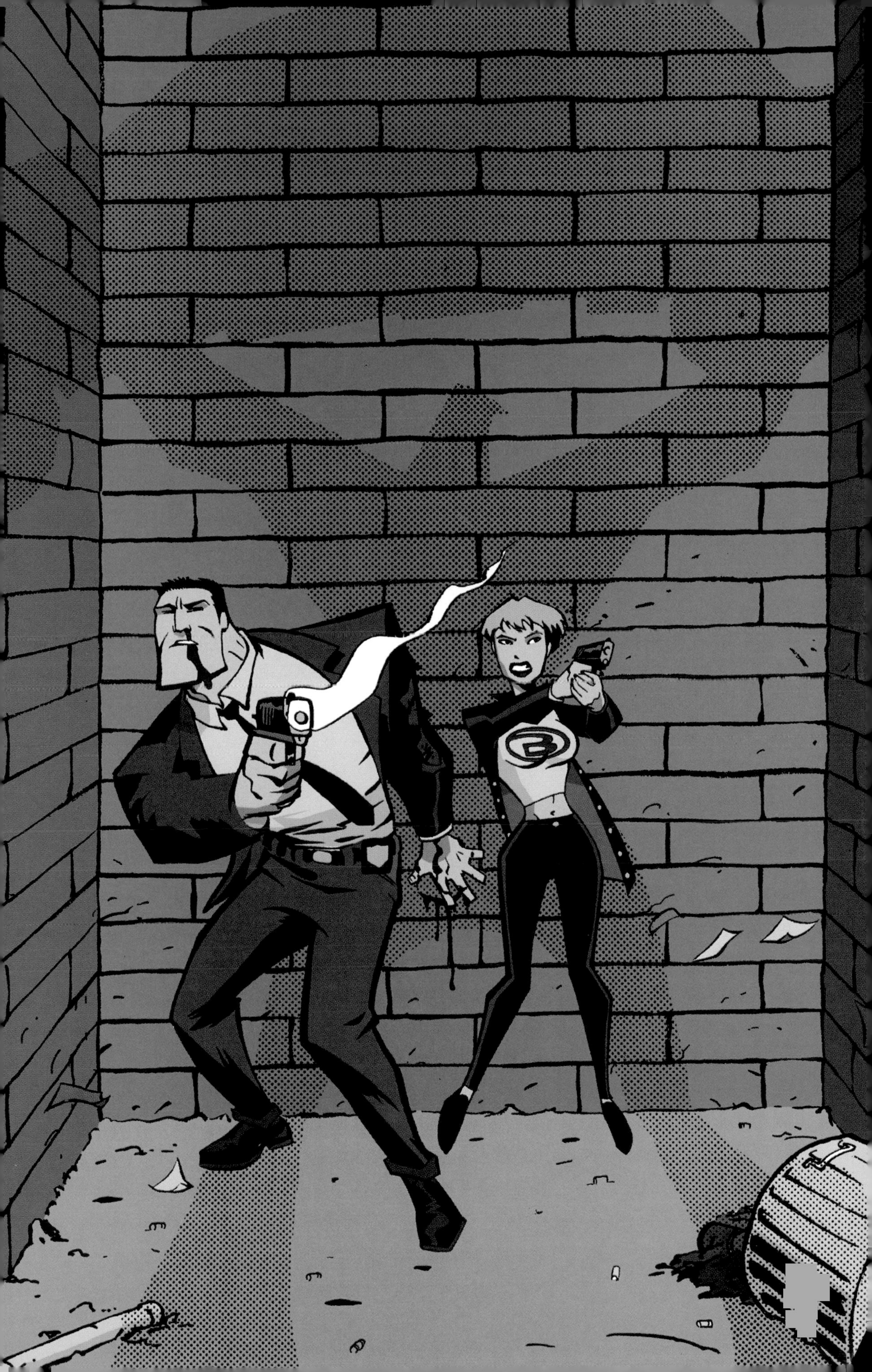

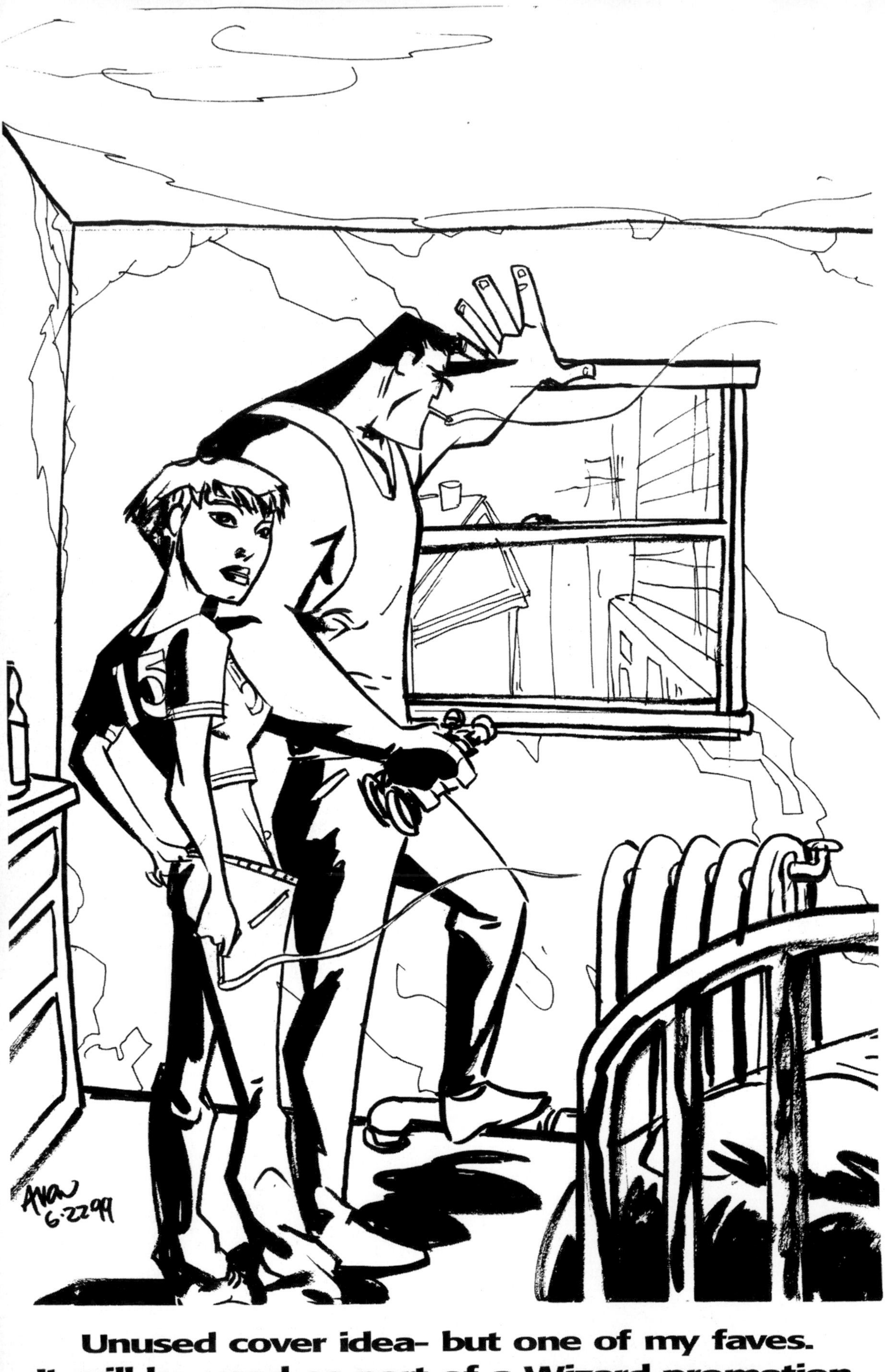
AVON
6·22·99

Unused cover idea– but one of my faves.
It will be used as part of a Wizard promotion.

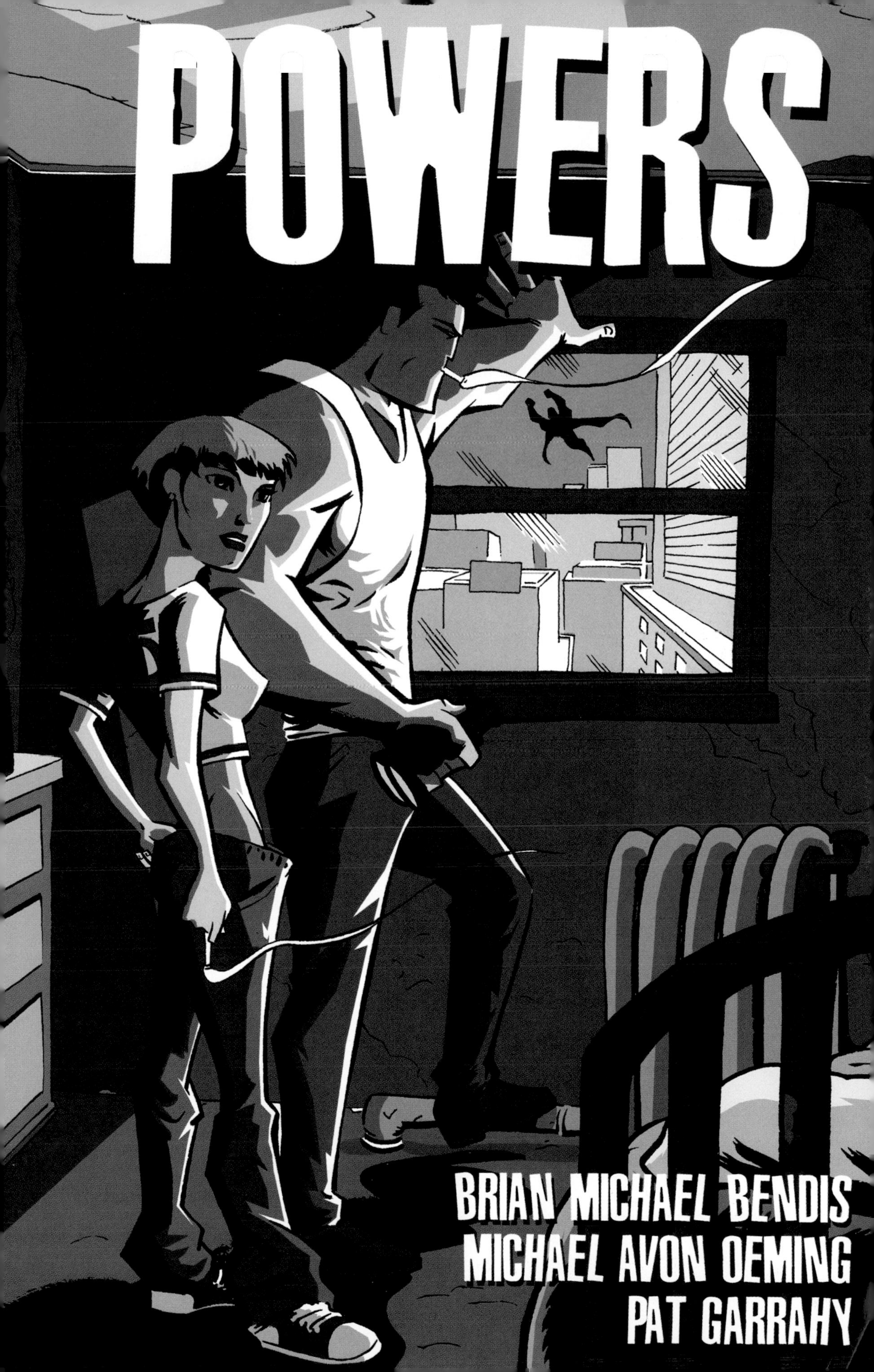
POWERS
BRIAN MICHAEL BENDIS
MICHAEL AVON OEMING
PAT GARRAHY

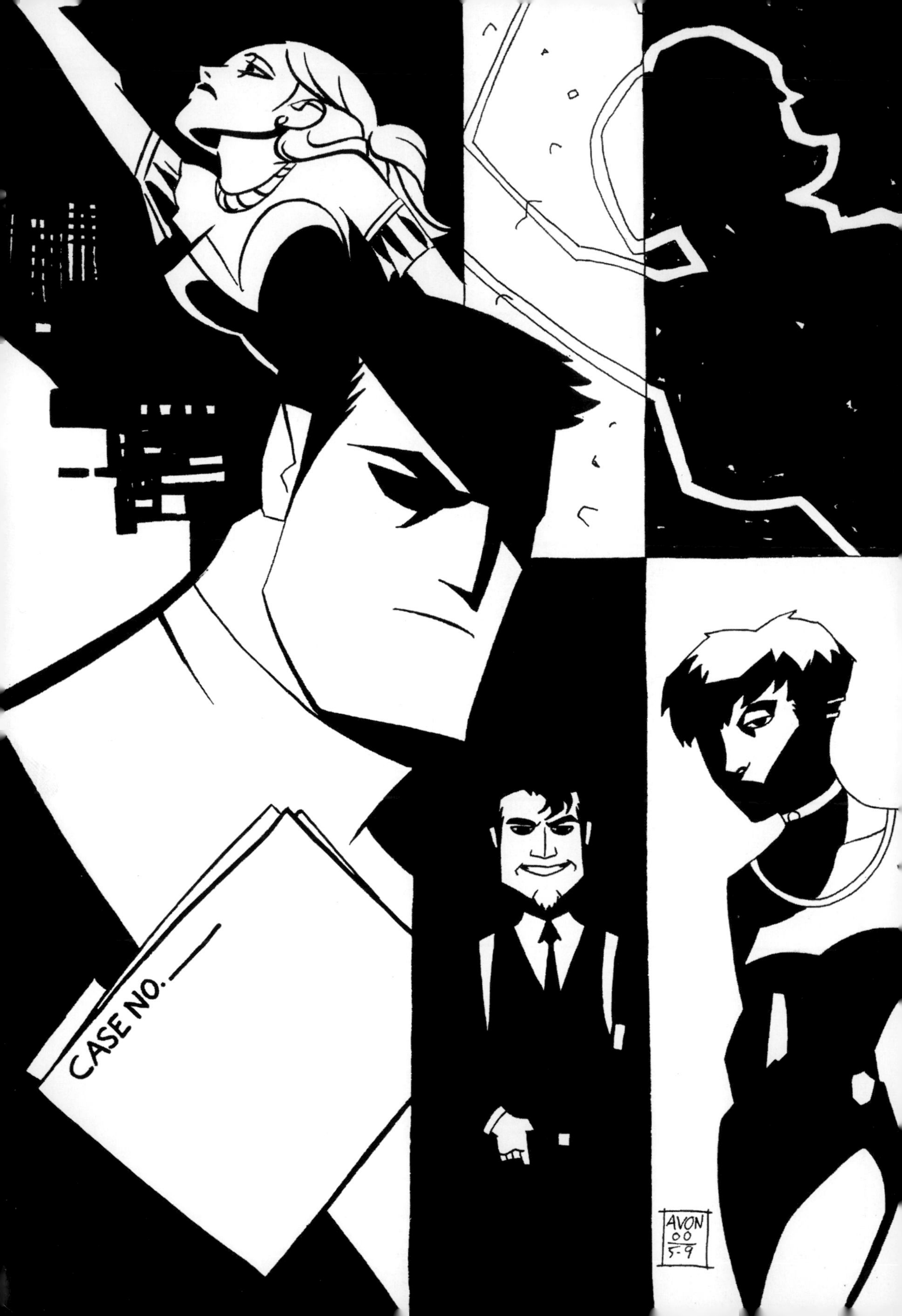
CASE NO.
AVON 00 5-9

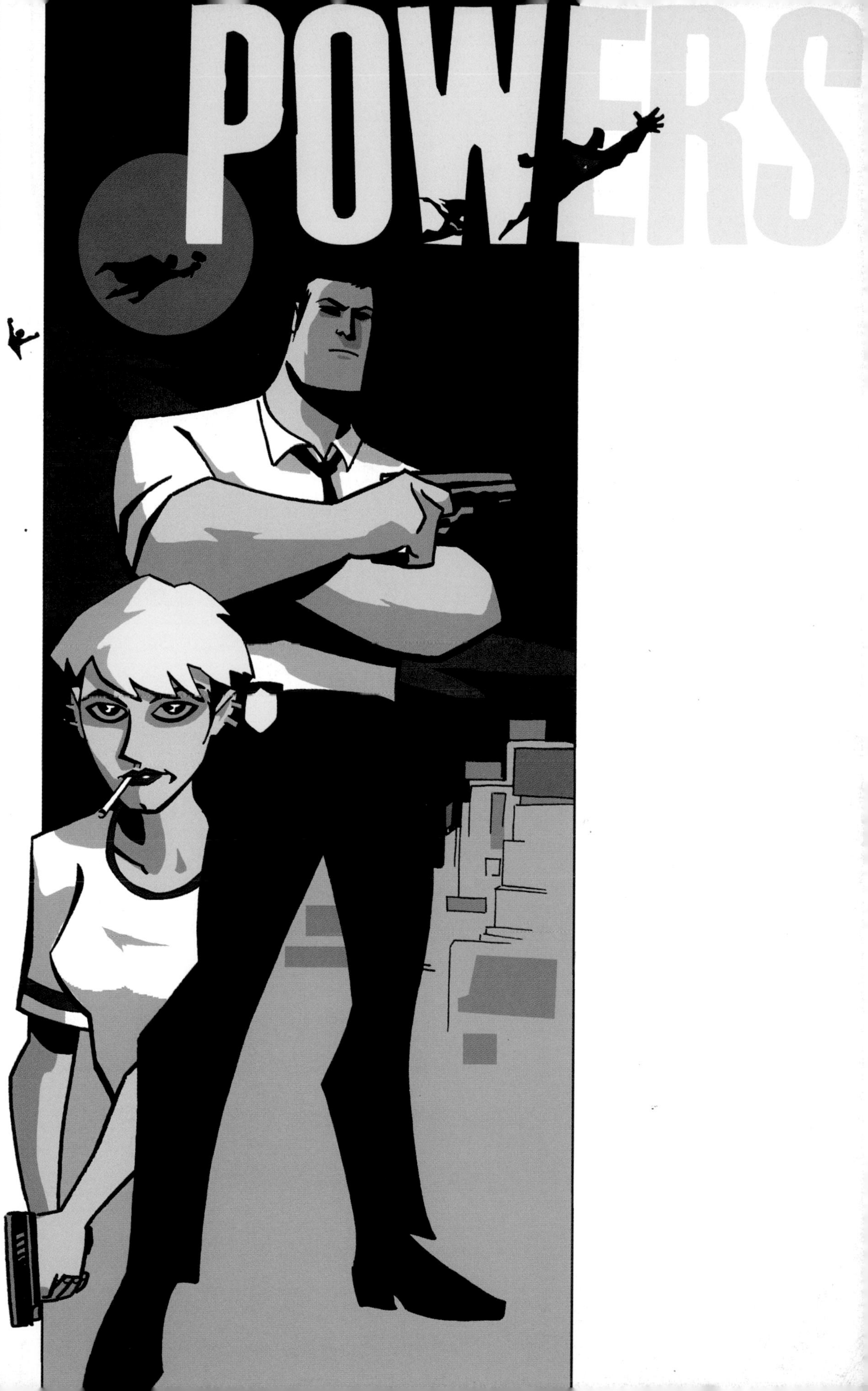
POWERS

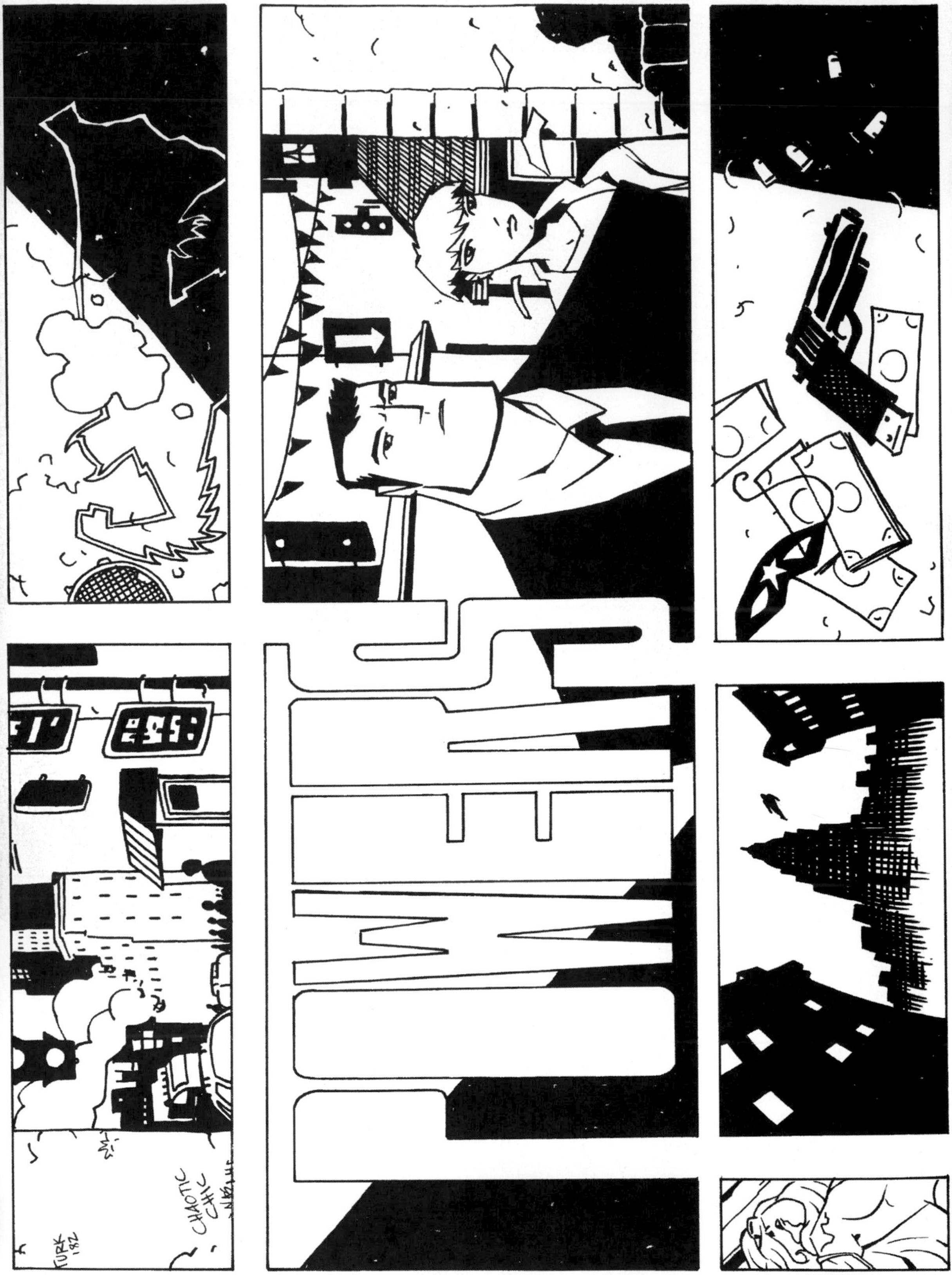
POWERS
CHAOTIC CHIC

Unused advertisement idea.

6- SQUEEZED OUT ANOTHER. YOU MAY WANT TO
RE-DO LETTERS

A Mike Oeming commision sketch.

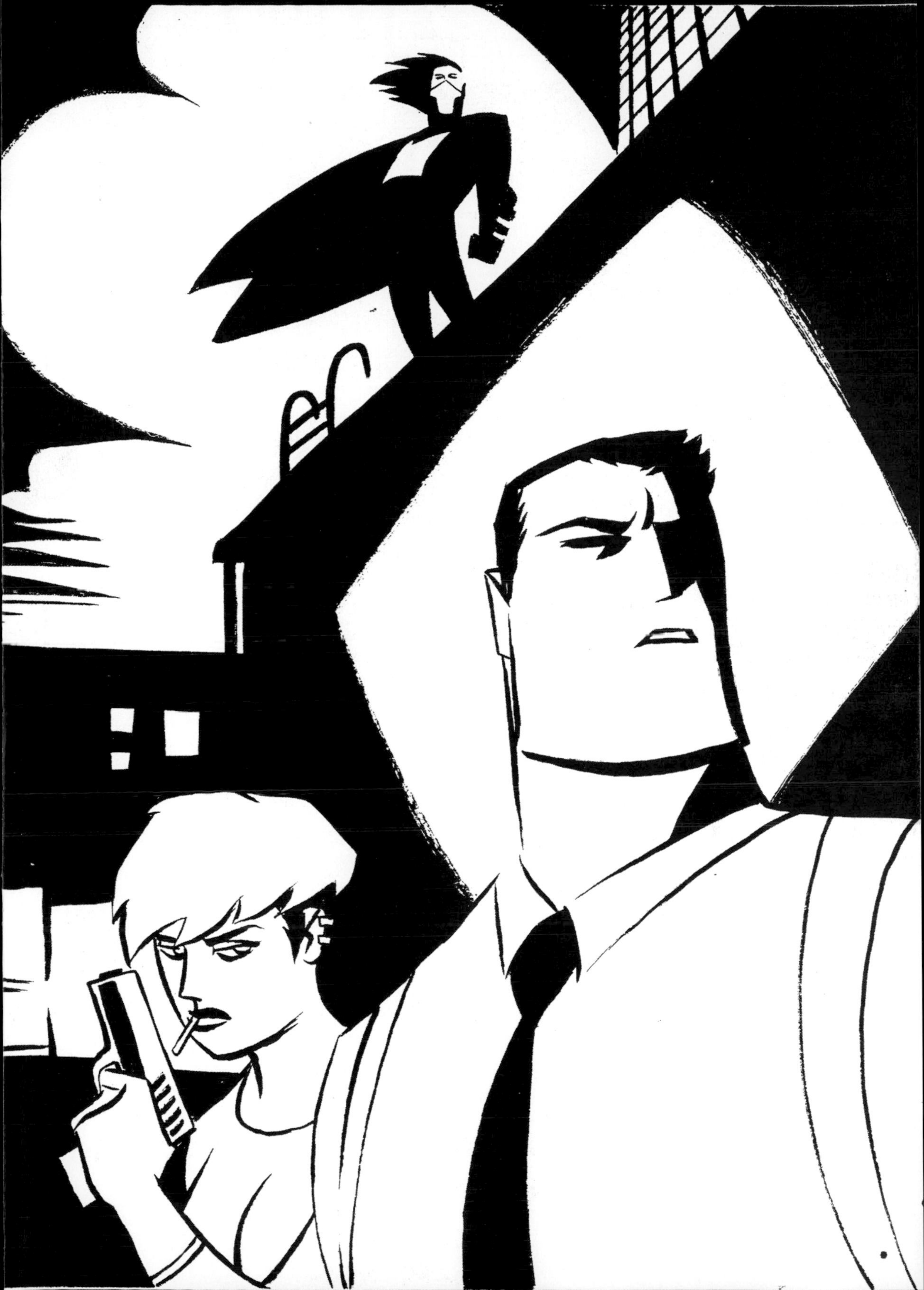

POWERS
THE CAMEOS

One of the best ideas we came up with for this book, and by 'best' I mean 'logistic nightmares,' was to ask well-known comic book creator friends of ours to lend us brand new super hero and villain creations to fill our cityscape.

This added an extra layer of fun to the whole thing. Many big name talents, talents people don't usually think of in this genre, were extremely generous by lending us their babies.

So, here on the following pages, for the first time, is a key to the identities of all the characters and their creators. Each character is copyright the creator named here. If no name is listed, that character is copyright Mike and myself and will be featured in an upcoming Powers storyarc.

We thank them all for being friends and pros.

DREI
DAVE JOHNSON

TWIGHLIGHT
DAVID MACK

THANKS AND DEDICATION

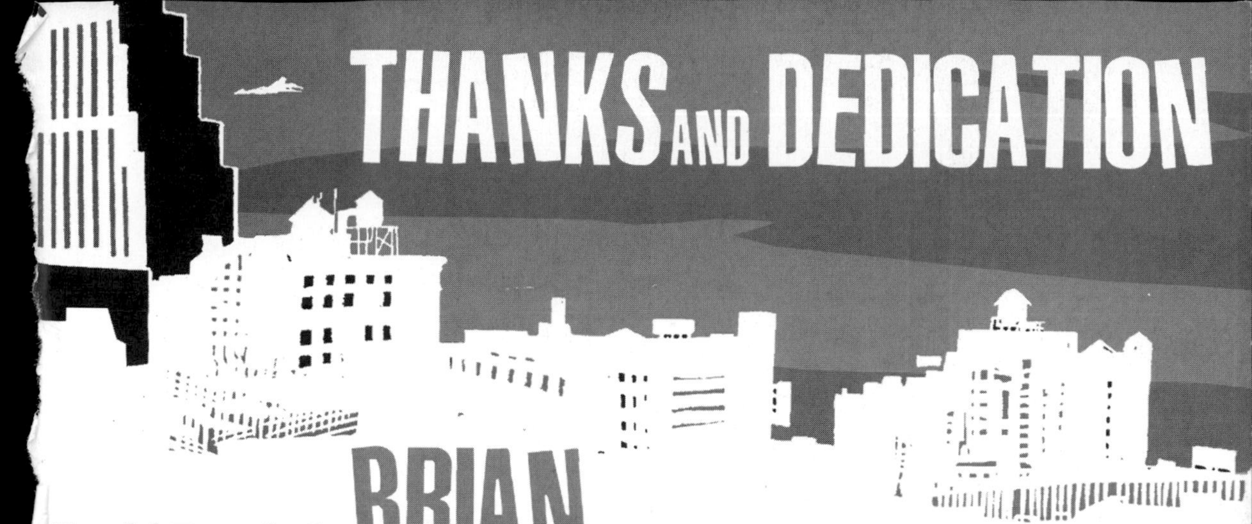

BRIAN

David Engel, Jim Valentino, Anthony Bozzi, Mace Neufeld, Brent Braun, Traci Hale, Joe Quesada, Bill Jemas, Kel Symons, Doug Belgrad, Jim McLaughlin, Randy Lander, Don Mcphereson, Jason Prichett, Justin Silvera, Chris Silberman, John Skrtic, Cliff Biggers, Ward Batty, Chris Lawrence, Warren Ellis, David Mack, James S. Rich, Joe Nozemack, Michael Doran, Matt Brady, Joel Meadows, Jared Bendis, Pat, K.C., Mike, Alisa, and the JINXWORLD messageboard.

MIKE

For Melissa and Ethan, the center of my world. Special thanks to Mom, Aunt Carol, Uncle Larry, Neil Vokes, the Bendis Board Posters and the Bordentown Police Department for all the support and help!

PAT

I'd like to thank the OCPStudios gents--Marshall Johnson, Josh Read, Mike Smith, James Dean Conklin, Tony Stocco, Ken Chang, and Scott Helmer. And I'd like to make sure to thank both my parents, 'cause I don't think I have thanked them previously in print.

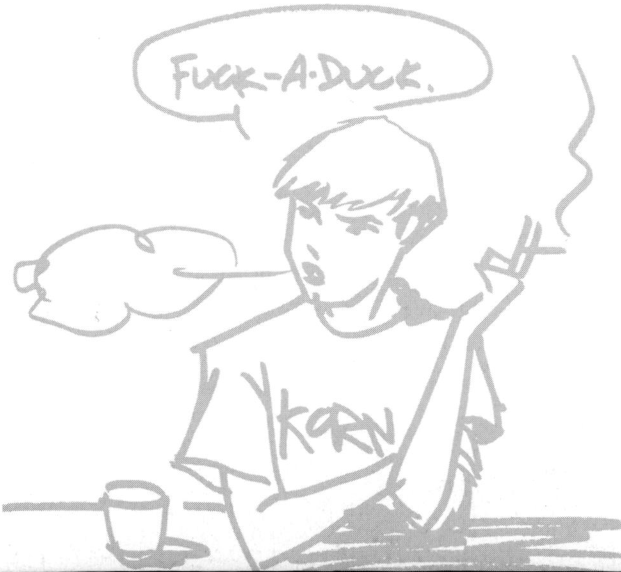
FUCK-A-DUCK.
KORN